International Relations

International Relations

Brief Seventh Edition

Jon C. W. Pevehouse
University of Wisconsin–Madison

Joshua S. Goldstein
American University, Washington, DC
University of Massachusetts Amherst

PEARSON

Boston   Columbus   Indianapolis   New York   San Francisco   Hoboken
Amsterdam   Cape Town   Dubai   London   Madrid   Milan   Munich   Paris   Montréal   Toronto
Delhi   Mexico City   São Paulo   Sydney   Hong Kong   Seoul   Singapore   Taipei   Tokyo

Editor in Chief: Dickson Musslewhite
Acquisitions Editor: Charlyce Owen-Jones
Program Manager: Rob DeGeorge
Editorial Assistant: Laura Hernandez
Field Marketing Manager:
   Brittan Pogue-Mohammed
Product Marketing Manager: Tricia Murphy
Digital Studio Project Manager: Tina Gagliostro
Project Manager: Carol O'Rourke

**Full Service Project Management and
Composition:** iEnergizer Aptara®, Ltd.
Full Service Project Manager: Kelly Ricci,
   iEnergizer Aptara®, Ltd.
Art Director: Kathryn Foot
Cover Photo: Aleksandar Radovanov/Fotolia
Procurement Specialist: Mary Ann Gloriande
Printer and Binder: RR Donnelley/Crawfordsville
Cover Printer: Phoenix/Lehigh

This seventh edition was written by Jon C. W. Pevehouse based on *International Relations Brief Edition, 2013–2014* Update by Joshua S. Goldstein and Jon C. W. Pevehouse.

For permission to use copyrighted material, grateful acknowledgment is made to the copyright holders on p. 391, which are hereby made part of this copyright page.

Library of Congress Cataloging-in-Publication Data

Names: Pevehouse, Jon C., author. | Goldstein, Joshua S., 1952- author.
Title: International relations / Jon C.W. Pevehouse, University of Wisconsin,
    Madison; Joshua S. Goldstein, American University, Washington, D.C.
    University of Massachusetts, Amherst.
Description: Brief seventh edition. | Boston : Pearson, 2017. | Previous
    editions list Joshua S. Goldstein as the first author.
Identifiers: LCCN 2015038245 | ISBN 9780134406350 | ISBN 0134406354
Subjects: LCSH: International relations.
Classification: LCC JZ1242 .G652 2017 | DDC 327—dc23 LC record available at
    http://lccn.loc.gov/2015038245

2 16

PEARSON

Student Edition
ISBN-10:   0-134-40635-4
ISBN-13: 978-0-134-40635-0

Instructor's Review Copy
ISBN-10:   0-134-41159-5
ISBN-13: 978-0-134-41159-0

A la Carte
ISBN-10:   0-134-41139-0
ISBN-13: 978-0-134-41139-2

For our children—Solomon and Ruth; Claire, Ava, and Carl

Brief Contents

Contents

> Note: Each chapter ends with a summary, key terms, and critical thinking questions.

Preface

We live in an increasingly interconnected world. These connections bring great benefits to our everyday lives: the ability to communicate instantaneously around the world and share our cultures and beliefs; the possibility of directly helping a person affected by an earthquake through a global network of charities; the ability to purchase a product made from parts manufactured in a dozen different countries, each using its specialized knowledge to create a better product—these are some of the potential benefits of the interconnected world. Yet these connections may also worsen existing problems: Terrorist networks use telecommunications to carry out attacks, global commerce can put undue strain on our natural environment, and millions of people still live with few of the global connections that are enjoyed by citizens of wealthier countries.

Despite these increasing connections and their implications for everyday life, many students begin college misinformed about basic facts of international relations (IR), such as the extent of poverty in and levels of foreign assistance to the developing world, and the trend toward fewer wars over the past two decades. An introductory textbook plays a key role in students' education about international affairs, and we have worked hard to make the Brief Seventh Edition of *International Relations* timely, accurate, visually appealing, and intellectually engaging. We hope this textbook can help a generation develop knowledge and critical thinking in order to find its voice and place in the changing world order.

IR is not only an important topic but also a fascinating one. The rich complexity of international relationships—political, economic, and cultural—provides a puzzle to try to understand. The puzzle is not only an intellectual challenge but also emotionally powerful. It contains human-scale stories in which the subject's grand themes—war and peace, intergroup conflict and community, integration and division, humans and their environment, poverty and development—play out.

New to the Seventh Edition

The Brief Seventh Edition of *International Relations* includes important revisions throughout to keep the text current in a time of historic changes in the international system.

Chapter 1:

- Completely updated economic and demographic data
- Updates on Middle East conflicts, including Syria, Libya, Yemen, and Iranian nuclear negotiations

- Updates on East Asian maritime tensions
- Discussion of the Ebola health crisis in West Africa

Chapter 2:

- New Policy Perspectives box feature
- Updates on the North Atlantic Treaty Organization's (NATO's) withdrawal from Afghanistan
- Discussion of Russian annexation of Crimea

Chapter 3:

- Revised discussion of Women in IR
- Updates on Arab Spring transitions and violence in the Middle East
- Discussion of congressional debate over Iran nuclear deal

Chapter 4:

- Revised listing of wars of the world and updated data on military forces worldwide
- Revised discussion of Islamic groups, including the rise of the Islamic State in Iraq and Syria (ISIS)
- Updated discussion of civil wars in Syria and Yemen
- New discussion of Ukrainian-Russian tensions and violence
- Revised discussion of maritime tensions in East Asia
- New discussion of Iran nuclear negotiations and the 2015 nuclear agreement

Chapter 5:

- Updated data and discussion on the continuing slow recovery from the global economic crisis of 2008–2009
- Discussion of controversial Transatlantic and Trans-Pacific trade agreements
- Updated discussion on continued struggles to complete the Doha Round of trade negotiations over new World Trade Organization mandates
- Updated discussions of state economic positions in the global economy, including Russian economic struggles
- Discussion of Chinese currency devaluations
- New discussion of virtual currencies such as bitcoin

Chapter 6:

- Completely updated data and discussion of current UN peacekeeping efforts
- Discussion of new UN Disabilities Treaty
- Updated discussion of International Criminal Court
- Updated discussion of the economic difficulties in Greece, including the possibility of the country's exit from the Eurozone
- Revised discussion of Eurozone countries

Chapter 7:

- Completely updated data on progress toward the UN Millennium Development Goals
- Discussion of European immigration crisis
- More focus on developments in BRIC countries (Brazil, Russia, India, and China)
- Updated discussion of foreign assistance based on updated data from 2014 and 2015
- Updated discussion of Chinese economic situation, including devaluations and stock market slides
- Revised discussion of international debt, including updated data

Chapter 8:

- Updated discussion of negotiations for a comprehensive global warming treaty
- Updates on attempts by China and the United States to move to smaller side agreements on environmental issues
- New discussion of Ebola in West Africa
- Revised discussion on the global fight against HIV/AIDS
- Revised discussion of the global digital divide, including updated data

In each chapter, we have updated the tables and figures with the most recent available data. This includes new data on gross domestic product (GDP), military forces, migration and refugees, debt, remittances, foreign aid, the HIV/AIDS epidemic, and UN peacekeeping operations, to name a few.

Finally, this Brief Seventh Edition of *International Relations* revises the photo program substantially. Dozens of new photos, many of them from 2014 and 2015, draw visual attention to current events while reinforcing key concepts in the text.

REVEL™

Educational technology designed for the way today's students read, think, and learn

When students are engaged deeply, they learn more effectively and perform better in their courses. This simple fact inspired the creation of REVEL: an immersive learning experience designed for the way today's students read, think, and learn. Built in collaboration with educators and students nationwide, REVEL is the newest, fully digital way to deliver respected Pearson content.

REVEL enlivens course content with media interactives and assessments—integrated directly within the authors' narrative—that provide opportunities for students to read about and practice course material in tandem. This immersive educational technology boosts student engagement, which leads to better understanding of concepts and improved performance throughout the course.

Learn more about REVEL

www.pearsonhighered.com/revel/

Structure of the Text

This text aims to present the current state of knowledge in IR in a comprehensive and accessible way—to provide a map of the subject covering its various research communities in a logical order. Common core principles—dominance, reciprocity, and identity—unify the text by showing how theoretical models apply across the range of topics in international security and political economy.

The overall structure of this text follows substantive topics, first in international security and then in international political economy (IPE). Chapter 1 introduces the study of IR; explains the collective goods problem and the core principles of dominance, reciprocity, and identity; and provides some geographical and historical context for the subject. Chapters 2 and 3 lay out the various theoretical approaches to IR: realist theories, liberal theories, and social theories (constructivist, postmodern, Marxist, peace studies, and gender theories). Chapter 4 introduces the main sources of international conflict and the conditions and manner in which such conflicts lead to war, terrorism, and other forms of violence. Chapter 5 introduces theoretical concepts in political economy (showing how theories of international security translate into IPE issue areas) and discusses trade relations and the politics of international money, banking, and multinational business operations. Chapter 6 shows how international organizations and law, especially the United Nations and the European Union, have evolved to become major global and regional influences and how human rights have become increasingly important. Chapter 7 addresses global North-South relations and population growth, and considers alternatives for economic development in the context of international business, debt, and foreign aid. Chapter 8 shows how environmental politics, telecommunications, and cultural exchange expand international bargaining and interdependence.

Pedagogical Elements

In a subject such as IR, in which knowledge is tentative and empirical developments can overtake theories, critical thinking is a key skill for college students to develop. At various points in the text, conclusions are left open-ended to let students reason their way through an issue and, in addition to the critical thinking questions at the end of each chapter, the boxed features support deeper and more focused critical thinking.

The Policy Perspectives feature in each chapter places students in the decision-making perspective of a national leader. This feature bridges international relations theory to policy problems while demonstrating the trade-offs often present in political decision making and highlighting the interconnectedness of foreign and domestic politics. The appendix, "Jobs and Careers in International Relations," helps students think about job possibilities in the field. These pages, devoted to careers in nongovernmental organizations, government and diplomacy, international business, and teaching and research, respond to the question, How will this class help me find a job? and include books and internet sites to further pursue the issue.

Many people find information—especially abstract concepts—easier to grasp when it is linked with pictures. Thus, the text uses color photographs extensively to illustrate important points. Photo captions reinforce main themes from the text and link them with the scenes pictured. Many of the photographs in this edition were taken in 2014 and 2015.

Students use different learning styles. Students who are visual learners should find not only the photos but also the many color graphics especially useful. The use of quantitative data also encourages critical thinking. Basic data, presented simply and appropriately at a global level, allow students to form their own judgments and to reason through the implications of different policies and theories. The text uses global-level data (showing the whole picture), rounds off numbers to highlight what is important, and conveys information graphically where appropriate.

Jon C. W. Pevehouse

Joshua S. Goldstein

Supplements

Pearson is pleased to offer several resources to qualified adopters of the Brief Seventh Edition *International Relations* and their students that will make teaching and learning from this text even more effective and enjoyable. Several of the supplements for this text are available at the Instructor Resource Center (IRC), an online hub that allows instructors to download quickly text-specific supplements. Please visit the IRC welcome page at www.pearsonhighered.com/irc to register for access.

INSTRUCTOR'S MANUAL/TEST BANK   This resource includes chapter summaries, learning objectives, lecture outlines, multiple-choice questions, true/false questions, and essay questions for each chapter. Available for download from the IRC.

PEARSON MYTEST   This powerful assessment generation program includes all of the items in the instructor's manual/test bank. Questions and tests can be easily created, customized, saved online, and then printed, allowing flexibility to manage assessments anytime and anywhere. To learn more, please visit www.mypearsontest.com or contact your Pearson representative.

POWERPOINT PRESENTATION   Organized around a lecture outline, these multimedia presentations also include photos, figures, and tables from each chapter. Available for download from the IRC.

Acknowledgments

Many scholars, colleagues, and friends have contributed ideas that influenced the various editions of this text. The text owes a special debt to the late Robert C. North, who suggested many years ago that the concepts of bargaining and leverage could be used to integrate IR theory across four levels of analysis. For help with military data issues, we thank the late Randall Forsberg. For suggestions, we thank our colleagues, and the students in our world politics classes. For help with data research, we thank Tana Johnson, Felicity Vabulas, Inken von Borzyskowski, Alex Holland, Lindsey Wagner, Monica Widmann, and Natalia Canas. Thanks to Mark Lilleleht for his assistance on the appendix, "Jobs and Careers in International Relations." Finally, we appreciate the years of support we received from our late colleague, teacher, and friend Deborah "Misty" Gerner.

About the Authors

Jon C. W. Pevehouse is Vilas Distinguished Achievement Professor of Political Science at the University of Wisconsin–Madison. He is an award-winning teacher and scholar. His research interests focus on international political economy, foreign policy, and international organizations. He is currently the editor of the leading professional journal in the field, *International Organization*. He received his BA from the University of Kansas and his Ph.D. from Ohio State University.

Joshua S. Goldstein is Professor Emeritus of International Relations, American University (Washington, DC) and Research Scholar, University of Massachusetts Amherst. He is an award-winning scholar who has written and spoken widely on war and society, including war's effects on gender, economics, and psychological trauma. His book *War and Gender* won the International Studies Association's Book of the Decade award.

To the Student

The topics studied by scholars are like a landscape with many varied locations and terrains. This textbook is a map that can orient you to the main topics, debates, and issue areas in international relations. Scholars use specialized language to talk about their subjects. This text is a phrase book that can translate such lingo and explain the terms and concepts that scholars use to talk about international relations. However, IR is filled with many voices speaking many tongues. The text translates some of those voices—of presidents and professors, free traders and feminists—to help you sort out the contours of the subject and the state of knowledge about its various topics. In this seventh edition, we have especially tried to streamline and clarify this complex subject to help you not just understand but deeply understand international relations. But ultimately, the synthesis presented in this text is the authors' own. Both you and your professor may disagree with many points. Thus, this textbook is only a starting point for conversations and debates.

With a combined map and phrase book in hand, you are ready to explore a fascinating world. The great changes in world politics in the past few years have made the writing of this textbook an exciting project. May you enjoy your own explorations of this realm.

J. C. W. P.

J. S. G.

A Note on Nomenclature

In international relations, names are politically sensitive; different actors may call a territory or an event by different names. This text cannot resolve such conflicts; it has adopted the following naming conventions for the sake of consistency. The United Kingdom of Great Britain (England, Scotland, Wales) and Northern Ireland is called Britain. Burma, renamed Myanmar by its military government, is referred to as Burma. The country of Bosnia and Herzegovina is generally shortened to Bosnia (with apologies to Herzegovinians). The former Yugoslav Republic of Macedonia is called Macedonia. The People's Republic of China is referred to as China. The Democratic Republic of the Congo (formerly called the Belgian Congo and then Zaire) is here called Democratic Congo. We refer to Cote D'Ivoire as Ivory Coast. Elsewhere, country names follow common usage, dropping formal designations such as "Republic of." We refer to the Sea of Japan, which some call the East Sea, and to the Persian Gulf, which is also called the Arabian Gulf. The 1991 U.S.-led multinational military campaign that retook Kuwait after Iraq's 1990 invasion is called the Gulf War, and the U.S. war in Iraq after 2003 is called the Iraq War. The war between Iran and Iraq in the 1980s is called the Iran-Iraq War.

Map

World States and Territories

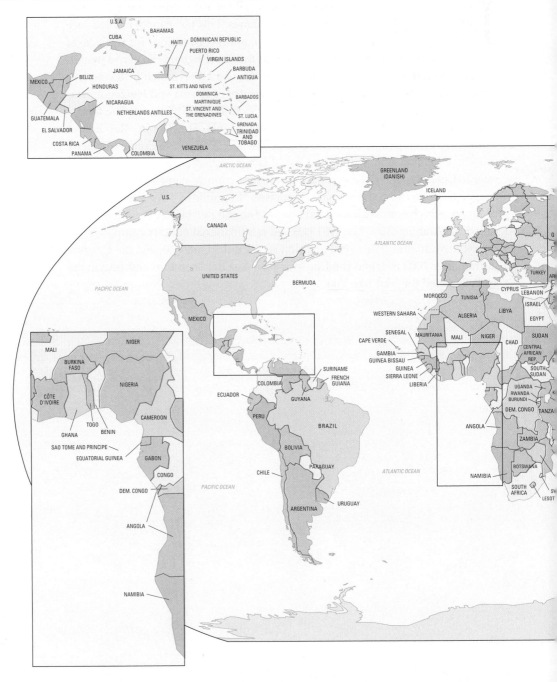

Map **xxi**

Chapter 1
The Globalization of International Relations

INTERNATIONAL SPACE STATION, 2010.

 ## Learning Objectives

1.1 Describe the properties of the collective action problem and how each core principle addresses the problem.

1.2 Evaluate whether states are still the key actors in international relations.

1.3 Identify at least three commonalities between states in the global North and states in the global South.

1.4 Explain at least two differences between the Cold War era and the post–Cold War era.

Globalization, International Relations, and Daily Life

1.1 Describe the properties of the collective action problem and how each core principle addresses the problem.

International relations is a fascinating topic because it concerns peoples and cultures throughout the world. The scope and complexity of the interactions among these groups make international relations a challenging subject to master.

Narrowly defined, the field of **international relations (IR)** concerns the relationships among the world's governments. But these relationships cannot be understood in isolation. They are closely connected with other actors (such as international organizations, multinational corporations, and individuals), with other social structures (including economics, culture, and domestic politics), and with geographical and historical influences. These elements together power the central trend in IR today—globalization.

Indeed, three key events of recent years reflect globalization. In 2014, an outbreak of the Ebola virus in Africa led to concerns of a global epidemic. Victims far from Africa—in Spain, the United States, and Great Britain—were quarantined, while new health-screening procedures to prevent the spread of the virus were implemented at hospitals and health clinics throughout those countries. The young protesters of the Arab Spring who overthrew several governments in 2011–2012 used Facebook and cell phones to plan and coordinate their revolutions. And the global economic recession of 2008–2009, which began with a collapse of the U.S. home mortgage market, spread quickly to other nations. Highly integrated global financial markets created a ripple effect across the globe that is still being felt today. Thus, three hallmarks of globalization—the ease of global travel, expanding communications technology, and integrated markets—propelled events that affected our daily lives.

Not only large-scale events influence our lives. The prospects for getting jobs after graduation depend on the global economy and international economic competition. Those jobs also are more likely than ever to entail international travel, sales, or communication. And the rules of the world trading system affect the goods that students consume every day, such as electronics, clothes, and gasoline.

Globalization has distinct positive impacts on our daily lives as well. As technology advances, the world is shrinking year by year. Better communication

international relations (IR) The relationships among the world's state governments and the connection of those relationships with other actors (such as the United Nations, multinational corporations, and individuals), with other social relationships (including economics, culture, and domestic politics), and with geographic and historical influences.

and transportation capabilities constantly expand the ordinary person's contact with people, products, and ideas from other countries. Globalization is internationalizing us.

In addition to feeling the influence of globalization and international relations on our daily lives, individual citizens can influence the world as well. Often, international relations is portrayed as a distant and abstract ritual conducted by a small group of people such as presidents, generals, and diplomats. Although leaders do play a major role in international affairs, many other people participate as well. College students and other citizens participate in international relations every time they vote in an election or work on a political campaign, buy a product or service traded on world markets, and watch the news. The choices we make in our daily lives ultimately affect the world we live in.

The purpose of this book is to introduce the field of IR, to organize what is known and theorized about IR, and to convey the key concepts used by political scientists to discuss relations among nations. This first chapter defines IR as a field of study, introduces the actors of interest, and reviews the geographical and historical aspects of globalization within which IR occurs.

Core Principles

The field of IR reflects the world's complexity, and IR scholars use many theories, concepts, and buzzwords in trying to describe and explain it. Underneath this complexity, however, lie a few basic principles that shape the field. We will lay out the range of theories and approaches in Chapters 2 and 3, but here we will present the most central ideas as free from jargon as possible.

IR revolves around one key problem: How can a group—such as two or more countries—serve its *collective* interests when doing so requires its members to forgo their *individual* interests? For example, every country has an interest in stopping global warming, a goal that can be achieved only by many countries acting together. Yet each country also has an individual interest in burning fossil fuels to keep its economy going. Similarly, all members of a military alliance benefit from the strength of the alliance, but each member separately has an interest in minimizing its own contributions in troops and money. Individual nations can advance their own short-term interests by seizing territory militarily, cheating on trade

TOUCHED BY WAR IR affects our lives in many ways. This woman's boyfriend died in Iraq in 2006.

agreements, and refusing to contribute to international efforts such as peace-keeping or vaccination campaigns. But if all nations acted this way, they would find themselves worse off, in a chaotic and vicious environment where mutual gains from cooperating on issues of security and trade would disappear.

This problem of shared interests versus conflicting interests among members of a group goes by various names in various contexts—the problem of "collective action," "free riding," "burden sharing," the "tragedy of the commons," or the "prisoner's dilemma." We will refer to the general case as the **collective goods problem**, that is, the problem of how to provide something that benefits all members of a group regardless of what each member contributes to it.

collective goods problem A tangible or intangible good, created by the members of a group, that is available to all group members regardless of their individual contributions; participants can gain by lowering their own contribution to the collective good, yet if too many participants do so, the good cannot be provided.

In general, collective goods are easier to provide in small groups than in large ones. In a small group, the cheating (or free riding) of one member is harder to conceal, has a greater impact on the overall collective good, and is easier to punish. The advantage of small groups helps explain the importance of the great power system in international security affairs and of the Group of Twenty (G20) industrialized countries in economic matters.

The collective goods problem occurs in all groups and societies, but it is particularly acute in international affairs because each nation is sovereign, with no central authority such as a world government to enforce on individual nations the necessary measures to provide for the common good. By contrast, in domestic politics *within* countries, a government can force individuals to contribute in ways that do not serve their individual self-interest, such as by paying taxes or paying to install antipollution equipment on vehicles and factories. If individuals do not comply, the government can punish them. Although this solution is far from perfect—cheaters and criminals sometimes are not caught, and governments sometimes abuse their power—it mostly works well enough to keep societies going.

Three basic principles—which we call dominance, reciprocity, and identity—offer possible solutions to the core problem of getting individuals to cooperate for the common good without a central authority to make them do so (see Table 1.1). These three principles are fundamental across the social sciences and recur in disciplines as diverse as the study of animal societies, child development, social psychology, anthropology, and economics, as well as political

Table 1.1 Core Principles for Solving Collective Goods Problems

Principle	Advantages	Drawbacks
Dominance	Order, Stability, Predictability	Oppression, Resentment
Reciprocity	Incentives for Mutual Cooperation	Downward Spirals; Complex Accounting
Identity	Sacrifice for Group, Redefine Interests	Demonizing an Out-Group

science. To explain each principle, we will apply the three principles to a small-scale human example and an IR example.

DOMINANCE   The principle of **dominance** solves the collective goods problem by establishing a power hierarchy in which those at the top control those below—a bit like a government but without an actual government. Instead of fighting constantly over who gets scarce resources, the members of a group can just fight occasionally over position in the "status hierarchy." Then social conflicts such as who gets resources are resolved automatically in favor of the higher-ranking actor. Fights over the dominance position have scripted rules that minimize, to some extent, the harm inflicted on the group members. Symbolic acts of submission and dominance reinforce an ever-present status hierarchy. Staying on top of a status hierarchy does not depend on strength alone, though it helps. Rather, the top actor may be the one most adept at forming and maintaining alliances among the group's more capable members. Dominance is complex and not just a matter of brute force.

> **dominance** A principle for solving collective goods problems by imposing solutions hierarchically.

In international relations, the principle of dominance underlies the great power system, in which a handful of countries dictate the rules for all the others. Sometimes a so-called *hegemon* or superpower stands atop the great powers as the dominant nation. The UN Security Council, in which the world's five strongest military powers hold a veto, reflects the dominance principle.

The advantage of the dominance solution to the collective goods problem is that, like a government, it forces members of a group to contribute to the common good. It minimizes open conflict within the group. However, the disadvantage is that this stability comes at a cost of constant oppression of, and resentment by, the lower-ranking members in the status hierarchy. Also, conflicts over position in the hierarchy can occasionally harm the group's stability and well-being, such as when challenges to the top position lead to serious fights. In the case of international relations, the great power system and the hegemony of a superpower can provide relative peace and stability for decades on end but then can break down into costly wars among the great powers.

RECIPROCITY   The principle of **reciprocity** solves the collective goods problem by rewarding behavior that contributes to the group and punishing behavior that pursues self-interest at the expense of the group. Reciprocity is very easy to understand and can be "enforced" without any central authority, making it a robust way to get individuals to cooperate for the common good.

> **reciprocity** A response in kind to another's actions; a strategy of reciprocity uses positive forms of leverage to promise rewards and negative forms of leverage to threaten punishment.

But reciprocity operates in both the positive realm ("You scratch my back and I'll scratch yours") and the negative ("An eye for an eye, a tooth for a tooth"). A disadvantage of reciprocity as a solution to the collective goods problem is that it can lead to a downward spiral as each side punishes what it believes to be negative acts by the other. Psychologically, most people overestimate their own good intentions and underestimate the value of the actions of their opponents or rivals. To avoid tit-for-tat escalations of conflict, one or both parties must act generously to get the relationship moving in a good direction.

In international relations, reciprocity forms the basis of most of the norms (habits; expectations) and institutions in the international system. Many central arrangements in IR, such as World Trade Organization (WTO) agreements, explicitly recognize reciprocity as the linchpin of cooperation. For instance, if one country opens its markets to another's goods, the other opens its markets in return. On the negative side, reciprocity fuels arms races as each side responds to the other's buildup of weapons. But it also allows arms control agreements and other step-by-step conflict-resolution measures, as two sides match each other's actions in backing away from the brink of war.

IDENTITY   A third potential solution to the collective goods problem lies in the identities of participants as members of a community. Although the dominance and reciprocity principles act on the idea of achieving individual self-interest (by taking what you can, or by mutually beneficial arrangements), the **identity** principle does not rely on self-interest. On the contrary, members of an identity community care about the interests of others in the community enough to sacrifice their own interests to benefit others. The roots of this principle lie in the family, the extended family, and the kinship group. But this potential is not limited to the close family; it can be generalized to any identity community that one feels a part of. As members of a family care about each other, so do members of an ethnic group, a gender group, a nation, or the world's scientists. In each case, individual members will accept solutions to collective goods problems that do not give them the best deal as individuals because the benefits are "all in the family," so to speak. A biologist retiring from a rich American university may give away lab equipment to a biologist in a poor country because they share an identity as scientists. A computer scientist from India may return home to work for lower pay after receiving training in Canada in order to help the community he or she cares about. Millions of people contribute to international disaster relief funds after tsunamis, earthquakes, or hurricanes because of a shared identity as members of the community of human beings.

identity A principle for solving collective goods problems by changing participants' preferences based on their shared sense of belonging to a community.

In IR, identity communities play important roles in overcoming difficult collective goods problems, including the issue of who contributes to development assistance, world health, and UN peacekeeping missions. The relatively large foreign aid contributions of Scandinavian countries, or the high Canadian participation in peacekeeping, cannot be explained well by self-interest but arise from these countries' self-defined identities as members of the international community. Even in military force and diplomacy (where dominance and reciprocity, respectively, rule the day), the shared identities of military professionals and of diplomats—each with shared traditions and expectations—can take the edge off conflicts. And military alliances also mix identity politics with raw self-interest, as shown by the unusual strength of the U.S.-British alliance, which shared interests alone cannot explain as well as shared identity does.

Nonstate actors, such as nongovernmental organizations or terrorist networks, also rely on identity politics to a great extent. The increasing roles of these actors—which include feminist organizations, churches, jihadists, and multinational corporations—have brought the identity principle to greater prominence in IR theory in recent years.

AN EVERYDAY EXAMPLE   To sum up the three core principles, imagine that you have two good friends, a man and a woman, who are in a romantic relationship. They love each other and enjoy the other's company, but they come to you for help with a problem: When they go out together, the man likes to go to the opera, whereas the woman enjoys going to boxing matches. (This is loosely based on a game theory scenario called "Battle of the Sexes.") Because of your training in international relations, you quickly recognize this as a collective goods problem in which the shared interest is spending time together and the conflicting individual interests are watching opera and watching boxing. (Of course, you know that the behavior of states is more complicated than that of individuals, but put that aside for a moment.) You might approach this problem in any of three ways.

First, you could say, "Traditionally, relationships work best when the man wears the pants. For thousands of years, the man has made the decision and the woman has followed it. I suggest you do the same, and buy season tickets to the opera." This would be a dominance solution. It could be a very stable solution, if the woman cares more about spending time with her true love than she cares about opera or boxing. It would be a simple solution that would settle all future conflicts. It would give one party everything he wants, and the other party some of what she wants (love, company, a stable relationship). This might be better for both of them than spending all their evenings arguing about where to go out. On the other hand, this solution might leave the woman permanently resentful at the manifestly unequal nature of the outcome. She might feel her love for her partner diminish over time by a longing for respect and a nostalgia for boxing. She might even meet another man who likes her *and* likes boxing.

Second, you could say, "Look, instead of fighting all the time, why don't you establish a pattern and trade off going to boxing one time and opera the next." This would be a reciprocity solution. You could set up agreements, accounting systems, and shared expectations to govern the implementation of this seemingly simple solution. For example, they could go to boxing on Friday nights and opera on Saturday nights. But what if opera season is shorter than boxing season? Then perhaps they would go to opera more often during its season and boxing more often when opera is out of season. What if one of them is out of town on a Friday night? Does that night count anyway or does it earn a credit for later? Or does the one who is in town go out alone? What if the man *hates* boxing but the woman only mildly dislikes opera? Do you set up a schedule of two operas for each boxing match to keep each side equally happy or unhappy? Clearly, reciprocity solutions can become very complicated (just look at the world trade rules in Chapter 5, for example), and they require constant monitoring to see if obligations are being met and cheating is being avoided. Your friends might find it an irritant in their relationship to keep close track of who owes whom a night at the opera or a boxing match.

TRAVEL COMPANIONS Collective goods are provided to all members of a group regardless of their individual contributions, just as these migrant workers crossing the Sahara desert in Niger in 2006 all depend on the truck's progress even while perhaps jostling for position among themselves. In many issue areas, such as global warming, the international community of nations is similarly interdependent. However, the provision of collective goods presents difficult dilemmas as players seek to maximize their own share of benefits.

Third, you could say, "Who cares about opera or boxing? The point is that you love each other and want to be together. Get past the superficial issues and strengthen the core feelings that brought you together. Then it won't matter where you go or what you're watching." This would be an identity solution. This approach could powerfully resolve your friends' conflict and leave them both much happier. Over time, one partner might actually begin to prefer the other's favorite activity after more exposure—leading to a change in identity. On the other hand, after a while self-interest could creep back in because that loving feeling might seem even happier with a boxing match or opera to watch. Indeed, one partner can subtly exploit the other's commitment to get past the superficial conflicts. "What's it matter as long as we're together," she says, "and oh, look, there's a good boxing match tonight!" Sometimes the identity principle operates more powerfully in the short term than the long term: The soldier who volunteers to defend the homeland might begin to feel taken advantage of after months or years on the front line, and the American college student who gives money once to tsunami victims may not want to keep giving year after year to malaria victims.

AN IR EXAMPLE Now consider the problem of nuclear proliferation. All countries share an interest in the collective good of peace and stability, which is hard to achieve in a world where more and more countries make more and more nuclear weapons. If individuals acquire dangerous weapons within a society, the government can take them away to keep everyone safe. But in the society of nations, no such central authority exists. In 2006, North Korea tested its first nuclear bomb, and Iran continues uranium enrichment that could lead to a nuclear bomb—defying UN resolutions in both cases.

One approach to nuclear proliferation legitimizes these weapons' ownership by just the few most powerful countries. The "big five" with the largest nuclear arsenals hold veto power on the UN Security Council. Through agreements like the Non-Proliferation Treaty (NPT) and the Proliferation Security Initiative, the existing nuclear powers actively try to keep their exclusive hold on these weapons and prevent smaller nations from getting them. This is a dominance approach. In 2003, when the United States thought Iraq's Saddam Hussein might have an active nuclear weapons program, as he had a decade earlier, it invaded Iraq and overthrew its government. Similarly, in 1982, when Iraq had begun working toward a nuclear bomb, Israel sent jets to bomb Iraq's nuclear facility, setting back the program by years. One drawback to these dominance solutions is the resentment they create among the smaller countries. Those countries point to an unenforced provision of the NPT stating that existing nuclear powers should get rid of their own bombs as other countries refrain from making new ones. And they ask what gives Israel the right to bomb another country, or the United States the right to invade one. They speak of a "double standard" for the powerful and the weak.

Reciprocity offers a different avenue for preventing proliferation. It is the basis of the provision in the NPT about the existing nuclear powers' obligation to disarm in exchange for smaller countries' agreement to stay nonnuclear. Reciprocity also underlies arms control agreements, used extensively in the Cold War to manage the buildup of nuclear bombs by the superpowers and used currently to manage the mutual reduction of their arsenals. Deterrence also relies on reciprocity. The United States warned North Korea in 2006 against selling its bombs (an action that would be in North Korea's short-term self-interest), threatening to retaliate against North Korea if any other actor used such a bomb against the United States. And when Libya gave up its nuclear weapons program in 2003, the international community gave it various rewards, including the ending of economic sanctions, in exchange.

The identity principle has proven equally effective, if less newsworthy, against nuclear proliferation. Many nations that have the technical ability to make nuclear weapons have *chosen* not to do so. They have constructed their national identities in ways that shape their self-interests and that make nuclear bombs undesirable. Some, like Sweden, do not intend to fight wars. Others, like Germany, belong to alliances in which they come under another nation's nuclear "umbrella" and do not need their own bomb. South Africa actually developed nuclear weapons in secret but then dismantled the program before apartheid ended, keeping the bomb out of the hands of the new majority-rule government. Nobody forced South Africa to do this (as in dominance), nor did it respond to rewards and punishments (reciprocity). Rather, South Africa's identity shifted. Similarly, Japan's experience of the catastrophic results of militarism, culminating in the destruction of two of its cities by nuclear bombs in 1945, continues generations later to shape Japan's identity as a country that does not want nuclear weapons, even though it has the know-how and even the stockpile of plutonium to make them.

Collective goods problems fascinate social scientists, and especially scholars of IR, precisely because they have no easy solutions. In later chapters, we will see how these three core principles shape the responses of the international community to various collective goods problems across the whole range of IR issues.

IR as a Field of Study

As part of political science, IR is about *international politics*—the decisions of governments about foreign actors, especially other governments. To some extent, however, the field is interdisciplinary, relating international politics to economics, history, sociology, and other disciplines. Some universities offer separate degrees or departments for IR. Most, however, teach IR in political science classes, in which the focus is on the *politics* of economic relationships, or the *politics* of environmental management, to take two examples. (The domestic politics of foreign countries, although overlapping with IR, generally makes up the separate field of *comparative politics*.)

Political relations among nations cover a range of activities—diplomacy, war, trade relations, alliances, cultural exchanges, participation in international organizations, and so forth. Particular activities within one of these spheres make up distinct **issue areas** on which scholars and foreign policy makers focus attention. Examples of issue areas include global trade, the environment, and specific conflicts such as the Arab-Israeli conflict. Within each issue area, and across the range of issues of concern in any international relationship, policy makers of one nation can behave in a cooperative manner or a conflictual manner—extending either friendly or hostile behavior toward the other nation. IR scholars often look at international relations in terms of the mix of **conflict and cooperation** in relationships among nations.

The scope of the field of IR may also be defined by the *subfields* it encompasses. Some scholars treat topics such as this text's chapters (for example, international law or international development) as subfields, but here we will reserve the term for two macro-level topics. Traditionally, the study of IR has focused on questions of war and peace—the subfield of **international security** studies. The movements of armies and of diplomats, the crafting of treaties and alliances, and the development and deployment of military capabilities were subjects that dominated the study of IR in the past, especially in the 1950s and 1960s, and they continue to hold a central position in the field. Since the Cold War, regional conflicts and ethnic violence have received more attention, while interdisciplinary peace studies programs and feminist scholarship have sought to broaden concepts of "security" further.

The subfield of **international political economy (IPE)**, a second main subfield of IR, concerns trade and financial relations among nations, and focuses on how nations have cooperated politically to create and maintain institutions that regulate the flow of international economic and financial transactions. Although these topics previously centered on relations among the world's richer nations, the widening of globalization and multilateral economic institutions such as the World Trade Organization has pushed IPE scholars to focus on developing states as well. In addition, they pay growing attention to relations between developed and developing nations (often labeled North-South relations), including topics such as economic dependency, debt, foreign aid, and technology transfer. Also newly important are problems of international environmental management and of global telecommunications. The subfield of IPE is expanding accordingly.

The same principles and theories that help us understand international security (in the first half of this text) also help us understand IPE (in the second half). Economics is important in security affairs, and vice versa.

issue areas Distinct spheres of international activity (such as global trade negotiations) within which policy makers of various states face conflicts and sometimes achieve cooperation.

conflict and cooperation The types of actions that states take toward each other through time.

international security A subfield of international relations (IR) that focuses on questions of war and peace.

international political economy (IPE) The study of the politics of trade, monetary, and other economic relations among nations, and their connection to other transnational forces.

Actors and Influences

1.2 **Evaluate whether states are still the key actors in international relations.**

The principal actors in IR are the world's governments. Scholars of IR traditionally study the decisions and acts of those governments in relation to other governments. The international stage is crowded with actors large and small who are intimately interwoven with the decisions of governments. These actors are individual leaders and citizens. They are bureaucratic agencies in foreign ministries. They are multinational corporations and terrorist groups. But the most important actors in IR are states.

State Actors

A **state** is a territorial entity controlled by a government and inhabited by a population. The locations of the world's states and territories are shown in the reference map at the front of this book.

A state government answers to no higher authority; it exercises *sovereignty* over its territory (to make and enforce laws, to collect taxes, and so forth). This sovereignty is recognized (acknowledged) by other states through diplomatic relations and usually by membership in the United Nations (UN). The population inhabiting a state forms a *civil society* to the extent that it has developed institutions to participate in political or social life. All or part of the population that shares a group identity may consider itself a *nation* (see p. 123). The state's government is a *democracy* to the extent that the government is controlled by the members of the population. In political life, and to some extent in IR scholarship, the terms *state, nation,* and *country* are used imprecisely, usually to refer to state governments. (Note that the word *state* in IR does not mean a state in the United States.)

With few exceptions, each state has a capital city—the seat of government from which it administers its territory—and often a single individual who acts in the name of the state. We will refer to this person simply as the "state leader." Often he or she is the *head of government* (such as a prime minister) or the *head of state* (such as a president, or a king or queen). In some countries, the same person is head of state and government. In other countries, the prime minister or the president or royalty is a symbolic leadership position. In any case, the most powerful political figure is the one we mean by "state leader," and these figures have been the key individual actors in IR. The state actor includes the individual leader as well as bureaucratic organizations such as foreign ministries that act in the name of the state. (What the United States calls *departments* are usually called *ministries* elsewhere. U.S. *secretaries* are *ministers* and the State Department corresponds with a foreign *ministry*.)

The **international system** is the set of relationships among the world's states, structured according to certain rules and patterns of interaction. Some such rules are explicit, some implicit. They include who is considered a member

state An inhabited territorial entity controlled by a government that exercises sovereignty over its territory.

international system The set of relationships among the world's states that is structured by certain rules and patterns of interaction.

POWERS THAT BE States are the most important actors in IR. A handful of states are considered great powers and one a "superpower." Here, leaders of Britain, the United States, and Germany watch a British-German soccer game (overtime shootout) together during a G8 summit at Camp David, 2012.

nation-states States whose populations share a sense of national identity, usually including a language and culture.

of the system, what rights and responsibilities the members have, and what kinds of actions and responses normally occur between states.

The modern international system has existed for only 500 years. Before then, people were organized into more mixed and overlapping political units such as city-states, empires, and feudal fiefs. In the past 200 years the idea has spread that nations—groups of people who share a sense of national identity, usually including a language and culture—should have their own states. Most large states today are such **nation-states**. But since World War II, the decolonization process in much of Asia and Africa has added many new states, some not at all nation-states. A major source of conflict and war at present is the frequent mismatch between perceived nations and actual state borders. When people identify with a nationality that their state government does not represent, they may fight to form their own state and thus to gain sovereignty over their territory and affairs. This substate nationalism is only one of several trends that undermine today's system of states. Others include the globalization of economic processes, the power of telecommunications, and the proliferation of ballistic missiles.

The independence of former colonies and, more recently, the breakup into smaller states of large multinational states (the Soviet Union and Yugoslavia) have increased the number of states in the world. The exact total depends on the status of a number of quasi-state political entities. The UN had 193 members in 2016.

Some other political entities are often referred to as states or countries, although they are not formally recognized as states. Taiwan is the most important of these. It operates independently in practice but is claimed by China (a claim recognized formally by outside powers) and is not a UN member. Formal colonies and possessions still exist; their status may change in the future. They include Puerto Rico (U.S.), Bermuda (British), Martinique (French), French Guiana, the Netherlands Antilles (Dutch), the Falkland Islands (British), and Guam (U.S.). Hong Kong reverted from British to Chinese rule in 1997 and retains a somewhat separate identity under China's "one country, two systems" formula. The status of the Vatican (Holy See) in Rome is ambiguous as is Palestine, which in 2012 joined the Vatican as the UN's only "nonmember observer state." Including various such territorial entities with states brings the world total to about 200 state or quasi-state actors. Other would-be states (such as Kurdistan and Western Sahara) do not fully control the territory they claim and are not widely recognized.

The population of the world's states varies dramatically: from China and India, with more than 1 billion people each, to microstates such as San

Figure 1.1 Largest Countries, 2014–2015

Source: Central Intelligence Agency. *World Factbook.* GDP estimates for 2014, population 2015.

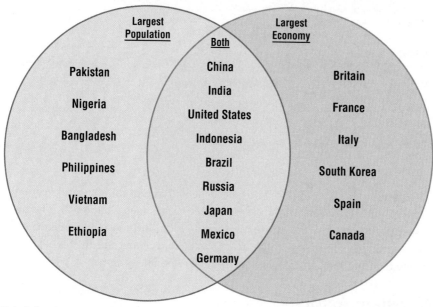

Largest Population	Both	Largest Economy
Pakistan	China	Britain
	India	
Nigeria	United States	France
Bangladesh	Indonesia	Italy
Philippines	Brazil	South Korea
	Russia	
Vietnam	Japan	Spain
Ethiopia	Mexico	Canada
	Germany	

Note: Left and center columns listed in population order, right column in GDP order. GDP calculated by purchasing parity.

Marino, with 32,000. With the creation of many small states in recent decades, the majority of states have fewer than 10 million people each, and more than half of the rest have 10 to 50 million each. But the 16 states with populations of more than 80 million people together contain about two-thirds of the world's population.

States also differ tremendously in the size of their total annual economic activity—**gross domestic product (GDP)**[1]—from the $17 trillion U.S. economy to the economies of tiny states such as the Pacific island of Tuvalu ($38 million). The world economy is dominated by a few states, just as world population is. Figure 1.1 lists the 15 largest countries by population and by economy. Each is an important actor in world affairs, especially the nine in the center that are largest in both population and economy.

gross domestic product (GDP) The size of a state's total annual economic activity.

---

[1] GDP is the total of goods and services produced by a nation; it is very similar to the gross national product (GNP). Such data are difficult to compare across nations with different currencies, economic systems, and levels of development. In particular, comparisons of GDP in capitalist and socialist economies, or in rich and poor countries, should be treated cautiously. GDP data used in this text are mostly from the World Bank. GDP data are adjusted through time and across countries for "purchasing-power parity" (how much a given amount of money can buy). See Summers, Robert, and Alan Heston. "The Penn World Table (Mark 5): An Expanded Set of International Comparisons, 1950–1988." *Quarterly Journal of Economics* 106 (2), 1991: 327–68. GDP and population data are for 2014 unless otherwise noted.

Table 1.2 Types of Nonstate Actors

Type		Who Are They?	Examples
IGOs[a]	Intergovernmental Organizations	Members are national governments	United Nations, NATO, Arab League
NGOs[a]	Nongovernmental Organizations	Members are individuals and groups	Amnesty International, Lions Clubs, Red Cross
MNCs	Multinational Corporations	Companies that span borders	ExxonMobil, Toyota, Wal-Mart
Others		Individuals, Cities, Constituencies, etc.	Bono, Iraqi Kurdistan, al Qaeda

[a]*Note:* IGOs and NGOs together make up International Organizations (IOs).

nonstate actors
Actors other than state governments that operate either below the level of the state (that is, within states) or across state borders.

intergovernmental organization (IGO)
An organization (such as the United Nations and its agencies) whose members are state governments.

nongovernmental organization (NGO)
A transnational group or entity (such as the Catholic Church, Greenpeace, or the International Olympic Committee) that interacts with states, multinational corporations (MNCs), other NGOs, and intergovernmental organizations (IGOs).

A few of these large states possess especially great military and economic strength and influence, and are called *great powers* (see Chapter 2). The most powerful of great powers, those with truly global influence, have been called *superpowers.* This term generally meant the United States and the Soviet Union during the Cold War, and now refers to the United States alone.

Nonstate Actors

National governments may be the most important actors in IR, but they are strongly influenced by a variety of **nonstate actors** (see Table 1.2). These actors are also called *transnational actors* when they operate across international borders.

First, states often take actions through, within, or in the context of **intergovernmental organizations (IGOs)**—organizations whose members are national governments. IGOs fulfill a variety of functions and vary in size from just a few states to nearly the whole UN membership. The Organization of Petroleum Exporting Countries (OPEC), the World Trade Organization (WTO), military alliances such as the North Atlantic Treaty Organization (NATO), and political groupings such as the African Union (AU) are all IGOs. Another type of transnational actor, **nongovernmental organizations (NGOs)**, are private organizations, some of considerable size and resources. Increasingly NGOs are being recognized, in the UN and other forums, as legitimate actors along with states, though not equal to them. Some of these groups have a political purpose; some, a humanitarian one; some, an economic or technical one. Sometimes NGOs combine efforts through transnational advocacy networks. There is no single pattern to NGOs. Together, IGOs and NGOs are referred to as international organizations (IOs). By one count there are more than 50,000 NGOs and 5,000 IGOs. IOs are discussed in detail in Chapter 6.

Multinational corporations (MNCs) are companies that span multiple countries. The interests of a large company doing business globally do not correspond with any one state's interests. MNCs often control greater resources, and operate internationally with greater efficiency, than many small states. They may prop up (or even create) friendly foreign governments, as the United Fruit Company did in the "banana republics" of Central America more than a century ago. But MNCs also provide poor states with much-needed foreign investment and tax revenues. MNCs in turn depend on states to provide protection, well-regulated markets, and a stable political environment. MNCs as international actors receive special attention in Chapters 5 and 7.

Various other nonstate actors interact with states, IOs, and MNCs. For example, the terrorist attacks since September 11, 2001, have demonstrated the increasing power that technology gives terrorists as nonstate actors. Just as Greenpeace can travel to a remote location and then beam video of its environmental actions there to the world, so too can al Qaeda place suicide bombers in world cities, coordinate their operations and finances through the Internet and global banking system, and reach a global audience with social media appeals. "Global reach," once an exclusive capability of great powers, now is available to many others, for better or worse.

Some nonstate actors are *substate actors:* they exist within one country but either influence that country's foreign policy or operate internationally, or both. For instance, the state of Ohio is entirely a U.S. entity but operates an International Trade Division to promote exports and foreign investment, with offices in Belgium, Japan, China, Canada, Israel, India, and Mexico. The actions of substate economic actors—companies, consumers, workers, investors—help create the context of economic activity against which international political events play out, and within which governments must operate.

In this world of globalization, of substate actors and transnational actors, states are still important. But to some extent they are being gradually pushed aside as companies, groups, and individuals deal ever more directly with each other across borders, and as the world economy becomes globally integrated. Now more than ever, IR extends beyond the interactions of national governments. Both state and nonstate actors are strongly affected by the revolution in information technologies now under way. The new information-intensive world promises to reshape international relations profoundly. Technological change dramatically affects actors' relative capabilities and even preferences. Telecommunications and computerization allow economics, politics, and culture alike to operate on a global scale as never before.

Levels of Analysis

The many actors involved in IR contribute to the complexity of competing explanations and theories. One way scholars of IR have sorted out this multiplicity of influences, actors, and processes is to categorize them into different *levels of analysis* (see Table 1.3). A level of analysis is a perspective on IR based on a set of similar actors or processes that suggests possible explanations to "why" questions. IR scholars have proposed various level-of-analysis schemes, most often with three main levels (and sometimes a few sublevels between).

Policy Perspectives

OVERVIEW International policy makers confront a variety of problems every day. Solving these problems requires difficult decisions and choices. Policy Perspectives is a box feature in each chapter that places you in a particular decision-making perspective (for example, the prime minister of Great Britain) and asks you to make choices concerning an important international relations issue.

Each box contains four sections. The first, Background, provides information about a political problem faced by the leader. This background information is factual and reflects real situations faced by these decision makers.

The second section, Domestic Considerations, reflects on the implications of the situation for domestic politics within the leader's government and society. How will the lives of ordinary citizens be affected?

The third section, Scenario, suggests a new problem or crisis confronting the leader. Although these crises are hypothetical, all are within the realm of possibility and would require difficult decisions by the leaders and their countries.

The fourth section, Choose Your Policy, asks you to make a choice responding to the Scenario.

With each decision, think about the trade-offs between your options. What are the risks and rewards in choosing one policy over another? Could alternative options address the problem within the given constraints effectively? Does one option pose bigger costs in the short term but fewer in the long term? Can you defend your decision to colleagues, the public, and other world leaders? How will your choice affect your citizens' lives and your own political survival?

As you consider each problem faced by the decision maker, try to reflect on the process and logic by which you have reached the decision. Which factors seem more important and why? Are domestic or international factors more important in shaping your decision? Are the constraints you face based on limited capability (for example, money or military power), or do international law or norms influence your decision as well? How do factors such as lack of time influence your decision?

You will quickly discover that there are often no "right" answers. At times, it is difficult to choose between two good options; at other times, one has to decide which is the least bad option.

The *individual* level of analysis concerns the perceptions, choices, and actions of individual human beings. Great leaders influence the course of history, as do individual citizens, thinkers, soldiers, and voters. Without Lenin, it is said, there might well have been no Soviet Union. If a few more people had voted for Nixon rather than Kennedy in the razor-close 1960 election, the Cuban Missile Crisis might have ended differently. The study of foreign policy decision making, discussed in Chapter 3, pays special attention to individual-level explanations of IR outcomes because of the importance of psychological factors in the decision-making process.

The *domestic* (or *state* or *societal*) level of analysis concerns the aggregations of individuals within states that influence state actions in the international arena, such as interest groups, political organizations, and government agencies. These groups operate differently (with different international effects) in different kinds of societies and states. Democracies may act differently from dictatorships, and democracies may act differently in an election year from the ways they do at other times. The politics of ethnic conflict and nationalism

Table 1.3 Levels of Analysis

Many influences affect the course of international relations. Levels of analysis provide a framework for categorizing these influences and thus for suggesting various explanations of international events. Examples include:

Global Level

North-South gap	Religious fundamentalism	Information revolution
World regions	Terrorism	Global telecommunications
European imperialism	World environment	Worldwide scientific and business
Norms	Technological change	communities

Interstate Level

Power	Wars	Diplomacy
Balance of power	Treaties	Summit meetings
Alliance formation	Trade agreements	Bargaining
and dissolution	IGOs	Reciprocity

Domestic Level

Nationalism	Dictatorship	Gender
Ethnic conflict	Domestic coalitions	Economic sectors and industries
Type of government	Political parties and elections	Military-industrial complex
Democracy	Public opinion	Foreign policy bureaucracies

Individual Level

Great leaders	Psychology of perception and decision	Citizens' participation (voting,
Crazy leaders	Learning	rebelling, going to war, etc.)
Decision making in crises	Assassinations, accidents of history	

plays an increasingly important role in the relations among states. Economic sectors within states, including the military-industrial sector, can influence their governments to take actions in the international arena that are good for business. Within governments, foreign policy agencies often fight bureaucratic battles over policy decisions.

The *interstate* (or *international* or *systemic*) level of analysis concerns the influence of the international system upon outcomes. Thus, it focuses on the interactions of states themselves, without regard to their internal makeup or the particular individuals who lead them. This level pays attention to states' relative power positions in the international system and the interactions among them. It has been traditionally the most important of the levels of analysis.

To these three levels can be added a fourth, the *global* level of analysis, which seeks to explain international outcomes in terms of global trends and forces that transcend the interactions of states. The changes of human technology, of certain worldwide beliefs, and of humans' relationship to the natural environment are all processes at the global level that influence international relations. The global level is also increasingly the focus of IR scholars studying transnational integration through worldwide scientific, technical, and business communities (see Chapter 8). Another pervasive global influence is the lingering effect of historical European imperialism.

Although IR scholars often focus their study mainly on one level of analysis, other levels bear on a problem simultaneously. There is no single correct level for a given "why" question. Rather, levels of analysis help suggest multiple explanations and approaches in trying to explain a given event. They remind scholars and students to look beyond the immediate and superficial aspects of an event to explore the possible influences of more distant causes. Note that the processes at higher levels tend to operate more slowly than those at the lower levels. Individuals go in and out of office often; the structure of the international system changes rarely.

Globalization

globalization The increasing integration of the world in terms of communications, culture, and economics; may also refer to changing subjective experiences of space and time accompanying this process.

Globalization encompasses many trends, including expanded international trade, telecommunications, monetary coordination, multinational corporations, technical and scientific cooperation, cultural exchanges of new types and scales, migration and refugee flows, and relations between the world's rich and poor countries. Although globalization clearly is very important, it is also rather vaguely defined and not well explained by any one theory. One popular conception of globalization is "the widening, deepening, and speeding up of worldwide interconnectedness in all aspects of contemporary social life. . . ." But at least three conceptions of this process compete.

One view sees globalization as the fruition of liberal economic principles (see Chapter 5). A global marketplace has brought growth and prosperity (not to all countries but to those most integrated with the global market). This economic process has made traditional states obsolete as economic units. States are thus losing authority to supranational institutions such as the International Monetary Fund (IMF) and the European Union (EU), and to transnational actors such as MNCs and NGOs. The values of technocrats and elite, educated citizens in liberal democracies are becoming global values, reflecting an emerging global civilization. The old North-South division is seen as less important because the global South is moving in divergent directions depending on countries' and regions' integration with world markets.

A second perspective is skeptical of these claims about globalization. These skeptics note that the world's major economies are no more integrated today than they were before World War I (when British

THINK GLOBALLY As the world economy becomes more integrated, markets and production are becoming global in scope. This container port in Shanghai ships goods to and from all over the world, 2013.

hegemony provided a common set of expectations and institutions). The skeptics also doubt that regional and geographic distinctions such as the North-South divide are disappearing in favor of a single global market. Rather, they see the North-South gap as increasing with globalization. Also, the economic integration of states may be leading not to a single world free-trade zone but to distinct and rival regional blocs in America, Europe, and Asia. The supposed emerging world civilization is disproved by the fragmenting of larger units (such as the Soviet Union) into smaller ones along lines of language, religion, and other such cultural factors.

A third school of thought sees globalization as more profound than the skeptics believe, yet more uncertain than the view of supporters of liberal economics. These "transformationalists" see state sovereignty as being eroded by the EU, the WTO, and other new institutions so that sovereignty is no longer an absolute but just one of a spectrum of bargaining leverages held by states. The bargaining itself increasingly involves nonstate actors. Thus, globalization diffuses authority. State power is not so much strengthened or weakened by globalization but transformed to operate in new contexts with new tools.

While scholars debate these conceptions of globalization, popular debates focus on the growing power of large corporations operating globally, the disruptive costs associated with joining world markets (for example, job loss and environmental impacts), the perception of growing disparities between the rich and the poor, and the collusion of national governments in these wrongs through their participation in IOs such as the WTO and the IMF. Policies to expand free trade are a central focus of antiglobalization protesters (see p. 187). Street protests have turned host cities into besieged fortresses in Seattle (1999); Washington, DC (2000 IMF and World Bank meetings); Quebec (2001 summit working toward a Free Trade Area of the Americas); and Genoa, Italy (2001 G8 summit). The key 2001 WTO meeting to launch a new trade round was held in Qatar, where protesters had little access. At the 2003 WTO meeting in Cancun, Mexico, thousands of protesters marched against the talks and the economic elites conducting them, but they were kept away from the WTO conference center. At the 2005 Hong Kong WTO meeting, protesters blocked nearby roads and some even tried to swim across Hong Kong harbor to disrupt the meeting. Just as scholars disagree on conceptions of globalization, so do protesters disagree on their goals and tactics. Union members from the global North want to stop globalization from shipping their jobs south. But workers in impoverished countries in the global South may desperately want those jobs as a first step toward decent wages and working conditions (relative to other options in their countries). Window-smashing anarchists meanwhile steal media attention from environmentalists seeking to amend the trade agenda. Thus, neither globalization nor the backlash to it is simple.

Globalization is changing both international security and IPE, as we will see in the coming chapters, but it is changing IPE more quickly and profoundly than security. The coming chapters address this broad range of topics, each affected by globalization. Chapter 3 shows how nonstate actors influence foreign policies of states. Chapter 5 looks at economic globalization, in trade, finance, and business, where globalization's influences are most apparent. Chapter 6 discusses global institutions, international law, and human rights, all of growing importance as globalization continues. Chapter 7 covers the global North-South divide, which is central to the concept of globalization. And Chapter 8 considers the information technology side of globalization as the world becomes wired in new ways, as well as the influence of globalization on our physical environment.

The *rest* of this chapter takes up two contextual aspects of globalization that shape the issue areas discussed in subsequent chapters—(1) the relations among the world's major regions, especially the rich North and poor South; and (2) the evolution of the international system over the past century, especially the past two decades of the post–Cold War era.

Global Geography

1.3   Identify at least three commonalities between states in the global North and states in the global South.

To highlight the insights afforded by a global level of analysis, this text divides the world into nine regions. These *world regions* differ from each other in the number of states they contain and in each region's particular mix of cultures, geographical realities, and languages. But each represents a geographical corner of the world, and together they reflect the overall larger divisions of the world.

North-South gap
The disparity in resources (income, wealth, and power) between the industrialized, relatively rich countries of the West (and the former East) and the poorer countries of Africa, the Middle East, and much of Asia and Latin America.

The global **North-South gap** between the industrialized, relatively rich countries of the North and the relatively poor countries of the South (see Chapter 7) is the most important geographical element at the global level of analysis. The regions used in this text have been drawn to separate (with a few exceptions) the rich countries from the poor ones. The North includes both the West (the rich countries of North America, Western Europe, and Japan) and the old East (the former Soviet Union and its bloc of allies).[2] The South includes Latin America, Africa, the Middle East, and much of Asia. The South is often called the *third world* (third after the West and East)—a term that is still widely used despite the second world's collapse. Countries in the South are also referred to as "developing" countries or "less-developed" countries (LDCs), in contrast to the "developed" countries of the North. The overall world regions are shown in Figure 1.2.

---

[2] Note that geographical designations such as the "West" and the "Middle East" are European-centered. From Korea, for example, China and Russia are to the west and Japan and the United States are to the east.

Figure 1.2 Nine Regions of the World

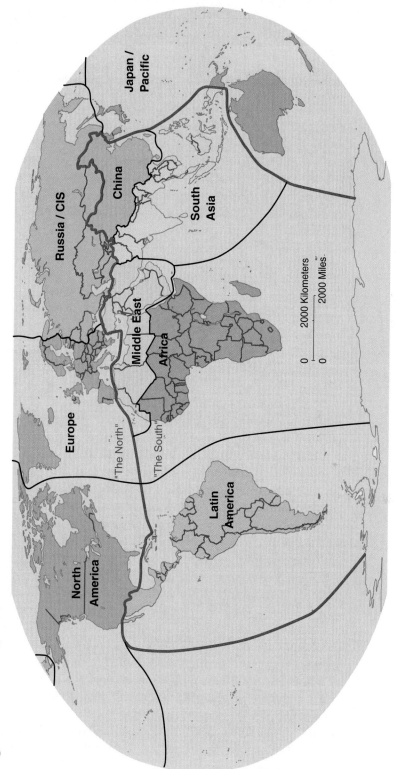

Table 1.4 Comparison of World Regions, 2014

Region	Population (Millions)	GDP (Trillion $)	GDP per Capita (Dollars)
The North			
North America	950	$18	$46,000
Europe	540	17	31,500
Japan/Pacific	240	8	30,000
Russia/CIS	280	4	11,000
The South			
China	1,395	15	10,000
Middle East	490	6	11,000
Latin America	615	7	12,000
South Asia	2,350	9	4,000
Africa	950	3	3,100
Total North	**1,400 (20%)**	**47 (55%)**	**33,000**
Total South	**5,800 (80%)**	**40 (45%)**	**7,000**
World Total	**7,200**	**$87**	**$12,000**

Note: Data adjusted for purchasing-power parity. 2014 GDP estimates (in 2015 dollars) are from Table 1.5; those for Russia, CIS, and China should be treated especially cautiously.

Source: World Bank Data

Most of these regions correspond with commonly used geographical names, but a few notes may help. *East Asia* refers to China, Japan, and Korea. *Southeast Asia* refers to countries from Burma through Indonesia and the Philippines. Russia is considered a European state, although a large section (Siberia) is in Asia. The *Pacific Rim* usually means East and Southeast Asia, Siberia, and the Pacific coast of North America and Latin America. *South Asia* only sometimes includes parts of Southeast Asia. Narrow definitions of the *Middle East* exclude both North Africa and Turkey. The *Balkans* are the states of southeastern Europe, bounded by Slovenia, Romania, and Greece.

Table 1.4 shows the approximate population and economic size (in terms of GDP) of each region in relation to the world as a whole. As the table shows, income levels per capita are, overall, more than five times as high in the North as in the South. *The North contains only 20 percent of the world's people but 55 percent of its goods and services.* The other 80 percent of the world's people, in the South, have only 45 percent of the goods and services. For individual countries within each world region, Table 1.5 shows total GDP for each country within a region (these definitions of regions will be used throughout the text). IR scholars have no single explanation of the huge North-South income gap (see Chapter 7).

Geography provides one context in which IR takes place; history provides another. The remainder of this chapter reviews the historical development of the international system since World War II.

Table 1.5 States and Territories with Estimated Total GDP, 2014 *(In billions of 2015 U.S. Dollars)*

North America

United States	17,000	Canada	1,700	Bahamas	10

Europe

Germany[a]	3,100	Norway	300	Latvia	40
Britain[a]	2,300	Portugal[a]	300	Bosnia and Herzegovina	40
France[a]	2,200	Denmark[a]	200	Albania	30
Italy[a]	2,000	Finland[a]	200	Estonia[a]	30
Spain[a]	1,400	Hungary[a]	200	Cyprus[a]	20
Netherlands[a]	800	Ireland[a]	200	Macedonia	20
Poland[a]	800	Slovakia[a]	100	Iceland	10
Belgium[a]	500	Bulgaria[a]	100	Malta[a]	10
Austria[a]	400	Serbia	90	Montenegro	9
Greece[a]	300	Croatia	90	Liechtenstein	4
Sweden[a]	400	Lithuania[a]	70	Andorra	4
Switzerland	400	Slovenia[a]	60	Monaco	1
Romania[a]	400	Luxembourg	50	San Marino	1
Czech Republic[a]	300				

Japan/Pacific

Japan	4,600	Fiji	6	Nauru	0
South Korea	1,600	Guam/Marianas[b]	4	Marshall Islands	0
Australia	1,100	Solomon Islands	1	Palau	0
New Zealand	100	Samoa	1	Kiribati	0
North Korea	40	Vanuatu	1	Tuvalu	0
Papua New Guinea	20	Tonga	1	Micronesia	0

Russia/CIS

Russia	2,200	Azerbaijan	100	Kyrgyzstan	20
Ukraine	400	Turkmenistan	70	Tajikistan	20
Kazakhstan	300	Georgia	30	Moldova	10
Belarus	200	Armenia	20	Mongolia	10
Uzbekistan	200				

China

China	14,000	Hong Kong[b]	400	Macau[b]	30
Taiwan[b]	900				

Middle East

Turkey	1,100	Morocco/W. Sahara	200	Oman	90
Iran	900	Kuwait	200	Libya	70
Saudi Arabia	800	Iraq	200	Yemen	60
Egypt	500	Qatar	200	Lebanon	60
United Arab Emirates	500	Syria	100	Jordan	40
Algeria	400	Tunisia	90	Bahrain	30
Israel/Palestine	300				

(continued)

Table 1.5 *(Continued)*

Latin America

Brazil	2,500	Bolivia	50	Suriname	5
Mexico	1,700	Panama	60	Guyana	5
Argentina	700	El Salvador	40	Belize	3
Colombia	500	Uruguay	40	Virgin Islands[b]	2
Venezuela	400	Paraguay	30	French Guiana[b]	2
Chile	300	Honduras	30	St. Lucia	2
Peru	300	Trinidad & Tobago	30	Antigua & Barbuda	2
Cuba	100	Jamaica	20	Grenada	1
Ecuador	100	Nicaragua	20	St. Vincent & Grenadines	1
Dominican Republic	100	Haiti	10	St. Kitts & Nevis	1
Puerto Rico[b]	70	Martinique[b]	7	Dominica	1
Guatemala	70	Barbados	7		
Costa Rica	60	Bermuda[b]	5		

South Asia

India	4,500	Bangladesh	300	Afghanistan	30
Indonesia	1,400	Singapore	300	Laos	20
Thailand	700	Sri Lanka	100	Bhutan	4
Pakistan	500	Burma (Myanmar)	70	East Timor	3
Malaysia	500	Nepal	40	Maldives	3
Philippines	400	Cambodia	40		
Vietnam	400	Brunei	30		

Africa

South Africa	600	Mauritius	20	Togo	7
Nigeria	500	Gabon	20	Somalia	6
Angola	100	Burkina Faso	20	Sierra Leone	6
Sudan	100	Chad	20	Burundi	5
Ethiopia	80	Mali	20	Central African Republic	4
Kenya	70	Namibia	20	Eritea	3
Ghana	70	Equatorial Guinea	20	Lesotho	3
Tanzania	60	Congo Republic	20	Djibouti	3
Cameroon	50	Malawi	20	Reunion[b]	3
Uganda	50	Zimbabwe	10	Gambia	3
Côte d'Ivoire (Ivory Coast)	40	Niger	10	Cape Verde	2
Botswana	30	Rwanda	10	Seychelles	2
Democratic Congo	30	Benin	10	Liberia	2
Zambia	30	Guinea	10	Guinea-Bissau	2
Mozambique	20	South Sudan	10	Comoros Islands	1
Senegal	20	Mauritania	10	São Tomé & Principe	0
Madagascar	20	Swaziland	7		

[a]European Union.
[b]Nonmember of UN.

Note: GDP data are inexact by nature. Estimates for Russia, CIS, China, and other nonmarket or transitional economies are particularly suspect and should be used cautiously. Numbers below 0.5 are listed as 0.

Sources: Data are authors' estimates based on World Bank calculations. Data are at purchasing-power parity. See footnote 1 on p. 13.

The Evolving International System

1.4 **Explain at least two differences between the Cold War era and the post–Cold War era.**

The basic structures and principles of international relations are deeply rooted in historical developments. The past 500 years, known as the "modern age," saw the rise of the international system of sovereign states. That era was dominated by recurring great power wars in Europe—in particular, the Thirty Years' War (1618–1648), the Napoleonic Wars (1803–1815), and the two World Wars (1914–1918 and 1939–1945). Such all-out wars among the world's most powerful armies, leaving whole continents in ruin, have not happened in the past 70 years and might never happen again. The history of these most recent 70 years is of particular importance to today's international system.

The Cold War, 1945–1990

The United States and the Soviet Union were the two superpowers of the post–World War II era: Each had its ideological mission (capitalist democracy versus communism), its networks of alliances and third world clients, and its deadly arsenal of nuclear weapons. Europe was divided, with massive military forces of the United States and its *NATO* allies on one side and massive forces of the Soviet Union and its *Warsaw Pact* allies on the other. Germany itself was split, with three-quarters of the country—and three-quarters of the capital city of Berlin—occupied by the United States, Britain, and France. The remainder, surrounding West Berlin, was occupied by the Soviet Union. In 1961, East Germany built the Berlin Wall separating East from West Berlin. It symbolized the division of Europe by what Winston Churchill had called the "iron curtain."

Despite the hostility of East-West relations during the **Cold War**, a relatively stable framework of relations emerged, and conflicts never escalated to all-out war between the largest states (see Figure 1.3). Although the Soviet bloc did not join Western economic institutions, all the world's major states joined the United Nations (unlike the ill-fated League of Nations).

The central concern of the West during the Cold War was that the Soviet Union might gain control of Western Europe—either through outright invasion or through communists' taking power in the war-weary and impoverished countries of Western Europe. This could have put the entire industrial base of the Eurasian landmass (from Europe to Siberia) under one state. The *Marshall Plan*—U.S. financial aid to rebuild European economies—responded to these fears, as did the creation of the NATO alliance. Half of the entire world's military spending was devoted to the European standoff. Much spending was also devoted to a superpower nuclear arms race, in which each superpower produced tens of thousands of nuclear weapons (see p. 168).

Through the policy of **containment**, adopted in the late 1940s, the United States sought to halt the expansion of Soviet influence globally on several levels

Cold War The hostile relations—punctuated by occasional periods of improvement, or détente—between the two superpowers, the United States and the Soviet Union, from 1945 to 1990.

containment A policy adopted in the late 1940s by which the United States sought to halt the global expansion of Soviet influence on several levels—military, political, ideological, and economic.

Figure 1.3 The Cold War, 1945–1990

Source: Gaddis, John Lewis. *We Now Know: Rethinking Cold War History.* Oxford, 1997. Zubok, Vladislav, and Constantine Pleshakov. *Inside the Kremlin's Cold War: From Stalin to Khrushchev.* Harvard, 1996. Garthoff, Raymond. *Détente and Confrontation: American-Soviet Relations from Nixon to Reagan.* Brookings, 1985. Larson, Deborah Welch. *Anatomy of Mistrust: U.S.-Soviet Relations During the Cold War.* Cornell, 1997. Trachtenberg, Marc. *A Constructed Peace: The Making of the European Settlement, 1945–1963.* Princeton, 1999.

	1940	1945	1950	1955	1960	1965	1970	1975	1980	1985	1990
Soviet Union		Stalin			Khrushchev		Brezhnev		Andropov / Chernenko	Gorbachev	
				Sputnik			nuclear parity with U.S.		military buildup	reforms (perestroika, glasnost)	
		A-bomb	Warsaw Pact								
United States	F. D. Roosevelt	Truman		Eisenhower	Kennedy	Johnson	Nixon	Ford	Carter	Reagan	Bush
			NATO	(nuclear superiority over USSR)		nuclear arms race			human rights	"Star Wars" (SDI)	
		containment policy							(Iran crisis)		
China		civil war (Nationalists-Communists)	Sino-Soviet alliance	People's Republic (Taiwan nationalist)	Sino-Soviet split	Soviet border clashes	U.S.-China rapprochement	death of Mao	neutral to pro-U.S.	student protests	
				Taiwan Straits crises (vs. U.S.)		A-bomb	joins UN				
						Cultural Revolution					
Confrontations		Berlin crisis		Soviet invasion of Hungary	Berlin Wall	USSR invades Czechoslovakia			U.S. invasion of Grenada		
		Greek civil war		U-2 incident	Berlin crisis						
				Cuban revolution	Cuban Missile Crisis						
		Korean War		Suez crisis		*Vietnam War*		*Afghanistan War*			
Proxy Wars						Indonesia	Arab-Israeli wars	Somalia vs. Ethiopia	Nicaragua		
								Chile coup	Cambodia	El Salvador	
										Angola	
Co-operation		Yalta summit		Geneva summit	Limited Test Ban Treaty	Non-Proliferation Treaty	SALT I	détente	SALT II	START talks	Paris summit (CFE)
											INF treaty

(WW II alliance)

at once—military, political, ideological, economic. The United States maintained an extensive network of military bases and alliances worldwide. Almost all of U.S. foreign policy in subsequent decades, from foreign aid and technology transfer to military intervention and diplomacy, came to serve the goal of containment.

The *Chinese communist revolution* in 1949 led to a Sino-Soviet alliance (*Sino* means "Chinese"). But China became fiercely independent in the 1960s following the **Sino-Soviet split**, when China opposed Soviet moves toward *peaceful coexistence* with the United States. In the late 1960s, young radicals, opposed to both superpowers, ran China during the chaotic and destructive *Cultural Revolution.* But feeling threatened by Soviet power, China's leaders developed a growing affiliation with the United States during the 1970s, starting with a dramatic visit to China by U.S. president Richard Nixon in 1972. During the Cold War, China generally tried to play a balancer role against whichever superpower seemed most threatening at the time.

In 1950, the *Korean War* broke out when communist North Korea attacked and overran most of U.S.-allied South Korea. The

IRON CURTAIN During the Cold War, the U.S. and Soviet sides sought spheres of influence. Europe was divided, and Germany itself was split, with its capital, Berlin, also divided. In 1961 the communist side built the Berlin Wall, seen here in 1962, to keep its population from leaving. It was dismantled as the Cold War ended in 1989.

United States and its allies (under UN authority obtained after the Soviets walked out of the Security Council in protest) counterattacked and overran most of North Korea. China sent "volunteers" to help North Korea, and the war bogged down near the original border until a 1953 truce. The Korean War hardened U.S. attitudes toward communism.

The Cold War thawed after Stalin died in 1953. The first **summit meeting** between superpower leaders took place in Geneva, Switzerland, in 1955. But the Soviet Union sent tanks to crush a popular uprising in Hungary in 1956 (an action it repeated in 1968 in Czechoslovakia), and the Soviet missile program that orbited *Sputnik* in 1957 alarmed the United States. In Cuba, after Fidel Castro's communist revolution in 1959, the United States attempted a counterrevolution in the botched 1961 *Bay of Pigs* invasion.

The **Cuban Missile Crisis** of 1962 ensued when the Soviet Union installed medium-range nuclear missiles in Cuba. The Soviet aims were to reduce the Soviet Union's strategic nuclear inferiority, to counter the deployment of U.S. missiles on

Sino-Soviet split A rift in the 1960s between the communist powers of the Soviet Union and China, fueled by China's opposition to Soviet moves toward peaceful coexistence with the United States.

summit meeting A meeting between heads of state, often referring to leaders of great powers, as in the Cold War superpower summits between the United States and the Soviet Union or today's meetings of the Group of Eight (G8) on economic coordination.

Cuban Missile Crisis (1962) A superpower crisis, sparked by the Soviet Union's installation of medium-range nuclear missiles in Cuba, that marks the moment when the United States and the Soviet Union came closest to nuclear war.

proxy wars Wars in the global South—often civil wars—in which the United States and the Soviet Union jockeyed for position by supplying and advising opposing factions.

Soviet borders in Turkey, and to deter another U.S. invasion of Cuba. U.S. leaders, however, considered the missiles threatening and provocative. As historical documents later revealed, nuclear war was quite possible. Some U.S. policy makers favored military strikes before the missiles became operational, when in fact some nuclear weapons in Cuba were already operational and commanders were authorized to use them in the event of a U.S. attack. Instead, President John F. Kennedy imposed a naval blockade to force their removal. The Soviet Union backed down, and the United States promised not to invade Cuba in the future. Leaders on both sides were shaken, however, by the possibility of nuclear war. They signed the *Limited Test Ban Treaty* in 1963, prohibiting atmospheric nuclear tests, and began to cooperate in cultural exchanges, space exploration, aviation, and other areas.

The two superpowers often jockeyed for position in the third world, supporting **proxy wars** in which they typically supplied and advised opposing factions in civil wars. The alignments were often arbitrary. For instance, the United States backed the Ethiopian government and the Soviets backed next-door rival Somalia in the 1970s; however, when an Ethiopian revolution caused the new government to seek Soviet help, the United States switched its support to Somalia.

One flaw of U.S. policy in the Cold War period was to see all regional conflicts through East-West lenses. Its preoccupation with communism led the United States to support unpopular pro-Western governments in a number of poor countries, nowhere more disastrously than in the *Vietnam War* in the 1960s. The war divided the U.S. public and ultimately failed to prevent a communist takeover. The fall of South Vietnam in 1975 appeared to signal U.S. weakness, especially combined with U.S. setbacks in the Middle East—the 1973 Arab oil embargo and the 1979 overthrow of the U.S.-backed shah of Iran.

In this period of apparent U.S. weakness, the Soviet Union invaded Afghanistan in 1979. Like the United States in Vietnam, the Soviet Union could not suppress rebel armies supplied by the opposing superpower. The Soviets withdrew after almost a decade of war that considerably weakened the Soviet Union. Meanwhile, President Ronald Reagan built up U.S. military forces to record levels and supported rebel armies in the Soviet-allied states of Nicaragua and Angola (and one faction in Cambodia) as well as Afghanistan. Superpower relations slowly improved after Mikhail Gorbachev, a reformer, took power in the Soviet Union in 1985. But some of the third world battlegrounds (notably Afghanistan and Angola) continued to suffer from brutal civil wars into the new century.

In June 1989, massive pro-democracy demonstrations in China's capital of Beijing (Tiananmen Square) were put down violently by the communist government. Around 1990, as the Soviet Union stood by, one Eastern European country after another replaced its communist government after mass demonstrations. The toppling of the Berlin Wall in late 1989 symbolized the end of the Cold War division of Europe. Germany formally reunified in 1990. The Soviet leader, Gorbachev, allowed these losses of power in hopes of concentrating on Soviet domestic restructuring under *perestroika* (economic reform) and *glasnost* (openness in political discussion). China remained a communist, authoritarian government but liberalized its economy and avoided military conflicts. In contrast to the Cold War era, China developed close ties with both the United States and Russia and joined the world's liberal trading regime.

Scholars do not agree on the important question of why the Cold War ended. One view is that U.S. military strength under President Reagan forced the Soviet Union into bankruptcy as it tried to keep up in the arms race. Others claim that the Soviet Union suffered from internal stagnation over decades and imploded because of weaknesses that had little to do with external pressure.

The Post–Cold War Era, 1990–2015

The post–Cold War era began with a bang while the Soviet Union was still disintegrating. In 1990, perhaps believing that the end of the Cold War had left a power vacuum in its region, Iraq occupied its neighbor Kuwait in an aggressive grab for control of Middle East oil. Western powers were alarmed—both about the example that unpunished aggression could set in a new era and about the direct threat to energy supplies for the world economy. The United States mobilized a coalition of the world's major countries (with almost no opposition) to counter Iraq. Working through the UN, the U.S.-led coalition applied escalating sanctions against Iraq.

When Iraq did not withdraw from Kuwait by the UN's deadline, the United States and its allies easily smashed Iraq's military and evicted its army from Kuwait in the *Gulf War.* But the coalition did not occupy Iraq or overthrow its government. The costs of the Gulf War were shared among the participants in the coalition, with Britain and France making military commitments while Japan and Germany made substantial financial contributions. This pass-the-hat financing was an innovation, one that worked fairly well.

The final collapse of the Soviet Union followed only months after the Gulf War. The 15 republics of the Soviet Union—Russia was just one—had begun taking power from a weakened central government, declaring themselves sovereign states. This process raised complex problems ranging from issues of national self-determination to the reallocation of property. In 1991, however, the Soviet Union itself broke apart. Russia and many of the other former republics struggled throughout the 1990s against economic and financial collapse, inflation, corruption, war, and military weakness. A failed Russian military coup attempt in 1991—and the role of Russian president Boris Yeltsin in opposing it—accelerated the collapse of the Soviet Union. Soon both capitalism and democracy were adopted as the basis of the economies and political systems of the former Soviet states. The republics became independent states and formed a loose coordinating structure—the *Commonwealth of Independent States (CIS).* Of the former Soviet republics, only the three small Baltic states and Georgia are nonmembers.

Western relations with Russia and the other republics have been mixed since the 1990s. Because of their own economic problems and a sense that Russia needed internal reform more than external aid, Western countries provided only limited aid for the region's harsh economic transition, which had drastically reduced living standards. Russia's brutal suppression of its secessionist province of Chechnya in 1995 and 1999 provoked Western fears. Russian leaders feared NATO expansion into Eastern Europe that placed threatening Western military forces on Russia's borders.

Despite these problems, the world's great powers increased their cooperation after the Cold War. Russia was accepted as the successor state to the Soviet Union and took its seat on the UN Security Council. Russia and the United States carried out major reductions in their nuclear weapons.

Just after the Gulf War in 1991, the former Yugoslavia broke apart, with several of its republics declaring independence. Ethnic Serbs, who were minorities in Croatia and Bosnia, seized territory to form a "Greater Serbia." With help from Serbia, which controlled the Yugoslav army, they killed hundreds of thousands of non-Serb Bosnians and Croatians and expelled millions more to create an ethnically pure state.

The international community recognized the independence of Croatia and Bosnia, admitting them to the UN and passing dozens of Security Council resolutions to protect their territorial integrity and their civilian populations. But in contrast to the Gulf War, the great powers showed no willingness to bear major costs to protect Bosnia. Instead, they tried to contain the conflict by assuming a neutral role as peacekeeper and intermediary. The UN sent almost 40,000 peacekeepers to Bosnia and Croatia, at a cost of more than $1 billion per year. NATO threatened military actions repeatedly, only to back down when costs appeared too high.

In 1995, Serbian forces overran two UN-designated "safe areas" in eastern Bosnia, expelling the women and slaughtering thousands of the men. Finally, two weeks of NATO airstrikes (the alliance's first-ever military engagement), along with losses to Croatia on the ground, induced Serb forces to come to terms. The treaty to end the war (authored by U.S. negotiators) formally held Bosnia together but granted Serbian forces autonomy on half of their territory, while placing about 60,000 heavily armed (mostly NATO) troops on the ground to maintain a cease-fire. Meanwhile, Serbian strongman Slobodan Milosevic was indicted for war crimes by the UN tribunal for the former Yugoslavia, was delivered to the tribunal in 2001, and died in 2006 near the end of a lengthy trial.

In contrast to their indecision early in the Bosnia crisis, the Western powers acted decisively in 1999 when Serbian forces carried out "ethnic cleansing" in the Serbian province of Kosovo, predominantly populated by ethnic Albanians. NATO launched an air war that escalated over ten weeks. NATO came under criticism from Russia and China for acting without explicit UN authorization and for interfering in Serbia's internal affairs. (The international community and the UN considered Kosovo, unlike Bosnia, to be part of Serbia.) In the end, Serbian forces withdrew from Kosovo and NATO has maintained a significant presence in the province ever since (4500 troops as of 2016). In 2008, with the UN Security Council still deadlocked over its status, Kosovo declared independence, bringing protests from Serbia and its allies. In 2010, the World Court declared Kosovo's *declaration* of independence legal, although its substantive status remains in dispute.

Other Western military intervention decisions since 1990 were less effective. In Somalia, a U.S.-led coalition sent tens of thousands of troops to suppress factional fighting and deliver relief supplies to a large population that was starving. When those forces were drawn into the fighting and sustained casualties, however, the United States abruptly pulled out. In Rwanda, in 1994, the genocide of more than half a million civilians in a matter of weeks was almost ignored by the international community. The great powers, burned by failures in Somalia and Bosnia, decided that their vital interests were not at stake. In 1997, the Rwanda conflict spilled into neighboring Zaire (now Democratic Congo), where rebels overthrew a corrupt dictator. Neighboring countries were drawn into the fighting, but the international community steered clear even as millions of civilians died of hunger and disease. The U.S. military intervened in Haiti to restore the elected president, but Haiti remains mired in poverty.

New rifts opened in 2001 between the United States and both China and Europe—on issues ranging from global warming to the proposed International Criminal Court. Russia and China signed a treaty of friendship in 2001, and European countries helped vote the United States off two important UN commissions.

These divisive issues receded when the United States was attacked by terrorists on September 11, 2001. The attacks destroyed the World Trade Center in New York and a wing of the Pentagon in Washington, DC, killing thousands of Americans and citizens of about 60 other countries. The attacks mobilized support for the United States by a very broad coalition of states. President Bush declared a "war on terrorism" that lasted for years and spanned continents, employing both conventional and unconventional means. In late 2001, U.S. and British forces and their Afghan allies ousted the Taliban regime in Afghanistan, which had harbored the al Qaeda network (led by Osama bin Laden).

The great power divisions reappeared, however, as the United States and Britain tried to assemble a coalition to oust Iraq's Saddam Hussein by force in early 2003. France and Germany (along with Russia and China) bitterly opposed the war, as did millions of protesters around the world. The dispute disrupted the Atlantic alliance for several years and weakened the UN's role as the U.S.-led coalition went forward despite its failure to win Security Council authorization for war.

The invasion itself was brief and decisive. A U.S. military force of 250,000 troops with advanced technology overpowered the Iraqi army in three weeks. Many Iraqis welcomed the end of a dictatorial regime, as had most Afghans in late 2001, but the war inflamed anti-American sentiment, especially in Muslim countries such as Egypt and Pakistan. Insurgent forces in Iraq gained strength as the U.S. occupation stretched on for years, and within several years, U.S. public opinion had turned against the protracted war. After a U.S. troop surge in 2007 and the arming of Sunni communities fed up with foreign Islamist radicals, violence in Iraq fell. U.S. forces withdrew from Iraq in 2009–2011, though some violence continued. Estimates of Iraqi deaths caused by the war range from tens of thousands to more than 600,000. Elections in 2010 and 2014 were relatively peaceful but left the country divided along ethnic lines.

In Afghanistan, fighting worsened in 2007 as the Taliban began an insurgency campaign from bases in Pakistan. Disputed elections, corruption, and "insider" attacks by members of Afghan security forces on NATO troops all made the foreigners' job difficult. NATO sent in tens of thousands of additional troops in 2009 but then began a withdrawal that drew down U.S. forces to around 13,000 troops by the beginning of 2016. One goal of the Afghan intervention was accomplished in 2011 when U.S. special forces killed Osama bin Laden in Pakistan. U.S. drone attacks on other militants inside Pakistan and elsewhere weakened al Qaeda but raised thorny legal and political issues.

Meanwhile, nuclear weapons programs in North Korea and Iran raised alarms. North Korea produced possibly a half-dozen nuclear bombs and tested three in 2006, 2009, and 2013. In 2012, it successfully tested an advanced long-range missile in defiance of a UN Security Council ban. Starting in 2004, Iran made and broke several agreements to suspend the enrichment of uranium that could be used to build nuclear weapons. In response, the UN Security Council passed a series of sanctions against Iran, demanding that it stop its enrichment program. In 2010, centrifuges key to its enrichment program began mysteriously destroying themselves, and investigation pinned the problem on the sophisticated Stuxnet computer virus, evidently a creation of Israeli and American defense scientists. It set back Iran's program by a year or more. Iran then agreed to scale back all nuclear activities in 2015 after reaching an agreement with Western powers to curtail its nuclear program in exchange for an end to economic sanctions. While some in the West are pleased with the agreement, others argue the agreement is not strong enough and question Iran's intentions to comply with the agreement.

The Arab Spring uprisings in 2011–2012 began with nonviolent protests in Tunisia and Egypt, both resulting in the overthrow of dictators and the holding of free elections. Egypt elected a leader of the long-banned Muslim Brotherhood as president, only to have the military overthrow him in 2013. In Libya and Syria, violent repression against protesters sparked violent uprisings, leading to the bloody overthrow of Libya's dictator with NATO air support, and a prolonged and agonizing civil war in Syria with a divided international community unable to respond effectively. Eventually, the Syrian war spilled into neighboring Iraq, while violence in Libya continued into 2016. These

FALL AFTER SPRING Peaceful trends mark the post–Cold War era, though war and terrorism continue. The Arab Spring popular uprisings beginning in 2011 brought some democratic reform to the Middle East. They overthrew governments in Tunisia, Egypt, and Libya; sparked civil war in Yemen and Syria; and reshaped the region's international dynamics. The future of democracy in the region is still uncertain. Here, supporters of former Islamist president Mohammed Morsi of Egypt—removed from office by the military—protest for his return to power, 2015.

conflicts in the Middle East led to a refugee crisis both in the region and in Europe as thousands of families fled the violence in hopes of resettling in a more stable country such as Germany. Yemen had its own revolution—a mix of peaceful protest, violent repression, ethnic conflict, and political compromise leading to a transitional government. By 2015, the transitional government (aided by Saudi Arabia and western allies) fought a bloody war against rebel groups (one aided by Iran, another by al Qaeda). And far away in Burma (Myanmar), a longstanding military regime finally made a concerted, if slow, move toward democracy.

The post–Cold War era may seem a conflict-prone period in which savage violence flares up with unexpected intensity around the world, in places such as Rwanda and Syria—even New York City. Yet *the post–Cold War era has been more peaceful than the Cold War era* (see pp. 68–69). Old wars have ended faster than new ones have begun. Latin America and parts of Africa have nearly extinguished wars in their regions, joining a zone of peace already encompassing North America, Europe, Japan and the Pacific, and China.

Warfare is diminishing even in the arc of conflict from Africa through the Middle East to South Asia. Since 1990, long bloody wars have ended in South Africa, Mozambique, Angola, southern Sudan, and Ethiopia-Eritrea, as did the various conflicts in Central America and the civil war in Sri Lanka. Wars in West Africa, Rwanda, and Indonesia have also wound down. After the Cold War, world order did not spiral out of control with rampant aggression and war.

However, the Israeli-Palestinian conflict, which saw rising expectations of peace in the 1990s, worsened after a proposed deal fell through in 2000. With the 2006 Palestinian election victory of the militant Islamist party Hamas, responsible for many violent attacks on Israel, hopes for a durable peace faded. In 2006, Israel fought a brief but intense war with Hezbollah guerrillas in southern Lebanon, while violent clashes between Israel and Hamas continued from 2009 to 2014. Israel deployed a new "Iron Dome" missile defense system against Hamas missiles in the 2012 and 2014 clashes. By 2015, Israelis had reelected a government promising to build more settlements on disputed land, while Palestinians joined the International Criminal Court in hopes of charging Israel with war crimes. Both moves brought denouncements from the opposing side, further diminishing hopes for peace.

In international economic relations, the post–Cold War era is one of globalization. New hubs of economic growth are emerging, notably in parts of Asia with remarkable economic growth. Globalization has created backlashes among people who are adversely affected or who believe their identities are threatened by foreign influences. The resurgence of nationalism and ethnic-religious conflict—occasionally in brutal form—results partly from that backlash. So does the significant protest movement against capitalist-led globalization.

With increasing globalization, transnational concerns such as environmental degradation and disease have become more prominent as well. Global warming looms as an ever-increasing danger that is underscored by the accelerating melting of arctic ice and increasing coastal flooding around the world. In 2014 and 2015, a virus known as Ebola killed thousands in western Africa and threatened to spread worldwide, triggering efforts to control the virus through quarantines. Major oil spills in the Gulf of Mexico and China in 2010 refocused international attention on the issue of pollution and the environment, especially in the context of the global race for natural resources.

China is becoming more central to world politics in the new century. Its size and rapid growth make China a rising power—a situation that some scholars liken to Germany's rise a century earlier. Historically, such shifts in power relations have caused instability in the international system. China's poor record on human rights makes it a frequent target of Western criticism from both governments and NGOs.

China holds (but seldom uses) veto power in the UN Security Council, and it has a credible nuclear arsenal. China adjoins several regional conflict areas and affects the global proliferation of missiles and nuclear weapons. It claims disputed territory in the resource-rich South China Sea and disputes ownership of islands with Japan in the East China Sea, but it has not fought a military battle in 25 years. China is the only great power from the global South. Its population size and rapid industrialization make China a big factor in the future of global environmental trends such as global warming. Economic turmoil in 2015 (high volatility in Chinese stock prices, lower factory output, and slowing investment) led some scholars to question the overall strength of the Chinese economy. Other experts suggested these were merely small bumps on the road to Chinese economic dominance. All these elements make China an important actor in the coming decades.

The transition to the post–Cold War era has been a turbulent time, full of changes and new possibilities both good and bad. It is likely, however, that the basic rules and principles of IR—those that scholars have long struggled to understand—will continue to apply, though their contexts and outcomes may change. Most central to those rules and principles is the concept of power, to which we now turn.

Chapter Review

Summary

- IR affects daily life profoundly; we all participate in IR.
- IR is a field of political science concerned mainly with explaining political outcomes in

international security affairs and international political economy.

- Theories complement descriptive narratives in explaining international events and outcomes, and although scholars do not agree on a single set of theories or methods, three core principles shape various solutions to collective goods problems in IR.

- States are the most important actors in IR; the international system is based on the sovereignty of about 200 independent territorial states of varying size.

- Nonstate actors such as intergovernmental organizations (IGOs), nongovernmental organizations (NGOs), and multinational corporations (MNCs) exert a growing influence on international relations.

- Four levels of analysis—individual, domestic, interstate, and global—suggest multiple explanations (operating simultaneously) for outcomes observed in IR.

- Globalization is conceived differently by various scholars but generally refers to the growing scope, speed, and intensity of connectedness worldwide. The process may be weakening, strengthening, or transforming the power of states. Antiglobalization activists oppose growing corporate power but disagree on goals and tactics.

- For nearly 50 years after World War II, world politics revolved around the East-West rivalry of the Cold War. This standoff created stability and avoided great power wars, including nuclear war, but turned poor states into proxy battlegrounds.

- The post–Cold War era holds hope of general great power cooperation despite the appearance of new ethnic and regional conflicts.

- The U.S. military campaign in Iraq overthrew a dictator but divided the great powers, heightened anti-Americanism worldwide, and led to years of insurgency and sectarian violence.

- The NATO campaign in Afghanistan against Taliban influence ended in 2014, although some NATO troops remain. U.S. Special Forces in 2011 killed Osama bin Laden in Pakistan, where drone attacks targeted other militants.

- The Arab Spring uprisings in 2011–2013 overthrew governments in Tunisia, Egypt, Libya, and Yemen, and sparked a brutal civil war in Syria. The outcomes of most of these regime transitions remain uncertain.

Key Terms

international relations (IR) 2
collective goods problem 4
dominance 5
reciprocity 5
identity 6
issue areas 10
conflict and cooperation 10
international security 10
international political economy
    (IPE) 10

state 11
international system 11
nation-states 12
gross domestic product
    (GDP) 13
nonstate actors 14
intergovernmental
    organizations (IGOs) 14
nongovernmental organizations
    (NGOs) 14

globalization 18
North-South gap 20
Cold War 25
containment 25
Sino-Soviet split 27
summit meeting 28
Cuban Missile Crisis 28
proxy wars 28

Critical Thinking Questions

1. Pick a current area in which interesting international events are taking place. Can you think of possible explanations for those events from each of the four levels of analysis? (See Table 1.3, p. 17.) Do explanations from different levels provide insights into different aspects of the events?

2. The Cold War is long over, but its influences linger. Can you think of three examples in which the Cold War experience continues to shape the foreign policies of today's states?

3. What do you expect will be the character of the twenty-first century? Peaceful? War-prone? Orderly? Chaotic? Why do you have the expectations you do, and what clues from the unfolding of events in the world might tell you whether your guesses are correct?

Chapter 2
Realist Theories

FRENCH FORCES INTERVENE IN MALI, 2013.

 Learning Objectives

2.1 Identify at least three assumptions of the theory of realism.

2.2 Describe two different ways to conceptualize and measure power.

2.3 Define anarchy and explain its importance in preventing international cooperation.

2.4 Explain the purpose of the North Atlantic Treaty Organization (NATO) alliance and how the purpose has changed over its history.

2.5 Describe the Prisoner's Dilemma game and explain how it is an analogy for the international system.

Realism

2.1 Identify at least three assumptions of the theory of realism.

No single theory reliably explains the wide range of international interactions, but one theoretical framework has historically held a central position in the study of international relations (IR). This approach, called realism, is favored by some IR scholars and vigorously contested by others, but almost all take it into account.

Realism (or *political realism*) is a school of thought that explains international relations in terms of power. The exercise of power by states toward each other is sometimes called *realpolitik,* or just *power politics.*

Modern realist theory developed in reaction to a liberal tradition that realists called **idealism.** Idealism emphasizes international law, morality, and international organization, rather than power alone, as key influences on international events. Idealists think that human nature is basically good. They see the international system as one based on a community of states that have the potential to work together to overcome mutual problems (see Chapter 3). For idealists, the principles of IR must flow from morality.

Idealists were particularly active between World War I and World War II, following the painful experience of World War I. U.S. president Woodrow Wilson led the effort to create the **League of Nations,** a forerunner of today's United Nations. But the U.S. Senate did not approve, and the League proved ineffective. U.S. isolationism between the world wars, along with declining British power and a Russia crippled by its own revolution, left a power vacuum in world politics that Germany and Japan filled in the 1930s. In an effort to appease German ambitions, Britain and France agreed in the **Munich Agreement** of 1938 to let Germany occupy part of Czechoslovakia. This "appeasement" seemed only to encourage Hitler's further conquests. Yet the lessons of the two world wars seem contradictory. From the failure of the Munich Agreement in 1938 to appease Hitler, many people have concluded that only a hardline foreign policy with preparedness for war will deter aggression and prevent war. Yet in 1914 it was just such hardline policies that apparently led Europe into a disastrous war, which might have been avoided by appeasement. Evidently the best policy would be sometimes harsh and at other times conciliatory.

After World War II, realists blamed idealists for looking too much at how the world *ought* to be instead of how it *really* is. Sobered by the experiences of

realism A broad intellectual tradition that explains international relations mainly in terms of power.

idealism An approach that emphasizes international law, morality, and international organization, rather than power alone, as key influences on international relations.

League of Nations An organization established after World War I and a forerunner of today's United Nations; it achieved certain humanitarian and other successes but was weakened by the absence of U.S. membership and by its own lack of effectiveness in ensuring collective security.

Munich Agreement A symbol of the failed policy of appeasement, this agreement, signed in 1938, allowed Nazi Germany to occupy part of Czechoslovakia. Rather than appease German aspirations, it was followed by further German expansions, which triggered World War II.

World War II, realists set out to understand the principles of power politics without succumbing to wishful thinking.

Realists ground themselves in a long tradition. The Chinese strategist *Sun Tzu*, who lived 2,000 years ago, advised the rulers of states how to survive in an era when war had become a systematic instrument of power for the first time. Sun Tzu argued that moral reasoning was not very useful to the state rulers of the day, faced with armed and dangerous neighbors. He showed rulers how to use power to advance their interests and protect their survival.

At roughly the same time, in Greece, *Thucydides* wrote an account of the Peloponnesian War (431–404 B.C.) focusing on relative power among the Greek city-states. He stated that "the strong do what they have the power to do and the weak accept what they have to accept." Much later, in Renaissance Italy (around 1500), *Niccolò Machiavelli* urged princes to concentrate on expedient actions to stay in power, including the manipulation of the public and military alliances. Realists see in these historical figures evidence that the importance of power politics is timeless and cross-cultural.

After World War II, scholar *Hans Morgenthau* argued that international politics is governed by objective, universal laws based on national interests defined in terms of power (not psychological motives of decision makers). He reasoned that no nation had "God on its side" (a universal morality) and that all nations had to base their actions on prudence and practicality. He opposed the Vietnam War, arguing in 1965 that a communist Vietnam would not harm U.S. national interests.

Similarly, in 2002, before the U.S. invasion of Iraq, leading realists figured prominently among the 33 IR scholars signing a *New York Times* advertisement warning that "war with Iraq is *not* in America's national interest." Thus realists do not always favor using military power, although they recognize the necessity of doing so at times. The target of the IR scholars' ad was the group of foreign policy makers in the Bush administration known as *neoconservatives*, who advocated more energetic use of American power, especially military force, to accomplish ambitious and moralistic goals such as democratizing the Middle East.

Thus, realists assume that IR can be best (though not exclusively) explained by the choices of states operating as autonomous actors rationally pursuing their own interests in an international system of sovereign states without a central authority. Table 2.1 summarizes some major differences between the assumptions of realism and idealism.

Table 2.1 Assumptions of Realism and Idealism

Issue	Realism	Idealism
Human Nature	Selfish	Altruistic
Most Important Actors	States	States and others including individuals
Causes of State Behavior	Rational pursuit of self-interest	Psychological motives of decision makers
Nature of International System	Anarchy	Community

For realists, ideologies do not matter much, nor do religions or other cultural factors with which states may justify their actions. Realists see states with very different religions, ideologies, or economic systems as quite similar in their actions with regard to national power. Thus, realism's foundation is the principle of dominance; alternatives based on reciprocity and identity will be reviewed in Chapter 3. Figure 2.1 lays out the various theoretical approaches to the study of IR that we discuss here and in Chapter 3.

Figure 2.1 Theories of IR

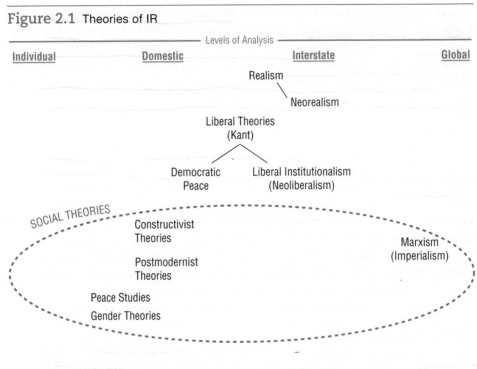

Power

2.2 Describe two different ways to conceptualize and measure power.

Power is a central concept in international relations—*the* central one for realists—but it is surprisingly difficult to define or measure.

Defining Power

power The ability or potential to influence others' behavior, as measured by the possession of certain tangible and intangible characteristics.

Power is often defined as the ability to get another actor to do what it would not otherwise have done (or not to do what it would have done). A variation on this idea is that actors are powerful to the extent that they affect others more than others affect them. These definitions treat power as influence. If actors get their way a lot, they must be powerful. One problem with this definition is that we seldom know what a second actor would have done in the absence of the first actor's power. There is a danger of circular logic: Power explains influence, and influence measures power.

Power is not influence itself, however, but the ability or potential to influence others. Many IR scholars believe that such potential is based on specific (tangible and intangible) characteristics or possessions of states—such as their sizes, levels of income, and armed forces. This is power as *capability.* Capabilities are easier to measure than influence and less circular in logic.

Measuring capabilities to explain how one state influences another is not simple, however. It requires summing up various kinds of potentials. States possess varying amounts of population, territory, military forces, and so forth. *The best single indicator of a state's power may be its total gross domestic product (GDP),* which combines overall size, technological level, and wealth. But even GDP is at best a rough indicator, and economists do not even agree how to measure it. The method followed in this text adjusts for price differences among countries, but an alternative method gives GDP estimates that are, on average, about 50 percent higher for countries in the global North and about

POWER AS INFLUENCE Power is the ability to influence the behavior of others. Military force and economic sanctions are among the various means that states and nonstate actors use to try to influence each other. In an effort to influence Iran's decision to pursue nuclear weapons, many Western powers and the United Nations had placed significant economic sanctions on Iran. This led to economic difficulties in Iran, especially the ability of Iranians to convert their currency (the rial) into U.S. dollars. Here, two women attempt to sell their money on the street to a money changer in Tehran, 2013.

50 percent lower for the global South, including China (see footnote 1 on p. 13). So GDP is a useful estimator of material capabilities but not a precise one.

Power also depends on nonmaterial elements. Capabilities give a state the potential to influence others only to the extent that political leaders can mobilize and deploy these capabilities effectively and strategically. This depends on national will, diplomatic skill, popular support for the government (its legitimacy), and so forth. Some scholars emphasize the *power of ideas*—the ability to maximize the influence of capabilities through a psychological process. This process includes the domestic mobilization of capabilities—often through religion, ideology, or (especially) nationalism. International influence is also gained by forming the rules of behavior to change how others see their own national interests. If a state's own values become widely shared among other states, that state will easily influence others. This has been called *soft power.* For example, the United States has influenced many other states to accept the value of free markets and free trade.

As the concept of soft power illustrates, dominance is not the only way to exert power (influence others). The core principles of reciprocity and (in the case of soft power) identity can also work. For example, a father who wants his toddler to stop screaming in a supermarket might threaten or actually administer a spanking (dominance); he might promise a candy bar at the checkout as a reward for good behavior (reciprocity); or he could invoke such themes as "Be a big boy/girl" or "You want to help Daddy, don't you?" (identity). Although realists emphasize dominance approaches, they do not dispute that states sometimes achieve their interests in other ways. Even realists recognize that power provides only a general understanding of outcomes. Real-world outcomes depend on many other elements, including accidents or luck.

Because power is a relational concept, a state can have power only relative to other states' power. *Relative power* is the ratio of the power that two states can bring to bear against each other. It matters little to realists whether a state's capabilities are rising or declining in absolute terms, only whether they are falling behind or overtaking the capabilities of rival states.

Estimating Power

The logic of power suggests that in wars, the more powerful state will generally prevail. Thus, estimates of the relative power of the two antagonists should help explain the outcome of each war. These estimates could take into account the nations' relative military capabilities and the popular support for each one's government, among other factors. But most important is the total size of each nation's economy—the total GDP. With a healthy enough economy, a state can buy a large army, popular support (by providing consumer goods), and even allies.

Elements of Power

State power is a mix of many ingredients. Elements that an actor can draw on over the *long term* include total GDP, population, territory, geography, and natural resources. These attributes change only slowly. Less tangible long-term power resources include political culture, patriotism, education of the population, and strength of the scientific and technological base. The credibility of its commitments (reputation for keeping its word) is also a long-term power base for a state. So is the ability of one state's culture and values to shape the thinking of other states consistently (the power of ideas).

Other capabilities allow actors to exercise influence in the *short term*. Military forces are such a capability—perhaps the most important kind. The size, composition, and preparedness of two states' military forces matter more in a short-term military confrontation than their respective economies or natural resources. Another capability is the military-industrial capacity to produce weapons quickly. The quality of a state's bureaucracy is another type of capability, allowing the state to gather information, regulate international trade, or participate in international conferences. Less tangibly, the *support* and *legitimacy* that an actor commands in the short term from constituents and allies are capabilities that the actor can use to gain influence. So is the *loyalty* of a nation's army and politicians to their leader.

Given the limited resources that any actor commands, trade-offs among possible capabilities always exist. Building up military forces diverts resources that might be put into foreign aid, for instance. Or buying a population's loyalty with consumer goods reduces resources available to the military. To the extent that one element of power can be converted into another, it is *fungible*. Generally, money is the most fungible capability because it can buy other capabilities.

Realists tend to see *military force* as the most important element of national power in the short term, and other elements such as economic strength, diplomatic skill, or moral legitimacy as being important to the extent that they are fungible into military power. Depending on the nature of the conflict in question, however, military power may be only one of many elements of power.

THE ECONOMICS OF POWER Military power such as tanks rests on economic strength, roughly measured by GDP. The large U.S. economy supports U.S. military predominance. In the 2003 U.S. invasion of Iraq, the United States could afford to send a large and technologically advanced military force to the Middle East. Here, U.S. forces enter Iraq, March 2003.

Morality can contribute to power by increasing the will to use power and by attracting allies. States have long clothed their actions, however aggressive, in rhetoric about their peaceful and defensive intentions. Of course, if a state over-uses moralistic rhetoric to cloak self-interest too often, it loses credibility even with its own population.

The use of geography as an element of power is called **geopolitics.** It is often tied to the logistical requirements of military forces. In geopolitics, as in real estate, the three most important considerations are location, location, location. States increase their power to the extent they can use geography to enhance their military capabilities, such as by securing allies and bases close to a rival power or by controlling key natural resources. Today, control of oil pipeline routes, especially in Central Asia, is a major geopolitical issue. Military strategists have also pointed out that the melting of the continental ice shelf (see Chapter 8) has opened new shipping routes for military purposes, creating a new geopolitical issue for Russia and the United States.

geopolitics The use of geography as an element of power, and the ideas about it held by political leaders and scholars.

The International System

2.3   Define anarchy and explain its importance in preventing international cooperation.

States interact within a set of long-established "rules of the game" governing what is considered a state and how states treat each other. Together these rules shape the international system.

The modern international system is sometimes dated from the *Treaty of Westphalia* in 1648, which ended the Thirty Years' War. It set out the basic rules that have defined the international system ever since—the sovereignty and territorial integrity of states as equal and independent members of an international system. Since then, states defeated in war might have been stripped of some territories but were generally allowed to continue as independent states rather than being subsumed by the victor. Key to this system was the ability of one state, or a coalition, to balance the power of another state so that it could not gobble up smaller units and create a universal empire.

Anarchy and Sovereignty

anarchy In IR theory, a term that implies not complete chaos but the lack of a central government that can enforce rules.

Realists believe that the international system exists in a state of **anarchy**—a term that implies not chaos or absence of structure and rules but rather the lack of a central government that can enforce rules. In domestic society within states, governments can enforce contracts, deter citizens from breaking rules, and carry out laws. Both democracies and dictatorships provide central government enforcement of a system of rules. Realists contend that no such central authority exists to enforce rules and ensure compliance with norms of conduct. This makes collective goods problems especially acute in IR. The power of one state is countered only by the power of other states. States must therefore rely on *self-help,* which they supplement with allies and the (sometimes) constraining power of international norms. In this anarchic world, realists emphasize prudence as a great virtue in foreign policy. Thus, states should pay attention not to the *intentions* of other states but rather to their *capabilities.*

norms The shared expectations about what behavior is considered proper.

Despite its anarchy, the international system is far from chaotic. Most state interactions adhere closely to **norms** of behavior—shared expectations about what behavior is considered proper. Norms change over time, slowly, but the most basic norms of the international system have changed little in recent centuries.

sovereignty A state's right, at least in principle, to do whatever it wants within its own territory; traditionally, sovereignty is the most important international norm.

Sovereignty—traditionally the most important norm—means that a government has the right, in principle, to do whatever it wants in its own territory. States are separate and autonomous, and they answer to no higher authority. In principle, all states are equal in status, if not in power. Sovereignty also means that states are not supposed to interfere in the internal affairs of other states. Although states do try to influence each other (exert power) on matters of trade, alliances, war, and so on, they are not supposed to meddle in the internal politics and decision processes of other states. More controversial is the claim by some states that sovereignty gives them the right to treat their own people in any fashion, including behavior that other states call genocide.

The lack of a "world police" to punish states if they break an agreement makes enforcement of international agreements difficult. For example, in the 1990s, North Korea announced it would no longer allow inspections of its nuclear facilities by other states, which put it in violation of the Non-Proliferation Treaty (NPT). The international community used a mix of positive incentives and threats to persuade North Korea to stop producing nuclear material. But in 2002, North Korea withdrew from the NPT and built perhaps a half-dozen nuclear bombs, one of which it exploded in 2006 (the world's first nuclear test in a decade). After reaching an agreement with the United States to stop producing nuclear weapons in 2008, North Korea refused to allow physical inspection of some of its nuclear facilities, arguing "it is an act of infringing upon sovereignty." These examples show the difficulty of enforcing international norms in the sovereignty-based international system.

In practice, most states have a hard time warding off interference in their affairs. "Internal" matters such as human rights or self-determination are more and more often concerns for the international community. Also, the integration of global economic markets and telecommunications makes it easier than ever for ideas to penetrate state borders.

PASSPORT PLEASE Sovereignty and territorial integrity are central norms governing the behavior of states. Terrorism and secessionist movements present two challenges to these norms, but the world's mostly stable borders uphold them. Every day, millions of people cross international borders, mostly legally and peacefully, respecting states' territorial integrity. Here, tightrope walker Nik Wallenda crosses the U.S.-Canadian border at Niagara Falls, 2012.

States are based on territory. Respect for the territorial integrity of all states, within recognized borders, is an important principle of IR. Many of today's borders are the result of past wars or were imposed arbitrarily by colonizers.

The territorial nature of the interstate system developed long ago when agrarian societies relied on agriculture to generate wealth. In today's world, in which trade and technology rather than land create wealth, the territorial state may be less important. Information-based economies are linked across borders instantly, and the idea that the state has a hard shell seems archaic. The accelerating revolution in information technologies may dramatically affect the territorial state system in the coming years.

States have developed norms of diplomacy to facilitate their interactions. Yet the norms of diplomacy can be violated. In 1979, Iranian students took over the U.S. embassy in Tehran, holding many of its diplomats hostage for 444 days—an episode that has soured American-Iranian relations ever since.

Realists acknowledge that the rules of IR often create a **security dilemma**— a situation in which actions taken by states to ensure their own security (such as deploying more military forces) threaten the security of other states. The responses of those other states (such as deploying more of their own military forces) in turn threaten the first state. The dilemma is a negative consequence of anarchy in the international system. If a world government could reliably detect and punish aggressors who arm themselves, states would not need to guard

security dilemma A situation in which actions that states take to ensure their own security (such as deploying more military forces) are perceived as threats to the security of other states.

against this possibility. Yet the self-help system requires that states prepare for the worst. Realists tend to see the dilemma as unsolvable, whereas liberals think it can be solved through the development of norms and institutions (see Chapters 3 and 6).

Balance of Power

balance of power
The general concept of one or more states' power being used to balance that of another state or group of states. The term can refer to (1) any ratio of power capabilities between states or alliances, (2) a relatively equal ratio, or (3) the process by which counterbalancing coalitions have repeatedly formed to prevent one state from conquering an entire region.

In the anarchy of the international system, the most reliable brake on the power of one state is the power of other states. The term **balance of power** refers to the general concept of one or more states' power being used to balance that of another state or group of states. Balance of power can refer to any ratio of power capabilities between states or alliances, or it can mean only a relatively equal ratio. Alternatively, balance of power can refer to the *process* by which counterbalancing coalitions have repeatedly formed in history to prevent one state from conquering an entire region. The theory of balance of power argues that such counterbalancing occurs regularly and maintains the stability of the international system. The system is stable because its rules and principles stay the same: State sovereignty does not collapse into a universal empire. This stability does not imply peace, however; it is instead a stability maintained by means of recurring wars that adjust power relations.

Alliances (to be discussed shortly) play a key role in the balance of power. Building up one's own capabilities against a rival is a form of power balancing, but forming an alliance against a threatening state is often quicker, cheaper, and more effective. Sometimes a particular state deliberately becomes a balancer (in its region or the world), shifting its support to oppose whatever state or alliance is strongest at the moment. Britain played this role on the European continent for centuries, and China played it in the Cold War.

In the post–Cold War era of U.S. dominance, balance-of-power theory would predict closer relations among Russia, China, and even Europe to balance U.S. power. And indeed, Russian-Chinese relations improved dramatically in areas such as arms trade and demilitarization of the border. French leaders have even criticized U.S. "hyperpower." But in recent years, with U.S. power seemingly stretched thin in Afghanistan and Iraq, its economy also weak, and Chinese power on the rise, more countries are balancing against China and fewer against the United States. In 2012 and 2013, Japan struck military agreements with former enemies South Korea and the Philippines and reaffirmed its U.S. ties in response to China's growing power.

World public opinion also reflects shifts in the balance of power. In 2003, as the Iraq War began, widespread anti-American sentiment revealed itself in Muslim countries. In Indonesia, Pakistan, Turkey, and Nigeria—containing half of the world's Muslims—more than 70 percent worried that the United States could become a threat to their own countries, a worry shared by 71 percent of Russians. A survey of 38,000 people in 44 nations showed a dramatic drop in support for the United States from 2002 to 2003. As Figure 2.2 illustrates, this decline in favorable views of the United States worldwide continued through 2007. But after 2008, with the United States seeking to exit its wars and exert its power less forcefully around the world, opinions turned upward. These shifts in public opinion can be both a cause and effect in international politics. Public opinion can make the governments in those countries more or less likely to cooperate with the United States on the world stage, and public opinion in these countries can change based on whether there is cooperation with (or hostility toward) the United States.

Figure 2.2 Views of the United States in Nine Countries, 2000–2014 (Percent favorable view in public opinion polls)

Source: Pew Global Attitudes Project. 2000 data from State Department surveys.

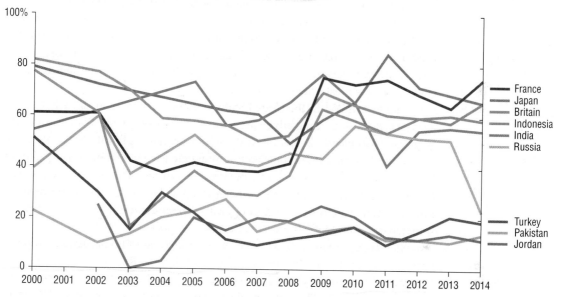

Great Powers and Middle Powers

The most powerful states in the world exert most of the influence on international events and therefore get the most attention from IR scholars. By almost any measure of power, a handful of states possess the majority of the world's power resources.

Although there is no firm dividing line, **great powers** are generally considered the half-dozen or so most powerful states. A system of great power relations has existed since around A.D. 1500, and the structure and rules of that system have remained fairly stable through time, although the particular members change. The structure is a balance of power among the six or so most powerful states, which form and break alliances, fight wars, and make peace, letting no single state conquer the others. Until the past century, the great power club was exclusively European. Sometimes great powers' status is formally recognized in an international structure such as the nineteenth-century Concert of

great powers Generally, the half-dozen or so most powerful states; the great power club was exclusively European until the twentieth century.

Europe or today's UN Security Council. In general, great powers are often defined as states that can be defeated militarily only by another great power. Great powers also tend to share a global outlook based on national interests far from their home territories.

The great powers generally have the world's strongest military forces and the strongest economies to pay for them. These large economies in turn rest on some combination of large populations, plentiful natural resources, advanced technology, and educated labor forces. Because power is based on these underlying resources, membership in the great power system changes slowly. Only rarely does a great power—even one defeated in a massive war—lose its status as a great power because its size and long-term economic potential change slowly. Thus, Germany and Japan, decimated in World War II, are powerful today.

In the *Concert of Europe* that dominated IR in the nineteenth century, the five most powerful states tried, with some success, to cooperate on major issues to prevent war—a possible precedent for today's UN Security Council. In this period, Britain became a balancer, joining alliances against whichever state emerged as the most powerful in Europe.

After World War II, the United States and the Soviet Union, allies in the war against Germany, became adversaries for 40 years in the Cold War. Europe was split into rival blocs—East and West—with Germany split into two states. The rest of the world became contested terrain where each bloc tried to gain allies or influence, often by sponsoring opposing sides in regional and civil wars. The end of the Cold War around 1990, when the Soviet Union collapsed, returned the international system to a more cooperative arrangement of the great powers somewhat similar to the Concert of Europe.

What states are great powers today? Although definitions vary, seven states appear to meet the criteria: the United States, China, Russia, Japan, Germany, France, and Britain. Together they account for more than half of the world's total GDP (see Figure 2.3). They include the five permanent members of the UN Security Council, who are also the members of the "club" openly possessing large nuclear weapons arsenals.

Notable on this list are the United States and China. The United States is considered the world's only superpower because of its historical role of world leadership (especially in and after World War II) and its predominant military might. China has the world's largest population; rapid economic growth (8–10 percent annually over 30 years, although 2015 brought some bumps to China's economy); and a large and modernizing military, including a credible nuclear arsenal. Indeed, in 2008, the U.S. National Intelligence Council's long-range planning report noted that China is poised to have a profound effect on the world over the next 20 years—perhaps more than any other state. Japan and Germany are economic great powers, but both countries have played constrained roles in international security affairs since World War II. Nonetheless, both have large and capable military forces, which they have begun to deploy abroad, especially in peacekeeping operations. Russia, France, and Britain were

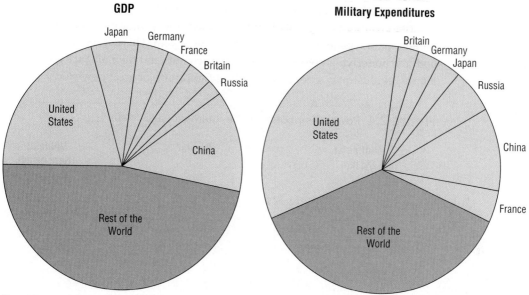

Figure 2.3 Great Power Shares of World GDP and Military Expenditures, 2014

Data sources: World Bank Development Indicators, 2015; SIPRI Yearbook, 2014.

Note: GDP calculated by purchasing-power method. China's GDP using alternate method would be about half as large.

winners in World War II and have been active military powers since then. Although much reduced in stature from their colonial heydays, they still qualify as great powers.

Middle powers rank somewhat below the great powers in terms of their influence on world affairs. A list of middle powers (not everyone would agree on it) might include midsized countries of the global North such as Canada, Italy, Spain, the Netherlands, Poland, Ukraine, South Korea, and Australia. It could also include large or influential countries in the global South such as India, Indonesia, Brazil, Argentina, Mexico, Nigeria, South Africa, Israel, Turkey, Iran, and Pakistan. Middle powers have not received as much attention in IR as have great powers.

middle powers States that rank somewhat below the great powers in terms of their influence on world affairs (for example, Brazil and India).

Power Distribution

With each state's power balanced by other states, the most important characteristic of the international system in the view of some realists is the *distribution* of power among states. Power distribution as a concept can apply to all the states in the world or to just the states in one region, but most often it refers to the great power system.

Neorealism, sometimes called *structural realism,* explains patterns of international events in terms of the system structure—the international distribution of power—rather than the internal makeup of individual states. Compared to traditional realism, neorealism is more "scientific" in the sense of proposing general laws to explain events, but neorealism has lost some of the richness of

neorealism A version of realist theory that emphasizes the influence on state behavior of the system's structure, especially the international distribution of power.

traditional realism, which took account of many complex elements (geography, political will, diplomacy, etc.). Recently, *neoclassical realists* have sought to restore some of these lost aspects.

Sometimes an international power distribution (world or regional) is described in terms of polarity (a term adopted from physics), which refers to the number of independent power centers in the system. This concept encompasses both the underlying power of various participants and their alliance groupings. Figure 2.4 illustrates several potential configurations of great powers.

Figure 2.4 Power Distribution in the International System

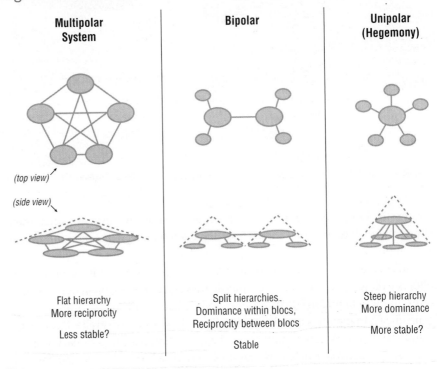

Multipolar System

(top view)

(side view)

Flat hierarchy
More reciprocity

Less stable?

Bipolar

Split hierarchies.
Dominance within blocs,
Reciprocity between blocs

Stable

Unipolar (Hegemony)

Steep hierarchy
More dominance

More stable?

Some might argue that peace is best preserved by a relatively equal power distribution (multipolarity) because then no country has an opportunity to win easily. The empirical evidence for this theory, however, is not strong. In fact, the opposite proposition has more support: Peace is best preserved by hegemony and next best by bipolarity.

Power transition theory holds that the largest wars result from challenges to the top position in the status hierarchy, when a rising power is surpassing (or threatening to surpass) the most powerful state. At such times, power is relatively equally distributed, and these are the most dangerous times for major wars. Status quo powers that are doing well under the old rules will try to maintain them, whereas challengers that feel locked out by the old rules may try to change them. When a rising power's status (formal position in the hierarchy) diverges from its

power transition theory A theory that the largest wars result from challenges to the top position in the status hierarchy, when a rising power is surpassing (or threatening to surpass) the most powerful state.

actual power, the rising power may suffer from relative deprivation: Its people may feel they are not doing as well as others or as well as they deserve, even though their position may be improving in absolute terms. Germany's rise in the nineteenth century gave it great power capabilities even though it was left out of colonial territories and other signs of status; this tension may have contributed to the two world wars.

It is possible that China and the United States will face a similar dynamic in the future. China may increasingly bristle at international rules and norms that it feels serves the interests of the United States. For its part, the United States may fear that growing Chinese economic and military power will be used to challenge U.S. power. In 2010, the U.S. military's strategic review questioned China's "long-term intentions," raising new questions about future power transitions. Yet China's economic stumbles in 2015 led some to question the inevitability of China's rise.

CHINA RISING Realists emphasize relative power as an explanation of war and peace. The modernization of China's military—in conjunction with China's rapidly growing economy—will increase China's power over the coming decades. Some observers fear instability in Asia if the overall balance of power among states in the region shifts rapidly. Here, the Chinese military celebrates China's first aircraft carrier in 2012.

Hegemony

Hegemony is one state's holding a preponderance of power in the international system, allowing it to single-handedly dominate the rules and arrangements by which international political and economic relations are conducted. Such a state is called a *hegemon.* Sometimes the term is used to refer to the complex of ideas that rulers use to gain consent for their legitimacy and keep subjects in line, reducing the need to use force to accomplish the same goal. By extension, such a meaning in IR refers to the hegemony of ideas such as democracy and capitalism, and to the global predominance of U.S. culture (see p. 368).

Most studies of hegemony point to two examples: Britain in the nineteenth century and the United States after World War II. Britain's predominance followed the defeat of its archrival France in the Napoleonic Wars. Both world trade and naval capabilities were firmly in British hands, as "Britannia ruled the waves." U.S. predominance followed the destruction caused by World War II. In the late 1940s, the U.S. GDP was more than half the world's total, U.S. vessels carried the majority of the world's shipping, the U.S. military could single-handedly defeat any other state or combination of states, and only the

hegemony One state's holding of a preponderance of power in the international system so that it can single-handedly dominate the rules and arrangements by which international political and economic relations are conducted.

United States had nuclear weapons. Over time, and as rival states rebuild after wars, hegemonic decline may occur, particularly when hegemons have overextended themselves with costly military commitments.

hegemonic stability theory The argument that regimes are most effective when power in the international system is most concentrated.

Hegemonic stability theory holds that hegemony provides some order similar to a central government in the international system: reducing anarchy, deterring aggression, promoting free trade, and providing a hard currency that can be used as a world standard. Hegemons can help resolve or at least keep in check conflicts among middle powers or small states. When one state's power dominates the world, that state can enforce rules and norms unilaterally, avoiding the collective goods problem. In particular, hegemons can maintain global free trade and promote world economic growth, in this view.

From the perspective of less powerful states, of course, hegemony may seem an infringement of state sovereignty, and the order it creates may seem unjust or illegitimate. For instance, China chafed under U.S.-imposed economic sanctions for 20 years after 1949, at the height of U.S. power, when China was encircled by U.S. military bases and hostile alliances led by the United States. To this day, Chinese leaders use the term *hegemony* as an insult, and the theory of hegemonic stability does not impress them.

Even in the United States there is considerable ambivalence about U.S. hegemony. U.S. foreign policy has historically alternated between *internationalist* and *isolationist* moods. In World War I, the country waited three years to weigh in and refused to join the League of Nations afterward. U.S. isolationism peaked in the 1930s; public opinion polls late in that decade showed 95 percent of the U.S. public opposed to participation in a future great European war, and about 70 percent opposed to joining with other nations to stop aggression.

Internationalists, such as Presidents Theodore Roosevelt and Woodrow Wilson, favored U.S. leadership and activism in world affairs. These views seemed vindicated by the failure of isolationism to prevent or avoid World War II. U.S. leaders after that war feared Soviet (and then Chinese) communism and pushed U.S. public opinion toward a strong internationalism during the Cold War. The United States became an activist, global superpower.

A second area of U.S. ambivalence is *unilateralism* versus *multilateralism* when the United States does engage internationally. Multilateral approaches—working through international institutions—augment U.S. power and reduce costs, but they limit U.S. freedom of action. In 2001, the United States declined to participate in international efforts such as a treaty on global warming (see pp. 337–338), a conference on racism, and an International Criminal Court (see p. 272). Unilateralist U.S. policies drew resistance from Europe and Canada. The international community's united front against terrorism pushed these disputes to the back burner, but they soon reemerged. The 2003 U.S.-led war in Iraq, with few allies and no UN stamp of approval, marked the peak of U.S. unilateralism. Since then, the NATO alliance has assumed new importance in Afghanistan and in the 2011 Libya campaign, and UN dues have been repaid.

Alliances

2.4 Explain the purpose of the North Atlantic Treaty Organization (NATO) alliance and how the purpose has changed over its history.

An *alliance* is a coalition of states that coordinate their actions to accomplish some end. Most alliances are formalized in written treaties, concern a common threat and related issues of international security, and endure across a range of issues and a period of time. If actors' purposes in banding together were shorter-term, less formal, or more issue specific, the association might be called a *coalition* rather than an alliance. Informal but enduring strategic *alignments* in a region are discussed shortly. But these terms are somewhat ambiguous. Two countries may have a formal alliance and yet be bitter enemies, as are Greece and Turkey. Or two countries may create the practical equivalent of an alliance without a formal treaty.

MARRIAGE OF CONVENIENCE Alliances generally result from a convergence of practical interests, not sentimental or ideological reasons. Here, a U.S. general gets rival Afghan warlords to patch up relations, 2002.

Purposes of Alliances

Alliances generally have the purpose of augmenting their members' power by pooling capabilities. For smaller states, alliances can be their most important power element, and for great powers, the structure of alliances shapes the configuration of power in the system. Of all the elements of power, none can change as quickly and decisively as alliances. Most alliances form in response to a perceived threat. When a state's power grows and threatens that of its rivals, the latter often form an alliance to limit that power. This happened to Iraq when it invaded Kuwait in 1990, as it had to Hitler's Germany in the 1940s and to Napoleon's France in the 1800s.

Realists emphasize the fluidity of alliances. They are not marriages of love but marriages of convenience. Alliances are based on national interests, and can shift as national interests change. This fluidity helps the balance-of-power process operate effectively. Examples of fluid alliances are many. Anticommunist Richard Nixon could cooperate with communist Mao Zedong in 1972. Joseph Stalin could sign a nonaggression pact with a fascist, Adolf Hitler, and then cooperate with the capitalist West against Hitler. The United States could back the Islamic militants in Afghanistan against the Soviet Union in the 1980s, then attack them in 2001. Every time history brings another such reversal in international alignments, many people are surprised. Realists are not so surprised.

The fluidity of alliances deepens the security dilemma (see p. 45). If there were only two states, each could match capabilities to have adequate defense but an inability to attack successfully. But if a third state is free to ally with either side, then each state has to build adequate defenses against the potential alliance of its enemy with the third state. The threat is greater and the security dilemma is harder to escape.

Alliance cohesion is the ease with which the members hold an alliance together. Cohesion tends to be high when national interests converge and when cooperation within the alliance becomes institutionalized and habitual. When states with divergent interests form an alliance against a common enemy, the alliance may come apart if the threat subsides. It did, for instance, with the World War II U.S.-Soviet alliance. Even when alliance cohesion is high, as in NATO during the Cold War, conflicts may arise over **burden sharing** (who bears the costs of the alliance).

Great powers often form alliances (or less formal commitments) with smaller states, sometimes called *client states*. Extended deterrence refers to a strong state's use of threats to deter attacks on weaker clients—such as the U.S. threat to attack the Soviet Union if it invaded Western Europe. Great powers face a real danger of being dragged into wars with each other over relatively unimportant regional issues if their respective clients go to war. If the great powers do not come to their clients' protection, they may lose credibility with other clients, but if they do, they may end up fighting a costly war.

NATO

At present, two important formal alliances dominate the international security scene. By far the more powerful is the **North Atlantic Treaty Organization (NATO)**, which encompasses Western Europe and North America. (The second is the U.S.-Japanese alliance.) Using GDP as a measure of power, the 28 NATO members possess nearly half the world total (roughly twice the power of the United States alone). Members are the United States, Canada, Britain, France, Germany, Italy, Belgium, the Netherlands, Luxembourg, Denmark, Norway, Iceland, Spain, Portugal, Greece, Turkey, Poland, the Czech Republic, Hungary, Lithuania, Estonia, Latvia, Slovenia, Slovakia, Bulgaria, Romania, Albania, and Croatia. At NATO headquarters in Brussels, Belgium, military staff members from the member countries coordinate plans and periodically direct exercises in the field. The NATO "allied supreme commander" has always been a U.S. general. In NATO, each state contributes its own military units—with its own national culture, language, and equipment specifications.

NATO was founded in 1949 to oppose and deter Soviet power in Europe. Its counterpart in Eastern Europe during the Cold War, the Soviet-led **Warsaw Pact**, was founded in 1955 and disbanded in 1991. During the Cold War, the United States maintained more than 300,000 troops in Europe, with advanced planes, tanks, and other equipment. After the Cold War ended, these forces

alliance cohesion The ease with which the members hold together an alliance; it tends to be high when national interests converge and when cooperation among allies becomes institutionalized.

burden sharing The distribution of the costs of an alliance among members; the term also refers to the conflicts that may arise over such distribution.

North Atlantic Treaty Organization (NATO) A U.S.-led military alliance, formed in 1949 with mainly West European members, to oppose and deter Soviet power in Europe. It is currently expanding into the former Soviet bloc.

Warsaw Pact A Soviet-led Eastern European military alliance, founded in 1955 and disbanded in 1991. It opposed the NATO alliance.

were cut to about 100,000. But NATO stayed together because its members believed that NATO provided useful stability, even though its mission was unclear. The first actual use of force by NATO was in Bosnia in 1994, in support of the UN mission there.

Currently, NATO troops from a number of member countries are fighting Taliban forces in Afghanistan. From 2003 to 2014, these forces, known as the International Security Assistance Forces (ISAF), were under NATO leadership. At its height (between 2010 and 2012), over 100,000 troops served in the ISAF, with NATO states providing the bulk of the forces. Non-NATO states, such as Australia, New Zealand, and Jordan, have also contributed troops to ISAF. In 2015, the NATO-led mission (now named Resolute Support) changed to providing support for Afghanistan's own military forces and the number of troops fell to under 13,000.

NATO's intervention in Libya in 2011 proved effective because air power turned the tide of the rebel war that overthrew Libya's dictator. With UN Security Council and Arab League backing for a no-fly zone, and European countries providing most of the combat planes, NATO rated the operation a great success.

The European Union has formed its own rapid deployment force, outside NATO. The decision to form this force grew in part from European military weaknesses demonstrated in the 1999 Kosovo war, in which the United States contributed the most power by far. Although this Eurocorps generally works *with* NATO, it also gives Europe more independence from the United States. In 2003, the European Union sent military forces as peacekeepers to Democratic Congo—the first multinational European military operation to occur outside NATO. In 2004, NATO and U.S. forces withdrew from Bosnia after nine years, turning over peacekeeping there to the European Union (as they had in Macedonia). But NATO forces, including U.S. soldiers, remain next door in Kosovo.

The biggest issue for NATO is its recent eastward expansion, beyond the East-West Cold War dividing line (see Figure 2.5). In 1999, former Soviet-bloc countries Poland, the Czech Republic, and Hungary joined the alliance. Joining in 2004 were Estonia, Latvia, Lithuania, Slovakia, Slovenia, Romania, and Bulgaria. In 2009, Albania and Croatia joined NATO, bringing the total number of members to 28. Georgia, Bosnia, Macedonia, and Montenegro all aspire to join NATO in the future. NATO expansion was justified as both a way to solidify new democracies and as protection against possible future Russian aggression. Yet the 2003 Iraq War bypassed NATO and divided NATO members. Longtime members France and Germany strongly opposed the war, and Turkey refused to let U.S. ground forces cross into Iraq.

Russian leaders oppose NATO's expansion into Eastern Europe as aggressive and anti-Russian. They view NATO expansion as reasserting dividing lines on the map of Europe, closer to Russia's borders. These fears strengthen nationalist and anti-Western political forces in Russia. To mitigate the problems, NATO created a category of symbolic membership—the Partnership for Peace—which

Figure 2.5 NATO Expansion

Note: All countries on map are members of NATO's Partnership for Peace program.

almost all Eastern European and former Soviet states, including Russia, joined. More recently, NATO cooperation with Ukraine and Georgia, the latter of which fought a short war against Russia in 2008, has also angered Russia. Tensions between Russia and NATO have run high since Russia's annexation of Crimea and its support of rebels in Ukraine. In response to NATO expansion, Russia has expanded its own military cooperation with states such as Venezuela, a government critical of U.S. foreign policy, and China, with whom it has conducted dozens of joint military exercises in the past five years.

Other Alliances

The second most important alliance is the **U.S.-Japanese Security Treaty,** a bilateral alliance. Under this alliance, the United States maintains nearly 50,000 troops in Japan (with weapons, equipment, and logistical support). Japan pays the United States several billion dollars annually to offset about half the cost of maintaining these troops. The alliance was created in 1951 against the potential Soviet threat to Japan.

Because of its roots in the U.S. military occupation of Japan after World War II, the alliance is very asymmetrical. The United States is committed to defend Japan if it is attacked, but Japan is not similarly obligated to defend the United States. The United States maintains troops in Japan, but not vice versa. The United States belongs to several other alliances, but Japan's only major alliance is with the United States. The U.S. share of the total military power in this alliance is also far greater than its share in NATO.

Japan's constitution renounces the right to make war and maintain military forces, although interpretation has loosened this prohibition over time. Japan maintains military forces, called the Self-Defense Forces, which are a powerful army by world standards but much smaller than Japan's economic strength could support. Japanese public opinion restrains militarism and precludes the development of nuclear weapons (after Japanese cities were destroyed by nuclear weapons in World War II). Nonetheless, some Japanese leaders believe that Japan's formal security role should expand commensurate with its economic power. In 2015, for example, Japan's parliament approved a new law allowing the use of military force overseas.

For its part, the United States has used the alliance with Japan as a base to project U.S. power in Asia, especially during the wars in Korea (1950–1953) and Vietnam (1965–1975), when Japan was a key staging area. The continued U.S. military presence in Japan (as in Europe) symbolizes the U.S. commitment to remain engaged in Asian security affairs.

Parallel with the U.S.-Japan treaty, the United States maintains military alliances with several other states, including South Korea and Australia. Close U.S. collaboration with militaries in other states such as Israel make them de facto U.S. allies.

The nine full members of the *Commonwealth of Independent States (CIS)* comprise the former Soviet republics except the Baltic states (Estonia, Latvia, and Lithuania). Russia, the official successor state to the Soviet Union, is the leading member and Ukraine is the second largest. Although some military coordination takes place through the CIS, initial plans for a joint military force did not succeed. Among the largest CIS members, Kazakhstan and Belarus are the most closely aligned with Russia, while Ukraine is the most independent (and in fact never officially ratified the CIS agreement). In 2009, Georgia withdrew from the CIS because of its military conflict with Russia.

For the present, international alignments—both military alliances and trade relationships—center on the United States (see Figure 2.6). Although several independent-minded states such as China, Russia, and France keep U.S.

U.S.-Japanese Security Treaty A bilateral alliance between the United States and Japan, created in 1951 against the potential Soviet threat to Japan. The United States maintains troops in Japan and is committed to defend Japan if attacked, and Japan pays the United States to offset about half the cost of maintaining the troops.

Figure 2.6 Current Alignment of Great and Middle Powers

Source: U.S. Department of Defense.

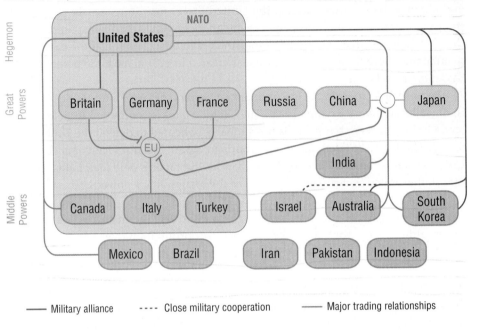

hegemony in check, little evidence exists of a coherent or formal rival power alignment emerging to challenge the United States.

Strategy

2.5 **Describe the Prisoner's Dilemma game and explain how it is an analogy for the international system.**

Actors use strategy to pursue good outcomes in bargaining with one or more other actors. States deploy power capabilities as leverage to influence each other's actions. Bargaining is interactive, and requires an actor to take account of other actors' interests even while pursuing its own. Sometimes bargaining communication takes place through actions rather than words.

Statecraft

Classical realists emphasize *statecraft*—the art of managing state affairs and effectively maneuvering in a world of power politics among sovereign states. Power strategies are plans actors use to develop and deploy power capabilities to achieve their goals.

A key aspect of strategy is choosing the kinds of capabilities to develop, given limited resources, in order to maximize international influence. This requires foresight because the capabilities required to manage a situation may

Policy Perspectives
Prime Minister of India, Narendra Modi

PROBLEM *How do you confront a fluid security environment by managing current and formal rivals?*

BACKGROUND As the world's largest democracy, your country faces many challenges both at home and abroad. In particular, in the past 50 years, you have fought wars against your two largest neighbors, China and Pakistan. Both states possess nuclear weapons, as do you. China and Pakistan have cooperated with each other in the past, including on sales of high-technology military goods such as missiles.

Your generally hostile relationship with Pakistan grows from a territorial dispute over half of the region of Kashmir, which both of you claim but India maintains control over. The territory is coveted not only by your respective governments but also by the publics in each country. While there has been cooperation between each country, tensions still run high over Kashmir. In the aftermath of the November 2008 terrorist attacks in Mombai, many in your country blamed Pakistan because it is home to Islamic militant groups.

Your hostilities with China have cooled over the years, but China remains a major rival in the region and you still maintain competing claims over territory. Like your own country, China is large economically as well as militarily, and it attempts to exert strong leadership in your region. In the past five years, however, your country has increased ties with China. You visited China in 2015, after China's leader visited India to sign trade and investment agreements. Your armies (the two largest in the world) have held joint training exercises, yet you also accuse one another of border violations.

DOMESTIC CONSIDERATIONS Within your country, neither Pakistan nor China are popular choices for allies. Your population is still angered by the Chinese victory in the 1962 Sino-Indian war and the disputed border territory that gave rise to the conflict. Yet your largely Hindu population is also angry at repeated attempts by Muslim Pakistan to gain control of Kashmir. Your advisers also remind you that China still has a healthy relationship with Pakistan, including sales of advanced weapons and large flows of military assistance. Indeed, the main political opposition parties argue that you have been too soft on both Pakistan and China. Any public backlash against your foreign policy on these issues could be widespread and bring calls for new elections that could unseat your government.

SCENARIO Imagine that the government of Pakistan begins to suffer from large-scale instability. Islamist militants are close to overthrowing the government there, giving them control of Pakistan's nuclear weapons. They are also calling for Muslims in Kashmir to rise up against Indian control, promising to assist a rebellion openly in that province by providing weapons and intelligence. Your own intelligence service considers the collapse of the current Pakistani government likely.

CHOOSE YOUR POLICY Do you push for closer relations with China as a result of instability in Pakistan? Can you trust China to support you in a dispute with Pakistan given those countries' close relationship? Do you ask China to help mediate between your government and Pakistan in the event of hostilities? Or do you continue your course as independently as possible, not trusting Chinese intentions toward your country?

need to be developed years before that situation presents itself. Yet the capabilities chosen often will not be fungible in the short term. Central to this dilemma is what kind of standing military forces to maintain in peacetime—enough to prevent a quick defeat if war breaks out but not so much as to overburden one's economy (see pp. 169–170).

Strategies also shape policies for when a state is willing to use its power capabilities. The *will* of a nation or leader is hard to estimate. Even if leaders make explicit their intention to fight over an issue, they might be bluffing.

The strategic actions of China in recent years exemplify the concept of strategy as rational deployment of power capabilities. China's central foreign policy goal is to prevent the independence of Taiwan, which China considers an integral part of its territory (as does the United Nations and, at least in theory, the United States). China may not have the military power to invade Taiwan successfully, but it has declared repeatedly that it will go to war if Taiwan declares independence. So far, even though such a war might be irrational on China's part, the threat has deterred Taiwan from formally declaring independence. China also breaks diplomatic relations with countries that recognize Taiwan. Chinese strategies mobilize various capabilities, including missiles, diplomats, and industrial conglomerates, in a coherent effort to influence the outcome of China's most important international issue. Strategy thus amplifies China's power.

deterrence The threat to punish another actor if it takes a certain negative action (especially attacking one's own state or one's allies).

The strategy of **deterrence** uses a threat to punish another actor if it takes a certain negative action (especially attacking one's own state or one's allies). If deterrence works, its effects are almost invisible; its success is measured in attacks that did not occur.

Most advocates of deterrence believe that conflicts are more likely to escalate into war when one party to the conflict is weak. In this view, building up military capabilities usually convinces the stronger party that a resort to military leverage would not succeed, so conflicts are less likely to escalate into violence.

compellence The threat of force to make another actor take some action (rather than, as in deterrence, refrain from taking an action).

A strategy of **compellence**, sometimes used after deterrence fails, refers to the threat of force to make another actor take some action (rather than refrain from taking an action). Generally, it is harder to get another state to change course (the purpose of compellence) than it is to get it to refrain from changing course (the purpose of deterrence).

One strategy used to try to compel compliance by another state is *escalation*—a series of negative sanctions of increasing severity applied in order to induce another actor to take some action. In theory, the less severe actions establish credibility—showing the first actor's willingness to exert its power on the issue—and the pattern of escalation establishes the high costs of future sanctions if the second actor does not cooperate. These actions should induce the second actor to comply, assuming that it finds the potential costs of the escalating punishments greater than the costs of compliance. But escalation can be quite dangerous. During the Cold War, many IR scholars worried that a conventional war could lead to nuclear war if the superpowers tried to apply escalation strategies.

An **arms race** is a reciprocal process in which two (or more) states build up military capabilities in response to each other. Because each wants to act prudently against a threat, the attempt to reciprocate leads to a runaway production of weapons by both sides. The mutual escalation of threats erodes confidence, reduces cooperation, and makes it more likely that a crisis (or accident) could cause one side to strike first and start a war rather than wait for the other side to strike. The arms race process was illustrated vividly in the U.S.-Soviet nuclear arms race, which created arsenals of tens of thousands of nuclear weapons on each side.

Rationality

Most realists (and many nonrealists) assume that those who wield power while engaging in statecraft behave as **rational actors** in their efforts to influence others. This view has two implications for IR.

First, the assumption of rationality implies that states and other international actors can identify their interests and put priorities on various interests: A state's actions seek to advance its interests. Many realists assume that the actor (usually a state) exercising power is a single entity that can "think" about its actions coherently and make choices. This is called the *unitary actor* assumption or sometimes the *strong leader* assumption. The assumption is a simplification because the interests of particular politicians, parties, economic sectors, or regions of a country often conflict. Yet realists assume that the exercise of power attempts to advance the **national interest**—the interests of the state itself.

But what are the interests of a state? Are they the interests of domestic groups (see Chapter 3)? The need to prevail in conflicts with other states (see Chapter 4)? The ability to cooperate with the international community for mutual benefit (see Chapter 6)? There is no simple answer. Some realists simply define the national interest as maximizing power—a debatable assumption. Others compare power in IR with money in economics—a universal measure. In this view, just as firms compete for money in economic markets, states compete for power in the international system.

COLD WAR THAW The unitary actor assumption holds that states make important decisions as though they were single individuals able to act in the national interest. In truth, factions and organizations with differing interests put conflicting pressures on state leaders. Here, U.S. president Barack Obama shakes hands with Cuban president Raul Castro in 2015. The United States has pledged to return to normal relations with Cuba after over 50 years of hostility. Yet various factions within the United States opposes this move, making the future of U.S.-Cuban relations uncertain.

arms race A reciprocal process in which two or more states build up military capabilities in response to each other.

rational actors Actors conceived of as single entities that can "think" about their actions coherently, make choices, identify their interests, and rank the interests in terms of priority.

national interest The interests of a state overall (as opposed to particular parties or factions within the state).

cost-benefit analysis
A calculation of the costs incurred by a possible action and the benefits it is likely to bring.

Second, rationality implies that actors are able to perform a **cost-benefit analysis**—calculating the costs incurred by a possible action and the benefits it is likely to bring. Applying power incurs costs and should produce commensurate gains. As in the problem of estimating power, one has to add up different dimensions in such a calculation. For instance, states presumably do not initiate wars that they expect to lose, except when they stand to gain political benefits, domestic or international, that outweigh the costs of losing the war. But it is not easy to tally intangible political benefits against the tangible costs of a war. Even victory in a war may not be worth the costs paid. Rational actors can miscalculate costs and benefits, especially when using faulty information (although this does not mean they are irrational). Finally, human behavior and luck can be unpredictable.

These assumptions about rationality and the actors in IR are simplifications that not all IR scholars accept. But realists consider these simplifications useful because they allow scholars to explain in a general way the actions of diverse actors.

The Prisoner's Dilemma

game theory A branch of mathematics concerned with predicting bargaining outcomes. Games such as Prisoner's Dilemma and Chicken have been used to analyze various sorts of international interactions.

Game theory is a branch of mathematics concerned with predicting bargaining outcomes. A game is a setting in which two or more players choose among alternative moves, either once or repeatedly. Each combination of moves (by all players) results in a set of payoffs (utility) to each player. The payoffs can be tangible items such as money or any intangible items of value. Game theory aims to deduce likely outcomes (what moves players will make), given the players' preferences and the possible moves open to them. Games are sometimes called formal models.

Game theory was first used extensively in IR in the 1950s and 1960s by scholars trying to understand U.S.-Soviet nuclear war contingencies. Moves were decisions to use nuclear weapons in certain ways, and payoffs were outcomes of the war. The use of game theory to study international interactions has become more extensive among IR scholars in recent years, especially among realists, who accept the assumptions about rationality. To analyze a game mathematically, one assumes that each player chooses a move rationally, to maximize its payoff.

zero-sum games
Situations in which one actor's gain is by definition equal to the other's loss, as opposed to a non-zero-sum game, in which it is possible for both actors to gain (or lose).

Different kinds of situations are represented by different classes of games, as defined by the number of players and the structure of the payoffs. One basic distinction is between **zero-sum games,** in which one player's gain is by definition equal to the other's loss, and *non-zero-sum games,* in which it is possible for both players to gain (or lose). In a zero-sum game there is no point in communication or cooperation between the players because their interests are diametrically opposed. But in a non-zero-sum game, coordination of moves can maximize the total payoff to the players, although each may still maneuver to gain a greater share of that total payoff.

The game called **Prisoner's Dilemma (PD)** captures the kind of collective goods problem common to IR. In this situation, rational players choose moves that produce an outcome in which all players are worse off than under a different set of moves. They all could do better, but as individual rational actors, they are unable to achieve this outcome. How can this be?

The original story tells of two prisoners questioned separately by a prosecutor. The prosecutor knows they committed a bank robbery but has only enough evidence to convict them of illegal possession of a gun unless one of them confesses. The prosecutor tells each prisoner that if he confesses and his partner doesn't confess, he will go free. If his partner confesses and he does not, he will get a long prison term for bank robbery (while the partner goes free). If both confess, they will get a somewhat reduced term. If neither confesses, they will be convicted on the gun charge and serve a short sentence. The story assumes that neither prisoner will have a chance to retaliate later, that only the immediate outcomes matter, and that each prisoner cares only about himself.

This game has a single solution: Both prisoners will confess. Each will reason as follows: "If my partner is going to confess, then I should confess too because I will get a slightly shorter sentence that way. If my partner is not going to confess, then I should still confess because I will go free that way instead of serving a short sentence." The other prisoner follows the same reasoning. The dilemma is that by following their individually rational choices, both prisoners end up serving a fairly long sentence when they could have both served a short one by cooperating (keeping their mouths shut).

In IR, the PD game has been used to gain insight into arms races. Consider the decisions of India and Pakistan about whether to build sizable nuclear weapons arsenals. Both have the ability to do so. Neither side can know whether the other is secretly building up an arsenal unless they reach an arms control agreement with strict verification provisions. To analyze the game, we assign values to each possible outcome—often called a *preference ordering*—for each player. This is not simple: If we misjudge the value a player puts on a particular outcome, we may draw wrong conclusions from the game.

The following preferences regarding possible outcomes are plausible: The best outcome would be that oneself but not the other player had a nuclear arsenal (the expense of building nuclear weapons would be worth it because one could then use them as leverage), second best would be for neither to go nuclear (no leverage but no expense), third best would be for both to develop nuclear arsenals (a major expense without gaining leverage), worst would be to forgo nuclear weapons oneself while the other player developed them (and thus be subject to blackmail).

The game can be summarized in a *payoff matrix* (see Figure 2.7). The first number in each cell is India's payoff, and the second number is Pakistan's. To

Prisoner's Dilemma (PD) A situation modeled by game theory in which rational actors pursuing their individual interests all achieve worse outcomes than they could have by working together.

Figure 2.7 Payoff Matrix in India-Pakistan PD Game

		Pakistan	
		Cooperate	Defect
India	Cooperate	(3,3)	(1,4)
	Defect	(4,1)	(2,2)

Note: First number in each group is India's payoff, second is Pakistan's. The number 4 is highest payoff, 1 lowest.

keep things simple, 4 indicates the highest payoff and 1 the lowest. As is conventional, a decision to refrain from building nuclear weapons is called "cooperation," and a decision to proceed with nuclear weapons is called "defection." The dilemma here parallels that of the prisoners just discussed. Each state's leader reasons: "If they go nuclear, we must; if they don't, we'd be crazy not to." The model seems to predict an inevitable Indian-Pakistani nuclear arms race, although both states would do better to avoid one.

This India-Pakistan example appeared in the first edition of this text in 1993. Since then, as predicted by the model, both sides have built nuclear weapons. In 1998, India detonated underground nuclear explosions to test weapons designs, and Pakistan promptly followed suit. In 2002, the two states nearly went to war, with projected war deaths of up to 12 million. A costly and dangerous arms race continues, and both sides now have dozens of nuclear missiles, and counting. This example illustrates why realists tend to be pessimistic about cooperative solutions to collective goods problems such as the one that the PD game embodies.

Another example of game theory, the game of Chicken, sheds light on the concept of deterrence. Deterrence involves convincing another actor not to undertake an action he or she otherwise would. Just as in the game of Chicken, when one driver commits to not swerving, state leaders attempt to convince others that they will respond harshly if they (or an ally) are attacked. But because not swerving risks disaster for both sides, it is difficult for one side to convince the other that he or she will risk crashing (fighting a war) if the other side decides not to swerve. Game theory often studies *interdependent decisions*—the outcome for each player depends on the actions of the other.

This chapter has focused on the concerns of realists—the interests of states, distribution of power among states, bargaining between states, and alliances of states. The chapter has treated states as unitary actors, much as one would analyze the interactions of individual people. The actions of state leaders have been treated as more or less rational in terms of pursuing definable interests through coherent bargaining strategies. But realism is not the only way to frame the major issues of international relations. Chapter 3 reexamines these themes critically, relying less on the core principle of dominance and more on reciprocity and identity.

Chapter Review

Summary

- Realism explains international relations in terms of power. Power can be conceptualized as influence or as capabilities that can create influence.

- The most important single indicator of a state's power is its GDP.

- Short-term power capabilities depend on long-term resources, both tangible and intangible. Realists consider military force the most important power capability.

- International anarchy—the absence of world government—means that each state is a sovereign and autonomous actor pursuing its own national interests.

- Seven great powers account for half of the world's GDP as well as the great majority of military forces and other power capabilities.

- Power transition theory says that wars often result from shifts in relative power distribution in the international system.

- Hegemony—the predominance of one state in the international system—can help provide stability and peace in international relations but with some drawbacks.

- States form alliances to increase their effective power. Alliances can shift rapidly, with major effects on power relations. The world's main alliances, including NATO and the U.S.-Japanese alliance, face uncertain roles in a changing world order.

- International affairs can be seen as a series of bargaining interactions in which states use power capabilities as leverage to influence the outcomes.

- Rational-actor approaches treat states as though they were individuals acting to maximize their own interests. These simplifications are debatable, but they allow realists to develop concise and general models and explanations.

- Game theory draws insights from simplified models of bargaining situations, such as the Prisoner's Dilemma.

Key Terms

realism 38
idealism 38
League of Nations 38
Munich Agreement 38
power 40
geopolitics 43
anarchy 44
norms 44
sovereignty 44

security dilemma 45
balance of power 46
great powers 47
middle powers 49
neorealism 49
power transition theory 50
hegemony 51
hegemonic stability theory 52
alliance cohesion 54

burden sharing 54
North Atlantic Treaty
    Organization (NATO) 54
Warsaw Pact 54
U.S.-Japanese Security
    Treaty 57
deterrence 60
compellence 60
arms race 61

Critical Thinking Questions

1. Using Table 1.5 on pp. 23–24 (with GDP as a measure of power) and the maps at the front of the text, pick a state and speculate about what coalition of nearby states might form with sufficient power to oppose the state if it became aggressive.

2. Choose a recent international event and list the power capabilities that participants used as leverage in the episode. Which capabilities were effective, and why?

3. The modern international system came into being at a time when agrarian societies relied primarily on farmland to create wealth. Now that most wealth is no longer created through farming, is the territorial nature of states obsolete? How might the diminishing economic value of territory change how states interact?

Chapter 3
Liberal and Social Theories

ANTINUCLEAR PROTESTERS IN GREAT BRITAIN, 2015.

 ## Learning Objectives

3.1 Distinguish two different theories to explain why democracies do not wage war on one another.

3.2 Compare the influence of public opinion and interest groups on the foreign policy process.

3.3 Explain three factors that can hamper individual decision making in an international crisis.

3.4 Illustrate how social theories could explain two countries moving from rivalry to alliance.

3.5 Describe the ways in which mediation can be used to resolve conflict in international relations.

3.6 Identify two problems in international relations where gender is an important factor in understanding those problems.

Liberal Traditions

3.1 **Distinguish two different theories to explain why democracies do not wage war on one another.**

If realism offers mostly dominance solutions to the collective goods problems of international relations (IR), several alternative theoretical approaches discussed in this chapter draw mostly on the reciprocity and identity principles (see Figure 2.1 in Chapter 2). Among other common elements, these approaches generally are more optimistic than realism about the prospects for peace.

The Waning of War

Although realists see the laws of power politics as relatively timeless and unchanging, liberal theorists generally see the rules of IR as slow, evolving incrementally through time and potentially becoming more and more peaceful. This evolution results primarily from the gradual buildup of international organizations and mutual cooperation (reciprocity) and secondarily from changes in norms and public opinion (identity). The main theories discussed in this chapter all hold that we are not doomed to a world of recurring war but can achieve a more peaceful world.

In recent years, a strong trend toward fewer and smaller wars has become evident. To many Americans, the world seems more war-prone and violent than ever because the country is at war on a scale not seen since Vietnam. Yet for the world as a whole, the current period is one of the least warlike ever.

First consider the long-term trend. In the first half of the twentieth century, world wars killed tens of millions and left whole continents in ruin. In the second half of that century, during the Cold War, proxy wars killed millions, and the world feared a nuclear war that could have wiped out our species. Now, in the early twenty-first century, wars like those in Afghanistan and Syria kill tens or even hundreds of thousands. We fear terrorist attacks that could destroy a city but not life on the planet. Generation by generation, the world has moved forward, unevenly but inexorably, from tens of millions killed to millions, to hundreds of thousands. This is still a large number and the impacts of war are still catastrophic. Perhaps if we could understand and sustain this trend, major wars might fade away altogether, though minor wars and terror attacks may continue to kill thousands of people.

Events in the post–Cold War era continue this long-term trend toward smaller wars. The late twentieth century and early twenty-first century saw the termination of lingering Cold War–era conflicts such as those in Angola, Northern Ireland, Guatemala, and southern Sudan (following South Africa and Mozambique earlier in the 1990s). Most of the wars that flared up after the Cold War ended, such as in Bosnia, Kosovo, Algeria, Rwanda, Burundi, and Uganda, have also come to an end. This waning of war continues in recent years. Liberia and Ivory Coast established power-sharing governments and brought in international peacekeepers—following in the path of Sierra Leone (which in 2003 held democratic elections). In 2005, the Irish Republican Army finished permanently dismantling its weaponry. In 2015, Colombia and the largest rebel group in that country agreed to a preliminary peace deal to be completed in 2016.

Today's most serious conflicts consist mainly of skirmishing rather than all-out battles. The last battles between heavily armed forces on both sides (with, for example, artillery, tanks, and airplanes) were the 2003 invasion of Iraq and the 2008 Russian-Georgian war, both short and one-sided affairs. The last great power war (with great powers fighting each other) ended more than 50 years ago.

In 2015, the world's most destructive war was in Syria, where a rebellion and the government's brutal suppression of it cost 200,000 lives over nearly five years. The war has spread into neighboring Iraq where Islamic militants, known as the Islamic State in Iraq and Syria (ISIS), captured significant territory. Military forces from several countries, including the United States, attacked the militants extensively in 2015. By 2015–2016, refugees fleeing this conflict had caused a crisis in Europe as they flooded into countries such as Hungary and Germany.

A deadly civil conflict in Ukraine, its military against pro-Russian separatists (supported by Russia), threatened political relations between Europe and Russia. In Afghanistan, the long war dragged on (but with fewer international troops), although with fewer outside troops, and in Democratic Congo, fighting flared again in the unstable east. Nigerian troops have moved against Islamist militants in the northern part of that country. By historical standards, these are all small wars.

Kant and Peace

What accounts for this positive trend toward peace in a world still feeling insecure and still violence-prone in many ways and places? Liberal theories of IR try to explain how peace and cooperation are possible.

Two hundred years ago, the German philosopher Immanuel Kant gave three answers. The first, based on the reciprocity principle, was that states could develop the organizations and rules to facilitate cooperation, specifically by forming a world federation resembling today's United Nations. This answer forms the foundation of present-day liberal institutionalism, discussed shortly.

Kant's second answer, operating at a lower level of analysis, was that peace depends on the internal character of governments. He reasoned that republics, with a legislative branch that can hold the monarch in check, will be more peaceful than autocracies. This answer, along with Kant's related point that citizens of any country deserve hospitality in any other country, is consistent with the reciprocity principle, but it also relies on the identity principle. Like the social theories discussed later in this chapter, it explains states' preferences based on the social interactions within the state. A variation on Kant's answer, namely, that *democracies* do not fight *each other*, is the basis of present democratic peace theory, also discussed later in this chapter. (Kant himself distrusted democracies as subjecting policy to mob rule rather than rationality, a view influenced by his witnessing the French Revolution.)

Kant's third answer, that trade promotes peace, relies on the assumption that trade increases wealth, cooperation, and global well-being—all while making conflict less likely in the long term because governments will not want to disrupt any process that adds to the wealth of their state. Moreover, as trade between states increases, they will find that they become mutually dependent on one another for goods. This mutual dependence between states is referred to as economic **interdependence.** Scholars often differentiate situations of *sensitivity,* where one state relies on another to provide an important good but can find alternate suppliers, with *vulnerability,* where there are few or no alternative suppliers.

interdependence A political and economic situation in which two states are simultaneously dependent on each other for their well-being. The degree of interdependence is sometimes designated in terms of "sensitivity" or "vulnerability."

Realists are skeptical, however, arguing that one state's reliance on another creates *more* tensions in the short term because states are nervous that another actor has an important source of leverage over them. We will return to this argument in Chapter 5.

Liberal Institutionalism

Now let us return to Kant's first answer to the question of how peace can evolve, namely, the ability of states to develop and follow mutually advantageous rules, with international institutions to monitor and enforce them. Liberal theories treat actors as capable of forgoing short-term individual interests in order to further the long-term well-being of a community to which they belong—and hence indirectly their own well-being. The core principle of reciprocity lies at the heart of this approach because international institutions operate by reciprocal contributions and concessions among formally equal members (peers). Indeed, in several important trade institutions, such as the World Trade Organization (WTO) and the European Union (EU), decisions require *consensus* among all members, making them all equal in governance. Kant argued that states, although autonomous, could join a worldwide federation like today's UN and respect its principles even at the cost of forgoing certain short-term individual gains. To Kant, international cooperation was a more rational option for states than resorting to war. Thus, in realist conceptions of rationality, war and violence appear rational (because they often advance short-term state interests), but in liberal theories, war and violence appear as irrational deviations that result from defective reasoning and harm the (collective, long-term) interests of warring states.

The **neoliberal** approach differs from earlier liberal approaches in that it concedes to realism several important assumptions—among them, that states are unitary actors rationally pursuing their self-interests in a system of anarchy. Neoliberals say to realists, "Even if we grant your assumptions about the nature of states and their motives, your pessimistic conclusions do not follow." States achieve cooperation because it is in their interest to do so, and they can learn to use institutions to ease the pursuit of mutual gains and the reduction of possibilities for cheating or taking advantage of another state.

Neoliberals use the *Prisoner's Dilemma (PD)* game (see p. 63) to illustrate their argument that cooperation is possible. Each actor can gain by individually defecting, but both lose when both defect. Similarly, in IR, states often have a mix of conflicting and mutual interests. The dilemma can be resolved if the game is played over and over again—an accurate model of IR, in which states deal with each other in repeated interactions. In that case, a strategy of strict reciprocity after an initial cooperative move (nicknamed *tit-for-tat*) can bring about mutual cooperation in a repeated PD game because the other player must conclude that any defection will merely provoke a like defection in response.

Thus, reciprocity in IR helps international cooperation emerge despite the absence of central authority. Through reciprocity, not a world government, norms and rules are enforced. But side by side with the potential for eliciting cooperation, reciprocity contains a danger of runaway hostility. When two sides both reciprocate but never manage to put relations on a cooperative footing, the result can be a drawn-out, nasty, tit-for-tat exchange of punishments. This characterizes Israeli relations with Palestinian militants over the years, for instance.

Building on the reciprocity principle, many norms mediate states' interactions. For example, diplomatic practices and participation in international organizations (IOs) are both strongly governed by shared expectations about the rules of correct behavior. As collective goods problems crop up in IR, states rely on a context of rules, norms, habits, and institutions that make it rational for all sides to avoid the self-defeating outcomes that would result from pursuing narrow, short-term self-interest. Neoliberals study historical and contemporary cases in IR to see how institutions and norms affect the possibilities for overcoming dilemmas and achieving international cooperation. (As we will soon see, some constructivists emphasize that these norms eventually function without states thinking about self-interest at all.) Thus, for neoliberals the emergence of international institutions is key to understanding how states achieve a superior rational outcome that includes long-term self-interest and not just immediate self-interest.

neoliberalism Shorthand for "neoliberal institutionalism," an approach that stresses the importance of international institutions in reducing the inherent conflict that realists assume in an international system; the reasoning is based on the core liberal idea that seeking long-term mutual gains is often more rational than maximizing individual short-term gains.

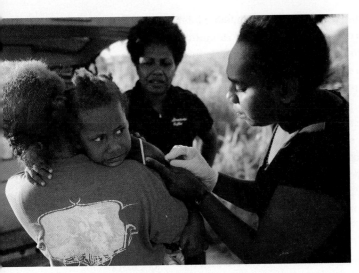

HEALTHY REGIME International regimes are sets of rules, norms, and procedures, not always codified into institutions, that govern the behavior of actors in IR. The world health regime includes states, IGOs such as the World Health Organization (WHO), nonprofit organizations such as the Gates Foundation, and others, all working with common expectations about activities to improve health and stem epidemics. Here, a UNICEF staff member vaccinates a child against measles after a devastating cyclone hit Vanuatu in 2015.

international regime A set of rules, norms, and procedures around which the expectations of actors converge in a certain international issue area (such as oceans or monetary policy).

International Regimes

Achieving good outcomes is not simple, though. Because of the contradictory interpretations that parties to a conflict usually have, it is difficult to resolve conflicts without a third party to arbitrate or an overall framework to set common expectations for all parties. These considerations underlie the creation of IOs.

An **international regime** is a set of rules, norms, and procedures around which the expectations of actors converge in a certain issue area (whether arms control, international trade, or Antarctic exploration). The convergence of expectations means that participants in the international system have similar ideas about what rules will govern their mutual participation: Each expects to play by the same rules. (This meaning of *regime* is not the same as that referring to the domestic governments of states, as in *regime change*.)

Regimes can help solve collective goods problems by increasing transparency— everyone knows what everyone else is doing, so cheating is riskier. The current revolution in information technologies is strengthening regimes particularly in this aspect. Also, with better international communication, states can identify conflicts and negotiate solutions through regimes more effectively.

The most common conception of regimes combines elements of realism and liberalism. States are seen as autonomous units maximizing their own interests in an anarchic context. Regimes do not play a role in issues in which states can realize their interests directly through unilateral applications of leverage. Rather, regimes come into existence to overcome collective goods dilemmas by coordinating the behaviors of individual states. Although states continue to seek their own interests, they create frameworks to coordinate their actions with those of other states if and when such coordination is necessary to realize self-interest (that is, in collective goods dilemmas).

Regimes do not substitute for the basic calculations of costs and benefits by states; rather, they open up new possibilities with more favorable cost-benefit ratios. Regimes facilitate and empower national governments faced with issues in which collective goods problems would otherwise prevent governments from achieving their ends. Regimes can be seen as *intervening variables* between the basic causal forces at work in IR—for realists, the relative power of state actors— and the outcomes such as international cooperation (or lack thereof). For realists in particular, regimes do not negate the effects of power; more often they codify and normalize existing power relations in accordance with the dominance principle. For example, the nuclear nonproliferation regime protects the status quo in which only a few states have nuclear weapons.

Because regimes depend on state power for their enforcement, some IR scholars argue that regimes are most effective when power in the international system is most concentrated—when there is a hegemon to keep order (see pp. 48–49). Yet regimes do not always decline with the power of hegemons that created them. Rather, they may take on a life of their own. Although hegemony may be crucial in *establishing* regimes, it is not necessary for *maintaining* them. Once actors' expectations converge around the rules embodied in a regime, the actors realize that the regime serves their own interests. Working through the regime becomes a habit, and national leaders may not seriously consider breaking out of the established rules.

In part, the survival of regimes rests on their embedding in permanent *institutions* such as the UN, the North Atlantic Treaty Organization (NATO), and the International Monetary Fund (IMF). These institutions become the tangible manifestation of shared expectations as well as the machinery for coordinating international actions based on those expectations. Formal institutions gain greater stability and weight than do noninstitutionalized regimes. With a staff and headquarters, an international institution can actively promote adherence to the rules in its area of political or economic life. These bureaucracies, however, can also promote policies that were not intended by the states that created the institutions.

The culmination of liberal institutionalism to date is the European Union (EU), which receives in-depth discussion in Chapter 6. After centuries of devastating wars, European states now enjoy a stable peace among themselves with strong international institutions to bind them.

Collective Security

The concept of **collective security,** which grows out of liberal institutionalism, refers to the formation of a broad alliance of most major actors in an international system for the purpose of jointly opposing aggression by any actor. Kant laid out the rationale for this approach. Because past treaties ending great power wars had never lasted permanently, Kant proposed a federation (league) of the world's states. Through such a federation, Kant proposed, the majority of states could unite to punish any one state that committed aggression, safeguarding the collective interests of all the nations while protecting the self-determination of small nations that all too easily became pawns in great power games.

After the horrors of World War I, the *League of Nations* was formed to promote collective security. But it was flawed in two ways. Its membership did not include all the great powers (and not the most powerful one, the United States),

collective security
The formation of a broad alliance of most major actors in an international system for the purpose of jointly opposing aggression by any actor; sometimes seen as presupposing the existence of a universal organization (such as the United Nations) to which both the aggressor and its opponents belong.

and its members proved unwilling to bear the costs of collective action to oppose aggression when it did occur in the 1930s. After World War II, the United Nations was created as the League's successor to promote collective security (see Chapter 6). Several regional intergovernmental organizations (IGOs) also currently perform collective security functions (deterring aggression) as well as economic and cultural ones—the *Organization of American States (OAS)*, the *Arab League*, and the *African Union (AU)*.

The success of collective security depends on two points. First, the members must keep their alliance commitments to the group (that is, members must not free-ride on the efforts of other members). When a powerful state commits aggression against a weaker one, it often is not in the immediate interest of other powerful states to go to war over the issue. Suppressing a determined aggressor can be very costly.

A second requisite for collective security is that enough members must agree on what constitutes aggression. The UN Security Council is structured so that aggression is defined by what all five permanent members, in addition to at least four of the other ten members, can agree on (see The Security Council on pp. 232–235). This collective security system does not work against aggression by a great power. When the Soviet Union invaded Afghanistan, or the United States mined the harbors of Nicaragua, or France blew up the Greenpeace ship *Rainbow Warrior,* the UN could do nothing—because those states can veto Security Council resolutions.

Collective security worked in 1990–1991 to reverse Iraq's conquest of Kuwait because the aggression brought all the great powers together and because they were willing to bear the costs of confronting Iraq. It was the first time since the founding of the UN that one member state had invaded, occupied, and annexed another—attempting to erase it as a sovereign state. The invasion was so blatant a violation of Kuwaiti sovereignty and territorial integrity that the Security Council had little trouble labeling it aggression and authorizing the use of force by a multinational coalition. The threat that Iraq posed to the world's oil supplies provided incentive for coalition members to contribute money or troops to solve the problem.

In 2002–2003, by contrast, the Security Council repeatedly debated Iraq's failure to keep the agreements it had made at the end of the Gulf War, in particular the promise to disclose and destroy all its weapons of mass destruction. But the great powers split, and a proposed U.S.-British resolution authorizing military force was withdrawn after France promised to veto it. Germany, Russia, and China also strongly opposed it. Public opinion around the world, especially in predominantly Muslim countries, also opposed the war. When the UN did not act, the United States, Britain, and Australia sent military forces to overthrow Saddam Hussein by force, comparing the UN to the toothless League of Nations (see pp. 38–39). However, the United States found no weapons of mass destruction in Iraq and then found itself in a prolonged counterinsurgency war. In retrospect, although the world's collective security system is creaky and not always effective, bypassing it to take military action also holds dangers.

The Democratic Peace

Kant argued that lasting peace would depend on states' becoming republics, with legislatures to check the power of monarchs (or presidents) to make war. He thought that checks and balances in government would act as a brake on the use of military force—compared to autocratic governments in which a single individual (or small ruling group) could make war without regard for the effect on the population.

Somewhat similarly, IR scholars have linked democracy with a kind of foreign policy fundamentally different from that of authoritarianism. One theory they considered was that democracies are generally *more peaceful* than authoritarian governments (fighting fewer, or smaller, wars). This turned out not to be true. Democracies fight as many wars as do authoritarian states. Indeed, the three most war-prone states of the past two centuries (according to political scientists who count wars) were France, Russia, and Britain. Britain was a democracy throughout, France for part of the period, and Russia not at all.

What *is* true about democracies is that, although they fight wars against authoritarian states, *democracies almost never fight each other.* No major historical cases contradict this generalization, which is known as the **democratic peace.** Why this is so is not entirely clear. Because there have not been many democracies for very long, the generalization could be just a coincidence, though this seems unlikely. It may be that democracies do not tend to have severe conflicts with each other because they tend to be capitalist states whose trade relations create strong interdependence (war would be costly because it would disrupt trade). Or citizens of democratic societies (whose support is necessary for wars to be waged) may simply not see the citizens of other democracies as enemies. By contrast, authoritarian governments of other states can be seen as enemies. Note that the peace among democracies gives empirical support to a long-standing liberal claim that, because it is rooted in the domestic level of analysis, contradicts realism's claim that the most important explanations are at the interstate level.

Over the past two centuries, democracy has become more widespread as a form of

democratic peace
The proposition, strongly supported by empirical evidence, that democracies almost never fight wars against each other (although they do fight against authoritarian states).

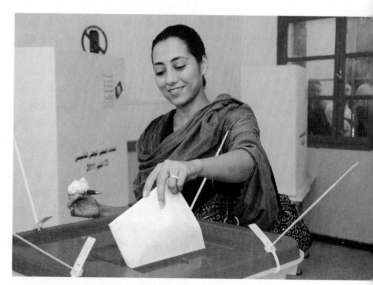

DEMOCRATIC TIDE Upsurges of democratic movements throughout the world in recent years testify to the power of the idea of democracy. Because democracies rarely fight each other, worldwide democratization might lead to lasting peace. Here, Tunisia holds its first free election after leading the Arab Spring and reversing decades of authoritarian rule, 2011.

government, and this trend is changing the nature of the foreign policy process worldwide. Many states do not yet have democratic governments (the most important of these is China). And existing democracies are imperfect in various ways—from political apathy in the United States and corruption in Japan to autocratic traditions in Russia. Nonetheless, the trend is toward democratization in most of the world's regions.

In recent decades, the trend has accelerated in several ways. New democracies emerged in several (though not all) states of the old Soviet bloc. Military governments gave way to democratically elected civilian governments throughout most of Latin America as well as in several African and Asian countries. South Africa, the last white-ruled African country, adopted majority rule in 1994. In the late 1990s, democracy replaced long-standing dictatorships in Indonesia and Nigeria, both regional giants. In 2004–2005, pro-democracy forces won victories in Ukraine, Afghanistan, Iraq, and Kyrgyzstan. In 2008, Pakistan's military-run government stepped down to make way for a democratically elected regime. And in 2011–2012, the Arab Spring revolutions catalyzed regime transitions in Tunisia, Egypt, Libya, and Yemen. While Tunisia has fared well on its path to democracy, the other states have experienced significant difficulties in establishing democratic rule. In 2012, Burma began a rapid transition toward democracy after decades of harsh military rule. However, military coups took place in Niger in 2010, Guinea-Bissau and Mali in 2012, Egypt in 2013, and Thailand in 2014. Iran rigged an election in 2009 and brutally cracked down on those protesting it.

We do not know where democratization will lead, but it is now conceivable that someday nearly all of the world's states will be democratically governed. As Kant envisaged, an international community based on peaceful relations may emerge. However, although mature democracies almost never fight each other, a period of *transition* to democracy may be more prone to war than either a stable democracy or a stable authoritarian government. Therefore the process of democratization does not necessarily bode well for peace in the short term. In early 2006, the first Iraqi elections were followed by a rise in sectarian violence, and then Palestinian elections brought to power the militant faction Hamas, which rejects Israel's right to exist.

Finally, it is important to note that while democracy is often associated with peace and cooperation, democratic institutions can make cooperation more difficult. For example, pressures for raising trade tariffs often arise from democratically elected legislatures. Some democratic countries may fail to join international organizations because of domestic opposition, as was the case with the United States and the League of Nations after World War I (see Chapter 1). Public opposition can also make attempts to expand existing cooperation difficult, as European Union leaders discovered after their proposal for a new EU constitution was defeated in democratic elections (see Chapter 10). Thus, while liberal scholars often extol the virtues of democracy, these same domestic institutions can make the process of international cooperation more complex.

Domestic Influences

3.2 **Compare the influence of public opinion and interest groups on the foreign policy process.**

Liberal institutionalism operates at the interstate level of analysis, but the democratic peace relies on the domestic level to explain IR events. In reality, a state's actions result from individual human choices—by citizenry, political leaders, diplomats, and bureaucrats—aggregated through the state's internal structures. Continuing in this vein, the next two sections examine the state from the inside out, trying to understand the processes and structures within states that make them behave as they do. We begin by examining the institutions that shape state behavior.

Bureaucracies

Of the many substate actors that influence states' actions in the international arena, those closest to the action are the bureaucratic agencies that states maintain to develop and carry out foreign policy. Different states maintain different foreign policy bureaucracies but all share some common elements. Almost all states maintain a *foreign service* of diplomats working in *embassies* in foreign capitals (and in *consulates* located in noncapital foreign cities), as well as diplomats who remain at home to coordinate policy. States appoint *ambassadors* as their official representatives to other states and to international organizations. Diplomatic activities are organized through a *foreign ministry* or the equivalent (for example, the U.S. State Department). In many democracies, some diplomats are *political appointees* who come and go with changes in government leaders, while others are *career diplomats* who come up through the ranks of the foreign service and tend to outlast changes in administration.

Diplomats provide much of the information that goes into making foreign policies, but their main role is to carry out rather than create policies. Nonetheless, foreign ministry bureaucrats often make foreign relations so routine that top leaders and political appointees can come and go without greatly altering the country's relations. The national interest is served, the bureaucrats believe, by the stability of overall national goals and positions in international affairs.

Tension is common between state leaders and foreign policy bureaucrats. Career diplomats try to orient new leaders and their appointees and to control the flow of information they receive (creating information screens). Politicians struggle to exercise power over the formal bureaucratic agencies because the latter can be too "bureaucratic" (cumbersome, routinized, conservative) to control easily. Also, these agencies are often staffed (at lower levels) mostly by career officials who may not owe loyalty to political leaders.

Sometimes state leaders appoint a close friend or key adviser to manage the foreign policy bureaucracy. President George H. W. Bush did this with his closest friend, James Baker, as did President George W. Bush in his second term with his former National Security Council (NSC) chief and confidante, Condoleezza

Rice. Chinese leader Mao Zedong put his loyal ally Zhou Enlai in charge of foreign policy. At other times, state leaders may appoint rivals with differing views of foreign policy—as President Barack Obama did with his former political rival Hillary Clinton.

Interagency tension also affects the formulation of foreign policy. Certain agencies traditionally clash, and an endless tug-of-war shapes the foreign policies that emerge. In an extreme example of interagency rivalry, the U.S. State Department and the Central Intelligence Agency (CIA) backed opposite sides in a civil war in Laos in 1960. In general, bureaucracies promote policies under which their own capabilities will be effective and their power will increase. Of special concern in many states is the institutional interest that military officers have in maintaining a strong military. If civilian state leaders allow officers' salaries to fall or the size of the military forces to be cut, they may well face institutional resistance from the military—in the extreme case, a military takeover of the government (see pp. 169–170). These issues were important factors (among several) in military coups in Thailand, Honduras, and Egypt in recent years.

In general, bureaucratic rivalry as an influence on foreign policy challenges the notion of states as unitary actors in the international system. Such rivalries suggest that a state does not have any single set of goals—a national interest—but that its actions may result from the bargaining of subunits, each with its own set of goals. Furthermore, such a perspective extends far beyond bureaucratic agencies because other substate actors have their own goals, which they seek to advance by influencing foreign policy.

Interest Groups

Foreign policy makers operate not in a political vacuum but in the context of the political debates in their society. In all states, societal pressures influence foreign policy, although these pressures are aggregated and made effective through different channels in different societies. In pluralistic democracies, interested parties influence foreign policy through interest groups and political parties. In dictatorships, similar influences occur but less visibly. Thus, foreign policies adopted by states generally reflect some kind of process of domestic coalition formation. Of course, international factors also affect domestic politics.

interest groups
Coalitions of people who share a common interest in the outcome of some political issue and who organize themselves to try to influence the outcome.

Interest groups are coalitions of people who share a common interest in the outcome of some political issue and who organize themselves to try to influence the outcome. For instance, French farmers have a big stake in international negotiations in the European Community (which subsidizes agriculture) and in world trade talks (which set agricultural tariffs). French farmers have turned out in large numbers to block roads, stage violent street demonstrations, and threaten to grind the national economy to a halt unless the government adopts their position. Similarly (but often less dramatically), interest groups form around businesses, labor unions, churches, veterans, senior citizens, members of an occupation, or citizens concerned about an issue such as the environment.

Lobbying is the process of talking with legislators or officials to influence their decisions on some set of issues. Three important elements that go into successful lobbying are the ability to gain a hearing with busy officials, the ability to present cogent arguments for one's case, and the ability to trade favors in return for positive action on an issue. These favors—legal and illegal—include campaign contributions, dinners at nice restaurants, trips to golf resorts, illicit sexual liaisons, and bribes. In many states, corruption is a major problem in governmental decision making (see pp. 309–310), and interest groups may induce government officials by illegal means to take certain actions.

Ethnic groups within one state often become interest groups concerned about their ancestral nation outside that state. Many members of ethnic groups feel strong emotional ties to their relatives in other countries; because the rest of the population generally does not care about such issues one way or the other, even a small ethnic group can have considerable influence on policy toward a particular country. Such ethnic ties are emerging as a powerful foreign policy influence in various ethnic conflicts in poor regions. The effect is especially strong in the United States, which is ethnically mixed and has a pluralistic form of democracy. For example, Cuban Americans organize to influence U.S. policy toward Cuba, as do Greek Americans on Greece, Jewish Americans on Israel, and African Americans on Africa. But whether or not a foreign country has a large constituency of ethnic nationals within another country, it can lobby that country's government.

Clearly, interest groups have goals and interests that may or may not coincide with the national interest as a whole (if indeed such an interest can be identified). As with bureaucratic agencies, the view of the state as a unitary actor can be questioned. Defenders of interest-group politics argue that various interest groups tend to push and pull in different directions, with the ultimate decisions generally reflecting the interests of society as a whole. But according to *Marxist* theories of international relations, the key domestic influences on foreign policy in capitalist countries are rich owners of big businesses. For instance, European imperialism benefited banks and big business, which made huge profits from exploiting cheap labor and resources in overseas colonies. During the Cold War, Marxists argued that Western foreign policies were driven by the profit motive of arms manufacturers.

Public Opinion

Many domestic actors seek to influence **public opinion**—the range of views on foreign policy issues held by the citizens of a state. Public opinion has greater influence on foreign policy in democracies than in authoritarian governments. But even dictators must pay attention to what citizens think. No government can rule by force alone: It needs legitimacy to survive. It must persuade people to accept (if not to like) its policies because, in the end, policies are carried out by ordinary people—soldiers, workers, and bureaucrats.

Because of the need for public support, even authoritarian governments spend great effort on *propaganda*—the public promotion of their official line—to

public opinion In IR, the range of views on foreign policy issues held by the citizens of a state.

win support for foreign policies. States use television, newspapers, and other information media in this effort. In many countries, the state owns or controls major mass media such as television and newspapers, mediating the flow of information to its citizens; however, new information technologies with multiple channels (such as the Internet) make this harder to do.

Journalists serve as the gatekeepers of information passing from foreign policy elites to the public. The media and government often conflict because of the traditional role of the press as a watchdog and critic of government actions and powers. The media try to uncover and publicize what the government wants to hide. Foreign policy decision makers also rely on the media for information about foreign affairs.

Yet the media also depend on government for information; the size and resources of the foreign policy bureaucracies dwarf those of the press. These advantages give the government great power to *manipulate* journalists by feeding them information to shape the news and influence public opinion. Government decision makers can create dramatic stories in foreign relations—through summit meetings, crises, and so forth. Bureaucrats can also *leak* secret information to the press to support their point of view and win bureaucratic battles. Finally, the military and the press have a running battle about journalists' access to military operations, but both sides gained from the open access given to journalists "embedded" with U.S. forces in Iraq in 2003.

In democracies, where governments must stand for election, an unpopular war can force a leader or party from office, as happened to U.S. president Lyndon Johnson in 1968 during the Vietnam War. Or a popular war can help secure a government's mandate to continue in power, as happened to Margaret Thatcher in Britain after the 1982 Falkland Islands War. During the war in Bosnia, officials in the U.S. State Department said privately that the main goal of U.S. policy was often just to keep the conflict there off the front pages of U.S. newspapers (an elusive goal, as it turned out).

In democracies, public opinion generally has *less effect on foreign policy than on domestic policy.* National leaders traditionally have additional latitude to make decisions in the international realm. This derives from the special need of states to act in a unified way to function effectively in the international system, as well as from the traditions of secrecy and diplomacy that remove IR from the realm of ordinary domestic politics. The *attentive public* in a democracy is the minority of the population that stays informed about international issues. This segment varies somewhat from one issue to another, but there is also a core of people who care in general about foreign affairs and follow them closely. The most active members of the attentive public on foreign affairs constitute a foreign policy *elite*—people with power and influence who affect foreign policy. This elite includes people within governments as well as outsiders such as businesspeople, journalists, lobbyists, and professors. Public opinion polls show that elite opinions sometimes (but not always) differ considerably from those of the general population and sometimes from those of the government as well.

Policy Perspectives
Prime Minister of Japan, Shinzo Abe

PROBLEM *How do you decide what foreign policy tools best balance domestic and international concerns?*

BACKGROUND Imagine that you are the prime minister of Japan. Since the end of the Korean War in 1953, relations with your neighbor to the west, North Korea, have been tense. Military tensions have persisted as North Korea has made and then broken several agreements regarding its nuclear program. North Korea tested nuclear weapons in 2006, 2009, and 2013, and it has also test-fired short-range ballistic missiles directly over Japan in an effort to intimidate your country. In late 2012, it tested a new long-range rocket in defiance of international warnings. You won election in 2012 on a hawkish platform, calling for large increases in defense spending and the deployment of antimissile weapons to protect your country from a North Korean launch.

For its part, North Korea has long demanded reparations for Japan's 35-year colonization of the Korean peninsula (1910–1945) and for Japan's actions in Korea during World War II. Japan has refused such reparations in the past but has provided limited aid in an attempt to encourage North Korea to denuclearize.

In the summer of 2008, the United States removed North Korea from its list of states that sponsor terrorism. This angered many in your country, who see this as giving in to North Korean demands for more aid in exchange for giving up its nuclear program. Your government vehemently protested this move by the United States, which the Japanese government called "extremely regrettable."

DOMESTIC CONSIDERATIONS Public opinion in Japan is very sensitive to relations with North Korea. In 2002, North Korea admitted to secretly abducting Japanese citizens in the 1970s and 1980s, transporting them to North Korea, and using them to train North Korean spies. North Korea claims that all 13 abductees have either returned to Japan or died, but many in Japan are skeptical of this claim. Many in Japan suspect more than 13 were abducted and have even demanded that North Korea return the bodies of the deceased. These abductions are an extremely sensitive issue in Japanese public opinion and past Japanese governments have demanded a resolution to the abduction issue before opening formal diplomatic relations with North Korea.

SCENARIO Now imagine that the United States is negotiating a new nuclear weapons agreement with North Korea. The United States asks that Japan contribute extensive foreign aid to North Korea to help ensure that a deal is reached. In return, North Korea will agree to allow increased inspections of all key nuclear sites and will rejoin the Non-Proliferation Treaty (see pp. 166–167). The United States is placing extensive pressure on your government to provide what it feels is critical aid.

CHOOSE YOUR POLICY How do you respond to U.S. pressure for more foreign aid? Do you risk a backlash from your public by increasing aid without having the abduction issue resolved? Do you resist pressure from the United States, your most important ally, and withhold the requested aid? Can you trust the North Korean government to hold up its end of the bargain after you give the economic aid? How do you balance a sensitive domestic political issue with a delicate set of international negotiations?

Governments sometimes adopt foreign policies for the specific purpose of generating public approval and hence gaining domestic legitimacy. This is the case when a government undertakes a war or foreign military intervention at a time of domestic difficulty, to distract attention and gain public support. Such a strategy takes advantage of the **"rally 'round the flag" syndrome**—the public's increased support for government leaders during wartime, at least in the short term. Citizens who would readily criticize their government's policies on education or health care often refrain from criticism when the government is at war and the lives of the nation's soldiers are on the line. Policies of this sort are often labeled *diversionary foreign policy*. Unfortunately, it is always difficult to tell whether a state adopts a foreign policy to distract the public because leaders would never admit to trying to divert public attention.

However, wars that go on too long or are not successful can turn public opinion against the government and even lead to a popular uprising to overthrow the government. In Argentina, the military government in 1982 led the country into war with Britain over the Falkland Islands. At first, Argentineans rallied around the flag, but after losing the war they rallied around the cause of getting rid of the military government and prosecuting its leaders. In 2006, President Bush's popularity, which had soared early in the Iraq War, plummeted as the war dragged on (see Figure 3.1), and voters threw his party out of power in Congress.

"rally 'round the flag" syndrome The public's increased support for government leaders during wartime, at least in the short term.

Figure 3.1 The "Rally 'Round the Flag" Syndrome

President Bush's approval rating demonstrates the "rally 'round the flag" syndrome, in which war triggers a short-term boost in public approval.

Source: Gallup Poll.

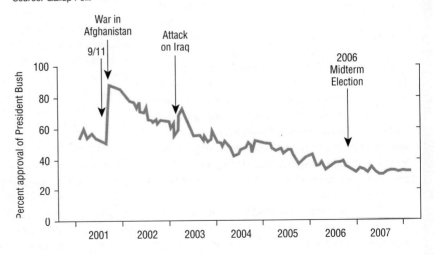

Legislatures

One conduit through which interest groups and public opinion may wield influence is legislatures. Some democracies, such as the United States, have presidential systems, in which legislative bodies are elected apart from the president (also referred to as an *executive*). In these systems, legislatures play a direct role in making foreign policy by passing budgets, regulating bureaucratic rules, creating trade law, even controlling immigration policy. Although executives may attend summits and talks, any agreement they sign must be approved by their domestic legislature.

Although few would argue that legislatures in presidential democracies do not influence foreign policy generally, different rules may apply to the use of military force. Some contend that legislatures, like public opinion, rally around the flag during times of international crises. For example, three days after the September 11, 2001, terrorist attacks, the U.S. Congress voted to give President Bush full authority to prosecute a war in Afghanistan. In October 2002, Congress passed a resolution authorizing the use of force in Iraq. Thus, legislatures rarely if ever challenge an executive on important military matters. An important exception to this occurred in 2015 when Republican legislators in the U.S. Congress tried to stop the nuclear agreement with Iran, but President Obama used his veto power to preserve it.

Others point to a different dynamic in which legislatures do stand up to executive power regarding military force. For example, because legislatures hold the "purse strings" (the ability to approve or reject new spending), they have the ability to stop a war in its tracks. In the United States, the War Powers Act, enacted during the close of the Vietnam War, requires the president to notify Congress when U.S. troops are deployed for combat. After this notification, the president has 60 days (plus a possible 30-day extension) to recall the troops unless Congress explicitly approves the military action. During the 2011 Libya air campaign, the Obama administration claimed that the War Powers Act did not apply because the action was not a war. However, during the American military campaign against ISIS forces in Iraq in 2014–2015, the Obama administration sought congressional approval for the use of force.

In parliamentary systems, such as Great Britain, executives (for example, prime ministers) are chosen by the political parties that hold a dominant position in the legislative bodies. Often parliamentary executives do not need to submit treaties or policies for formal approval by the legislature, yet legislatures still hold power regarding foreign policy. In many parliamentary systems, if a foreign (or domestic) policy is controversial, parties that do not have a majority in the legislature can try to call elections—meaning that the country votes again on which parties will hold seats in the legislature. If different parties win a majority of seats, a new executive is appointed. Thus, in parliamentary systems, legislatures play a key role in designing and implementing foreign policy.

Making Foreign Policy

3.3 Explain three factors that can hamper individual decision making in an international crisis.

Foreign policies are the strategies that governments use to guide their actions in the international arena. Foreign policies spell out the objectives that state leaders have decided to pursue in a given relationship or situation. But in general,

**foreign policy
process** The process
by which foreign
policies are arrived at
and implemented.

IR scholars are less interested in specific policies than in the **foreign policy process**—how policies are arrived at and implemented.

States establish various organizational structures and functional relationships to create and carry out foreign policies. Officials and agencies collect information about a situation through various channels; they write memoranda outlining possible options for action; they hold meetings to discuss the matter; they sometimes meet privately to decide how to steer the meetings. Such activities, broadly defined, are what is meant by the phrase "the foreign policy process." IR scholars are especially interested in exploring whether certain kinds of policy processes lead to certain kinds of decisions—whether certain processes produce better outcomes (for the state's self-defined interests) than do others.

Foreign policy outcomes result from multiple forces at various levels of analysis. While the previous section discussed the state-level institutions, here the focus is on individual decision makers and the groups they operate within. Whether at the institutional or individual level of analysis, the study of foreign policy processes runs counter to realism's assumption of a unitary state actor.

Models of Decision Making

The foreign policy process is a process of *decision making*. States take actions because people in governments—*decision makers*—choose those actions. Decision making is a *steering* process in which adjustments are made as a result of feedback from the outside world. Decisions are carried out by actions taken to change the world, and then information from the world is monitored to evaluate the effects of these actions. These evaluations—along with information about other, independent changes in the environment—go into the next round of decisions (see Figure 3.2).

Figure 3.2 Decision Making as Steering

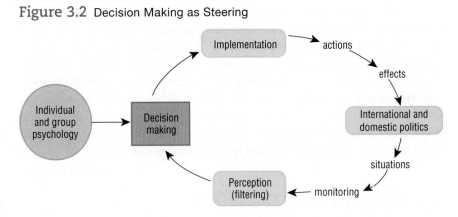

rational model A
model in which decision makers calculate
the costs and benefits
of each possible
course of action, then
choose the one with
the highest benefits
and lowest costs.

A common starting point for studying the decision-making process is the **rational model.** In this model, decision makers set goals, evaluate their relative importance, calculate the costs and benefits of each possible course of action, and then choose the one with the highest benefits and lowest costs (see Figure 3.3).

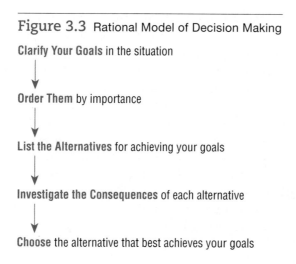

Figure 3.3 Rational Model of Decision Making

Clarify Your Goals in the situation

Order Them by importance

List the Alternatives for achieving your goals

Investigate the Consequences of each alternative

Choose the alternative that best achieves your goals

The choice may be complicated by *uncertainty* about the costs and benefits of various actions. In such cases, decision makers must attach probabilities to each possible outcome of an action. For example, will pressuring a rival state to give ground in peace talks work or backfire? Some decision makers are relatively *accepting of risk,* whereas others are *averse to risk.* These factors affect the importance that decision makers place on various alternative outcomes that could result from an action.

Of course, one may believe decision makers are rational but not accept the realist assumption that states may be treated as unitary actors. Governments are made up of individuals who may rationally pursue their goals. Yet the goals of different individuals involved in making a decision may diverge, as may the goals of different state agencies. For example, the U.S. secretary of state may have a different goal than the secretary of defense, just as the Central Intelligence Agency may view a situation differently than the National Security Council does. The rational model of decision making is somewhat complicated by uncertainty and the multiple goals of decision makers. Thus, the rational model may imply that decision making is simpler than is actually the case.

An alternative to the rational model of decision making is the **organizational process model.** In this model, foreign policy decision makers generally skip the labor-intensive process of identifying goals and alternative actions, relying instead for most decisions on standardized responses or *standard operating procedures.* For example, the U.S. State Department every day receives more than a thousand reports or inquiries from its embassies around the world and sends out more than a thousand instructions or responses to those embassies. Most are never seen by the top decision makers (the secretary of state or the president); instead, they are handled by low-level decision makers who apply general principles—or who simply try to make the least controversial, most

organizational process model A decision-making model in which policy makers or lower-level officials rely largely on standardized responses or standard operating procedures.

standardized decision. The organizational process model implies that much of foreign policy results from "management by muddling through."

government bargaining model A model that sees foreign policy decisions as flowing from a bargaining process among various government agencies that have somewhat divergent interests in the outcome ("where you stand depends on where you sit"). Also called *bureaucratic politics model.*

Another alternative to the rational model is the **government bargaining model** (or *bureaucratic politics model*), in which foreign policy decisions result from the bargaining process among various government agencies with somewhat divergent interests in the outcome. In 1992, the Japanese government had to decide whether to allow sushi from California to be imported—a weakening of Japan's traditional ban on importing rice (to maintain self-sufficiency in its staple food). The Japanese Agriculture Ministry, with an interest in the well-being of Japanese farmers, opposed the imports. The Foreign Ministry, with an interest in smooth relations with the United States, wanted to allow the imports. The final decision to allow imported sushi resulted from the tug-of-war between the ministries. Thus, according to the government bargaining model, foreign policy decisions reflect (a mix of) the interests of state agencies.

Individual Decision Makers

Every international event is the result, intended or unintended, of decisions made by individuals. IR does not just happen. President Harry Truman, who decided to drop U.S. nuclear bombs on two Japanese cities in 1945, had a sign on his desk: "The buck stops here." As leader of the world's greatest power, he had nobody to pass the buck to. If he chose to use the bomb (as he did), more than 100,000 civilians would die. If he chose not to, the war might drag on for months, with tens of thousands of U.S. casualties. Truman had to choose. Some people applaud his decision; others condemn it. But for better or worse, Truman as an individual had to decide, and take responsibility for the consequences. Similarly, the decisions of individual citizens, although they may not seem important when taken one by one, create the great forces of world history.

BOMBS AWAY Foreign policies often deviate from rationality as a result of the misperceptions and biases of decision makers and populations. Here, in 2014, North Korea's dictator Kim Jong-Un watches a rocket test. His country's nuclear weapons program and their delivery vehicles are a significant concern in the West. These weapons will pose a much greater threat if Kim, who took over in 2011, is an irrational madman than if he turns out to be a shrewdly rational actor.

The study of individual decision making revolves around the question of rationality. To what extent are national leaders (or citizens) able to make rational decisions in the national interest—if indeed such an interest can be defined? Individual rationality is not equivalent to state rationality: States might filter individuals' irrational decisions to arrive at rational choices, or states might distort individually rational decisions and end up with irrational state choices. But realists tend to assume that both states and individuals are rational and that the goals or interests of states correlate with those of leaders.

The most simplified rational-actor models assume that interests are the same from one actor to another. If this were so, individuals could be substituted for each other in various roles without changing history very much. States would all behave similarly to each other (or rather, the differences between them would reflect different resources and geography, not differences in the nature of national interests). Individual decisions would reflect the *values* and *beliefs* of the decision maker.

Individual decision makers not only have differing values and beliefs but also have unique personalities—their personal experiences, intellectual capabilities, and personal styles of making decisions. Some IR scholars study individual psychology to understand how personality affects decision making.

Beyond individual *idiosyncrasies* in goals or decision-making processes, individual decision making diverges from the rational model in at least three *systematic* ways. First, decision makers suffer from **misperceptions** and **selective perceptions** (taking in only some kinds of information) when they compile information on the likely consequences of their choices. Decision-making processes must reduce and filter the incoming information on which a decision is based; the problem is that such filtration often is biased. **Information screens** are subconscious filters through which people put the information coming in about the world around them. Often they simply ignore any information that does not fit their expectations. Information is also screened out as it passes from one person to another in the decision-making process. For example, prior to the September 2001 terrorist attacks, U.S. intelligence agencies failed to interpret available evidence adequately because too few analysts were fluent in Arabic.

Misperceptions can affect the implementation of policy by low-level officials as well as its formulation by high-level officials. For example, in 1988, officers on a U.S. warship in the Persian Gulf shot down a civilian Iranian jet that they believed to be a military jet attacking them. The officers were trying to carry out policies established by national leaders, but because of misperceptions, their actions instead damaged their state's interests.

Second, the rationality of individual cost-benefit calculations is undermined by emotions that decision makers feel while thinking about the consequences of their actions—an effect referred to as *affective bias*. (*Positive* and *negative affect* refer to feelings of liking or disliking someone.) As hard as a decision maker tries to be rational in making a decision, the decision-making process is bound to be influenced by strong feelings held about the person or state toward which a decision is directed.

Third, *cognitive biases* are systematic distortions of rational calculations based not on emotional feelings but simply on the limitations of the human brain in making choices. The most important bias seems to be the attempt to produce *cognitive balance*—or to reduce *cognitive dissonance*. These terms refer to

misperceptions The mistaken processing of the available information about a decision; one of several ways—along with affective and cognitive bias—in which individual decision making diverges from the rational model.

selective perceptions When individuals are more likely to perceive information that is consistent with their beliefs, while ignoring information that is inconsistent with those beliefs.

information screens The subconscious or unconscious filters through which people put the information coming in about the world around them.

the tendency people have to try to maintain mental models of the world that are logically consistent (this seldom succeeds entirely).

One implication of cognitive balance is that decision makers place greater value on goals that they have put much effort into achieving—the *justification of effort*. This is especially true in a democracy, in which politicians must face their citizens' judgment at the polls and so do not want to admit failures. The Vietnam War trapped U.S. decision makers in this way in the 1960s. After sending half a million troops halfway around the world, U.S. leaders found it difficult to admit to themselves that the costs of the war were greater than the benefits.

Decision makers also achieve cognitive balance through *wishful thinking*—an overestimate of the probability of a desired outcome. A variation of wishful thinking is to assume that an event with a *low probability* of occurring will *not* occur. This could be a dangerous way to think about catastrophic events such as accidental nuclear war or a terrorist attack.

Cognitive balance often leads decision makers to maintain a hardened image of an *enemy* and to interpret all of the enemy's actions in a negative light (because the idea of bad people doing good things would create cognitive dissonance). A *mirror image* refers to two sides in a conflict maintaining very similar enemy images of each other ("we are defensive, they are aggressive," etc.). A decision maker may also experience psychological *projection* of his or her own feelings onto another actor.

Another form of cognitive bias, related to cognitive balance, is the use of *historical analogies* to structure one's thinking about a decision. This can be quite useful or quite misleading, depending on whether the analogy is appropriate. Each historical situation is unique in some way, and when a decision maker latches onto an analogy and uses it as a shortcut to a decision, the rational calculation of costs and benefits may be cut short as well. In particular, decision makers often assume that a solution that worked in the past will work again—without fully examining how similar the situations really are. For example, U.S. leaders incorrectly used the analogy of Munich in 1938 to convince themselves that appeasement of communism in the Vietnam War would lead to increased communist aggression in Asia. Vietnam in turn became a potent analogy that made U.S. leaders shy of involvement in overseas conflicts such as Bosnia; this was called the "Vietnam syndrome."

All of these psychological processes—misperception, affective biases, and cognitive biases—interfere with the rational assessment of costs and benefits in making a decision. Two specific modifications to the rational model of decision making have been proposed to accommodate psychological realities.

First, the model of *bounded rationality* takes into account the costs of seeking and processing information. Nobody thinks about every single possible course of action when making a decision. Instead of **optimizing,** or picking the very best option, people usually work on the problem until they come up with a "good enough" option that meets some minimal criteria; this is called **satisficing** (finding a satisfactory solution). The time constraints faced by top decision

optimizing Picking the very best option; contrasts with satisficing, or finding a satisfactory but less than best solution to a problem. The model of "bounded rationality" postulates that decision makers generally "satisfice" rather than optimize.

satisficing The act of finding a satisfactory or "good enough" solution to a problem.

makers in IR—who are constantly besieged with crises—generally preclude their finding the very best response to a situation. These time constraints were described by U.S. Secretary of Defense William Cohen in 1997: "The unrelenting flow of information, the need to digest it on a minute-by-minute basis, is quite different from anything I've experienced before. . . . There's little time for contemplation; most of it is action."

Second, **prospect theory** provides an alternative explanation (rather than simple rational optimization) of decisions made under risk or uncertainty. According to this theory, decision makers go through two phases. In the *editing phase*, they frame the options available and the probabilities of various outcomes associated with each option. Then, in the *evaluation phase*, they assess the options and choose one. Prospect theory holds that evaluations take place by comparison with a *reference point*, which is often the status quo but might be some past or expected situation.

Individual decision making thus follows an imperfect and partial kind of rationality at best. Not only do the goals of different individuals vary but decision makers also face a series of obstacles in receiving accurate information, constructing accurate models of the world, and reaching decisions that further their own goals. The rational model is only a simplification at best and must be supplemented by an understanding of individual psychological processes that affect decision making.

prospect theory A decision-making theory that holds that options are assessed by comparison to a reference point, which is often the status quo but might be some past or expected situation. The model also holds that decision makers fear losses more than they value gains.

Group Psychology

In one respect, groups promote rationality by balancing out the blind spots and biases of any individual. Advisers or legislative committees may force a state leader to reconsider a rash decision. And the interactions of different individuals in a group may result in the formulation of goals that more closely reflect state interests rather than individual idiosyncrasies. However, group dynamics also introduce new sources of irrationality into the decision-making process.

Groupthink refers to the tendency for groups to reach decisions without accurately assessing their consequences because individual members tend to go along with ideas they think the others support. The basic phenomenon is illustrated by a simple psychology experiment. A group of six people is asked to compare the lengths of two lines projected onto a screen. When five of the people are secretly instructed to say that line A is longer—even though anyone can see that line B is actually longer—the sixth person is likely to agree with the group rather than believe his or her own eyes.

groupthink The tendency of groups to validate wrong decisions by becoming overconfident and underestimating risks.

Unlike individuals, groups tend to be overly optimistic about the chances of success and are thus more willing to take risks. Participants suppress their doubts about dubious undertakings because everyone else seems to think an idea will work. Also, because the group diffuses responsibility from individuals, nobody feels accountable for actions.

In a spectacular case of groupthink, President Ronald Reagan's close friend and director of the U.S. CIA bypassed his own agency and ran covert operations

Figure 3.4 Some Psychological Pitfalls of Decision Making

Note: Conflictland could be Vietnam in 1968, Bosnia in 1994, or Iraq in 2006.

spanning three continents using the NSC staff in the White House basement. The NSC sold weapons to Iran in exchange for the freedom of U.S. hostages held in Lebanon and then used the Iranian payments to fund Nicaraguan Contra rebels illegally. The *Iran-Contra scandal* resulted when these operations, managed by an obscure NSC aide named Oliver North, became public.

The U.S. war in Iraq may also provide cautionary examples to future generations about the risks of misinformation, misperception, wishful thinking, and groupthink in managing a major foreign policy initiative. Some of the problems of individual and group psychology in the policy process—be they in Vietnam, Bosnia, or Iraq—are illustrated in Figure 3.4.

The *structure of a decision-making process*—the rules of the decision makers, how voting is conducted, and so forth—can affect the outcome, especially when no single alternative appeals to a majority of participants. Experienced participants in foreign policy formation are familiar with the techniques for manipulating decision-making processes to favor outcomes they prefer. The structure of decision making also reflects the composition of a decision group.

State leaders often rely on an inner circle of advisers in making foreign policy decisions. The composition and operation of the inner circle vary across governments. Some groups depend heavily on *informal* consultations in addition to formal meetings. Some leaders create a "kitchen cabinet"—a trusted group of friends who discuss policy issues with the leader even though they have no formal positions in government. Russian president Boris Yeltsin relied on the advice of his bodyguard, who was a trusted friend.

Crisis Management

The difficulties in reaching rational decisions, both for individuals and for groups, are heightened during a crisis. *Crises* are foreign policy situations in which outcomes are very important and time frames are compressed. Crisis

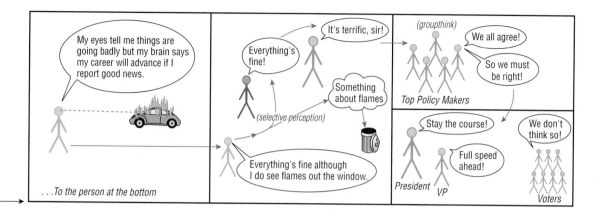

decision making is harder to understand and predict than is normal foreign policy decision making.

In a crisis, decision makers operate under tremendous time constraints. The normal checks on unwise decisions may not operate. Communications become shorter and more stereotyped, and information that does not fit a decision maker's expectations is more likely to be discarded simply because there is no time to consider it. In framing options, decision makers tend to restrict the choices, again to save time, and tend to overlook creative options while focusing on the most obvious ones.

Groupthink occurs easily during crises. During the 1962 Cuban Missile Crisis, President John F. Kennedy created a small, closed group of advisers who worked together intensively for days on end, cut off from outside contact. Even the president's communication with Soviet leader Nikita Khrushchev was rerouted through Kennedy's brother Robert and the Soviet ambassador, cutting out the State Department. Recognizing the danger of groupthink, Kennedy left the room from time to time—removing the authority figure from the group—to encourage free discussion. The group managed to identify an option (a naval blockade) between their first two choices (bombing the missile sites or doing nothing).

WORKING UNDER STRESS Crisis management takes a high toll psychologically and physiologically. President Eduard Shevardnadze of Georgia seems to show this strain in 1992—just the beginning of years of civil war and perpetual crisis in that country. Shevardnadze, formerly a Soviet foreign minister, had returned to lead his native Georgia when the Soviet Union dissolved. He left office in 2003 after a popular uprising against corruption.

Participants in crisis decision making not only are rushed but also experience severe psychological *stress,* amplifying the biases just discussed. Decision makers tend to overestimate the hostility of adversaries and to underestimate their own hostility toward those adversaries. More and more information is screened out in making decisions.

Whether decision makers are in crisis mode or normal routines, their decisions are shaped by the government and society in which they work. Foreign policy is constrained and shaped by substate actors such as government agencies, political interest groups, and industries. Foreign policy is a complex outcome of a complex process. It results from the struggle of competing themes, competing domestic interests, and competing government agencies. No single individual, agency, or guiding principle determines the outcome.

Beyond the challenges to realist theories from liberal theories and foreign policy analysis, several more sweeping critiques have emerged. These include constructivism, postmodernism, Marxist theories, peace studies, and gender theories of IR.

Social Theories

3.4   Illustrate how social theories could explain two countries moving from rivalry to alliance.

Several distinct approaches in IR theory may be grouped together as *social theories,* meaning that they rely on social interaction to explain individuals' and states' preferences. These theories contrast with the assumption of fixed, timeless preferences in most theories based on realism (states want more power) and liberalism (states, interest groups, and individuals want peace and prosperity).

Constructivism

constructivism A movement in IR theory that examines how changing international norms and actors' identities help shape the content of state interests.

Constructivism, a fast-growing approach in IR, asks how states construct their interest through their interactions with one another. It is best described as an approach rather than a theory because, when stripped to its core, it says nothing about IR per se. However, its lessons about the nature of norms, identity, and social interactions can provide powerful insights into the world of IR. In fact, most constructivist explanations draw heavily on the identity principle to explain international behavior.

Constructivism is interested in how actors define their national interests, threats to those interests, and their relationships with one another. Realists (and neoliberals) tend simply to take state interests as given. Thus, constructivism puts IR in the context of broader social relations. States decide what they want based not only on material needs but also on "social" interaction. Just as a shopper may decide to buy a particular smartwatch because it will be perceived as cool (that is, more socially acceptable), so states may chose policies based on what they perceive will be "popular" with other states. Yet just as shoppers may have limits placed on which smartwatch they can afford to buy (limited resources), constructivists also recognize that power is not absent from international relations.

For example, why is the United States concerned when North Korea builds nuclear weapons but not when Great Britain does? Realists would quickly answer that North Korea poses a bigger threat, yet from a pure military power perspective, Great Britain is a *far* superior military force to North Korea. Yet no one would argue that Great Britain is a threat to the United States no matter how many nuclear weapons it builds and no matter how deep disagreements about foreign policy become. Constructivist scholars would point out the shared history, shared alliances, and shared norms that tell Americans and the British they are not a threat to one another, although they are very powerful militarily. The identity of the potential adversary matters, not just its military capabilities and interests.

Constructivists hold that these state identities are complex and changing and arise from interactions with other states—often through a process of *socialization*. Some constructivist scholars contend that, over time, states can conceptualize one another so that there is no danger of a security dilemma, arms races, or the other effects of anarchy. They point to Europe as an example—a continent that was the center of two military conflicts in the first half of the twentieth century that killed millions. By the end of that century, war had become unthinkable. European identities are now intertwined with the European Union, not with the violent nationalism that led to two world wars. For constructivists, power politics, anarchy, and military force cannot explain this change. Institutions, regimes, norms, and changes in identity are better explanations.

Societies as a whole also change over time in what they consider to be threatening. Two hundred years ago, pirates were the scourge of the high seas. These nonstate actors invaded ports, pillaged goods, committed murder, and flaunted all international authority. It would not be hard to consider such behavior as terrorism, even though the pirates had no political goals in their violence. Even if the pirates' behavior is not terrorism, no one would doubt the costs associated with piracy. Many states, including the United States, used their navies in attempts to eradicate pirates. Yet despite the danger and harm historically caused by these actors, today we celebrate pirates by making them sports mascots, naming amusement rides after them, and glorifying them in movies.

Of course, one could argue that pirates are no longer a threat—even though numerous acts of piracy still occur on the high seas. Even apart from the high-profile pirate hijackings near Somalia in 2008–2009, the threat from piracy has remained high for many years. Yet we find it acceptable to play down the piracy threat by incorporating them into popular culture. No doubt someone from two centuries ago would find such acceptance odd.

How odd? Imagine in 200 years your great-great-grandchildren riding a terrorist-themed ride at Disneyland or watching the latest *Terrorists of the Persian Gulf* movie. Constructivists are quick to point out that what societies or states consider dangerous is not universal or timeless. Social norms and conventions change, and these changes can have tremendous implications for foreign policy.

Another field of constructivist research also relies heavily on international norms and their power to constrain state action. Although realists (and neoliberals) contend that states make decisions based on a *logic of consequences* ("What will happen to me if I behave a certain way?"), constructivist scholars note that there is a powerful *logic of appropriateness* ("How should I behave in this situation?"). For example, some cases of humanitarian intervention—military intervention by a state or states to protect citizens or subjects of another state—seem difficult to explain in realist or liberal terms. Why, for example, did the United States in 1992 send troops to Somalia—a country of minimal strategic and economic importance to the United States—as Somalia descended into political chaos and faced the possibility of mass starvation (see p. 31)? A constructivist explanation might point to changing norms about which kinds of people are worthy of protection. In the nineteenth century, European powers occasionally intervened to protect Christian subjects of the Ottoman Empire from massacres, but they generally ignored non-Christian victims. However, as decolonization enshrined the principle of self-determination and as human rights became widely valued, the scope of humanitarian intervention expanded. Although the international community does not always respond effectively to humanitarian crises, it is no longer acceptable to view only Christians as deserving protection.

Examples of identity principles can be found in the developing world as well. Some constructivists have argued that countries in Latin America, Africa, and the Middle East have adopted or changed policies in response to international norms—not because it provided large benefits but rather because it was perceived as the appropriate course of action. For example, many developing states have raced to create science bureaucracies and/or begin technological modernization of their militaries. Constructivists point out that the reason developing states choose to spend their limited resources on such projects is their desire to be perceived as "modern" by the international system. Ironically, many states that

CONSTRUCTING IDENTITIES Constructivist theories, based on the core principle of identity, see actors' preferences as constructed by the actors rather than given "objectively." These theories may do better than realist or liberal approaches in explaining major changes in a state's foreign policy goals and image in the world that arise from internal changes and new self-concepts rather than external constraints or opportunities. Examples might include the breakup of the Soviet Union and the election of Barack Obama as U.S. president. Iran's identity as an Islamic revolutionary state affects its foreign policies. Here, the morals police close a barber shop in Iran for giving Western-style haircuts, 2008.

build science bureaucracies have few scientists, and many states that build advanced militaries have few enemies. Thus, constructivists emphasize that identities and norms must be used to explain this seemingly puzzling behavior.

How are these international norms spread around the world? In an age of global communication and relative ease of transportation, many possibilities exist. Some contend that individuals labeled *norm entrepreneurs,* through travel, writing, and meeting with elites, change ideas and encourage certain types of norms. Some point to broad-based social movements and nongovernmental organizations, such as the anti-apartheid movement encouraging the development of a global norm of racial equality. Others show how international organizations (such as the UN and NATO) can diffuse norms of what is appropriate and inappropriate behavior. In each case, however, new ideas and norms, rather than power and self-interest, drive state behavior.

Research in the constructivist tradition has expanded rapidly in recent years. Scholars have examined the role of the European Union in socializing elites in new member states as well as the role of the United Nations in conferring legitimacy on the use of force as a source of its power. Others have investigated how international organizations gain authority through their expertise (for example, the IMF on international financial issues) to make decisions that run counter to what their member states desire. Finally, constructivist scholars have begun to investigate how notions of identity and symbolism are important for understanding terrorist movements and counterterrorism policy.

Of course, like any approach or theory of IR, constructivism has its critics. Realists suggest that norms are simply covers for state (or personal) interests. Liberals argue that some constructivist scholars pay too little attention to the formal institutions and the power politics within them. Moreover, both realists and liberals make the criticism that it is difficult to tell when a person's identity or beliefs are genuine or adopted strategic reasons to bring material benefits (such as more aid, trade, or membership into an exclusive organization). Despite these criticisms, constructivist thinking and its emphasis on the identity principle will continue to be at the core of IR research for years to come.

Postmodernism

Postmodernism is a broad approach to scholarship that has left its mark on various academic disciplines, especially the study of literature. Because of their literary roots, postmodernists pay special attention to *texts* and to *discourses*—how people write and talk about their subject (IR). Postmodern critiques of realism thus center on analyzing realists' words and arguments. A central idea of postmodernism is that there is no single, objective reality but a multiplicity of experiences and perspectives that defy easy categorization. For this reason, postmodernism itself is difficult to present in a simple or categorical way. Postmodern scholarship in IR preceded, set the stage for, and has largely been supplanted by constructivism.

postmodernism An approach that denies the existence of a single fixed reality and pays special attention to texts and to discourses—that is, to how people talk and write about a subject.

From a postmodern perspective, realism cannot justify its claim that states are the central actors in IR and that states operate as unitary actors with coherent sets of objective interests (which they pursue through international power politics). Postmodern critics of realism see nothing objective about state interests and certainly nothing universal (in that one set of values or interests applies to all states).

More fundamentally, postmodernism calls into question the whole notion of states as actors. States have no tangible reality; they are "fictions" that we (as scholars and citizens) construct to make sense of the actions of large numbers of individuals. For postmodernists, the stories told about the actions and policies of states are just that—stories. They are filtered through an interpretive process that distorts the actual experiences of those involved.

Contrary to realism's claim that states are unitary actors, postmodernists see multiple realities and experiences lurking below the surface of the fictional entities (states) that realists construct. The Soviet Union, for example, was treated by realists as a single actor with a single set of objective interests. Indeed, it was considered the second most important actor in the world. Realists were amazed when the Soviet Union split into 15 pieces, each containing its own fractious groups and elements. It became clear that the "unitary state" called the Soviet Union had masked (and let realists ignore) the divergent experiences of constituent republics, ethnic groups, and individuals.

Postmodernists seek to "deconstruct" such constructions as states, the international system, and the associated stories and arguments (texts and discourses) with which realists portray the nature of international relations. To *deconstruct* a text—a term borrowed from literary criticism—means to tease apart the words in order to reveal hidden meanings, looking for what might be omitted or included only implicitly. The hidden meanings not explicitly addressed in the text are often called the **subtext.** Omissions are an aspect of subtext, as when realist theories of IR omit women and gender, for example. In its emphasis on states, realism omits the roles of individuals, domestic politics, economic classes, multinational corporations (MNCs), and other nonstate actors. In its focus on the great powers, realism omits the experiences of poor countries. In its attention to military forms of leverage, it omits the roles of various nonmilitary forms of leverage. By contrast, postmodernists celebrate the diversity of experiences that make up IR without needing to make sense of them by simplifying and categorizing.

subtext Meanings that are implicit or hidden in a text rather than explicitly addressed.

Marxism

Historically most important among social theories, Marxist approaches to IR hold that both IR and domestic politics arise from unequal relationships between **economic classes.** This emphasis on classes—implying that the domestic and economic attributes of societies shape external relations with other states—contrasts with the realist approach to IR, with its separation of domestic and international

economic classes A categorization of individuals based on economic status.

politics. We will discuss Marxist theories of IR in Chapter 7 because they concern primarily the global divisions of North and South arising from the history of imperialism. Here we will show, briefly, how Marxist theories as social theories contrast with the realist paradigm.

Marxism is a branch of socialism that holds that the more powerful classes oppress and exploit the less powerful by denying them their fair share of the surplus they create. The oppressed classes try to gain power in order to seize more of the wealth for themselves. This process, called *class struggle,* is one way of looking at the political relationships between richer and poorer people and ultimately between richer and poorer world regions.

Marxism includes both communism and other approaches. In the mid-nineteenth century, *Karl Marx* emphasized labor as the source of economic surplus. At that time, the Industrial Revolution was accompanied by particular hardship among industrial workers (including children) in Europe. Marxists still believe that the surplus created by labor should be recaptured by workers through political struggle. Today, Marxism is most influential in countries of the global South, where capital is scarce and labor conditions are wretched.

One important class in revolutions during the past century (contrary to Marx's expectations) has been *peasants.* Marxists traditionally consider peasants backward, ignorant, individualistic, and politically passive compared to the better-educated and class-conscious proletariat. But in practice, the successful third world revolutions have been peasant rebellions (often led by Marxists talking about the proletariat). The largest was the Chinese revolution in the 1930s and 1940s.

Marx's theories of class struggle were oriented toward *domestic* society in the industrializing countries of his time, not toward poor countries or international relations. Traditional Marxists looked to the advanced industrialized countries for revolution and socialism, which would grow out of capitalism. In their view, the third world would have to develop through its own stages of accumulation from feudalism to capitalism before taking the revolutionary step to socialism. What actually happened was the opposite. Proletarian workers in industrialized countries enjoyed rising standards of living and did not make revolutions. Meanwhile, in the backward third world countries, oppressed workers and peasants staged a series of revolutions, successful and failed.

Why did revolutions occur in backward rather than advanced countries? The answer largely shapes how one sees North-South relations today. Marxists have mostly (but not exclusively) followed a line of argument developed by *V. I. Lenin,* founder of the Soviet Union, before the Russian Revolution of 1917. Russia was then a relatively backward state, as the global South is today, and most Marxists considered a revolution there unlikely (looking instead to Germany).

Lenin's theory of imperialism argued that European capitalists were investing in colonies where they could earn big profits and then using part of these profits to *buy off* the working class at home. But Lenin saw that, after the scramble for colonies in the 1890s, few areas of the world remained to be colonized.

Marxism A branch of socialism that emphasizes exploitation and class struggle and includes both communism and other approaches.

Imperialist expansion could occur only at the expense of other imperialist states, leading to interimperialist competition and wars such as World War I. Seizing on Russia's weakness during that war, Lenin led the first successful communist revolution there in 1917.

Lenin's general idea still shapes a major approach to North-South relations—the idea that industrialized states exploit poor countries (through both formal and informal colonization) and buy off their own working classes with the profits. Through this *globalization of class relations*, world accumulation concentrates surplus in the rich parts of the world and away from the poor ones. Revolutions, then, would be expected in poor regions.

Many revolutionaries in poor countries sought to break loose from exploitation by the European colonizers. After European colonization ended, the United States, as the world's richest country (with large investments in the global South and a global military presence), became the target of revolutionaries agitating against exploitation in poor countries. In a number of countries, imperialists were thrown out (often violently, sometimes not) and revolutionary nationalists took power.

One of the most important such revolutions was in China, where Mao Zedong's communists took power in 1949 on a Leninist platform adapted to the largely peasant-based movement they led. Mao declared that "China has stood up"—on its own feet, throwing off foreign domination and foreign exploitation. In India at the same time, the movement led by Gandhi used different means (nonviolence) to achieve similar ends—national independence from colonialism. Indonesia threw out the Dutch. Lebanon threw out the French. Cuba threw out the Americans. This pattern was repeated, with variations, in dozens of countries.

According to the revolutionaries in these countries, exploitation of poor countries by rich ones takes away the economic surplus of the global South and concentrates the accumulation of wealth in the rich parts of the world. By breaking free of such exploitation, poor states can then retain their own surplus and begin to accumulate their own wealth. Eventually they can generate their own self-sustaining cycles of accumulation and lift themselves out of poverty.

However, such an approach has not worked well. A policy of self-reliance does not foster growth (see p. 182). And within a single poor country, trade-offs arise between concentrating or distributing wealth. For former colonies, the realities of economic development after independence have been complex. These realities are discussed in Chapter 7.

Not all Marxist approaches favor a policy of self-reliance after revolution. *Leon Trotsky*, a Russian revolutionary, believed that after the 1917 revolution, Russia would never be able to build socialism alone and should make its top priority the spreading of revolution to other countries to build a worldwide alliance. Trotsky's archrival Stalin wanted to build "socialism in one country," and he prevailed (and had Trotsky killed). Most revolutions since then, including China's, have had a strongly nationalist flavor.

Marxist theories in IR entered a low-visibility phase after the collapse of the Soviet Union and China's turn toward capitalism—events that seemed to discredit Marxist theories. In recent years, however, Marxists and former Marxists have taken power in a number of Latin American countries. Venezuela and Bolivia, as a result, have become active allies of Cuba, forming an anti-American coalition (although America's normalization with Cuba in 2105 could bring tensions to this coalition). In Nicaragua, the former communist leader whom U.S.-organized rebels fought in the 1980s won election as president in 2006. In Nepal, Maoists reached a peace deal and then won national elections. These events, along with China's continuing formal adherence to Marxism, suggest that Marxist theories of IR have ongoing importance in the post–Cold War era.

Peace Studies

3.5   Describe the ways in which mediation can be used to resolve conflict in international relations.

Peace studies challenges fundamental concepts behind both realism and neoliberalism. In particular, peace studies seeks to shift the focus of IR away from the interstate level of analysis and toward a broad conception of social relations. Peace studies connects war and peace with individual responsibility, economic inequality, gender relations, cross-cultural understanding, and other aspects of social relationships. Peace studies also seeks the potentials for peace not in the transactions of state leaders but in the transformation of entire societies (through social revolution) and in transnational communities (bypassing states and ignoring borders to connect people and groups globally).

Another way in which peace studies seeks to broaden the focus of inquiry is to reject the supposed objectivity of traditional (realist and liberal) approaches. Most scholars of peace studies think that a good way to gain knowledge is to participate in action—not just to observe objectively. This lack of objectivity has been criticized as *normative bias* because scholars impose their personal norms and values on the subject. Scholars in peace studies respond, however, that realism itself has normative biases and makes policy prescriptions.

SHADOW OF WAR Militarism in a culture, or the lack thereof, can influence foreign policy. In societies at war, children's psychological trauma contributes to intergroup conflicts decades later. Generations of Palestinians have grown up in a society affected by violent conflict. This Palestinian girl, walking between Israeli troops and Palestinian stone-throwers in the West Bank in 2010, has lived around violent conflict her whole life, as have her parents and grandparents.

conflict resolution
The development and implementation of peaceful strategies for settling conflicts.

mediation The use of a third party (or parties) in conflict resolution.

positive peace A peace that resolves the underlying reasons for war; not just a cease-fire but a transformation of relationships, including elimination or reduction of economic exploitation and political oppression.

The development and implementation of peaceful strategies for settling conflicts—using alternatives to violent forms of leverage—are known by the general term **conflict resolution.** These methods are at work, competing with violent methods, in almost all international conflicts. Recently the use of conflict resolution has been increasing, becoming more sophisticated, and succeeding more often.

Most conflict resolution uses a third party whose role is **mediation** between two conflicting parties. If both sides agree in advance to abide by a solution devised by the mediator, the process is called *arbitration*. In that case, both sides present their arguments to the arbitrator, who decides on a "fair" solution. Arbitration often uses a panel of three people, one chosen by each side and a third on whom both sides agree.

Conflicting parties (and mediators) can also use *confidence-building* measures to gradually increase trust. By contrast, *linkage* lumps together diverse issues so that compromises on one can be traded off against another in a grand deal.

Peace studies scholars argue that war is not just a natural expression of power but one closely tied to *militarism*, the glorification of war, military force, and violence through TV, films, books, political speeches, toys, games, sports, and other such avenues. Militarism also refers to the structuring of society around war—for example, the dominant role of a military-industrial complex in a national economy. Militarism may underlie the propensity of political leaders to use military force. Historically, militarism has had a profound influence on the evolution of societies. War has often been glorified as a "manly" enterprise that ennobles the human spirit (especially before World War I, which changed that perspective). Not only evil acts but also exemplary acts of humanity are brought forth by war—sacrifice, honor, courage, altruism on behalf of loved ones, and bonding with a community larger than oneself.

Examples of less militarized cultures show that realism's emphasis on military force is not universal or necessary. Costa Rica has had no army for 50 years (just lightly armed forces), even during the 1980s when wars occurred in neighboring Nicaragua and Panama. Japan since World War II has developed strong norms against war and violence.

Positive peace refers to a peace that resolves the underlying reasons for war—peace that is not just a cease-fire but a transformation of relationships. Under positive peace, not only do state armies stop fighting each other, they stop arming, stop forming death squads against internal protest, and reverse the economic exploitation and

GIVE PEACE A CHANCE Peace demonstrators play a role in many conflicts. Here, demonstrators respond to an outbreak of violence in Belfast, Northern Ireland, 2013.

political oppression that scholars in peace studies believe are responsible for social conflicts that lead to war.

Proponents of this approach see broad social and economic issues—assumed by realists to be relatively unimportant—as inextricably linked with positive peace. Some scholars define poverty, hunger, and oppression as forms of violence—which they call *structural violence* because it is caused by the structure of social relations rather than by direct actions such as shooting people. Structural violence in this definition kills and harms many more people each year than do war and other forms of direct political violence. Positive peace is usually defined to include the elimination of structural violence because it is considered a source of conflict and war.

Positive peace encompasses a variety of approaches to social change. These include alternative mechanisms for conflict resolution to take the place of war; popular pressure on governments through peace movements and political activism; strengthening of norms against the use of violence; the development of international or global identity transcending national, ethnic, and religious divisions; and egalitarian relations within societies in the economic, social, and political realms. Positive peace is usually defined to include political equality and human rights as well.

The creation of a **world government** has long been debated by scholars and pursued by activists. Some scholars believe progress is being made (through the UN) toward the eventual emergence of a world government. Others think the idea is impractical or even undesirable (merely adding another layer of centralized control, when peace demands decentralization and freedom).

world government
A centralized world governing body with strong enforcement powers.

Scholars in peace studies also study how to achieve the conditions for positive peace. Most peace studies scholars share a skepticism that state leaders, if left to themselves, would ever achieve positive peace. Rather, they believe the practice of IR will change only as a result of pressures from individuals and groups. The most commonly studied method of exerting such pressure is through **peace movements**—people taking to the streets in protest against war and militarism.

peace movements
Movements against specific wars or against war and militarism in general, usually involving large numbers of people and forms of direct action such as street protests.

The philosophies of *nonviolence* and *pacifism* are based on a unilateral commitment to refrain from using any violent forms of leverage in bargaining. No state today follows such a strategy; indeed, it is widely believed that in today's world, a state that adopted a nonviolent philosophy would risk exploitation or conquest. *Mahatma Gandhi* emphasized that nonviolence must be *active* in seeking to prevent violence and stand up against injustice. Protesters in the Arab Spring movements in 2011 followed Dr. King's example as well as specific strategies recommended by an American, Gene Sharp, whose ideas were taught to young Arab activists at earlier workshops in Europe. These nonviolent approaches worked spectacularly in Tunisia and Egypt; were swept aside by a violent rebellion in Libya; and gave way to wars in Syria, where war claimed nearly 200,000 lives in 2011–2014, and in Yemen, where war and rebellion claimed over 8,000 lives in that same period.

Gender Theories

3.6 Identify two problems in international relations where gender is an important factor in understanding those problems.

Scholarship on gender has cut a broad swath across academic disciplines, from literature to psychology, to history. In recent years, it has made inroads in international relations, once considered one of the fields most resistant to feminist arguments.

Why Gender Matters

Gender scholarship encompasses a variety of strands of work, but all have in common the insight that gender matters in understanding how IR works—especially in issues relating to war and international security. *Feminist scholarship* in various disciplines seeks to uncover hidden assumptions about gender in how we study a subject. What scholars traditionally claim to be universal often turns out to be true only of males. Some feminist IR scholars argue that the core assumptions of realism—especially of anarchy and sovereignty—reflect the ways in which *males* tend to interact and to see the world. In this view, the realist approach simply assumes male participants when discussing foreign policy decision making, state sovereignty, or the use of military force.

This critique is somewhat complex. Because the vast majority of heads of state, diplomats, and soldiers *are* male, it may be realistic to study them as males. What the feminist critics then ask is that scholars explicitly recognize the gendered nature of their subject (rather than implicitly assuming all actors are male). In this view, our understanding of male actors in IR can be increased by considering how their gender identity affects their views and decision processes. And females also influence IR (more often through nonstate channels than males do)—influences often ignored by realism. Some feel that women scholars tend to be more interested in these roles and effects than are their male colleagues, who largely ignore gender topics. One list of "fifty key thinkers" in IR includes four women, three of whom it lists as gender scholars, while none of the 46 males are listed as gender scholars. And when a survey in 2014 listed the 20 most influential IR scholars, only 3 were women.

Beyond revealing the hidden assumptions about gender in a field of scholarship, feminist scholars often *challenge traditional concepts of gender* as well. In IR, these traditional concepts revolve around the

A GUY THING Feminists from various theoretical traditions agree that the gender makeup of international summits and national governments matters. Here, China's old (left) and new (right) ruling group mark the transition of power, 2012.

assumptions that males fight wars and run states, whereas females are basically irrelevant to IR. Such gender roles are based in the broader construction of masculinity as suitable to *public* and political spaces, whereas femininity is associated with the sphere of the *private* and domestic.

Like realists (see p. 38), gender theorists follow a long line of tradition.[1] Not long before Thucydides, the ancient Greek poetess Sappho wrote love poems to women on the island of Lesbos. Just before Machiavelli, the Italian-born writer Christine de Pisan praised women's abilities to make peace. A century after Hobbes, Mary Wollstonecraft in Britain argued for equal rights for women. And a century before Morgenthau founded American realism, the American Susan B. Anthony worked tirelessly for pacifism, abolitionism, and suffrage.

Beyond a basic agreement that gender is important, there is no single feminist approach to IR but several *strands* of scholarship and theory. Although they are interwoven (all paying attention to gender and to the status of women), they often run in different directions. On some core issues, the different strands of feminism have conflicting views, creating debates *within* feminism.

One strand, **difference feminism,** values the unique contributions of women *as* women. Difference feminists do not think women do all things as well as men, or vice versa. Because of their greater experience with nurturing and human relations, women are seen as potentially more effective than men (on average) in conflict resolution and group decision making. Difference feminists believe gender differences are not just social constructions and cultural indoctrination (although these contribute to gender roles, too). Some difference feminists believe there is a core biological essence to being male or female (sometimes called *essentialism*), but the majority think gender differences are more culturally than biologically determined. In either case, women's perspectives create a *standpoint* from which to observe, analyze, and criticize the traditional perspectives on IR.

Another strand, **liberal feminism,** rejects these claims as being based on stereotyped gender roles. Liberal feminists see the "essential" differences in men's and women's abilities or perspectives as trivial or nonexistent—men and women are equal. They deplore exclusion of women from positions of power in IR but do not believe that including women would change the nature of the international system. Liberal feminists seek to include women more often as subjects of study—such as women state leaders, women soldiers, and other women operating outside the traditional gender roles in IR.

A third approach combines feminism with postmodernism, discussed earlier in this chapter. **Postmodern feminism** tends to reject the assumptions about gender made by both difference and liberal feminists. Where difference feminists consider gender differences important and fixed, and liberal feminists consider those differences trivial, postmodern feminists find them important but arbitrary and flexible.

difference feminism
A strand of feminism that believes gender differences are not just socially constructed and that views women as inherently less warlike than men (on average).

liberal feminism A strand of feminism that emphasizes gender equality and views the "essential" differences in men's and women's abilities or perspectives as trivial or nonexistent.

postmodern feminism
An effort to combine feminist and postmodernist perspectives with the aim of uncovering the hidden influences of gender in IR and showing how arbitrary the construction of gender roles is.

---

[1]Thanks to Francine D'Amico for this idea.

The Masculinity of Realism

Difference feminism provides a perspective from which to reexamine the core assumptions of realism. Some difference feminists have argued that realism emphasizes autonomy and separation because men find separation easier to deal with than interconnection.

This view rests on a psychological theory that boys and girls grow up from a young age with different views of separateness and connection. In this theory, because a child's primary caretaker is almost always female in the early years, girls form their gender identity around the perception of similarity with their caretaker (and by extension the environment in which they live), but boys perceive their difference from the caretaker. From this experience, boys develop social relations based on individual autonomy, but girls' relations are based on connection. As a result, women are held to be more likely than men to fear abandonment, whereas men are more likely to fear intimacy.

In *moral* reasoning, according to this theory, boys tend to apply abstract rules and stress individual rights, but girls pay more attention to the concrete contexts of different situations and to the responsibility of group members for each other. In playing *games*, boys resolve disputes through arguments about the rules and then keep playing, but girls are more likely to abandon a game rather than argue over the rules and risk the social cohesion of their group. In *social relations*, boys form and dissolve friendships more readily than girls, who are more likely to stick loyally with friends. (The empirical evidence in psychological research for these theorized gender differences is mixed at best.)

Realism, of course, rests on the concept of states as separate, autonomous actors that make and break alliances freely while pursuing their own interests (but not interfering in each other's internal affairs). Such a conception of autonomy parallels the masculine psyche just described. Thus, some feminist scholars find in realism a hidden assumption of masculinity. Furthermore, the sharp distinction that realists draw between international politics (anarchic) and domestic politics (ordered) parallels the distinction in gender roles between the public (masculine) and private (feminine) spheres. Thus, realism constructs IR as a man's world.

By contrast, an international system based on *feminine* principles might give greater importance to the interdependence of states than to their autonomy, stressing the responsibility of people to care for each other with less regard for states and borders. In the struggle between the principles of human rights and of sovereignty (noninterference in internal affairs), human rights would receive priority. In the choice of forms of leverage when conflicts arise between states, violence might be less prevalent.

From this difference-feminist perspective, neoliberalism has gone backward from traditional liberalism by accepting the realist assumption of separate unitary states as the important actors and downplaying substate and transnational actors, including women. Neoliberalism's conception of cooperation as rule-based interactions among autonomous actors also reflects masculinist assumptions.

Gender in War and Peace

In addition to its emphasis on autonomy and anarchy, realism stresses military force as the key form of leverage in IR. Here, too, many difference feminists see in realism a hidden assumption of masculinity. They see war as not only a male occupation but as the quintessentially male occupation. In this view, men are inherently the more warlike sex and women the more peaceful one. Thus, although realism may accurately portray the importance of war and military force in IR, it merely reflects the male domination of the international sphere to date—not a necessary, eternal, or inescapable logic of relations among states.

Difference feminists find much evidence to support the idea of war as a masculine pursuit. Anthropologists have found that in all known cultures, males are the primary (and usually the only) combatants in warfare, despite the enormous diversity of those cultures in so many other ways. One supposed link between war and masculinity is the male sex hormone testosterone (along with related hormones), which some biologists have connected with aggressive behavior in animals.

WOMAN POWER Difference feminists see women as inherently less warlike than men and more adept at making peace because of their potential and actual experiences as mothers. In this view, women play distinct roles in politics and also have distinct needs. During the rule of the Taliban in Afghanistan and parts of Pakistan, girls were barred from attending schools. Malala Yousafzai advocated for human rights, especially the education of women, in Pakistan. She survived an assassination attempt in 2012 and went on to become the youngest person to win the Nobel Peace Prize in 2014.

However, complex behaviors such as aggression and war cannot be said to be biologically *driven* or predetermined because humanity's most striking biological capability is flexibility.

Difference feminists emphasize women's unique abilities and contributions as *peacemakers*. They stress women's roles as *mothers* and potential mothers. Because of such caregiving roles, women are presumed to be more likely than men to oppose war and more likely to find alternatives to violence in resolving conflicts. Both biologically and anthropologically, no firm evidence connects women's caregiving functions (pregnancy and nursing) with any particular kinds of behavior such as reconciliation or nonviolence. The role of women varies considerably from one society to another. Although they rarely take part in combat, women often provide logistical support to male warriors and sometimes help drive the men into a war frenzy by dancing, shaming nonparticipating males, and other activities supportive of war.

Nonetheless, the idea of women as peacemakers has a long history. In ancient Athens, the (male) playwright Aristophanes, in the play *Lysistrata*, speculated about how women might end the unpopular Peloponnesian War with Sparta, then in progress (in part by withholding sex from men). Women have formed their own organizations to work for peace on many occasions. In 1852, *Sisterly Voices* was published as a newsletter for women's peace societies. During World War I, Jane Addams and other feminists founded the Women's Peace Party (now called the Women's International League for Peace and Freedom).

After World War I, the *suffrage* movement won the right for women to vote. Difference feminists thought that women would vote for peace and against war, thus changing the nature of foreign policy, but women generally voted as their husbands did. Nonetheless, U.S. public opinion on foreign policy issues since the 1930s partially vindicates difference feminists. A **gender gap** in polls finds women about 10 percentage points lower than men on average in their support for military actions. This gender gap shrinks, however, when broad consensus on a military action exists, as when U.S. forces attacked terrorist supporters in Afghanistan in late 2001. In 1995, the UN-sponsored Beijing conference on women brought together women activists from around the world and helped deepen feminists' engagement with global issues such as North-South inequality. Through these various actions, difference feminists began developing a feminist practice of international relations that could provide an alternative to the masculine practice of realism.

gender gap Refers to polls showing women lower than men on average in their support for military actions, as well as for various other issues and candidates.

In 2000, the UN Security Council passed Resolution 1325, mandating greater inclusion of women and attention to gender in UN peacekeeping and reconstruction. But in several locations, UN peacekeepers participated in local prostitution, rape, and even sex trafficking. In 2004, Secretary-General Annan called "shameful" the reported behavior of UN troops from several countries serving in Democratic Congo. Investigators there found hundreds of cases of sexual crimes by UN personnel.

As a result of Resolution 1325, "gender advisers" have begun to accompany international peacekeeping and relief operations to provide practical advice on more effective operations in the context of local cultures' gender relations. For example, the head of a group of Swedish men sent to build a bridge in Sri Lanka initially said, "Our task is to build a bridge; we don't need to worry about gender issues." When asked how it would be used, he replied, "By car mostly," but when asked, "The women too?" he said, "No, they'll probably walk." As a result of this gender perspective, the bridge was redesigned to include a pedestrian walkway.

Women in IR

Liberal feminists are skeptical of difference-feminist critiques of realism. They believe that when women are allowed to participate in IR, they play the game basically the same way men do, with similar results. They think that women can practice realism—based on autonomy, sovereignty, anarchy, territory, military force, and all the rest—just as well as men can. Thus, liberal feminists tend to reject the critique of realism as masculine. Liberal feminism focuses on the integration of women into the overwhelmingly male preserves of foreign policy making and the military. (In practice, many feminist scholars draw on both difference feminists' and liberal feminists' views in various proportions.)

Female state leaders do not appear to be any more peaceful, or any less committed to state sovereignty and territorial integrity, than are male leaders (see Table 3.1). Of course, women in traditionally male roles may have been selected (or self-selected) on the basis of their suitability to such roles: They may not act the way "average" women would act. Some have even suggested that women in power tend to be more warlike to compensate for being females in traditionally male roles. But overall, women state leaders, like men, seem capable of leading in war or in peace as circumstances demand.

Table 3.1 Notable Women State Leaders of Recent Decades

Leader	Country	Record in Office	Time Frame
Park Geun-hye	S. Korea	Inherits conflict with N. Korea	2013–
Julia Gillard	Australia	Arranged to host U.S. Marine base	2010–2013
Yingluck Shinawatra	Thailand	Tensions with military; secessionist war	2011–2014
Rosa Otunbayeya	Kyrgyz Republic	First woman president of former communist Central Asian state. Calmed ethnic tensions.	2010–2011
Sheikh Hasina Wajed	Bangladesh	Attempting to consolidate democratic transition	2008–
Angela Merkel	Germany	Only current woman leader of a great power; put limits on German troops with NATO forces in Afghanistan	2005–
Ellen Johnson-Sirleaf	Liberia	Struggling to keep country calm after civil war	2006–
Margaret Thatcher	Britain	First woman to lead a great power in a century; went to war to recover Falkland Islands from Argentina	1982
Indira Gandhi	India	Led war against Pakistan	1971
Golda Meir	Israel	Led war against Egypt and Syria	1973
Benazir Bhutto	Pakistan	Struggled to control own military; assassinated 2007	late 1980s
Corazon Aquino	Philippines	Struggled to control own military	late 1980s
Tansu Çiller	Turkey	Led a harsh war to suppress Kurdish rebels	mid-1990s
Violetta Chamorro	Nicaragua	Kept the peace between factions after civil war	1980s
Chandrika Kumaratunga	Sri Lanka	Tried to make peace with separatists, but returned to war	1990s and since
Megawati Sukarnoputri	Indonesia	Struggled to keep country calm; lost re-election bid	2000s

Note: Other states, such as Finland, Norway, New Zealand, Denmark, Brazil, Thailand, and Iceland, have had women leaders when war and peace were not major political issues in those countries.

Source: D'Amico, Francine, and Peter R. Beckman, eds. *Women in World Politics: An Introduction.* Bergin & Garvey, 1995. Nelson, Barbara J., and Najma Chowdhury, eds. *Women and Politics Worldwide.* Yale, 1994. Genovese, Michael A., ed. *Women as National Leaders: The Political Performance of Women as Heads of Government.* Sage, 1993. McGlen, Nancy E., and Meredith Reid Sarkees. *Women in Foreign Policy: The Insiders.* Routledge, 1993.

In the U.S. Congress, it is hard to compare men's and women's voting records on foreign policy issues because there have been so few women. The U.S. Senate, which approves treaties and foreign policy appointments, was 98–99 percent male until 1992 (but dropped to 80 percent male in 2013). Women never chaired the foreign policy committees (Armed Services and Foreign Relations) in the Senate or House until 2011.

Globally, the number of women serving in legislatures is increasing. A 2015 UN report found that women comprised over 22 percent of members of parliaments across the world, up from 7 percent in 1995. As of 2015, 10 women served as head of state and 14 served as head of government. Some nations set aside a certain number of seats for females in parliament. Yet female candidates often capture more seats than are set aside. In Rwanda, for example, women make up over 50 percent of the lower house of parliament, even though the law requires only 30 percent female representation.

Liberal feminists also believe that women soldiers, like women politicians, have a range of skills and abilities comparable to men's. About 200,000 women soldiers serve in the U.S. military (15 percent of the total), and nearly 2 million women are veterans. Women perform well in a variety of military roles, including logistical and medical support, training, and command. In 2015, the first two women graduated from the U.S. Army's elite Ranger School. Women have had success in other countries that have allowed them into the military (or, in a few cases, drafted them).

Although women have served with distinction in military forces, they have been excluded from combat roles in most of those forces. In some countries, military women are limited to traditional female roles such as nurses and typists. Even when women may hold nontraditional positions such as mechanics and pilots (as in the United States), most women remain in the traditional roles. This is beginning to change. In 2013, the U.S. military lifted the ban on women serving in combat units.

There are some historical examples of individual women who served in combat (sometimes disguised as men, sometimes not). In the fifteenth century, Joan of Arc rallied French soldiers to defeat England, turning the tide of the Hundred Years' War. (The English burned her at the stake as a

COMBAT HERO Women soldiers have performed as well as men in military tasks, as predicted by liberal feminists. But in state armies, women are barred from virtually all infantry combat units worldwide. Guerrilla forces more often include women, and female U.S. military police in Iraq often participate in fighting. Here, in 2005, a sergeant from the Kentucky National Guard receives the silver star for heroism in combat after fighting off an ambush in Iraq.

witch after capturing her.) Women have often participated in combat in rebel forces fighting guerrilla wars in Vietnam, Nicaragua, and elsewhere, as well as in terrorist or paramilitary units in countries such as Peru, Germany, Italy, and Palestine. Women in Eritrea's guerrilla forces became part of that country's regular army after independence and then served in frontline combat units during Eritrea and Ethiopia's trench warfare in the late 1990s. In recent years, U.S. women soldiers have found themselves in combat (present mobile tactics and fluid front lines make it hard to separate combat from support roles). In the 2003 Iraq War, women flew all types of airplanes and helicopters, and one woman was in the first group of U.S. prisoners of war (POWs) captured early in the war. During the subsequent years of war in Iraq, U.S. women military police have acquitted themselves well in numerous firefights. All these cases suggest that (at least some) women are able to hold their own in combat.

The main reason that military forces exclude women from combat seems to be fear about what effect their presence might have on the male soldiers, whose discipline and loyalty have traditionally been thought to depend on male bonding and single-minded focus. Liberal feminists reject such arguments and maintain that group bonding in military units does not depend on gender segregation. (After all, similar rationales were once given for racial segregation in U.S. military forces.)

The effect of war on noncombatant women has also received growing attention. Attacks on women in Algeria, Rwanda, Bosnia, Afghanistan, Democratic Congo, and Sudan pointed to a possible new trend toward women as military targets. Systematic rape was used as a terror tactic in Bosnia and Rwanda, and the Japanese army in World War II operated an international network of sex slaves known as "comfort women." Rape has long been treated as a normal if regrettable by-product of war, but recently certain instances of rape were declared war crimes (see pp. 271–275).

In sum, liberal feminists reject the argument that women bring uniquely feminine assets or liabilities to foreign and military affairs. They do not critique realism as essentially masculine in nature but do criticize state practices that exclude women from participation in international politics and war.

Difference Feminism Versus Liberal Feminism?

The arguments of difference feminists and liberal feminists may seem totally at odds. But the evidence in favor of both positions can be reconciled to some extent by bearing in mind that the character and ability of an individual are not the same as that of his or her group. Rather, the qualities of individuals follow a bell curve distribution, with many people clustered in the middle and fewer people very high or low on a given capability.

Gender differences posited by difference feminists mean that one bell curve is shifted from the other, even though the two may still overlap quite a bit

Figure 3.5 Overlapping Bell Curves

Bell curves show that individuals differ in capabilities such as physical strength or peacemaking ability. Although the genders differ on average, for most individuals (in the area of overlap) such differences do not come into play. Liberal feminists emphasize the area where the curves overlap; difference feminists emphasize the overall group differences.

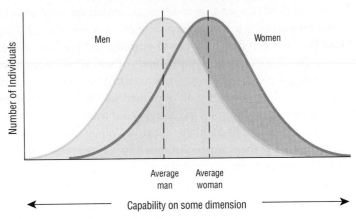

(see Figure 3.5). To take a simple example, a few women are physically larger than almost all men, and a few men are smaller than almost all women. But, on average, men are somewhat larger than women. On different dimensions of capability, the women's curve is above the men's on average, but there is still much overlap.

Liberal feminists emphasize the overlap of the two bell curves. They say that individual women—*most* women on most relevant dimensions—are well within the male curve and thus can perform equally with the men. Indeed, women in nontraditional gender roles may well perform better than their male counterparts because presumably women who self-select into such roles (such as by joining the military or running a government) are near the high end of the female bell curve, whereas the men are closer to the middle of the male curve.

Difference feminists are more interested in the shift in the two bell curves, not their overlap. On average, in this perspective, women tend to see international relations in a somewhat different way than men do. Although *individuals* selected to participate in foreign policy and the military may not differ from their male counterparts, women as a group differ. Women voters display different concerns regarding IR than men (as shown by the gender gap in opinion polls and voting patterns).

By this logic, then, profound differences in IR—and a shift away from the utility of realism in explaining state behavior—would occur only if many women participated in key foreign policy positions. A *few* women politicians or women soldiers do not change the masculine foundations of IR. But a world in which *most* politicians or soldiers were female might be a different story. Of course, these theories of difference feminists have never been tested because women have never attained predominance in foreign policy making in any country—much less in the international system as a whole.

In addition to the liberal and difference strands of feminism, a third strand, postmodern feminism, is connected with the rise of postmodernism.

Postmodern Feminism

One line of criticism directed at realism combines feminism and postmodernism. *Postmodern feminism* seeks to deconstruct realism with the specific aim of uncovering the pervasive hidden influences of gender in IR while showing how arbitrary the construction of gender roles is. Feminist postmodernists agree with difference feminists that realism carries hidden meanings about gender roles, but they deny that there is any fixed, inherent meaning in either male or female genders. Rather, feminist postmodernists look at the interplay of gender and power in a more open-ended way. Postmodern feminists criticize liberal feminists for trying merely to integrate women into traditional structures of war and foreign policy. They criticize difference feminists as well, for glorifying traditional feminine virtues.

Postmodern feminists have tried to deconstruct the language of realism, especially when it reflects influences of gender and sex. For instance, the first atomic bombs had male gender (they were named "Fat Man" and "Little Boy"). The plane that dropped the atomic bomb on Hiroshima (the *Enola Gay*) had female gender; it was named after the pilot's mother. Similarly, pilots have pasted pinup photos of nude women onto conventional bombs before dropping them. In all these cases, postmodern feminists would note that the feminine gender of vehicles, targets, or decorations amplifies the masculinity of the weapon itself.

All three strands of feminist theories provide explanations that often differ from both realist and liberal theories. For example, in the case of response to aggression, feminists might study the need for state leaders to prove their manhood by standing up to the bad guys. This is connected with the male role as protector of the orderly domestic sphere (home, family, country) against the dangerous and anarchic outside world. Since 2001, gender roles have become increasingly visible on both sides of the "war on terror," with both women's positions in society and men's concepts of masculinity becoming contested territory between the West and armed Islamic groups. Traditional theories of IR that ignore these issues may lack explanatory power as a result.

Each of these alternatives to realism has certain advantages and disadvantages as they attempt to explain world events. However, all of these theories and approaches must try to understand international conflicts and the use of military force. Chapter 4 takes up these issues.

Chapter Review

Summary

- Liberals dispute the realist notion that narrow self-interest is more rational than mutually beneficial cooperation. Neoliberalism argues that even in an anarchic system of autonomous rational states, cooperation can emerge through the building of norms, regimes, and institutions.

- Reciprocity can be an effective strategy for reaching cooperation in ongoing relationships but carries a danger of turning into runaway hostility or arms races.

- Collective goods are benefits received by all members of a group regardless of their individual contribution. Shared norms and rules are important in getting members to pay for collective goods.

- International regimes—convergent expectations of state leaders about the rules for issue areas in IR—help provide stability in the absence of a world government.

- In a collective security arrangement, a group of states agrees to respond together to aggression by any participating state.

- Foreign policies are strategies that governments use to guide their actions toward other states. The foreign policy process is the set of procedures and structures that states use to arrive at foreign policy decisions and to implement them.

- Domestic constituencies (interest groups) have distinct interests in foreign policies and often organize politically to promote those interests.

- Public opinion influences governments' foreign policy decisions (more so in democracies than in authoritarian states), but governments also manipulate public opinion.

- Legislatures can provide a conduit for public opinion and interests groups to influence foreign policy. Executives and legislators may differ on how best to achieve a state's national interest.

- Democracies have historically fought as many wars as authoritarian states, but democracies have almost never fought wars against other democracies. This is called the democratic peace.

- In the rational model of decision making, officials choose the action whose consequences best meet the state's established goals. By contrast, in the organizational process model, decisions result from routine administrative procedures; in the government bargaining (or bureaucratic politics) model, decisions result from negotiations among governmental agencies with different interests in the outcome.

- The actions of individual decision makers are influenced by their personalities, values, and beliefs as well as by common psychological factors that diverge from rationality.

- Foreign policy decisions are also influenced by the psychology of groups (including groupthink), the procedures used to reach decisions, and the roles of participants. During crises, the potentials for misperception and error are amplified.

- Constructivists reject realist assumptions about state interests, tracing those interests in part to social interactions and norms.

- Postmodern critics reject the entire framework and language of realism, with its unitary state actors. Postmodernists argue that no simple categories can capture the multiple realities experienced by participants in IR.

- Marxists view international relations, including global North-South relations, in terms of a struggle between economic classes (especially workers and owners) that have different roles in society and different access to power.

- Mediation and other forms of conflict resolution are alternative means of exerting leverage on participants in bargaining.

- Positive peace not only implies the absence of war but also addresses the conditions that scholars in peace studies connect with violence—especially injustice and poverty.

- Feminist scholars of IR agree that gender is important in understanding IR but diverge into several strands regarding their conception of the role of gender.

- Difference feminists argue that real (not arbitrary) differences between men and women exist. Men think about social relations more often in terms of autonomy (as do realists), but women think in terms of connection. Difference feminists argue that men are more warlike on average than women.

- Liberal feminists disagree that women have substantially different capabilities or tendencies as participants in IR. They argue that women are equivalent to men in almost all IR roles. As evidence, liberal feminists point to historical and present-day women leaders and women soldiers.

- Postmodern feminists seek to uncover gender-related subtexts implicit in realist discourse, including sexual themes connected with the concept of power.

Key Terms

Critical Thinking Questions

1. Democracies almost never fight wars with each other, so do existing democracies have a national security interest in seeing democratization spread to China and other authoritarian states? If so, how can that interest be reconciled with the long-standing norm of noninterference in the internal affairs of other sovereign states?

2. India and Pakistan are neighbors and enemies. Given the problems of misperception and bias in foreign policy decision making, what steps could you propose that each government adopt to keep these problems from interfering in the rational pursuit of national interests?

3. Peace studies claims that internal characteristics of states (at the domestic level of analysis) strongly affect the propensity for war or potential for lasting peace. For one society, show how internal characteristics—social, economic, and/or cultural—influence that society's external behavior.

4. Would IR operate differently if most state leaders were women? What would the differences be? What evidence (beyond gender stereotypes) supports your answer?

Chapter 4
Conflict, War, and Terrorism

ANTI-INDIAN PROTESTERS AND INDIAN SECURITY FORCES IN KASHMIR, 2015.

 Learning Objectives

4.1 Distinguish two different theories about the causes of war at two different levels of analysis.

4.2 Identify at least four different international conflicts where religion plays a role in creating or exacerbating the conflict.

4.3 Summarize two different international territorial disputes and evaluate the prospects for their peaceful settlement.

115

4.4 Compare the influence of technology on the instruments of leverage used in land, sea, and air conflicts.

4.5 Assess potential advantages and disadvantages to two different approaches to counterterrorism.

4.6 Contrast the effectiveness of the global regime to prevent the spread of nuclear weapons with the global regime to prevent the spread of chemical weapons.

4.7 Explain how tensions in civil-military relations can undermine military operations and even threaten political stability.

The Wars of the World

4.1 Distinguish two different theories about the causes of war at two different levels of analysis.

Chapter 3 discussed the decreasing number and size of wars in the world (see pp. 68–69). This chapter will focus on the remaining wars, and historical cases, to explain the causes of international conflicts.

Figure 4.1 shows the 15 wars in progress in December 2015. The largest are in Syria and neighboring Iraq. Of the 15 wars, 14 wars are in the global South. All but Ukraine and Russia (Chechnya) are in a zone of active fighting (outlined on the map) spanning parts of Africa, the Middle East, and South Asia.

In four smaller zones (dotted lines on the map), dozens of wars of recent decades have ended. Some of the countries in these zones still face difficult post-war years with the possibility of sliding back into violence. In Sierra Leone, for example, a ten-year civil war ended in 2002, but occasional political instability has threatened to reignite that conflict. But most peace agreements in the world's postwar zones are holding up.

Types of War

Many different activities are covered by the general term *war*. Consequently, it is not easy to say how many wars are going on in the world at the moment. But most lists of wars set some minimum criteria—for instance, a minimum of a thousand battle deaths—to distinguish war from lower-level violence such as violent strikes or riots.

hegemonic war War for control of the entire world order— the rules of the international system as a whole. Also called *world war, global war, general war,* or *systemic war.*

Wars are diverse. Wars tend to arise from different situations and play different sorts of roles in bargaining over conflicts. Starting from the largest wars, we may distinguish the following main categories.

Hegemonic war is a war over control of the entire *world order*—the rules of the international system as a whole, including the role of world hegemony (see p. 51). This class of wars (with variations in definition and conception) is also

Figure 4.1 Wars in Progress, December 2015

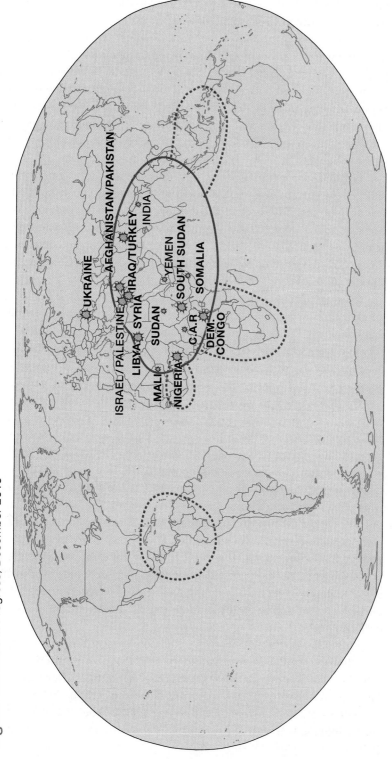

UKRAINE

AFGHANISTAN/PAKISTAN

INDIA

IRAQ/TURKEY

SYRIA

YEMEN

SOUTH SUDAN

SOMALIA

LIBYA

ISRAEL/PALESTINE

SUDAN

C.A.R.

DEM. CONGO

MALI

NIGERIA

☀ Estimated deaths over 1,000 per year

☀ Estimated deaths under 1,000 per year

— Zone of active wars

⋯⋯ Zones of transition from wars in recent decades

known as *world war, global war, general war,* or *systemic war.* The last hegemonic war was World War II. This kind of war probably cannot occur any longer without destroying civilization.

total war Warfare by one state waged to conquer and occupy another; modern total war originated in the Napoleonic Wars, which relied on conscription on a mass scale.

Total war is warfare by one state waged to conquer and occupy another. The goal is to reach the capital city and force the surrender of the government, which can then be replaced with one of the victor's choosing. Total war as we know it began with the mass destruction of the Napoleonic Wars, which introduced large-scale conscription and geared the entire French national economy toward the war effort. In total war, with the entire society mobilized for the struggle, the entire society of the enemy is considered a legitimate target.

limited war Military actions that seek objectives short of the surrender and occupation of the enemy.

Limited war includes military actions carried out to gain some objective short of the surrender and occupation of the enemy. For instance, the U.S.-led war against Iraq in 1991 retook the territory of Kuwait but did not go on to Baghdad to topple Saddam Hussein's government. Many border wars have this character: After occupying the land it wants, a state may stop and defend its gains, as Russia did after expelling Georgian troops from disputed Georgian provinces in 2008, for example.

Raids are limited wars that consist of a single action—a bombing run or a quick incursion by land. In 2007, Israeli warplanes bombed a facility in Syria that Israel believed to be a nuclear research facility. Raids fall into the gray area between wars and nonwars because their destruction is limited and they are over quickly. Raiding that is repeated or fuels a cycle of retaliation usually becomes a limited war or what is sometimes called *low-intensity conflict.*

civil war A war between factions within a state trying to create, or prevent, a new government for the entire state or some territorial part of it.

Civil war refers to war between factions within a state trying to create, or prevent, a new government for the entire state or some territorial part of it. (The aim may be to change the entire system of government, merely to replace the people in it, or to split a region off as a new state.) The U.S. Civil War of the 1860s is a good example of a secessionist civil war. The war in El Salvador in the 1980s is an example of a civil war for control of the entire state (not secessionist). Civil wars often seem to be among the most brutal wars. The 50,000 or more deaths in the civil war in El Salvador, including many from massacres and death squads, were not based on ethnic differences. Of course, many of today's civil wars emerge from ethnic conflicts as well. In Chad, for example, a rebel group composed of rival clans to the president's nearly overthrew the government in 2007. Sustaining a civil war usually requires a source of support for rebels, from neighboring states, diaspora ethnic communities, or revenue from natural resources or illegal drugs.

guerrilla war Warfare without front lines and with irregular forces operating in the midst of, and often hidden or protected by, civilian populations.

Guerrilla war, which includes certain kinds of civil wars, is warfare without front lines. Irregular forces operate in the midst of, and often hidden or protected by, civilian populations. The purpose is not to confront an enemy army directly but rather to harass and punish it and thus gradually limit its operation and effectively liberate territory from its control. Rebels in most civil wars use such methods. U.S. military forces in South Vietnam fought against Vietcong guerrillas in the 1960s and 1970s, with rising frustration. (Efforts to combat a guerrilla army—counterinsurgency—are discussed on p. 149.) Without a fixed front line, there is much territory that neither side controls; both sides exert military leverage over the same places at the same time. Thus, guerrilla wars hurt civilians, who suffer most when no military force firmly controls a location, opening the door to banditry, personal vendettas, sexual violence, and other such lawless behavior. The situation is doubly painful because conventional armies fighting against guerrillas often cannot distinguish them from civilians and punish both together. In one famous case in South Vietnam, a U.S. officer who had ordered an entire village burned to deny its use as a sanctuary by the Vietcong commented, "We had to destroy the village to save it." Warfare increasingly is irregular and guerrilla-style; it is less and less often an open conventional clash of large state armies.

In all types of war, the abstractions and theories of international relations (IR) scholars hardly capture the horrors experienced by those on the scene, both soldiers and civilians. War suspends basic norms of behavior and, especially over time, traumatizes participants and bystanders. Soldiers see their best friends blown apart before their eyes; they must kill and maim their fellow human beings; some experience lifelong psychological traumatic stress as a result. Civilians experience terror, violence, and rape; they lose loved ones and homes; they too often live with trauma afterward. The violence of war does not resemble war movies but instead creates a nearly psychotic experience of overwhelming confusion, noise, terror, and adrenaline. Soldiers in professional armies train to keep functioning in these conditions—but still have an incredibly difficult job—whereas those in irregular forces and civilian populations caught in civil wars have little hope of coping. The horrors of war are magnified in cases of genocide and massacre, of child soldiers, and of brutal warfare that continues over years.

Scholars and policy makers are paying more attention in recent years to the difficult transitions from war to peace around the world—postwar reconciliation, conflict resolution, transitional governments representing opposing factions, economic reconstruction, and so forth. These efforts often address collective goods problems among the parties, as when Somali clan elders in 2007 agreed that all would be better off by giving up their guns to the new

GIVING UP THE GUNS Once armed groups stop shooting, a long process of postwar transition ensues. Disarming and demobilizing militias is the most critical aspect of this transition, but also the most difficult because it leaves disarmed groups vulnerable. Here, a major armed group turns in weapons under an amnesty in the Niger Delta region of Nigeria, 2009.

central government but none wanted to go first. After the shooting stops, international peacekeepers and nongovernmental organizations (NGOs) focus on Security Sector Reform (SSR) to create professional military and police forces instead of warlord militias. The process of Disarmament, Demobilization, and Reintegration (DDR) deals with the common problem of what to do with irregular forces after civil wars end.

truth commissions
Governmental bodies established in several countries after internal wars to hear honest testimony and bring to light what really happened during these wars, and in exchange to offer most of the participants asylum from punishment.

In several countries where long internal wars in the 1990s had led to dehumanization and atrocities—notably in South Africa—new governments used **truth commissions** to help the society heal and move forward. The commissions' role was to hear honest testimony from the period, to bring to light what really happened during these wars, and in exchange to offer most of the participants asylum from punishment. Sometimes international NGOs helped facilitate the process. However, human rights groups objected to a settlement in Sierra Leone in 1999 that brought into the government a faction that had routinely cut off civilians' fingers as a terror tactic. (Hostilities did end, however, in 2001.) Thus, after brutal ethnic conflicts give way to complex political settlements, most governments try to balance the need for justice and truth with the need to keep all groups on board.

Experts have debated how much truth and reconciliation are necessary after long conflicts. Some now argue that in some circumstances, tribunals and government-sponsored panels to investigate past crimes could lead to political instability in transitional states. Other experts disagree, noting that the work of such panels can be essential to building trust, which is important for democracy.

Theories of the Causes of War

The Roman writer Seneca said nearly 2,000 years ago: "Of war men ask the outcome, not the cause." This is not true of political scientists. They want to know why countries fight.

conflict A difference in preferred outcomes in a bargaining situation.

The term **conflict** in IR generally refers to armed conflict. Conflict itself is ever present in the international system—the condition against which bargaining takes place. In conflict bargaining, states develop capabilities that give them leverage to obtain more favorable outcomes than they otherwise would achieve. Whether fair or unfair, the ultimate outcome of the bargaining process is a settlement of the particular conflict. Rarely do conflicts lead to violence, however.

The question of when conflict becomes violent can be approached in different ways. Descriptive approaches, favored by historians, tend to focus narrowly on specific, direct causes of the outbreak of war, which vary from one war to another. For example, one could say that the assassination of Archduke Franz Ferdinand in 1914 "caused" World War I. More theoretical approaches, favored by many political scientists, tend to focus on the search for general explanations, applicable to a variety of contexts, about why wars break out. For example, one can see World War I as caused by shifts in the balance of power among European states, with the assassination being only a catalyst.

One way to organize the many theories offered by political scientists to explain why wars begin is to use the levels of analysis concept from Chapter 1. Using this framework reminds us that most important events in IR have multiple causes at different levels of analysis.

THE INDIVIDUAL LEVEL   On the *individual* level of analysis, theories about war center on rationality. One theory, consistent with realism, holds that the use of war and other violent means of leverage in international conflicts is normal and reflects *rational* decisions of national leaders.

An opposite theory holds that conflicts often escalate to war because of *deviations* from rationality in the individual decision-making processes of national leaders (see Chapter 3)—information screens, cognitive biases, groupthink, and so forth. A related theory holds that the education and mentality of whole populations of individuals determine whether conflicts become violent. Here, public nationalism or ethnic hatred—or even an innate tendency toward violence in human nature—may pressure leaders to solve conflicts violently.

Neither theory holds up very well. Some wars clearly reflect rational calculations of national leaders, whereas others clearly were mistakes and cannot be considered rational. Certainly some individual leaders seem prone to turn to military force to try to settle conflicts on favorable terms. But a maker of war can become a maker of peace, as did Egypt's Anwar Sadat. Individuals of many cultural backgrounds and religions lead their states into war, as do both male and female leaders.

THE DOMESTIC LEVEL   The *domestic* level of analysis draws attention to the characteristics of states or societies that may make them more or less prone to use violence in resolving conflicts. During the Cold War, Marxists frequently said that the aggressive and greedy *capitalist* states were prone to use violence in international conflicts, whereas Western leaders claimed that the expansionist, ideological, and totalitarian nature of *communist* states made them especially prone to using violence. In truth, both types of society fought wars regularly.

Likewise, rich industrialized states and poor agrarian ones both go to war. Anthropologists have found that a wide range of *preagricultural* hunter-gatherer societies were much more prone to warfare than today's societies. Thus, the potential for warfare seems to be universal across cultures, types of society, and time periods—although the importance and frequency of war vary greatly from case to case.

Some argue that domestic political factors shape a state's outlook on war and peace. For example, the democratic peace suggests that democracies almost never fight other democracies (see Chapter 3), although both democracies and authoritarian states fight wars. Others claim that domestic political parties, interest groups, and legislatures play an important role in whether international conflicts become international wars.

WHY WAR? Political scientists do not agree on a theory of why great wars like World War II occur and cannot predict whether they could happen again. The city of Stalingrad (Volgograd) was decimated during Germany's invasion of the Soviet Union, 1943.

Few useful generalizations can tell us which societies are more prone or less prone to war. The same society may change greatly over time. For example, Japan was prone to using violence in international conflicts before World War II, but it has been averse to such violence since then. If general principles explain why some societies at some times are more peaceful than others and why they change, political scientists have not yet identified them.

THE INTERSTATE LEVEL   Theories at the *interstate* level explain wars in terms of power relations among major actors in the international system. *Power transition theory* holds that conflicts generate large wars at times when power is relatively equally distributed and a rising power is threatening to overtake a declining hegemon (see pp. 50–51).

At this level, too, incompatible theories compete. Deterrence is supposed to stop wars by building up power and threatening its use. But the theory of arms races holds that wars are caused, not prevented, by such actions. No general formula has been discovered to tell us in what circumstances each of these principles holds true.

Some political scientists study war from a statistical perspective, analyzing data on types of wars and the circumstances under which they occurred. Current research focuses on the effects of factors such as democracy, government structure, trade, and international organizations in explaining the escalation or settlement of "militarized interstate disputes."

THE GLOBAL LEVEL   At the *global* level of analysis, a number of theories of war have been proposed. Of the several variations on the idea that major warfare in the international system is *cyclical,* one approach links large wars with *long economic waves* (also called *Kondratieff cycles*) in the world economy, of about 50 years' duration. Another approach links the largest wars with a 100-year cycle based on the creation and decay of world orders (see pp. 51–52). These *cycle theories* at best can explain only general tendencies toward war in the international system over time.

Thus, on all the levels of analysis, competing theories offer different explanations for why some conflicts become violent and others do not. Political scientists cannot yet confidently predict which of the world's many international conflicts will lead to war. We can gain insight, however, by studying various types of conflicts to understand better what states fight about.

Conflicts of Ideas

4.2   Identify at least four different international conflicts where religion plays a role in creating or exacerbating the conflict.

The following sections discuss six types of international conflict: ethnic, religious, ideological, territorial, governmental, and economic. The first three are conflicts over ideas, the last three conflicts over interests. These six types of conflict are not mutually exclusive, and they overlap considerably in practice. For example, the conflicts between Russia and Ukraine after the 1991 Soviet breakup were complex. *Ethnic* Russians living in Ukraine, and ethnic Ukrainians living in Russia, experienced ethnic conflict. There are *religious* differences between Ukrainian and Russian forms of Christianity. In addition, the two new states had a *territorial* dispute over the Crimean peninsula, which Soviet leader Nikita Khrushchev had transferred to Ukraine in the 1950s. The two states also had *economic* conflicts over trade and money after the Soviet breakup, which created new borders and currencies. These multiple conflicts did not lead to the use of military force, however, until 2014. After protesters forced the resignation of Ukraine's pro-Russian president, Russia annexed Crimea. Russia also supported a rebellion in the eastern portion of Ukraine where many ethnic Russians lived. So the types of conflict discussed here come into play in combination rather than separately.

We will look first at the most difficult types of conflict, in which intangible elements such as ethnic hatred, religious fervor, or ideology come into play—conflicts of ideas. These identity-based sources of international conflict today have been shaped historically by nationalism as the link between identity and internationally recognized statehood. Therefore we will briefly review the development of nationalism before examining the three types of conflicts of ideas.

Nationalism

Nationalism—devotion to the interests of one's own nation over the interests of other states—may be the most important force in world politics in the past two centuries. A nation is a population that shares an identity, usually including a language and culture. But nationality is a difficult concept to define precisely. To some degree, the extension of political control over large territories such as France created the commonality necessary for nationhood—states created nations. At the same time, however, the perceived existence of a nation has often led to the creation of a corresponding state as a people win sovereignty over their own affairs—nations create states.

Around A.D. 1500, countries such as France and Austria began to bring entire nations together into single states. These new nation-states were very large and powerful, and they overran smaller neighbors. Over time, they conquered and incorporated many small territorial units. Eventually the idea of

nationalism Identification with and devotion to the interests of one's nation. It usually involves a large group of people who share a national identity and often a language, culture, or ancestry.

nationalism itself became a powerful force and ultimately contributed to the disintegration of large, multinational states such as Austria-Hungary (in World War I), the Soviet Union, and Yugoslavia.

The principle of *self-determination* implies that people who identify as a nation should have the right to form a state and exercise sovereignty over their affairs. Self-determination is a widely praised principle in international affairs today (although not historically). But it is generally secondary to the principles of sovereignty (noninterference in other states' internal affairs) and territorial integrity, with which it frequently conflicts. Self-determination does not give groups the right to change international borders, even those imposed arbitrarily by colonialism, in order to unify a group with a common national identity. Generally, though not always, self-determination has been achieved by violence. When the borders of (perceived) nations do not match those of states, conflicts almost inevitably arise. Today such conflicts are widespread—in Quebec, Israel-Palestine, India-Pakistan, Chechnya, Sri Lanka, Tibet, and many other places.

The process of popular mobilization intensified greatly in the French Revolution and the subsequent Napoleonic Wars, when France instituted a universal draft and a centrally run "command" economy. Its motivated citizen armies, composed for the first time of Frenchmen rather than mercenaries, marched longer and faster. People participated in part because they were patriotic. Their nation-state embodied their aspirations and brought them together in a common national identity.

The United States meanwhile had followed the example of the Netherlands by declaring independence from Britain in 1776. Latin American states gained independence early in the nineteenth century, and Germany and Italy unified their nations out of multiple political units (through war) later in that century.

Before World War I, socialist workers from different European countries had banded together as workers to fight for workers' rights. In that war, however, most abandoned such solidarity and instead fought for their respective nations; nationalism thus proved a stronger force than socialism. Before World War II, nationalism helped Germany, Italy, and Japan build political orders based on *fascism*—an extreme authoritarianism girded by national chauvinism. And in World War II, it was nationalism and patriotism (not communism) that rallied the Soviet people to sacrifice by the millions to turn back Germany's invasion.

In the past 50 years, nations by the dozens have gained independence and statehood. Jews worked persistently in the first half of the twentieth century to create the state of Israel, and Palestinians aspired in the second half to create a Palestinian state. While multinational states such as the Soviet Union and Yugoslavia have fragmented in recent years, ethnic and territorial units such as Ukraine, Slovenia, and East Timor have established themselves as independent nation-states. Others, such as Montenegro and Kurdistan, seek to do so and already run their own affairs. The continuing influence of nationalism in today's world is evident. It affects several of the main types of conflict that occupy the rest of this chapter.

Ethnic Conflict

Ethnic conflict is quite possibly the most important source of conflict in the numerous wars now occurring throughout the world. **Ethnic groups** are large groups of people who share ancestral, language, cultural, or religious ties and a common *identity* (individuals identify with the group). Although conflicts between ethnic groups often have material aspects—notably over territory and government control—ethnic conflict itself entails a dislike or hatred that members of one ethnic group systematically feel toward another ethnic group. In this regard, ethnic conflict is based not on tangible causes (what someone does) but on intangible ones (who someone is).

ethnic groups Large groups of people who share ancestral, language, cultural, or religious ties and a common identity.

Ethnic groups often form the basis for nationalist sentiments. Not all ethnic groups identify as nations; for instance, within the United States, various ethnic groups coexist (sometimes uneasily) with a common *national* identity as Americans. But in locations where millions of members of a single ethnic group live as the majority population in their ancestors' land, they usually think of themselves as a nation. In most such cases they aspire to have their own state with its formal international status and territorial boundaries.

Territorial control is closely tied to the aspirations of ethnic groups for statehood. All states' borders deviate to some extent (sometimes substantially) from the actual location of ethnic communities. Members of the ethnic group are left outside its state's borders, and members of other ethnic groups are located within the state's borders. The resulting situation can be dangerous, with part of an ethnic group controlling a state and another part living as a minority within another state controlled by a rival ethnic group.

Other ethnic groups lack any home state. Kurds share a culture, and many aspire to create a state of Kurdistan. But Kurds live in four states—Turkey, Iraq, Iran, and Syria—all of which strongly oppose giving up part of their own territory for a new Kurdish state (see Figure 4.2). Kurds enjoyed autonomy in part of northern Iraq under U.S. protection in the 1990s, and quasi-autonomous status in a post-Saddam Iraq. The Kurds' success in the 2010 Iraqi elections gave them a strong position to retain this status. In the Syrian civil war that began in 2011, Kurdish areas gained considerable autonomy while straddling the fence politically between the government and the rebels. By 2014–2015, Kurdish fighters received significant international military support (not form Turkey) in fighting Islamic State in Iraq and Syria (ISIS) militants who were capturing territory in northern Iraq and Syria. By late 2015, however, Turkey began military operations against both the Kurds and ISIS militants. Whether the Kurds are able to further their aims of independent territory in the region remains to be seen.

Ethnic conflicts often involve pressures to redraw borders by force. When ethnic populations are minorities in territories

Figure 4.2 Kurdish Areas

Ethnic populations often span international borders. The shaded region shows the approximate area of Kurdish settlements.

controlled by rival ethnic groups, they may even be driven from their land or (in rare cases) systematically exterminated. By driving out the minority ethnic group, a majority group can assemble a more unified, more contiguous, and larger territory for its nation-state, as ethnic Serbs did through "ethnic cleansing" after the breakup of Yugoslavia.

Outside states often worry about the fate of "their people" living as minorities in neighboring states. For instance, Albania is concerned about ethnic Albanians who are the majority population in the Serbian province of Kosovo. But as Kosovo moved toward independence from Serbia, Serbia worried about the minority of ethnic Serbs living in Kosovo. Similar problems have fueled wars between Armenia and Azerbaijan and between India and Pakistan. The dangerous combination of ethnic conflict and territorial disputes could lead to more wars in the future.

genocide An intentional and systematic attempt to destroy a national, ethnic, racial, or religious group, in whole or in part. It was confirmed as a crime under international law by the UN Genocide Convention (1948).

In extreme cases, governments use **genocide**—systematic extermination of ethnic or religious groups in whole or in part—to try to destroy scapegoated groups or political rivals. Under its fanatical policies of racial purity, Nazi Germany exterminated 6 million Jews and millions of others, including homosexuals, Roma, and communists. The mass murders, now known as the Holocaust, along with the sheer scale of war unleashed by Nazi aggression, are considered among the greatest *crimes against humanity* in history. Responsible German officials faced justice in the *Nuremberg Tribunal* after World War II (see p. 271). The pledges of world leaders after that experience "never again" to allow genocide have been found wanting as genocide recurred in the 1990s in Bosnia and Rwanda, and most recently in Darfur, Sudan.

In Rwanda, where the Hutu group is the majority and the Tutsi group the minority, a Hutu-nationalist government in 1994 slaughtered an estimated 800,000 Tutsis (and Hutus opposed to the government) in a matter of weeks. The weak international response to this atrocity reveals how frail are international norms of human rights compared to norms of noninterference in other states' internal affairs—at least when no strategic interests are at stake. The Hutu ultranationalists quickly lost power when Tutsi rebels defeated the government militarily, but the war spread into Democratic Congo, where the ultranationalists took refuge and where fighting continues over 20 years later.

In Sudan, the warring sides (largely northern Muslims versus southern Christians) in a decades-long civil war signed a peace agreement in 2003, ending a war that had killed more than a million people. The agreement called for withdrawing government forces from the south of the country, establishing a power-sharing transitional government and army, and holding a referendum in the rebel areas in six years. These processes led to the successful independence of South Sudan in 2011. But following this peace agreement, rebels in the western Darfur region began to protest their exclusion from the peace agreement. In response, the government helped Arab (Muslim) militias raid black African (also Muslim) Darfur villages, wantonly killing, raping, and burning. In 2004, the government and some of the Darfur rebels reached a tentative peace agreement, and the African Union and United Nations sent in a joint peacekeeping mission in 2007. After years of Sudanese government delays and other frustrations, the force had 23,000 uniformed personnel on the ground by 2011 and most of that force remains there as of 2016. The international community's ineffective response to the mass murders in Darfur, like that in Rwanda in 1994, shows the limited reach of international norms in today's state-based international system.

In cases of both genocide and less extreme scapegoating, ethnic hatreds do not merely bubble up naturally. Rather, politicians provoke and channel hatred to strengthen their own power. Often, in ethnically divided countries, political parties form along ethnic lines, and party leaders consolidate their positions in their own populations by exaggerating the dangers from the other side. The existence of a threat from an out-group promotes the cohesion of an in-group, thereby creating a somewhat self-reinforcing process of ethnic division.

ethnocentrism The tendency to see one's own group (in-group) in favorable terms and an out-group in unfavorable terms.

CAUSES OF ETHNIC HOSTILITY   Why do ethnic groups frequently dislike each other? Often, long-standing historical conflicts exist over specific territories or natural resources, or over one ethnic group's economic exploitation or political domination of another. They become driven not by tangible grievances (though these may well persist) but by processes described by social psychology. The ethnic group is a kind of extended *kinship* group—a group of related individuals sharing some ancestors. Even when kinship relations are not very close, a *group identity* makes a person act as though the other members of the ethnic group were family. Perhaps as technology allows far-flung groups to congregate in cyberspace, there will be less psychological pressure to collect ethnic groups physically in a territorial nation-state.

Ethnocentrism, or *in-group bias*, is the tendency to see one's own group in favorable terms and an *out-group* in unfavorable terms. No *minimum criterion* of similarity or kin relationship is needed to evoke the group identity process, including in-group bias. In psychological experiments, even trivial differentiations can evoke these processes. If people are assigned to groups based on a known but unimportant characteristic (such as preferring circles to triangles), before long the people in each group show in-group bias and begin to dislike the other group's

FIGHTING THE OUT-GROUP Ethnic conflicts play a role in many international conflicts. Ethnocentrism based on an in-group bias can promote intolerance and ultimately dehumanization of an out-group, as in genocides in Darfur (Sudan), Rwanda, and Bosnia; South African apartheid; the persecution of Jews and other minorities in Nazi Germany; and slavery in the United States. In 2014, Ukraine erupted in violence, pitting pro-European forces in western Ukraine against pro-Russian forces in eastern Ukraine. Here, a pro-Russian rebel moves to take a position against Ukrainian government forces, 2014.

members. Just as the reciprocity principle has its negative side (see p. 6), so does the identity principle. The same forces that allow sacrifice for a group identity, as in the European Union, also allow the formation of in-group bias.

In-group biases are stronger when the other group looks different, speaks a different language, or worships in a different way (or all three). All too easily, an out-group can be *dehumanized* and stripped of all human rights. This dehumanization includes the common use of animal names—"pigs," "dogs," and so forth—for members of the out-group. U.S. propaganda in World War II depicted Japanese people as apes. Especially in wartime, dehumanization can be extreme. The restraints on war that have evolved in regular interstate warfare, such as not massacring civilians (see pp. 271–275), are easily discarded in interethnic warfare.

Experience in Western Europe shows that education over time can overcome ethnic animosities between traditionally hostile nations, such as France and Germany. After World War II, these states' governments rewrote the textbooks for a new generation. Previously, each state's textbooks had glorified its past deeds, played down its misdeeds, and portrayed its traditional enemies in unflattering terms. In a continent-wide project, new textbooks that gave a more objective and fair rendition were created. By contrast, present-day Japanese textbooks that gloss over Japan's crimes in World War II continue to inflame relations with both China and Korea.

Ethnic groups are only one point along a spectrum of kinship relations—from nuclear families through extended families, villages, provinces, and nations, up to the entire human race. Loyalties fall at different points along the spectrum. It is unclear why people identify most strongly at one level of group identity. In Somalia, loyalties are to clans; in Serbia, they are to the ethnic group; in the United States and elsewhere, multiethnic countries command people's primary loyalty. States reinforce their citizens' identification with the state through flags, anthems, pledges of allegiance, and so forth. Perhaps someday people will shift loyalties further, developing a *global identity* as humans first and members of states and ethnic groups second.

Religious Conflict

One reason ethnic conflicts often transcend material grievances is that they find expression as *religious* conflicts. Because religion is the core of a community's value system in much of the world, people whose religious practices differ are easily disdained and treated as unworthy or even inhuman. When overlaid on ethnic and territorial conflicts, religion often surfaces as the central and most visible division between groups. For instance, most people in Azerbaijan are Muslims; most Armenians are Christians.

Nothing inherent in religion mandates conflicts—in many places, members of different religious groups coexist peacefully. But religious differences hold the potential to make existing conflicts more intractable because religions involve

Policy Perspectives
President of Liberia, Ellen Johnson-Sirleaf

PROBLEM *How do you prevent civil war while retaining control of your government?*

BACKGROUND Imagine you are the president of Liberia. Your election in the spring of 2006 as the first woman president in Africa was hailed as a breakthrough for Liberia. The election ended decades of political violence that devastated your own country as well your neighbors Ivory Coast and Sierra Leone. The violence ended when former Liberian president Charles Taylor went into exile in Nigeria. Tens of thousands of people lost their lives or were subject to human rights abuses, including torture and mutilation, in the wars begun under Taylor's rule.

Recently, however, there is optimism within your country and from the international community. Rebel groups have remained quiet, and Charles Taylor was convicted in a war crimes trial in 2013 and is now in prison. Economic aid has begun to stream into your country to assist in development. Your country is resource rich and has the potential to become a middle-income country because of its vast natural agricultural and mineral resources. And you won the 2011 Nobel Peace Prize for helping end the war.

DOMESTIC CONSIDERATIONS Tremendous challenges lie ahead. Economically, your country is underdeveloped, with years of civil war leading to increases in corruption and economic stagnation. Many of the powerful economic actors in your country benefit from the corruption and graft, which you have pledged to end. Unemployment is very high, with hundreds of thousands of young men unemployed. Until recently, roving bands of fighters controlled pockets of territory. Armed police have occasionally returned to the streets to restore order, and in late 2008, a mass breakout from the country's only maximum security prison allowed over 100 criminals to escape.

SCENARIO Now imagine that a group that was involved in the civil war begins to reopen the war. The group has taken refuge in Sierra Leone and now begins to make cross-border raids against your country. Although Sierra Leone does not support the group, its government has limited resources to devote to the issue.

One option is to negotiate directly with the group. Negotiations could lead to peace, but they might require power sharing in your government, which could derail your attempts to lessen corruption.

Another option is to use military force against the rebels. But international donors would discourage you from endangering the fragile peace in Liberia, with the implicit threat of an aid cutoff if you are perceived to be too hardline. In addition, the reemergence of a civil war would make your proposed democratic and economic reforms more difficult to implement. Your military is not well trained, and you are very uncertain about the possibility of success against the rebels. A strong military response to the rebels, however, could discourage future aggression and establish that you are a tough leader.

CHOOSE YOUR POLICY How do you handle this new threat from the rebels? Do you adopt a hardline policy against them in hopes of defeating them? Or do you attempt reconciliation in hopes of minimizing the prospect of further bloodshed, but at the price of bringing your enemies into the government and thus undermining some of your goals?

core values, which are held as absolute truth. This is increasingly true as *fundamentalist* movements have gained strength in recent decades. (The reasons for fundamentalism are disputed, but it is clearly a global-level phenomenon.) Members of these movements organize their lives and communities around their religious beliefs; many are willing to sacrifice, kill, and die for those beliefs. Fundamentalist movements have become larger and more powerful in recent decades in Christianity, Islam, Judaism, Hinduism, and other religions. Such movements challenge the values and practices of **secular** political organizations—those created apart from religious establishments.

secular Created apart from religious establishments, with a high degree of separation between religious and political organizations.

Among the secular practices threatened by fundamentalist movements include the rules of the international system, which treat states as formally equal and sovereign whether they are "believers" or "infidels." As transnational belief systems, religions are often taken as a higher law than state laws and international treaties. This runs counter to the norms of the international system and to the assumptions of realism.

ISLAMIST MOVEMENTS   Currently, violent conflicts are being fought in the name of all the world's major religions. But special attention is due to conflicts involving Islamic groups and states. Islamist actors are active participants in 13 of the world's 15 wars in progress (see p. 117). In addition, the U.S. "war on terror" is directed against a network of Islamic terror groups. However, most Islamist movements are not violent.

Islam A broad and diverse world religion whose divergent populations include Sunni Muslims, Shi'ite Muslims, and many smaller branches and sects from Nigeria to Indonesia, centered in the Middle East and South Asia.

Islam, the religion practiced by **Muslims**, is broad and diverse. Its divergent populations include Sunni Muslims (the majority), Shi'ite Muslims (concentrated in Iran, southern Iraq, southern Lebanon, and Bahrain), and many smaller branches and sects. Most countries with mainly Muslim populations belong to the Islamic Conference, an intergovernmental organization (IGO). The world's predominantly Islamic countries stretch from Nigeria to Indonesia, centered historically in the Middle East (see Figure 4.3) but with the largest populations in South and Southeast Asia. Many international conflicts around this zone involve Muslims on one side and non-Muslims on the other, as a result of geographical and historical circumstances including colonialism and oil.

Muslims See *Islam*.

Islamist Political ideology based on instituting Islamic principles and laws in government. A broad range of groups using diverse methods come under this category.

Islamist groups advocate basing government and society on Islamic law. These groups vary greatly in the means they employ to pursue this goal. Most are nonviolent—charities and political parties. Some are violent—militias and terrorist networks. In the 1990s Islamic parties gained ground in Turkey—a secular state in which the military has intervened repeatedly to prevent religious politics—and a former Islamist leader has been prime minister since 2003, making Turkey an important model of moderate Islam. Islamist parties have also led Iraq's government and played central roles in the Arab Spring countries, initially winning elections in Tunisia and Egypt. Armed Islamist factions became key players in the Syrian civil war in 2013. By 2014, one group, the Islamic State in Iraq and Syria (ISIS), had become the strongest of these groups and captured significant territory in Syria and neighboring Iraq. Their rapid expansion in both

Figure 4.3 Members of the Islamic Conference and Areas of Conflict

Shaded countries are members of the conference; numbered regions are areas of conflict between Muslims and non-Muslims or secular authorities.

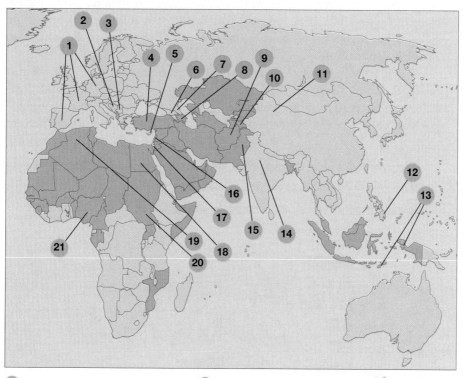

1 Germany, France, Spain	8 Armenia/Azerbaijan	15 Pakistan
2 Bosnia-Herzegovina	9 Afghanistan	16 Lebanon
3 Serbia/Kosovo	10 Tajikistan	17 Israel/Palestine
4 Turkey	11 Western China	18 Egypt
5 Cyprus	12 Philippines	19 Algeria
6 Georgia	13 East Timor/Indonesia	20 Sudan
7 Southern Russia/Chechnya	14 India	21 Nigeria

countries triggered military action against them by several North Atlantic Treaty Organization (NATO) states, Russia, and regional powers.

If Islamist movements seek changes primarily in domestic policies, why do they matter for IR? Islamist politics may lead to different foreign policies, but the more important answer is that some Islamist movements have become a transnational force shaping world order and global North-South relations in important ways.

In several countries, Islamists reject Western-oriented secular states in favor of governments more explicitly oriented to Islamic values. These movements reflect long-standing *anti-Western* sentiment in these countries—against the old European colonizers who were Christian—and are in some ways *nationalist* movements expressed through religious channels. In some Middle Eastern countries with authoritarian governments, religious institutions (mosques) have been the only available avenue for political opposition. Religion has therefore become a means to express opposition to the status quo in politics and culture.

Public opinion in both Muslim and non-Muslim countries shows some misconceptions and differences in opinion (see Figure 4.4). Support for Islamist radicals varies greatly among countries. A 2010 poll recalls "mirror image" perceptions (see p. 88). In five Western industrialized countries, 40–80 percent

Figure 4.4 Public Opinion in Muslim and Non-Muslim Countries

Source: Pew Global Attitudes Survey, 2005, 2010, and 2014.

How often is suicide bombing or violence against civilians justified in order to defend Islam?

Percent responding
often or sometimes in 2014

Lebanon	29%
Indonesia	9%
Pakistan	3%
Turkey	18%
Jordan	15%
Egypt	24%

Non-Muslims think Muslims are:

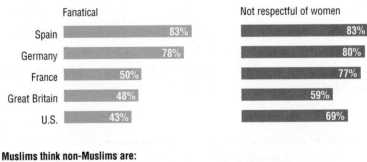

Fanatical		Not respectful of women	
Spain	83%	Spain	83%
Germany	78%	Germany	80%
France	50%	France	77%
Great Britain	48%	Great Britain	59%
U.S.	43%	U.S.	69%

Muslims think non-Muslims are:

Fanatical		Not respectful of women	
Jordan	68%	Jordan	53%
Turkey	67%	Turkey	39%
Egypt	61%	Egypt	52%
Indonesia	41%	Indonesia	50%
Pakistan	24%	Pakistan	52%

thought Muslims were "fanatical" and 60–80 percent thought Muslims did not respect women. But in three of five *Muslim* countries, more than 60 percent thought non-Muslims were "fanatical" and in four of those five countries, a majority thought non-Muslims did not respect women.

The more radical Islamist movements not only threaten some existing governments—especially those tied to the West—but also undermine traditional norms of state sovereignty. They reject Western political conceptions of the state (based on individual autonomy) in favor of a more traditional Islamic orientation based on community. Some aspire to create a single political state encompassing most of the Middle East, as existed in the *caliphate* of A.D. 600–1200. Such a development would create a profound challenge to the present international system—particularly to its current status quo powers—and would therefore be opposed at every turn by the world's most powerful states.

Islamists in Middle Eastern countries, like revolutionaries elsewhere, derive their main base of strength from championing the cause of the poor masses against rich elites. Like other revolutionaries throughout the global South, Islamist movements in countries such as Turkey, Egypt, and Lebanon draw their base of support from poor slums, where the Islamists sometimes provide basic services unmet by the government.

In a 2010 public opinion poll in Morocco and Saudi Arabia, a plurality of respondents identified primarily as Muslims, more than identified primarily as citizens of their states or as Arabs. But in Jordan, Lebanon, Egypt, and the United Arab Emirates (UAE), the pattern was reversed, with large majorities identifying primarily as citizens of their states. Islamist movements tap into the public's identification with issues that may not affect them materially but affect their identities as Muslims, across national borders—especially the Arab-Israeli conflict. The public in Muslim countries also cared about wars in the 1990s in Bosnia, Azerbaijan, and Chechnya, where Christian armed forces attacked Muslim civilians. Islamists see all these conflicts as part of a broad regional (or even global) struggle of Islam against Western, Christian imperialism—a struggle dating back to the Crusades almost 1,000 years ago. From the perspective of some outsiders, the religious conflicts boiling and simmering at the edges of the Islamic world look like an expansionist threat to be contained. The view from within looks more like being surrounded and repressed.

The 2003 Iraq War greatly inflamed anti-American feeling and helped radicalize politics across the Muslim world, especially in Arab countries that saw the U.S. invasion as a humiliation to Arab dignity. However, the presidency of Barack Hussein Obama, whose middle name reflects Muslim family roots in Kenya, increased America's favorability ratings in Bahrain, Jordan, and Egypt. By 2010, though, many of those numbers had begun to fall again as the Arab world began to express frustration in the Middle East peace process and the U.S. decision to stay in Afghanistan. By 2015, American favorability ratings in the Arab world were lower than in many years past.

ARMED ISLAMIST GROUPS Anti-American and anti-Western sentiments in predominantly Islamic countries have accelerated the growth of violent Islamist groups as well. Although they are in the minority, they have disproportionate effects on IR and receive the most public attention.

Armed Islamist groups vary tremendously, and in some cases they violently disagree with each other (see Table 4.1). In particular, divisions between the Sunni and Shi'ite wings of Islam have led to violence. This split played out prominently in Iraq, where Saddam Hussein was a Sunni ruling over a Shi'ite majority (brutally repressing their rebellion after the 1991 Gulf War) and earlier fighting a long deadly war against Shi'ite Iran. After the U.S.-led overthrow of Saddam in 2003, Shi'ite parties took power and Shi'ite militias exacted revenge, while some Sunnis waged a relentless insurgency that turned into deadly waves of sectarian violence. The violence in Iraq has since diminished, but the Sunni–Shi'ite relationship there remains unsettled.

Table 4.1 Major Armed Islamist Groups

Group	Country	Branch of Islam	Actions
Islamic Republic of Iran	Iran	Shi'ite	Only Islamic revolution to successfully control a state (since 1979); held off secular Iraq in 1980s war; now attempting to build nuclear weapons.
Hezbollah	Lebanon	Shi'ite	Fought Israeli army in 2006. Part of ruling coalition in Lebanon.
Mahdi Army	Iraq	Shi'ite	Clashed with U.S. forces in Iraq; major faction in Iraqi government.
Al-Nusra Front	Syria	Sunni	Leading rebel militia in civil war.
Ansar Dine	Mali	Sunni	Controlled north of country in 2012; took hostages in Algeria in 2013.
Hamas	Palestine (Gaza)	Sunni	Forces have killed hundreds of Israeli civilians and fought a war against Israel in 2008 and 2014. Won Palestinian elections in 2006. Controls Gaza Strip.
al Shabab	Somalia	Sunni	Controlled most of country in 2007–2012. Allied with al Qaeda. Ousted by African Union in 2012. Attacks in Kenya in 2014.
Moro Islamic Liberation Front	Philippines	Sunni	Forces have fought for independence of certain regions in the Muslim-populated southern Philippine Islands.
al Qaeda	World (Pakistan?)	Sunni	9/11 attacks and European bombings. Weakened by deaths of top leaders.
Taliban	Afghanistan	Sunni	Major insurgent group fighting foreign forces; controlled country in 1996–2001.
The Islamic State (ISIS)	Syria/Iraq	Sunni	Emerged from Sunni militant groups in Iraq; re-emerged as key actor in Syrian civil war; targeted by international airstrikes in 2014–2015.
Houthis	Yemen	Shi'ite	Took control of much of Yemen in 2014; supported by Iran; attacked by Saudi Arabia.

Islamist guerrilla fighters/terrorists are also active in Chechnya (Russia), Kashmir (India), Central Asia, Indonesia, and Europe.

Source: U.S. Department of Defense

Since 2011, the Sunni-Shi'ite divide has centered on Syria, where the ruling family is Alawite (an offshoot of Shi'ism) and the majority Sunni. Civil war there has also taken on sectarian overtones, reinforced by outside backers—Shi'ite Iran for the government along with the Shi'ite Lebanese militia Hezbollah, and Sunni Turkey and Arab Gulf states for the rebels.

By 2014, Islamist rebels that had emerged in Syria united with Sunnis from Iraq to form ISIS. This group quickly gained adherents and achieved quick military victories, especially in Sunni populated areas of Iraq. The group gained global attention as they released videos showing the beheadings of their hostages. Their quick military advances and videos led to a significant military effort to reestablish Iraqi government control and defeat ISIS. Actors ranging from Kurdish guerillas to Iran, to Jordan, to the United States worked to undermine ISIS. By 2015, Islamist groups in Libya, Yemen, and Egypt carried out terrorist attacks claiming ties to ISIS.

Regionally, Iran and Saudi Arabia represent the split, facing each other over the Persian Gulf (also called the Arabian Gulf) and engaging in a major arms race, with the Saudis stocking in jets and missiles while the Iranians race to build a nuclear weapon. These countries came into open diplomatic conflict when Saudi Arabia attacked Iran-supported rebels in Yemen in 2014–2015.

In Iran, a popular uprising in 1979 overthrew the U.S.-backed shah and installed an Islamic government in which the top religious leaders (ayatollahs) can overturn the laws passed by the parliament. The rejection of international norms by some Islamists was dramatically illustrated when Iran refused to protect U.S. diplomats in Iran in 1979. In 2009, a disputed presidential election led to the harsh repression of protesters. In 2012, Iran's currency lost half its value as harsh international sanctions hurt the economy, and Israel threatened military attack if necessary to stop Iran's nuclear ambitions.

Iran strongly supports—with money, arms, and training—the Hezbollah militia in Lebanon and the government in Syria. Hezbollah runs hundreds of schools, hospitals, and other charities, but it is also included on the U.S. list of terrorist organizations. Hezbollah fought Israel for years, winning popular support throughout the Arab world, even among Sunnis. Hezbollah took a leading role in Lebanon's government in 2011, despite a UN tribunal's indictment of its members for the 2005 assassination of Lebanon's prime minister.

On the Sunni side, the major militant Islamist groups, and some less violent ones, are Salafis. They adhere to some version of Wahhabism, a fundamentalist interpretation of Islamic law with roots in Saudi Arabia. The most important center of this fundamentalist movement currently is in Afghanistan and the next-door tribal areas of western Pakistan. Militants following the same philosophy are also active across Northern Africa in 2015, notably in Nigeria, Mali, Libya, and Somalia.

In Afghanistan, an Islamic government was established in 1992 after a civil war (and following a decade of ill-fated Soviet occupation). Rival Islamic factions then continued the war with even greater intensity for several years. By

1997, a faction called Taliban had taken control of most of Afghanistan and imposed an extreme interpretation of Islamic law. With beatings and executions, the regime forced women to wear head-to-toe coverings, girls to stay out of school, and men to grow beards, among other repressive policies.

The incendiary mixture in Afghanistan in the 1990s—unending war, grinding poverty, Islamic fundamentalism, and an ideologically driven government—allowed Afghanistan to become a base for worldwide terrorist operations, culminating in the September 11, 2001, attacks. In response, the United States exerted its power to remove the Taliban from power in Afghanistan and disrupt the al Qaeda terrorist network headquartered there. Despite U.S. and NATO successes, the Taliban continues to attack NATO forces and civilians. In late 2015, Taliban forces captured a large city (Kunduz), which government military forces struggled to re-capture.

The Taliban's defeat in Afghanistan in 2001 led its members, with like-minded Pakistani militants, to establish bases in the lawless "tribal areas" of western Pakistan, a much larger neighbor with nuclear weapons. Pakistan's intelligence service is widely believed to use Islamist militants to exert influence in both Afghanistan and in Kashmir, a territory Pakistan and India dispute. In late 2008, Pakistan-based terrorists attacked Mumbai, India, and killed about 150 civilians there. Pro-democracy forces ousted Pakistan's military ruler and installed an elected government in 2008, although not until after the movement's leader, Benazir Bhutto, had been assassinated.

The war in Afghanistan has strained relations between Pakistan and the United States and its NATO allies. These strains worsened in 2011, when U.S. forces found and killed Osama bin Laden in a Pakistani city. Pakistanis objected to the intrusion that violated their sovereignty, while Americans wondered whether the Pakistani military had colluded in hiding bin Laden.

Al Qaeda is a transnational group—more a network or movement than a central organization in recent years—that recruits fighters from various countries, encourages and sometimes trains them, and helps them fight in foreign conflicts (such as in Afghanistan in the 1980s, Iraq after 2003, or Syria today).

Although al Qaeda as a "brand" has picked up followers in northern Africa in recent years, it has lost steam in Asia and Europe, where the years after 2001 saw various terror bombings from Bali, Indonesia, to Morocco, Saudi Arabia, Russia, the Philippines, Indonesia, Iraq, and Turkey. In 2004, bombings of trains in Madrid killed hundreds and apparently tipped an election against the pro-American Spanish government—thus inducing Spain to pull its troops out of Iraq. The next year, the London subway was the target.

In Saudi Arabia—home to the world's largest oil reserves, Islam's holiest sites, and the roots of Wahhabism—al Qaeda has long hoped to overthrow the monarchy. In 1979, Islamist militants briefly seized control of the Grand Mosque in Mecca.

Saudi Arabia's neighbor to the south, Yemen, has an active branch of al Qaeda–affiliated fighters who have tried several times to bomb U.S.-bound aircraft and who seized territory in the south of the country in 2011–2012 while the government was paralyzed by political unrest in the capital (part of the Arab Spring). Yemen is the poorest country in the Middle East and has suffered from decades of civil conflict. The United States operates a vigorous campaign of drone attacks to combat the Yemeni militants. By 2015, Yemen was near full-scale civil war, with several groups fighting each another. One minority group known as the Houthis (allied with Iran but opposed to al Qaeda) fought to take control of the government. In response, Saudi Arabia (Iran's rival) attacked the Houthi rebels to restore control to the government. In the midst of this chaos, new Islamic fighters claiming allegiance to ISIS began carrying out suicide bombings.

ISLAMIC STATE? In some Muslim-populated countries, Islam is a political rallying point—especially in authoritarian countries in which the mosque is a rare permitted gathering point. Some Islamist politicians are developing new models of government, mixing democracy and Islamic tradition, especially in the countries most affected by the Arab Spring protests. Other Islamist groups, such as the Islamic State in Iraq and Syria (ISIS), fight violently for a state founded on Islamic law. Here, ISIS forces parade through an Iraqi city after its capture in 2014.

Somalia's al Shabab fighters, affiliated with al Qaeda, were ousted from most cities and towns in 2012 by an African Union force, but not before taking revenge on Ethiopia and Uganda, which had contributed troops to support the Somali government. Al Shabab carried out deadly bombings in Uganda during the 2010 World Cup finals. In 2011, although the African Union force in Somalia pushed al Shabab out of the capital, a terrible famine, caused by drought and war, gripped the Shabab-held areas of the country and forced refugees into Kenya. In response, Kenya also sent military forces into Somalia to attack al Shabab. In 2015, the U.S. military claimed to have killed a key al Shabab leader using a drone.

In Libya, the overthrow of a dictator in 2011 (with NATO assistance) empowered armed Islamist groups that had formerly been repressed. They killed the U.S. ambassador in 2012, and they joined ethnic rebels from Mali, who had been fighting as mercenaries for the Libyan dictator, to seize northern Mali, using large quantities of weapons they brought from Libya. The Islamists swept aside the ethnic rebels and took power for themselves, but by 2013, they were ousted by a military intervention by France and neighboring African countries to return control to the government of Mali.

In the West African country of Nigeria, an Islamist group known as Boko Haram has attacked government officials and civilians since 2009. Most notably, the group attacked several girls' schools in 2014, taking young girls hostages in each attack. The Nigerian government has declared a state of emergency and has deployed thousands of troops to northern provinces, where the group is strongest.

In Palestine, the radical Islamist faction Hamas is another important Sunni Islamist militia, though not connected with al Qaeda or the Taliban. Centered in the Gaza Strip, Hamas sent suicide bombers who killed hundreds of Israelis after 2000, then won free parliamentary elections in 2006 because it was seen as less corrupt than the dominant party. However, Palestine remains divided, with the Palestinian Authority controlling the West Bank and Hamas controlling Gaza.

The two great powers to face Islamist violence within their borders are Russia in its far south and China in its far west. The predominantly Sunni Muslim republic of Chechnya, a Russian province, tried to split away from Russia in the early 1990s after the Soviet Union collapsed. After destructive wars in 1994–1995 and 1999–2000, the threat abated, although Chechen guerrillas then turned to airline hijackings, hostage taking, and suicide bombings. In 2004, hundreds of children died after Chechen terrorists took over a school and held them hostage. In 2005, Russian forces killed the Chechen separatist leader they held responsible, and political violence in Chechnya is now sporadic.

Overall, conflicts involving Islamist movements are more complex than simply religious conflicts; they concern power, economic relations, ethnic chauvinism, and historical empires as well.

IDEOLOGICAL SPLIT Ideology plays only a limited role in most international conflicts. After revolutions, ideologies such as Marxism may affect foreign policy, but over the following decades, countries such as China or the Soviet Union typically revert to a foreign policy based more on national interests than ideology. Nonetheless, ideological clashes still occur, as between the freedom-loving United States and authoritarian North Korea. Here the different styles of the two countries are on display as the New York Philharmonic performs a rare concert in North Korea, 2008.

Ideological Conflict

To a large extent, ideology, like religion, symbolizes and intensifies conflicts between groups and states more than it causes them. But ideologies have a somewhat weaker hold on core values and absolute truth than religions do.

For realists, ideological differences among states do not matter much because all members of the international system pursue their national interests in the context of relatively fluid alliances. Over the long run, even countries that experience revolutions based on strong ideologies tend to lose their ideological fervor—be it Iran's Islamic fundamentalism in 1979, China's Maoist communism in 1949, Russia's Leninist communism in 1917, or even U.S. democracy in 1776. In each case, the revolutionaries expected that their assumption of power would dramatically alter their state's foreign policy because, in each case, their ideology had profound international implications. Yet within a few decades, each of these revolutionary governments turned to the pursuit of national interests above ideological ones.

Sometimes even self-proclaimed ideological struggles are not really ideological. In Angola in the 1980s, the United States backed a rebel army called UNITA against a Soviet-aligned government—supposedly a struggle of democracy against Marxism. In truth, the ideological differences were quite arbitrary. The government mouthed Marxist rhetoric to get the Soviet Union to give it aid (a policy it reversed as soon as Soviet aid dried up). The rebels who used democratic rhetoric to get U.S. support had earlier received Chinese support and mouthed Maoist rhetoric. This conflict, which finally ended in 2002, really had nothing to do with ideology. It was a power struggle between two armed, ethnically based factions fighting to control Angola's oil, diamonds, and other wealth.

In the short term, revolutions *do* change international relations—they make wars more likely—but not because of ideology. Rather, the sudden change of governments can alter alliances and change the balance of power. With calculations of power being revised by all parties, it is easy to miscalculate or to exaggerate threats on both sides. But revolutions are seldom exported to other states.

Conflicts of Interest

4.3 Summarize two different international territorial disputes and evaluate the prospects for their peaceful settlement.

If conflicts of ideas can be intractable because of psychological and emotional factors, conflicts about material interests are somewhat easier to settle based on the reciprocity principle. In theory, given enough positive leverage—a payment in some form—any state should agree to another state's terms on a disputed issue.

Territorial Disputes

Among the international conflicts that concern tangible "goods," those about territory have special importance because of the territorial nature of the state (see pp. 43–47). Conflicts over control of territory are really of two varieties: territorial disputes (about where borders are drawn) and conflicts over control of entire states within existing borders (discussed next under Control of Governments). Consider first differences over where borders between two states should be drawn—that is, who controls a disputed piece of land. Because states value home territory with an almost fanatical devotion, border disputes tend to be among the most intractable in IR. States seldom yield territory in exchange for money or any other positive reward. Nor do states quickly forget territory that they lose involuntarily. For example, in 2002, Bolivian public opinion opposed a gas export pipeline through Chile to the sea because Chile had seized the coastline from Bolivia in 1879. The goal of regaining territory lost to another state is

irredentism A form of nationalism whose goal is to regain territory lost to another state; it can lead directly to violent interstate conflicts.

called **irredentism**. This form of nationalism often leads directly to serious interstate conflicts.

Because of their association with the integrity of states, territories are valued far beyond any inherent economic or strategic value they hold. For example, after Israel and Egypt made peace in 1978, it took them a decade to settle a border dispute at Taba, a tiny plot of beachfront on which Israeli developers had built a hotel just across the old border. The two states finally submitted the issue for binding arbitration, and Egypt ended up in possession. For Egypt, regaining every inch of territory was a matter of national honor and a symbol of its sovereignty and territorial integrity.

The value states place on home territory seems undiminished despite the apparent reduction in the inherent value of territory as technology has developed. Historically, territory was the basis of economic production—agriculture and the extraction of raw materials. Winning wars meant gaining territory, which meant increasing wealth. Today, however, much more wealth derives from trade and technology than from agriculture. The costs of most territorial disputes appear to outweigh any economic benefits that the territory in question could provide. Exceptions exist, however, such as the capture of diamond-mining areas in several African countries by rebels who use the diamond revenues to finance war. But in 2002, 40 states created a program of UN certification for legitimate diamonds, trying to keep the "conflict diamonds" off the international market.

SECESSION   Efforts by a province or region to secede from an existing state are a special type of conflict over borders—not the borders of two existing states but the efforts to draw international borders around a new state. Dozens of secession movements exist around the world, of varying sizes and political effectiveness, but they succeed in seceding only rarely. The existing state almost always tries to hold on to the area in question. For example, in the 1990s, the predominantly Albanian population of the Serbian province of Kosovo fought a war to secede from Serbia. NATO intervention, including sustained bombing of Serbia (not approved by the UN), led to the withdrawal of Serbia's army from Kosovo and its replacement with European and American peacekeeping troops who have been there ever since. Most of the Kosovo population wants to secede and become an internationally recognized state, but Serbians argue that Kosovo is historically and presently under Serbian sovereignty. While the UN and the great powers negotiated over the future of Kosovo, with Russia insisting there be no promise of independence, Kosovars took matters into their own hands. In 2008, Kosovo declared independence without UN approval. Several countries, including the United States and the largest EU states, recognized Kosovo's independence, angering Serbia, Russia, and China. In 2011, South Sudan successfully gained independence with UN membership and the support of Sudan.

Wars of secession can be large and deadly, and they can easily spill over international borders or draw in other countries. This spillover is particularly likely if members of an ethnic or a religious group span two sides of a border, constituting the majority group in one state and a majority in a nearby region of another state, but a minority in the other state as a whole. In the Kosovo case, Albanian Muslims are the majority in Albania and in Kosovo but the minority in Serbia. The same pattern occurs in Bosnia-Serbia, Moldova-Russia, and India-Pakistan. In some cases, secessionists want to merge their territories with the neighboring state, which amounts to redrawing the international border. International norms frown on such an outcome.

The strong international norms of sovereignty and territorial integrity treat secession movements as domestic problems of little concern to other states. The general principle seems to be this: "We existing states all have our own domestic problems and disaffected groups or regions, so we must stick together behind sovereignty and territorial integrity." Thus, for instance, Russia and China opposed the secession of Kosovo from Serbia because of its implications for Chechnya and Taiwan, respectively.

SHOULD I STAY OR SHOULD I GO? Efforts by a region to secede from a state are a frequent source of international conflict, but international norms generally treat such conflicts as internal matters unless they spill over borders. Increasingly, autonomy agreements are resolving secession conflicts. Here, a voter leaves the polls in the 2014 referendum on Scottish independence. Scots voted to remain part of Great Britain in the election.

This principle does have limits, however. In August 2008, after fighting broke out between the Georgian military and the Georgian province of South Ossetia, Russia intervened militarily on behalf of South Ossetia and Abkhazia, resulting in a brief war between Russia and Georgia. Russia then recognized both Georgian provinces as independent, a move denounced by the United States and the EU and not accepted by the UN.

Messy border problems can result when multinational states break up into pieces. In such cases, borders that had been internal become international; because these borders are new, they may be more vulnerable to challenge. In the former Yugoslavia, ethnic groups had intermingled and intermarried, leaving mixed populations in most of the Yugoslav republics. When Yugoslavia broke up in 1991–1992, several republics declared their independence as separate states. Two of these, Croatia and Bosnia, contained minority populations of ethnic Serbs. Serbia seized effective control of significant areas of Croatia and Bosnia that contained Serbian communities or linked such populations geographically. Non-Serbian populations in these areas were driven out or massacred—euphemistically called **ethnic cleansing**. Then, when Croatia reconquered most of its territory in 1995, Serbian populations fled. Ethnic nationalism, whipped up by opportunistic politicians, proved stronger than multiethnic tolerance in both Serbia and Croatia.

ethnic cleansing
Euphemism for forced displacement of an ethnic group or groups from a territory, accompanied by massacres and other human rights violations; it has occurred after the breakup of multinational states, notably in the former Yugoslavia.

The breakup of a state need not lead to violence, however. Serbia split peacefully from Montenegro (a former Yugoslav republic) in 2006. Czechoslovakia split into the Czech Republic and Slovakia in a cooperative manner. And the breakup of the Soviet Union mostly did not lead to violent territorial disputes between republics, even when ethnic groups spanned new international borders.

The norm against forceful redrawing of borders does not apply to cases of decolonization. Only the territorial integrity of existing, recognized states is protected by international norms. Colonies and other territorial possessions historically had value only as property to be won, lost, sold, or traded in political deals and wars. The transfer of Hong Kong from British to Chinese control in 1997 illustrates how colonial territory is dispensable (Britain's perspective) while home territory is nearly sacred (China's perspective). From neither perspective do the views of the inhabitants carry much weight.

Increasingly, autonomy for a region has become a realistic compromise between secession and full control by a central government. In 2005, spurred partly by the devastating tsunami a year earlier, separatists in Aceh province, Indonesia, disbanded, giving up on independence, and instead participated in regional elections in 2006. The Indonesian government withdrew its 24,000 troops from Aceh and offered the province limited self-rule along with 70 percent of the oil, gas, and mineral wealth earned there.

INTERSTATE BORDERS   Border disputes between existing states are taken more seriously by the international community, but they are less common than secessionist conflicts. Because of the norm of territorial integrity, few important border conflicts remain among long-established states. At one time, huge chunks of territory passed between states at the stroke of a pen. Since the end of World War II, however, only a minuscule amount of territory has changed hands between established states through force (this does not apply to the formation of new states and the fragmenting of old ones).

Furthermore, when territorial disputes do occur between established states, they *can* be settled peacefully. In 2006, Nigeria withdrew its troops from the potentially oil-rich Bakassi Peninsula, which it ceded to Cameroon's sovereignty. The resolution of the dispute, dating from colonial times, followed more than a decade of painstaking progress through the World Court, the personal mediation of the UN Secretary General when Nigeria initially rejected the Court's decision, and the promise of outside powers to monitor implementation of the agreement. Why would Nigeria—a country with nine times Cameroon's population, more than triple its gross domestic product (GDP), and a much stronger military—voluntarily cede territory? Doing so would seem to run counter to the predictions of realism in particular and the dominance principle in general. Liberal theories would do better at explaining this outcome: Nigeria acted in its own self-interest because turning the dispute over to the World Court and bringing in the UN to assist with implementation brought the kind of stability needed for foreign investment to develop the area's resources, primarily oil.

LINGERING DISPUTES   Today, the few remaining interstate border disputes generate important international conflicts. Among the most difficult are the borders of *Israel*. The 1948 cease-fire lines resulting from Israel's war of independence expanded in the 1967 war. Israel returned the Sinai Peninsula to Egypt, but the remaining territories occupied in 1967—the *West Bank* near Jordan, the *Gaza Strip* near Egypt, and the *Golan Heights* of Syria—are central to the Arab-Israeli conflict. In particular, Israel's ongoing construction of Jewish settlements in the West Bank, bitterly opposed by Palestinians and considered illegal by most international actors, remains a contentious sticking point. Israeli-Palestinian agreements since 1993 tried to move toward Palestinian autonomy in parts of the West Bank and Gaza, and negotiations seemed headed toward creation of a state of Palestine there. That effort completely stalled in the twenty-first century, however, notwithstanding the 2012 upgrading of Palestine's UN status to nonmember "state," a symbolic gesture.

Another serious border dispute is in the *Kashmir* area, where India, Pakistan, and China intersect. The Indian-held part of Kashmir is predominantly inhabited by Muslims, a group that is the majority in Pakistan but a minority in India. A *Line of Control* divides the disputed province. Pakistan accuses India of oppressing Kashmiris and thwarting an international agreement to decide Kashmir's future by a popular referendum. India accuses Pakistan of aiding and infiltrating Islamic radicals who carry out attacks in Indian-occupied Kashmir. The two countries went to war twice over the issue, and they nearly did so again in 2002—that time armed with nuclear-armed missiles. A cease-fire took hold in 2003 and stopped most of the incessant low-level fighting along the Line of Control, although sporadic skirmishes continue, with some of the worst fighting in years breaking out late in 2014.

Many of the world's other remaining interstate territorial disputes—and often the most serious ones—concern the control of small islands, which often provide strategic advantages, natural resources (such as offshore oil), or fishing rights. International law now gives an island's owner fishing and mineral rights in surrounding seas for 200 miles in each direction. Six countries claim the tiny *Spratly Islands* in the South China Sea (see Figure 4.5). In 2002, they agreed to avoid confrontations over the islands, and they remain calm. Japan and China also dispute tiny islands, as do Japan and South Korea, Iran and the United

Figure 4.5 Disputed Islands

The Spratly Islands exemplify contemporary conflicts over territory and natural resources around islands. All or part of the Spratlys are claimed by China, Vietnam, Malaysia, Brunei, the Philippines, and Taiwan.

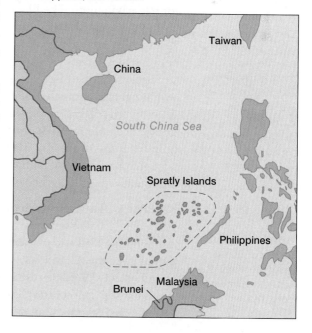

LOCATION, LOCATION, LOCATION Control of islands, and of the large exclusive economic zone (EEZ) that surrounds them under the law of the sea, has created a number of complicated interstate conflicts. Japan claims Okinotori, shown here in 2005, as an island with an EEZ, but China calls it merely a "rock" without surrounding economic rights.

Arab Emirates, Spain and Morocco, Argentina and Britain, and Russia and Japan. In 2005, Japan and China argued over whether Okinotori—an uninhabited coral reef with two tiny protrusions smaller than a house—was an "island" (with surrounding economic rights) or just a "rock." The two navies and air forces have confronted each other there repeatedly, though without violence. In 2015, Japan deployed its largest naval vessel (a helicopter carrier) since World War II to patrol the area, yet it also held talks with China over the disputed islands.

TERRITORIAL WATERS States treat **territorial waters** near their shores as part of their national territory. Definitions of such waters are not universally agreed upon, but norms have developed in recent years, especially since the *UN Convention on the Law of the Sea (UNCLOS)* (see p. 343). Waters within three miles of shore have traditionally been recognized as territorial, but there

territorial waters
The waters near states' shores generally treated as part of national territory. The UN Convention on the Law of the Sea provides for a 12-mile territorial sea and a 200-mile exclusive economic zone covering exclusive fishing and mineral rights (but allowing for free navigation by all).

are disputes about how far out national sovereignty extends and for what purposes. UNCLOS generally allows a 12-mile limit for shipping and a 200-mile *exclusive economic zone (EEZ)* covering fishing and mineral rights (but allowing for free navigation). The EEZs together cover a third of the world's oceans. In 2010, Russia and Norway agreed to divide portions of the Arctic Ocean into EEZs for the purposes of oil and gas extraction, ending a 40-year dispute between those states.

Because of the EEZs, sovereignty over a single tiny island can now bring with it rights to as much as 100,000 square miles of surrounding ocean. But these zones overlap greatly, and shorelines do not run in straight lines; numerous questions of interpretation thus arise about how to delineate territorial and economic waters. In the Sea of Okhotsk, Russia's EEZ includes all but a small "doughnut hole" of international waters in the middle. Non-Russian boats have fished intensively in the "hole," which depletes fish stocks in Russia's EEZ.

airspace The space above a state that is considered its territory, in contrast to outer space, which is considered international territory.

AIRSPACE The **airspace** above a state is considered the territory of the state. To fly over a state's territory, an airplane must have that state's permission. For example, in a 1986 raid on Libya, U.S. bombers based in Britain had to fly a long detour over the Atlantic Ocean because France (between Britain and Libya) would not let U.S. planes use its airspace.

Outer space, by contrast, is considered international territory like the oceans. International law does not define exactly where airspace ends and outer space begins. However, orbiting satellites fly higher than airplanes, move very fast, and cannot easily change direction to avoid overflying a country. And very few states can shoot down satellites. Because satellites have become useful to all the great powers as intelligence-gathering tools, and because all satellites are extremely vulnerable to attack, a norm of demilitarization of outer space has developed. No state has ever attacked the satellite of another.

Control of Governments

Despite the many minor border disputes that continue to plague the world, most struggles to control territory do not involve changing borders or fighting over islands. Rather, they are conflicts over which governments will control entire states within their existing borders.

In theory, states do not interfere in each other's governance because of the norm of sovereignty. In practice, however, states often have strong interests in other states' governments and try to influence who holds power in those states. Conflicts over governments take many forms, some mild and some severe, some deeply entwined with third parties, and some more or less bilateral. Sometimes a state merely exerts subtle influences on another state's elections; at other times, a state supports rebel elements seeking to overthrow the second state's government.

Such a conflict erupted in 2013–2014, when Ukraine's then pro-Russian president cracked down on pro-Western protesters. Opposition forces succeeded in forcing the president to resign, but his supporters in eastern Ukraine, aided by Russia, took up arms against the new pro-Western government. Meanwhile, Russia annexed the Crimean peninsula, which it said desired to reunite with Russia. In 2015, multiple cease-fires between Ukrainian forces and pro-Russian rebels failed as eastern provinces in Ukraine tried to break away.

Occasionally, one state invades another in order to change its government. The Soviet Union did this in Czechoslovakia in 1968; the United States did not do so in Iraq in 1991 but did in 2003. The international community frowns on such overt violations of national sovereignty.

Economic Conflict

Economic competition is the most pervasive form of conflict in international relations because economic transactions are pervasive. Every sale made and every deal reached across international borders entails a resolution of conflicting interests. Costa Rica wants the price of coffee, which it exports, to go up; Canada, which imports coffee, wants it to go down. In a global capitalist market, all economic exchanges involve some conflict of interest.

However, such economic transactions also contain a strong element of mutual economic gain in addition to the element of conflicting interests (see Chapters 3 and 5). These mutual gains provide the most useful leverage in bargaining over economic exchanges: States and companies enter into economic transactions because they profit from doing so. The use of violence would usually diminish such profit by more than could be gained as a result of the use of violence. Thus, economic conflicts do not usually lead to military force and war.

Another kind of economic conflict that affects international security concerns *military industry*—the capacity to produce military equipment, especially high-technology weapons such as fighter aircraft or missiles. There is a world trade in such items, but national governments try (not always successfully) to control such production—to try to ensure that national interests take priority over those of manufacturers and that the state is militarily self-sufficient in case of war. Economic competition (over who profits from such sales) is interwoven with security concerns (over who gets access to the weapons). In 2009, proponents of a bailout for the U.S. automobile industry argued that the industry could provide vital production capacity in time of war, as it had during World War II. The transfer of knowledge about high-tech weaponry and military technologies to potentially hostile states is a related concern.

Economic competition also becomes a security issue when it concerns trade in *strategic materials* needed for military purposes, such as special minerals or alloys for aircraft production and uranium for atomic weapons. Few countries are self-sufficient in these materials; the United States imports about half the strategic materials it uses. Nearly every country must import at least some strategic materials for its economy to function.

DRUG TRAFFICKING   As a form of illegal trade across international borders, drug trafficking is smuggling, which deprives states of revenue and violates states' legal control of their borders. But smuggling in general is an economic issue rather than a security one. Unlike other smuggled goods, however, drugs are treated as a security threat because of their effect on national (and military) morale and efficiency. Drug trafficking has also become linked with security concerns because military forces participate regularly in operations against the heavily armed drug traffickers.

The U.S. government is trying to prevent *cocaine cartels* based in Colombia from supplying U.S. cities. Such cocaine derives mostly from coca plants grown by peasants in mountainous areas of Peru, Bolivia, and Colombia itself. For poor peasants, the cocaine trade may be their only access to a decent income. More important for international security, rebel armies can fund their operations primarily through control of the trade in illicit drugs. In Mexico, a major supplier of illegal drugs to the next-door United States, deadly violence among drug gangs has spiraled out of control in the past decades, claiming tens of thousands of lives.

In Latin America, the long history of U.S. military intervention makes state cooperation with U.S. military forces a sensitive political issue. In 1989, U.S. forces invaded Panama; arrested its leader, dictator Manuel Noriega; and convicted him in U.S. courts of complicity in drug trafficking through Panama.

All six types of conflict discussed in this chapter can be pursued through peaceful or violent means. The rest of this chapter examines how states and armed nonstate groups use capabilities of violence to pursue their goals in international conflicts.

Conventional Military Forces

4.4   Compare the influence of technology on the instruments of leverage used in land, sea, and air conflicts.

A state leader in a conflict can apply various kinds of leverage to influence an outcome (see Figure 4.6). One set of levers represents nonviolent means of influencing other states, such as foreign aid, economic sanctions, and personal diplomacy (less tangible means are the use of norms, morality, and other ideas). A second set of levers—the subject of the rest of this chapter—involves violent actions. They set armies marching or missiles flying.

Figure 4.6 Military and Nonmilitary Means of Leverage

Conventional armed force is the most commonly used military form of leverage.

Source: U.S. Department of Defense

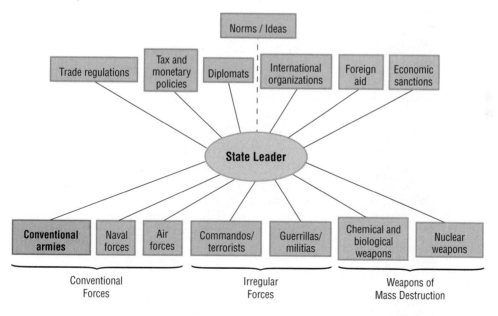

Great powers continue to dominate the makeup of world military forces. Table 4.2 summarizes the most important forces of the great powers. Together, they account for about 60 percent of world military spending, 30 percent of the world's soldiers, nearly 50 percent of conventional weapons, 98 percent of nuclear weapons, and 90 percent of arms exports. (The table also indicates the

Table 4.2 Estimated Great Power Military Capabilities, 2014

	Military Expenditures[a] (Billions of US $)	Active Duty Soldiers[b] (Millions)	Heavy Weapons[b]				Arms Exported[a] (Billions of US $)
			Tanks	Carriers/ Warships/ Submarines	Combat Airplanes	Nuclear Weapons[c]	
United States	580	1.4	2,785	10 / 98 / 59	3,500	7,300	18
Russia	90	0.8	2,800	0 / 34 / 47	1,800	8,000	11
China	190	2.3	6,540	0 / 71 / 65	1,150	250	2
France	65	0.2	200	0 / 22 / 6	300	300	3
Britain	55	0.2	225	0 / 19 / 6	200	225	3
Germany	45	0.2	400	0 / 16 / 5	240	0	2
Japan	60	0.2	700	0 / 50 / 18	600	0	0
Approximate % of world total	65%	30%	70%	100 / 70 / 50%	40%	98%	90%

Problematic data: Russian and Chinese military expenditure estimates vary. U.S. and Russian nuclear warheads include deployed strategic weapons (1,950 U.S., 1,740 Russian) with the remainder held in reserve or retired (awaiting destruction).

Data on soldiers exclude reserves. Tanks include only post-1980 modern main battle tanks. Warships are cruisers, destroyers, and frigates. Carriers include only supercarriers. Airplanes are fourth-generation. Nuclear warheads include both strategic and tactical weapons. Arms exports are for orders placed, 2013.

Sources: Author's estimates based on data provided by the following sources:

[a]2014 data from Stockholm International Peace Research Institute.

[b]2014 data from Institute for International and Strategic Studies. *The Military Balance 2015.*

[c]Federation of American Scientists data for 1/1/2015.

Source: U.S. Department of Defense

sizable military forces maintained by Germany and Japan despite their nontraditional roles in international security since World War II.)

Military capabilities divide into three types: conventional forces, irregular
forces (terrorism, militias), and weapons of mass destruction (nuclear, chemical,
and biological weapons). Conventional forces are most important—they are
active in all 15 wars currently in progress.

Land Forces: Controlling Territory

Whatever their ultimate causes and objectives, most wars involve a struggle to
control territory. Territory holds a central place in warfare because of its importance in the international system, and vice versa. Borders define where a state's
own military forces and rival states' military forces are free to move. *Armies* are
adapted to take, hold, or defend territory. Military forces with armed foot soldiers can *occupy* a territory militarily. Although inhabitants may make the soldiers' lives unhappy through violent or nonviolent resistance, generally only
another organized military force can displace occupiers.

Foot soldiers are called the *infantry.* They use assault rifles and other light
weapons (such as mines and machine guns) as well as heavy artillery of various
types. Artillery is extremely destructive and not very discriminating: It usually
causes the most damage and casualties in wars. *Armor* refers to tanks and
armored vehicles. In open terrain, such as desert, mechanized ground forces
typically combine armor, artillery, and infantry. In close terrain, such as jungles
and cities, however, foot soldiers are more important.

Counterinsurgency has received growing attention in recent years because
of Iraq and Afghanistan, but it is central to nearly all the wars currently in
progress worldwide. Counterinsurgency warfare often includes programs to
try to "win the hearts and minds" of populations so that they stop sheltering
the guerrillas.

counterinsurgency
An effort to combat
guerrilla armies,
often including pro-
grams to "win the
hearts and minds" of
rural populations so
that they stop shel-
tering guerrillas.

In some ways, because counterinsurgency warfare is as much about political gains as military strategy, it is the most complex type of warfare. While bat-
tling armed factions of an insurgency, a government must essentially conduct a
public relations campaign to persuade the population to abandon the movement
and provide public services (such as education and welfare programs) to show
its responsiveness to the population. In addition, a government must be strong
militarily, but it cannot be too brutal in the application of force lest more of the
population begin to support the guerrillas.

U.S. military forces conducted counterinsurgency campaigns in Iraq and
Afghanistan for several years. The campaigns have included the use of lethal
military force, payments to key tribal leaders to support American efforts, assisting the formation of local government, and training new police and military
forces to combat the insurgency. These types of activities place tremendous
stress on militaries, which are usually trained only to fight wars, not undertake
rebuilding distant governments.

Counterinsurgency campaigns are costly and labor-intensive. For example, the U.S. Army's counterinsurgency manual suggests that 20 troops should be deployed for every 1,000 citizens to be protected from insurgents. Few states can afford such campaigns for long periods of time. Indeed, even including allied forces, the U.S. never reached such a ratio of troops-to-population in Iraq or Afghanistan. Such a ratio would require 600,000 troops for Afghanistan, compared with the 130,000 that were actually deployed there at the war's peak in 2010 (down to less than 13,000 by 2015).

A common tool of guerrillas, insurgents, and the governments fighting them is **landmines**, which are simple, small, and cheap containers of explosives with a trigger activated by contact or sensor. These mines were a particular focus of public attention in the 1990s because, in places such as Angola, Afghanistan, Cambodia, and Bosnia, they were used extensively by irregular military forces that never disarmed them. Long after such a war ends, landmines continue to maim and kill civilians who try to reestablish their lives in former war zones. Public opinion and NGOs have pressured governments to restrict the future use of landmines. A treaty to ban landmines was signed by more than 100 countries at a 1997 conference organized by Canada. Russia and Japan signed on shortly afterward, but not China or the United States (which said mines would be needed to slow any North Korean invasion of South Korea). By 2014, more than 48 million landmines had been destroyed under the treaty, with 87 countries eliminating their stockpiles.

landmines Concealed explosive devices, often left behind by irregular armies, that kill or maim civilians after wars end. Such mines number more than 100 million, primarily in Angola, Bosnia, Afghanistan, and Cambodia. A movement to ban landmines is underway; more than 100 states have agreed to do so.

Naval Forces: Controlling the Seas

Navies are adapted primarily to control passage through the seas and to attack land near coastlines. Controlling the seas in wartime allows states to move their own goods and military forces by sea while preventing enemies from doing so.

In 2008–2012, navies of the Western powers responded to the rapid growth of piracy in three of the world's vital shipping lanes—off Somalia south of the Suez Canal, the Straits of Malacca in Indonesia connecting the Indian Ocean with East Asia, and more recently the waters off West Africa. The Somali pirates, taking advantage of near-anarchy in that country, established safe havens onshore and ventured out to capture dozens of ships, holding the vessels, cargoes, and crews for ransom. Shipping companies generally paid up, millions of dollars per ship, rather than lose valuable goods and people. The pirates pushed the limits by capturing first a Ukrainian freighter loaded with tanks and weapons and then a huge Saudi oil tanker with $100 million of oil. Racing to ships in very small, fast boats, armed with automatic rifles and grenade launchers, they toss up grappling hooks, climb the sides, and subdue the crew, typically within about ten minutes. The world's navies patrolled the area to deter piracy (see Figure 4.7), but with incomplete success because of the sheer size of the oceans.

In 2008, the UN Security Council unanimously called for international cooperation in fighting the surge in hijackings. U.S. special forces killed the hijackers

Figure 4.7 Pirate Attacks Near Somalia, January to September 2008

Source: Based on UNOSAT map, October 2, 2008.

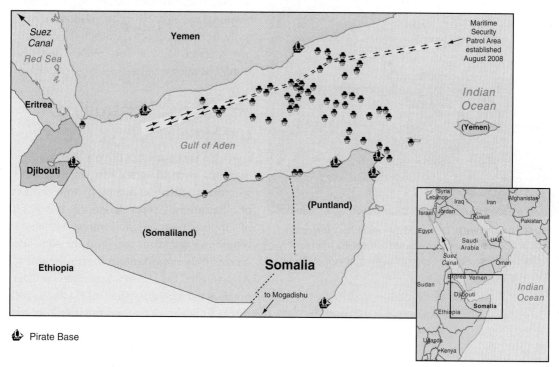

Pirate Base

of one American ship in 2009, European Union attack helicopters raided an onshore pirate base in 2012, and a Somali rescue freed a ship in late 2012. Many cargo ships began carrying armed guards. All these measures led to a sharp decline in Somali hijackings in 2012.

Aircraft carriers—mobile platforms for attack aircraft—are instruments of **power projection** that can attack almost any state in the world. Merely sending an aircraft carrier sailing to the vicinity of an international conflict implies a threat to use force—a modern version of nineteenth-century "gunboat diplomacy." Aircraft carriers are extremely expensive and typically require 20 to 25 supporting ships for protection and supply. Few states can afford even one. Only the United States operates large carriers, known as supercarriers—11 of them, costing more than $5 billion each. In 2016, the U.S. Navy plans to commission a newly designed supercarrier costing $14 billion. China has acquired and renovated one carrier, which it announced was entering service as of 2012, although only for training purposes. Eight other countries (France, India, Russia, Spain, Brazil, Italy, Thailand, and the United Kingdom) maintain smaller carriers that use helicopters or small airplanes.

Surface ships, which account for the majority of warships, rely increasingly on guided missiles and are in turn vulnerable to attack by missiles (fired from

power projection
The ability to use military force in areas far from a country's region or sphere of influence.

ships, planes, submarines, or land). Because the ranges of small missiles now reach from dozens to hundreds of miles, naval warfare emphasizes detection at great distances without being detected oneself—a cat-and-mouse game of radar surveillance and electronic countermeasures.

Air Forces: Controlling the Skies

Air forces serve several purposes—strategic bombing of land or sea targets; "close air support" (battlefield bombing); interception of other aircraft; reconnaissance; and airlift of supplies, weapons, and troops. Missiles—whether fired from air, land, or sea—are increasingly important. In the Soviet war in Afghanistan, the U.S.-made portable Stinger missiles used by guerrillas took a heavy toll on the Soviet air force. In 2003, the threat from shoulder-fired missiles kept the Baghdad airport closed to commercial air traffic for more than a year.

PROJECTING POWER Different types of military forces are adapted to different purposes. Aircraft carriers are used for power projection in distant regions, such as in the Afghanistan and Iraq campaigns.

Traditionally, and still to some extent, aerial bombing resembles artillery shelling in that it causes great destruction with little discrimination. This has changed somewhat as smart bombs improve accuracy. Laser-guided bombs follow a sensor pointed at the target from the air or ground. Other bombs use Global Positioning System (GPS) navigation (see p. 153) to hit targets through clouds, smoke, or sandstorms. Most of the bombing in the 1991 Gulf War was high-altitude saturation bombing using dumb bombs. But in the 2003 Iraq War, the massive air campaign early in the war used smart bombs entirely and hit far more targets with fewer bombs.

The increasing sophistication of electronic equipment and the high-performance requirements of attack aircraft make air forces expensive—totally out of reach for some states. Thus, rich states have huge advantages over poor ones in air warfare. Despite the expense, air superiority is often the key to the success of ground operations, especially in open terrain. The U.S. bombings of Iraq (1991 and 2003), Serbia (1999), and Afghanistan (2001) demonstrated a new effectiveness of air power, applied not against the morale of enemy populations (as in World War II) but directly at battlefield positions. The U.S. ability to decimate distant military forces while taking only very light casualties is historically unprecedented. The 2003 attack on Iraq demonstrated the usefulness of air power but also its limits. A massive precision bombing raid on Baghdad a few days into the war destroyed hundreds of targets of value to Saddam Hussein's government. It was designed to "shock and awe" enemy commanders into giving up. However, U.S. forces still had to slug it out on the ground to get to Baghdad. Clearly, this war could not have been won from the air. As ground soldiers have pointed out, "Nobody ever surrendered to an airplane."

Air forces are a likely area for attention in any future U.S.-China arms race. China has spent large sums in the past ten years rejuvenating its aging air force capabilities. The United States continues to invest heavily in its own air force, creating new technologies to stay ahead of Chinese advances. And while air power may be less useful in small-scale warfare, states continue to build their air forces in the event of more large-scale conflicts.

Coordinating Forces: Logistics and Intelligence

All military operations rely heavily on logistical support such as food, fuel, and ordnance (weapons and ammunition). Military logistics is a huge operation, and in most armed forces the majority of soldiers are not combat troops. Global reach capabilities combine long-distance logistical support with various power-projection forces. These capabilities allow a great power to project military power to distant corners of the world and to maintain a military presence in most of the world's regions simultaneously. Only the United States today fully possesses such a capability—with worldwide military alliances, air and naval bases, troops stationed overseas, and aircraft carriers.

Space forces are military forces designed to attack in or from outer space. Ballistic missiles, which travel through space briefly, are not generally included in this category. Only the United States and Russia have substantial military capabilities in space. China put an astronaut in orbit in 2003 and successfully launched a lunar orbiter in 2007, but it has fewer space capabilities overall. The development of space weapons has been constrained by the technical challenges and expenses of space operations and by norms against militarizing space.

The far more common uses of space by the military are for command and coordination purposes. Satellites are used extensively for military purposes. Satellites perform military surveillance and mapping, communications, weather assessment, and early warning of ballistic missile launches. Satellites also provide navigational information to military forces—army units, ships, planes, and even guided missiles in flight. Locations are calculated to within about 50 feet by small receivers, which pick up beacons transmitted from a network of 24 U.S. satellites known as a *Global Positioning System (GPS)*. Handheld receivers are available commercially, so the military forces of other countries can free-ride on these satellite navigation beacons. Poorer states can buy satellite photos on the commercial market—including high-resolution pictures that Russia sells for hard currency. In fact, access to such information has diffused to the point that the terrorists who attacked Mumbai, India, in 2008 planned their attack using satellite images available through Google

Earth and coordinated it in real time from Pakistan using satellite phones. In the 2006 war between Hezbollah and Israel in Lebanon, Hezbollah forces used GPS jammers to complicate Israeli air support and targeting operations. But generally, in outer space, great powers have the advantage over smaller or poorer states.

Intelligence gathering also relies on various other means such as electronic monitoring of telephone lines and other communications, reports from embassies, and information in the open press. The U.S. military operates a massive intelligence-gathering operation, especially for information relevant to battlefield deployments and other tactical matters. Satellite intelligence is supplemented by monitoring a very high volume of electronic communications, such as radio and telephone conversations. Terrorists in remote Afghanistan had to use couriers because the U.S. military could monitor their electronic communications.

The largest U.S. military intelligence agency is the National Security Agency (NSA), whose mission is encoding U.S. communications and breaking the codes of foreign communications. The NSA employs more mathematics Ph.D.s than anyone else in the world, is the second largest electricity consumer in the state of Maryland, has a budget larger than that of the Central Intelligence Agency (CIA), and is believed to have the most powerful computer facility in the world. The various intelligence operations taken together are very large and are growing in importance as the information revolution proceeds and as the war on terrorism makes the NSA's mission more central. The full extent of the NSA's operations were revealed in 2013 when a former NSA contractor leaked millions of documents revealing that the NSA had secretly gathered massive amounts of data, including telephone and Internet records, on American citizens and foreign diplomats. The revelation of these programs led to outrage among U.S. allies and to calls for expanded oversight of spy agencies by the American public.

Evolving Technologies

Technological developments have changed the nature of military force in several ways. First, the resort to force in international conflicts now has more profound costs and consequences. Great powers in particular can no longer use force to settle disputes among themselves without risking massive destruction and economic ruin. Also, military engagements now occur across greater standoff distances between opposing forces. Missiles of all types are accelerating this trend. These technological advances undermine the territorial basis of war and the "hard shell" of the state itself. In recent years, this trend has accelerated with the use of unmanned drone aircraft, including drones armed with missiles, in U.S. military efforts in Pakistan, Yemen, and Libya. In addition to America's thousands of drones, other countries have been rapidly acquiring them. China, Russia, India, Pakistan, Turkey, Italy, Germany, France, and Iran also have heavy and medium-weight attack drones. An Iranian-made drone was shot down over Israel in 2012. Britain and Israel have used drones for attacks, but most drones worldwide are used for surveillance. U.S. underwater sea drones for mine clearing, produced by Germany, were sent to the Persian Gulf in 2012 as tensions with Iran escalated. Drones are now used even by businesses and private citizens. In late 2014, a European soccer match between Serbia and Albania was interrupted by a drone carrying an Albanian nationalist flag flying near midfield. The incident led to diplomatic tension between the two countries.

Electronic warfare (now broadened to *information warfare*) refers to the uses of the electromagnetic spectrum (radio waves, radar, infrared, etc.) in war and is critical to all technologically advanced military forces. *Stealth technology* uses special radar-absorbent materials and unusual shapes in the design of aircraft, missiles, and ships to scatter enemy radar. However, stealth is extremely expensive (the B-2 stealth bomber costs about $2 billion) and is prone to technical problems. Strategies for *cyberwar*—disrupting enemy computer networks to degrade command and control, or even hacking into bank accounts electronically—may figure prominently in future wars, though they have not yet. The United States decided against using cyberattacks to disable Libya's air defenses in 2011 out of fear of the precedent such an action could set. In the future, terrorist attacks also could target computer networks, including the Internet and critical infrastructure such as electric grids.

SMALL IS BEAUTIFUL The information revolution is making smaller weapons and smaller dispersed units more potent. A "revolution in military affairs" is driving changes in U.S. military strategy, including the expanding use of unmanned drones. This insect-size drone shown in 2011 could collect real-time intelligence in complex urban environments.

electronic warfare Use of the electromagnetic spectrum (radio waves, radar, infrared, etc.) in war, such as employing electromagnetic signals for one's own benefit while denying their use to an enemy.

Cyberattacks are an issue of growing importance in international relations, with Chinese, Russian, and American hackers constantly probing each other's systems. In 2010, the U.S.-Israeli Stuxnet virus targeted Iran's nuclear centrifuges, and in 2012, the Flame virus was found on thousands of computers across the Middle East, mostly in Iran. It could grab screenshots and keystrokes, and remotely turn on computer microphones to help the creators (again, presumably Americans and Israelis) spy on operations in the Iranian nuclear program. A few months later, probably in response, a virus deleted files on the computers of a major Saudi oil company, replacing them with an image of a burning American flag. In 2015, the United States and China agreed to stop online surveillance on each other, but many are skeptical whether either side will abide by the agreement.

ASYMMETRICAL CONFLICT Terrorist attacks often reflect the weakness of the perpetrators and their lack of access to other means of leverage. Terror can sometimes amplify a small group's power and affect outcomes. Al Qaeda's September 11, 2001, attacks, staged by a relatively small nonstate actor, ultimately led to the withdrawal of U.S. troops from Saudi Arabia, drew the United States into a counterinsurgency war in Iraq, and brought al Qaeda itself a surge of recruits for new attacks worldwide.

Terrorism

4.5 Assess potential advantages and disadvantages to two different approaches to counterterrorism.

The U.S. State Department listed 59 foreign terrorist organizations in 2015. Some are motivated by religion (for example, al Qaeda) but others by class ideology (for example, Shining Path in Peru) or by ethnic conflict and nationalism (for example, Basque Fatherland and Liberty). Earlier in this chapter (pp. 134–138) we discussed conflicts involving armed Islamist militias and terrorist networks. Here we discuss terrorism itself as a tactic. Since September 2001, governments and citizens have paid much more attention to terrorism than before. But terrorism itself is not new.

Terrorism refers to political violence that targets civilians deliberately and indiscriminately. Beyond this basic definition, other criteria can be applied, but the definitions become politically motivated: One person's freedom fighter is another's terrorist. More than guerrilla warfare, terrorism is a shadowy world of faceless enemies and irregular tactics marked by extreme brutality.

Traditionally, the purpose of terrorism is to demoralize a civilian population in order to use its discontent as leverage on national governments or other parties to a conflict. Related to this is the aim of creating drama in order to gain media attention for a cause. Terrorism is seldom mindless; rather, it is usually a calculated use of violence as leverage. However, motives and means of terrorism vary widely, having in common only that some actor is using violence to influence other actors.

Thus, the primary effect of terrorism is psychological. In part, the effectiveness of terrorism in capturing attention is due to the dramatic nature of the incidents, especially as shown on television news. Terrorism also gains attention because of the randomness of victims. Although only a few dozen people may be injured by a bomb left in a market, millions of people realize "It could have been me" because they, too, shop in markets. Attacks on airplanes augment this fear because many people already fear flying. Terrorism thus amplifies a small amount of power by its psychological effect on large populations; this is why it is usually a tool of the weak. However, al Qaeda's attacks follow a somewhat different pattern, planned less to create fear than simply to kill as many Americans and their allies as possible—and ultimately to touch off apocalyptic violence that al Qaeda followers believe will bring about God's intervention. The psychological effect is aimed at Muslim populations worldwide rather than at Americans.

In the shockingly destructive attack on the World Trade Center, tangible damage was far greater than in previous terrorist attacks—reaching into thousands of lives and tens of billions of dollars. The psychological impact was even stronger than the physical damage—changing the U.S. political and cultural landscape instantly. And the same terrorist network was trying to obtain nuclear weapons (see pp. 160–162) with which to kill not thousands but hundreds of thousands of Americans.

The classic cases of terrorism—from the 1970s to the 2001 attacks—are those in which a *nonstate* actor uses attacks against *civilians* by secret *nonuniformed* forces, operating across *international borders,* as leverage against state actors. Radical political factions or separatist groups hijack or blow up airplanes or plant bombs in cafés, clubs, or other crowded places. For example, Chechen radicals seized a school in Beslan, a small city in the Caucasus region in 2004. For three days, they held nearly 1,200 children, parents, and teachers without food or water. When Russian troops stormed the school, more than 300 people died, including 172 children. Such tactics create spectacular incidents that draw attention to the terrorists' cause. For example, the bombing of the Boston Marathon in 2013 was an unsophisticated attack by two brothers, yet it preoccupied news media for weeks afterward. It is often a tactic of desperation, and it almost always reflects weakness in the power position of the attacker.

Yet the persistence of terrorism is in some ways puzzling because the tactic has a mixed record of success. Suicide bombers were arguably effective at convincing the United States to leave Lebanon in 1983, but the Chechen terrorists' 2004 school attack marked their end as a serious force in Chechnya. The Palestinians did not win a state through terrorism. Videos of beheadings of hostages by ISIS fighters rallied global efforts to defeat that movement in Iraq and Syria. In addition, even large numbers of suicide bombers have yet to be effective at gaining a state for the Tamils in Sri Lanka or providing leverage for Hamas or Islamic Jihad against Israel. Clearly, terrorist activities do not reliably achieve political ends.

Terrorists are more willing than states are to violate the norms of the international system because, unlike states, they do not have a stake in that system. Conversely, when a political group gains some power or legitimacy, its use of terrorism usually diminishes.

Some research has attempted systematically to analyze when particular types of terrorism, such as suicide bombings, are effective at achieving the goals of terrorist organizations. According to one study, suicide bombings, rather than an irrational use of violence by terrorist groups, follow strategic patterns (see Figure 4.8). In particular, they occur most frequently against democracies rather than autocracies, presumably because the attacks are thought to be strongly influenced by public opinion. Still, this same study concludes that this terror tactic has not been particularly successful at achieving significant goals.

Figure 4.8 Location of Suicide Attacks, 1980–2008

Source: Based on Carnegie Corporation of New York.

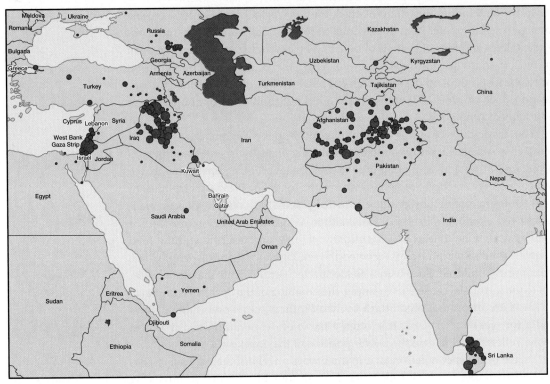

· 1   ● 11–25

● 2–10   ● 26–100   ⬤ 101–410

States themselves carry out acts designed to terrorize their own populations or those of other states, but scholars tend to avoid the label "terrorism" for such acts, preferring to call them repression or war. In fact, no violent act taken during a civil or international war—by or toward a warring party—can necessarily fit neatly into the category of terrorism. The narrowest definition of terrorism would exclude acts either by or against *uniformed military forces* rather than civilians. This definition would exclude the killing of 243 U.S. Marines by a car bomb in Lebanon in 1983 and the 2001 attack on the Pentagon because they were directed at military targets. It would also exclude the bombing of German cities in World War II, although the purpose was to terrorize civilians. But in today's world of undeclared war, guerrilla war, civil war, and ethnic violence, a large gray zone surrounds clear cases of terrorism. Disagreements about whether terrorism included Palestinian attacks on Israel, and Pakistani attacks in Kashmir, scuttled efforts to pass a UN treaty on terrorism in late 2001.

state-sponsored terrorism The use of terrorist groups by states, usually under control of a state's intelligence agency, to achieve political aims.

State-sponsored terrorism refers to the use of terrorist groups by states—usually under control of the state's intelligence agency—to achieve political aims. In 1988, a bomb scattered pieces of Pan Am flight 103 over the Scottish countryside. Combing the fields for debris, investigators found fragments of a tape recorder with a sophisticated plastic explosive bomb. The U.S. and British governments identified the Libyan intelligence agents responsible and, in 1992, backed by the UN Security Council, they demanded that Libya turn over the two agents for trial. When Libya refused, the UN imposed economic sanctions. In 1999, Libya turned over the suspects for trial—two received life in prison while a third was acquitted—and the UN suspended its sanctions. In 2003, Libya formally took responsibility for the bombing, struck a multibillion-dollar compensation deal with victims' families, and regained a normal place in the international community.

As of 2015, the United States has accused three states of supporting international terrorism—Iran, Syria, and Sudan. All have been on the list for more than a decade. The U.S. government has barred U.S. companies from doing business in those states. However, these kinds of unilateral U.S. sanctions are of limited effect. Syria can do business with Egypt, as can Iran with Russia. North Korea was removed from the list in 2008 in exchange for promises to halt its nuclear weapons program. Cuba was removed from the list in 2015 after normalization of relations with the United States.

COUNTERTERRORISM   Just as the methods used by terrorists have become more diverse over the past decades, so have the policies implemented to prevent terrorist incidents. Debates over how best to prevent terrorist attacks are often heated because there are also debates about why individuals engage in terrorist attacks in the first place.

Policies to combat terrorism can be placed along a spectrum involving more or less force in confronting terrorism and terrorist organizations. On the nonviolent end of the spectrum are calls for economic development. Advocates of these programs point out that, in very poor states, people will be especially vulnerable to recruitment by terrorist organizations. With no bright future ahead of them and little opportunities to better themselves, people will naturally lose hope, become angry, and undertake seemingly irrational acts because they feel they have nothing to lose. And although there is little direct evidence that factors like poverty correlate directly with terrorist activities, it is clear that very poor states with weak central governments have served as recruiting grounds for international terrorist organizations.

In the middle of the spectrum are policing activities. These involve efforts by domestic police, usually in cooperation with other countries' police forces, to apprehend or kill terrorists while breaking up terrorist organizations. In one famous example of effective counterterrorist policing, the government of Peru, using an elite investigative team of the national police force, arrested the leader of the Shining Path movement, which at one point controlled over 20,000 well-armed militia members and had assassinated several Peruvian political leaders. The police arrested the movement's leader after staking out a dance studio (which he lived above) and digging through trash from the studio to find clues. After his capture, the Shining Path movement largely collapsed.

At the other end of the counterterrorism spectrum is organized military conflict. States may undertake small- or large-scale conflicts to counter terrorist organizations. In 1998, the United States launched cruise missile strikes against a plant in Sudan believed to be producing chemical weapons for al Qaeda but turned out to be making infant formula. In addition, the U.S.-led war in Afghanistan was a response to the 9/11 attacks on the United States.

Of course, nearly every state that undertakes counterterrorism policies uses some combination of these methods. In the United States, for example, foreign aid is often justified in terms of assisting development and economic growth to decrease the possibility that the poor and uneducated can be drafted easily into terrorist organizations. The FBI and local law enforcement cooperate with many international partners to track and detain suspected terrorists, while U.S. soldiers assist other states with training and weapons in their fight against terrorists. Finally, the war in Afghanistan was a large war undertaken against the Taliban government that had protected al Qaeda.

Weapons of Mass Destruction

4.6 Contrast the effectiveness of the global regime to prevent the spread of nuclear weapons with the global regime to prevent the spread of chemical weapons.

weapons of mass destruction (WMDs) Nuclear, chemical, and biological weapons, all distinguished from conventional weapons by their enormous potential lethality and their relative lack of discrimination in whom they kill.

Weapons of mass destruction (WMDs) comprise three general types: nuclear, chemical, and biological weapons. They are distinguished from conventional weapons by their enormous potential lethality, given their small size and modest costs, and by their relative lack of discrimination in whom they kill. When deployed on ballistic missiles, they can be fired from the home territory of one state and wreak great destruction on the home territory of another state. Until now, this has never happened. But the mere threat of such an action undermines the territorial integrity and security of states in the international system. Of central concern today are the potentials for proliferation—the possession of weapons of mass destruction by more and more states and nonstate actors.

Nuclear Weapons

Nuclear weapons are, in sheer explosive power, the most destructive weapons available to states. A single weapon the size of a refrigerator can destroy a city. Defending against nuclear weapons is extremely difficult at best. To understand the potentials for nuclear proliferation, one has to know something about how nuclear weapons work. There are two types. *Fission* weapons (atomic bombs or A-bombs) are simpler and less expensive than fusion weapons (also called thermonuclear bombs, hydrogen bombs, or H-bombs).

When a fission weapon explodes, one type of atom (element) is split into new types with less total mass. The lost mass is transformed into energy according to Albert Einstein's famous formula, $E = mc^2$, which shows that a little bit of mass is equivalent to a great deal of energy. In fact, the fission bomb that destroyed Nagasaki, Japan, in 1945 converted to energy roughly the amount of mass in a penny.

The two elements that can be split in this way, uranium-235 (U-235) and plutonium, are known as **fissionable material**. Fission weapons work by taking subcritical masses of the fissionable material—amounts not dense enough to start a chain reaction—and compressing them into a critical mass, which explodes. In the simplest design, one piece of uranium is propelled down a tube (by conventional explosives) into another piece of uranium. A more efficient but technically demanding design arranges high explosives precisely around a hollow sphere of plutonium to implode the sphere and create a critical mass.

fissionable material
The elements uranium-235 and plutonium, whose atoms split apart and release energy via a chain reaction when an atomic bomb explodes.

Although these designs require sophisticated engineering, they are well within the capabilities of many states and some private groups. The obstacle is obtaining fissionable material. Only 10 to 100 pounds or less are required for each bomb, but even these small amounts are not easily obtained. U-235, which can be used in the simplest bomb designs, is especially difficult to make. Extracting the fissionable U-235, referred to as enriching the uranium up to weapons grade (or high grade), is slow, expensive, and technically complex—a major obstacle to proliferation. But North Korea, Iran, Iraq, and Libya all built infrastructure to do so in recent years. North Korea promised to end its uranium program and dismantle its nuclear complex (after testing a plutonium bomb in 2006 and 2009), but by 2015, experts estimated North Korea would possess over 100 bombs by 2020. In 2015, Iran reached an agreement with the five permanent members of the UN Security Council (plus Germany) that allowed it to continue to process uranium to low levels of enrichment while allowing international inspections of nuclear sites. Skeptics of the agreement worry that Iran will not comply with the deal, while advocates argue that even if Iran continues to work on a weapon, its program will be slowed by many years.

Plutonium is more easily produced, which can be done from low-grade uranium in nuclear power reactors. But a plutonium bomb is more difficult to build than a uranium one—another obstacle to proliferation. Plutonium is also used in commercial breeder reactors, which Japan and other countries have built recently—another source of fissionable material.

Fusion weapons are extremely expensive and technically demanding; they are for only the richest, largest, most technologically capable states. Here, two small atoms (variants of hydrogen) fuse together into a larger atom, releasing energy. This reaction occurs only at very high temperatures (the sun "burns" hydrogen through fusion). Weapons designers use fission weapons to create these high energies and trigger an explosive fusion reaction. The explosive power of fusion weapons can reach hundreds of times that of fission nuclear weapons. In the post–Cold War era, such megabombs have become irrelevant because they are too powerful for any actor to use productively and too difficult for terrorists or small states to build.

Ballistic Missiles and Other Delivery Systems

Delivery systems for getting nuclear weapons to their targets—much more than the weapons themselves—are the basis of states' nuclear arsenals and strategies (discussed shortly). Inasmuch as nuclear warheads can be made quite small—weighing a few hundred pounds or even less—they are adaptable to a wide variety of delivery systems.

During the Cold War, nuclear delivery systems were divided into two categories. *Strategic* weapons could hit an enemy's homeland. *Tactical* nuclear weapons were designed for battlefield use. Both superpowers integrated tactical nuclear weapons into their conventional air, sea, and land forces using a variety of delivery systems—gravity bombs, artillery shells, short-range missiles, land-mines, depth charges, and so forth.

However, the tens of thousands of nuclear warheads integrated into super-power conventional forces posed dangers such as theft or accident. Their actual use would have entailed grave risks of escalation to strategic nuclear war, putting home cities at risk. Thus, both superpowers phased out tactical nuclear weapons almost entirely when the Cold War ended.

The main strategic delivery vehicles are **ballistic missiles**; unlike airplanes, they are extremely difficult to defend against. Ballistic missiles carry a warhead up along a trajectory—typically out of the atmosphere, at least 50 miles high—before descending. In addition, some missiles fire from fixed sites (silos), whereas others are mobile, firing from railroads or large trailer trucks (making them hard to target). The longest-range missiles are **intercontinental ballistic missiles (ICBMs)**, with ranges of more than 5,000 miles.

Of special interest today are short-range ballistic missiles (SRBMs), with ranges under 1,000 miles. In regional conflicts, the long range of more powerful missiles may not be necessary. The largest cities of Syria and Israel are only 133 miles from each other; the capital cities of Iraq and Iran are less than 500 miles apart, as are those of India and Pakistan. All of these states are among the 33 that own ballistic missiles. Short-range and some medium-range ballistic missiles are cheap enough to be bought or made by small middle-income states.

Many short-range ballistic missiles are highly inaccurate but still very difficult to defend against. With conventional warheads, they have more psychological than military utility (demoralizing an enemy population). With nuclear, chemical, or biological warheads, however, these missiles could be deadlier. The **cruise missile** is a small winged missile that can navigate across thousands of miles of previously mapped terrain to reach a target. Cruise missiles can be launched from ships, submarines, airplanes, or land.

The proliferation of ballistic missiles has been difficult to control. Through the **Missile Technology Control Regime**, industrialized states try to limit the

---

ballistic missiles
The major strategic delivery vehicle for nuclear weapons; it carries a warhead along a trajectory (typically rising at least 50 miles high) and lets it drop on the target.

intercontinental ballistic missiles (ICBMs) The longest-range ballistic missiles, able to travel 5,000 miles.

cruise missile A small winged missile that can navigate across thousands of miles of previously mapped terrain to reach a particular target; it can carry either a nuclear or a conventional warhead.

Missile Technology Control Regime A set of agreements through which industrialized states try to limit the flow of missile-relevant technology to developing countries.

flow of missile-relevant technology to states in the global South, but they have had limited success. Short- and medium-range missiles (with ranges up to about 2,000 miles) apparently are being developed by Iran, Israel, Saudi Arabia, Pakistan, India, North Korea, and possibly Argentina and Brazil. In 2008, Iran alarmed the West by testing a missile that could reach Israel, Egypt, and parts of Europe. In 2012, North Korea, evidently in cooperation with Iran, successfully tested a long-range missile capable of transcontinental distances.

Small states or terrorists that acquired nuclear weapons could deliver them through innovative means such as by car, by boat, or in diplomatic pouches. The United States runs a Container Security Initiative aimed at preventing weapons of mass destruction from reaching U.S. shores in seaborne shipping containers. But doing so without impeding international trade is a daunting challenge.

Chemical and Biological Weapons

A *chemical weapon* releases chemicals that disable and kill people. The chemicals vary from lethal ones such as nerve gas to merely irritating ones such as tear gas. Different chemicals interfere with the nervous system, blood, breathing, or other body functions. Some can be absorbed through the skin; others must be inhaled. Some persist in the target area long after their use; others disperse quickly.

It is possible to defend against most chemical weapons by dressing troops in protective clothing and gas masks and following elaborate procedures to decontaminate equipment. But protective suits are hot, and antichemical measures reduce the efficiency of armies. Civilians are much less likely to have protection against chemicals than are military forces. Chemical weapons are by nature indiscriminate about whom they kill. Several times, chemical weapons have been used deliberately against civilians (notably by the Iraqi government against Iraqi Kurds in the 1980s).

Use of chemical weapons in war has been rare. Mustard gas, which produces skin blisters and lung damage, was widely used in World War I. After the horrors of that war, the use of chemical weapons was banned in the 1925 Geneva Protocol, which is still in effect today. In World War II, both sides were armed with chemical weapons but neither used them for fear of retaliation (the same was true in the Gulf War). Since then (with possibly a few unclear exceptions), only Iraq

VULNERABLE Civilians are more vulnerable to chemical weapons than soldiers are. A treaty aims to ban chemical weapons worldwide. Here, Israeli kindergarteners prepare against a chemical warfare threat from Iraqi Scud missiles during the Gulf War, 1991.

has violated the treaty—against Iran in the 1980s. Unfortunately, Iraq's actions not only breached a psychological barrier against using chemical weapons but also showed such weapons to be cheap and effective against human waves of attackers without protective gear. This stimulated dozens more poor states to begin acquiring chemical weapons.

Chemical weapons are a cheap way for states to gain weapons of mass destruction. Production of chemical weapons can use similar processes and facilities as for pesticides, pharmaceuticals, and other civilian products, which makes it difficult to find chemical weapons facilities in suspect countries or to deny those states access to the needed chemicals and equipment.

Chemical Weapons Convention (1992) An agreement that bans the production and possession of chemical weapons and includes strict verification provisions and the threat of sanctions against violators and nonparticipants in the treaty.

The 1925 Geneva Protocol did not ban the production or possession of chemical weapons, only their use, and several dozen states built stockpiles of them. The United States and the Soviet Union maintained large arsenals of chemical weapons during the Cold War but have reduced them greatly in the past decade. The 1992 **Chemical Weapons Convention** to ban the production and possession of chemical weapons has been signed by all the great powers and nearly all other states, with a few exceptions, including Egypt, Angola, and North Korea. The new treaty includes strict verification provisions and the threat of sanctions against violators, including (an important extension) those who are nonparticipants in the treaty. From 1997 to 2014, the treaty organization oversaw the elimination of more than half of the world's chemical weapons (nearly 60,000 metric tons). In 2013, Syria admitted to possessing chemical weapons and agreed to the destruction of its weapons that were used against rebel groups in that country's civil war.

Biological weapons resemble chemical ones, but they use deadly microorganisms or biologically derived toxins. Some use viruses or bacteria that cause fatal diseases, such as smallpox, bubonic plague, and anthrax. Others cause nonfatal, but incapacitating, diseases or diseases that kill livestock. Theoretically, a single weapon could spark an epidemic in an entire population, but this would pose too great a danger, so less contagious microorganisms are preferred.

Biological Weapons Convention (1972) An agreement that prohibits the development, production, and possession of biological weapons but makes no provision for inspections.

Biological weapons have rarely been used in war (Japan tried some on a few Chinese villages in World War II). Their potential strikes many political leaders as a Pandora's box that could let loose uncontrollable forces if opened. Thus, the development, production, and possession of biological weapons are banned by the 1972 **Biological Weapons Convention**, signed by more than 100 countries, including the great powers. The superpowers destroyed their stocks of biological weapons and had to restrict their biological weapons complexes to defensive research rather than the development of weapons. However, because the treaty makes no provision for inspection and because biological weapons programs are, like chemical ones, relatively easy to hide, several states remain under suspicion of having biological weapons. UN inspections of Iraq in the mid-1990s uncovered an active biological weapons program. Evidence surfaced after the collapse of the Soviet Union that a secret biological weapons program had been under way there as well. Today, the United States and perhaps a dozen other countries maintain biological weapons research (not banned by the treaty). Researchers try to ascertain the military implications of advances in biotechnology.

Proliferation

Proliferation is the spread of weapons of mass destruction—nuclear weapons, ballistic missiles, and chemical or biological weapons—into the hands of more actors. The implications of proliferation for international relations are difficult to predict but clearly profound. Ballistic missiles with weapons of mass destruction remove the territorial protection offered by state borders and make each state vulnerable to others. Some realists, who believe in rationality, reason that in a world where the use of military force could lead to mutual annihilation, there would be fewer wars—just as during the arms race of the Cold War, the superpowers did not blow each other up. Other IR scholars who put less faith in the rationality of state leaders are much more alarmed by proliferation. They fear that, with more and more nuclear (or chemical/biological) actors, miscalculation or accident—or fanatical terrorism—could lead to disaster.

proliferation The spread of weapons of mass destruction (nuclear, chemical, or biological weapons) into the hands of more actors.

The leaders of the great powers tend to side with the second group. They have tried to restrict weapons of mass destruction to the great powers. Proliferation erodes the great powers' advantage relative to middle powers. There is also a widespread fear that these weapons may fall into the hands of terrorists or other nonstate actors who would be immune from threats of retaliation (with no territory or cities to defend). Evidence captured during the 2001 war in Afghanistan showed that al Qaeda was trying to obtain weapons of mass destruction and would be willing to use them. Lax security at the vast, far-flung former Soviet nuclear complex increased fears that fissionable materials could reach terrorists.

SOMETHING TO HIDE The most important hurdle in making nuclear weapons is access to fissionable materials (plutonium and uranium). Iran's enrichment of uranium could give that country nuclear bombs within the decade. Fueling Western suspicions, Iran has not been forthcoming with international inspectors. Iran bulldozed this large site and removed its topsoil in 2004 before letting inspectors in. Western states and the UN Security Council have applied sanctions against Iran, and a controversial nuclear deal was agreed to in 2015.

Nuclear proliferation could occur simply by a state or nonstate actor's buying (or stealing) one or more nuclear weapons or the components to build one. The means to prevent this include covert intelligence, tight security measures, and safeguards to prevent a stolen weapon from being used. In 2007, two teams of armed assailants broke into the South African nuclear facility where atomic bombs had once been designed and produced. After reaching the control room and shooting one guard, they were repelled, leaving a mystery along with doubts about the security of such nuclear facilities. As political unrest occurs in nuclear states, notably Pakistan, thoughts often turn toward the safety of nuclear weapons.

A stronger form of nuclear proliferation is the development by states of nuclear complexes to produce their own nuclear weapons on an ongoing basis. Here, larger numbers of weapons are involved and strong potentials exist for arms races in regional conflicts and rivalries. The relevant regional conflicts are those between Israel and the Arab states, Iran and its neighbors, India and Pakistan, the two Koreas, and possibly Taiwan and China. India and Pakistan each have dozens of nuclear weapons and the missiles to deliver them. North Korea tested bombs in 2006, 2009, and 2013. In addition, South Africa reported in 1993 that it had built several nuclear weapons but then dismantled them in the 1980s (before white minority rule ended).

Israel has never officially admitted that it has nuclear weapons, but it is widely believed to have a hundred or more. Israel wants these capabilities to convince Arab leaders that military conquest of Israel is impossible. In 2007, Israeli warplanes destroyed a site in Syria thought to be a nuclear reactor of North Korean design. Syria quickly cleared all traces of the building after the attack.

Non-Proliferation Treaty (NPT) (1968)
A treaty that created a framework for controlling the spread of nuclear materials and expertise, including the International Atomic Energy Agency (IAEA), a UN agency based in Vienna that is charged with inspecting the nuclear power industry in NPT member states to prevent secret military diversions of nuclear materials.

The **Non-Proliferation Treaty (NPT)** of 1968 created a framework for controlling the spread of nuclear materials and expertise. The International Atomic Energy Agency (IAEA), a UN agency based in Vienna, is charged with inspecting the nuclear power industry in member states to prevent secret military diversions of nuclear materials. However, a number of potential nuclear states (such as Israel) have not signed the NPT, and even states that have signed may sneak around its provisions by keeping some facilities secret (as Iraq and Iran did). In 2006, a deal between the United States and India to share nuclear technology led many states to question the NPT because those benefits were supposedly reserved for signatories only. Nonetheless, the deal received final U.S. and Indian approval in 2008.

North Korea withdrew from the IAEA in 1993 and then bargained with Western leaders to get economic assistance, including safer reactors, in exchange for freezing its nuclear program. North Korea's leader died months later, but the compromise held up. In 1999, North Korea allowed inspection of a disputed underground complex and agreed to suspend missile tests in exchange for aid and partial lifting of U.S. trade sanctions. Then, in 2002, the United States confronted North Korea with evidence of a secret uranium enrichment program, which the North Koreans then admitted. North Korea then pulled out of the agreement and out of the IAEA, restarted its nuclear reactor, and apparently turned its existing plutonium into a half-dozen bombs within months, one of which was tested in 2006. North Korea again agreed to give up its program in 2008, yet after another nuclear test in 2009, it began processing nuclear material again. It tested another device in 2013.

Iran denies, but appears to be, working to develop nuclear weapons. Since 2003, Iran first agreed to suspend its uranium enrichment program and allow surprise IAEA inspections, and then it restarted enrichment, suspended it again, and restarted it again. In 2005, U.S.-backed efforts by Europe to reach a deal faltered. In 2006, the UN Security Council condemned Iran's actions and imposed mild sanctions. Iran insisted on its right to enrich uranium for what it called peaceful purposes. In 2008, Iran's behavior led to further UN Security Council sanctions, and in 2009, after a secret underground processing facility was discovered, Iran was engaged in talks over the program with Western powers. An interim deal was reached in late 2013 whereby Iran agreed to slow uranium processes in exchange for relief from sanctions. A final deal was reached in mid-2015 that allowed Iran to continue enrichment of uranium, but only to low levels that could not be used to make a weapon. Iran also agreed to allow increased inspections of its nuclear sites. In exchange, Western powers agreed to lift sanctions against Iran, although some of these sanctions will not be lifted until Iran dismantles certain parts of its nuclear program.

Nuclear Strategy and Arms Control

The term *nuclear strategy* refers to decisions about how many nuclear weapons to deploy, what delivery systems to put them on, and what policies to adopt regarding their possible use. The main reason for possessing nuclear weapons is to deter another state from a nuclear or conventional attack by threatening ruinous retaliation. Under **mutually assured destruction (MAD)**, neither side can prevent the other from destroying it. The acronym implies that the strategy, though "rational," is actually insane (mad) because it could destroy both sides.

Defense has played little role in nuclear strategy to date because no effective defense against missile attack exists. However, the United States is spending billions of dollars a year to try to develop defenses that could shoot down incoming ballistic missiles. The program is called the **Strategic Defense Initiative (SDI)**, or Star Wars.

In 2004, the United States began deploying both a prototype missile intercept system based in Alaska and a destroyer in the Sea of Japan that could try to shoot down a North Korean missile in its boost phase. It also moved to put in place—against strong Chinese opposition—a missile-defense collaboration in Asia that would include Japan, Australia, possibly India, and Taiwan. Four Japanese destroyers are to join the U.S. one, and Patriot missiles based in Japan would try to shoot down incoming missiles. But North Korea has more than 600 ballistic missiles capable of hitting Japan.

The United States is deploying a multilayer system with 24 ground-based interceptor missiles in Alaska and California (directed toward the North Korean threat), 21 ship-based interceptors, about 500 Patriot missiles for short-range ballistic missile threats, and a series of radars and control centers. It is testing an airplane-based laser system and had concluded agreements with Poland and the Czech Republic to build missile defenses in those countries before reversing these plans in favor of a sea-based system to guard against any Iranian threat with a radar system based in Turkey. In 2012 and 2014, Israel used a new "Iron Dome" defense system to shoot down short-range missiles fired by Hamas in large numbers.

mutually assured destruction (MAD) The possession of second-strike nuclear capabilities, which ensures that neither of two adversaries could prevent the other from destroying it in an all-out war.

Strategic Defense Initiative (SDI) A U.S. effort, also known as Star Wars, to develop defenses that could shoot down incoming ballistic missiles. It was spurred by President Ronald Reagan in 1983.

During the Cold War, the superpowers' nuclear forces grew and technologies developed. These evolving force structures were codified by a series of arms control agreements. *Arms control* is an effort by two or more states to regulate by formal agreement their acquisition of weapons, using the reciprocity principle to solve the collective goods problem of expensive arms races that ultimately benefit neither side (see p. 6). Arms control is broader than just nuclear weapons—for instance, after World War I, the great powers negotiated limits on sizes of navies—but in the Cold War, nuclear weapons were the main focus of arms control. Arms control agreements typically require long, formal negotiations with many technical discussions, culminating in a treaty. Some arms control treaties are multilateral, but during the Cold War, most were bilateral (U.S.-Soviet). Some stay in effect indefinitely; others have a limited term.

Several treaties in the 1970s locked in the superpowers' basic parity in nuclear capabilities under MAD. The U.S. arsenal peaked in the 1960s at more than 30,000 warheads; the Soviet arsenal peaked in the 1980s at more than 40,000. More recent arms control agreements substantially reduced nuclear forces after the end of the Cold War. Under the 2002 U.S.-Russian Strategic Offensive Reductions Treaty, each side was to reduce deployed warheads from about 6,000 to 2,200. In March 2010, the sides signed a treaty (referred to as New START), which will further lower the number of warheads to 1,550 and also create additional verification mechanisms. Overall, the U.S. and Russian nuclear arsenals are down to one-third of their peak levels and dropping, and the majority of remaining warheads are not deployed. The reciprocity principle that helped fuel the arms race also enables its step-by-step reversal.

China, France, and Britain each have several hundred weapons—France's and Britain's mostly on submarine-launched missiles and China's mostly on long-range bombers and intermediate-range missiles.

Comprehensive Test Ban Treaty (CTBT) (1996) A treaty that bans all nuclear weapons testing, thereby broadening the ban on atmospheric testing negotiated in 1963.

A **Comprehensive Test Ban Treaty (CTBT)** to halt all nuclear test explosions was signed in 1996 after decades of stalemate. It aims to impede the development of new types of nuclear weapons. However, the treaty does not take effect until signed and ratified by all 44 states believed capable of building at least a crude nuclear weapon. India did not sign the CTBT and defied it in 1998 with five nuclear tests. Pakistan followed suit with its own tests. The U.S. Senate voted in 1999 against ratifying the CTBT. Russia ratified it in 2000. Although no nuclear tests occurred worldwide in 1999–2005, North Korea's nuclear tests in 2006, 2009, and 2013 dealt more setbacks to the CTBT.

Efforts to control *conventional* arms trade through arms control treaties have had little success. In the early 1990s, the five permanent members of the Security Council, which account for most weapons sales to the Middle East, tried to negotiate limits on the supply of weapons to that region. But no participant wanted to give up its own lucrative arms sales to the region, which each naturally saw as justified (again, showing the difficulty of overcoming collective goods problems).

All the weapons of mass destruction are relatively difficult and expensive to build, yet they provide only specialized capabilities that are rarely if ever actually used. This is why most states that could technically acquire them have decided not to do so. Such cost-benefit thinking also applies more broadly to states' decisions about the acquisition of all kinds of military forces.

States and Militaries

4.7 Explain how tensions in civil-military relations can undermine military operations and even threaten political stability.

Given the range of military capabilities available to states (at various costs), how many and what types should state leaders choose to acquire? This question confronts all states, but they answer it in different ways.

Military Economics

States vary widely in military spending, from Costa Rica, with almost no military spending at all, to North Korea, which devotes 20 percent or more of all economic activity to military purposes. If military budgets are too low, states may be unprepared to meet a security threat. But if leaders set military budgets too high, they will overburden the national economy in the long run.

World military spending is about 2.4 percent of the total goods and services in the world economy—about $1.8 trillion every year, or roughly $1 million every 20 seconds. Most is spent by a few big states, about 40 percent by the United States alone. (U.S. spending is expected to fall steadily in the coming years as its wars end, but other countries are increasing their spending rapidly.) World military spending is a vast flow of money that could, if redirected to other purposes, change the world profoundly and improve major world problems. Of course, "the world" does not spend this money or choose how to direct it; states do. World military spending decreased by about one-third overall in the 1990s, although it slowly began to increase again after 1998 and has jumped back up by one-quarter since 2001.

INTO THE STREETS Through a hierarchical chain of command, states control the actions of millions of individual soldiers, creating leverage in the hands of state leaders. But armed forces still sometimes defy civilian control. Here, an anti-coup protester in Thailand berates soldiers after a military coup in that country, 2014.

Most arms sales worldwide go to the global South. In recent decades, about half of these arms imports have been in the Middle East, but lately, India and China have taken a growing share. The great majority of international arms exports come from the United States, with Russia, France, and Britain also ranking. In the immediate post–Cold War era, global arms sales fell but have since climbed back to near–Cold War levels.

Activists have called attention to the sales of small arms, especially assault rifles, to unstable conflict zones where irregular armies commit brutalities. In 2001, 140 states agreed to a voluntary pact to curb small-arms sales to conflict zones. In the fall of 2009, the UN General Assembly voted nearly unanimously to begin work on an Arms Trade Treaty. The treaty passed the General Assembly in 2013 with only Iran, North Korea, and Syria voting no. The treaty entered into force in December 2014. While 73 countries have ratified the treaty, ratification by the U.S. Senate appears unlikely.

Control of Military Forces

military governments States in which military forces control the government; they are most common in poor countries, where the military may be the only large modern institution.

coup d'état The seizure of political power by domestic military forces—that is, a change of political power outside the state's constitutional order.

civil-military relations The relations between a state's civilian leaders and the military leadership. In most countries, the military takes orders from civilian leaders. In extreme cases, poor civil-military relations can lead to military coups.

Although militaries are instruments of state power, in many states the military forces themselves control the government. These **military governments** are mostly in the global South, where the military may be the only large modern institution in a country. A **coup d'état** is the seizure of political power by domestic military forces—a change of political power outside the state's constitutional order. In 2014, military leaders took power in Thailand, deposing its leaders. Coup leaders move quickly to seize centers of power—official state buildings as well as television stations and transmitters—before other units of the military can put down the coup attempt or unleash a civil war. Civilian politicians in power and uncooperative military officers are arrested or killed. The coup leaders try to create a sense of inevitability around the change in government while claiming their actions will bring long-term stability.

CIVIL-MILITARY RELATIONS   Beyond overcoming chaos and complexity, state leaders sometimes must confront challenges from within their own military ranks as well. Many states, especially democratic states, adhere to a principle of *civilian supremacy*. This is the idea that civilian leaders (who are either elected or appointed) are at the top of the chain of command. Civilians, not military officers, decide when and where the military fights. The officers, by contrast, are supposed to control how the military fights.

This division of labor between civilians and militaries inevitably leads to tensions. The interaction of civilian with military leaders—called **civil-military relations**—is an important factor in how states use force. Military leaders may undermine the authority of civilian leaders in carrying out foreign policies, or they may even threaten civilian supremacy if certain actions are taken in international conflicts. Military officers also want autonomy of decision once force is committed in order to avoid the problems created in the Vietnam War when President Johnson sat in the White House situation room daily picking targets for bombing raids. Even more complicated was NATO's 1999 bombing of Serbia, where specific targets had to be approved by politicians in multiple countries. In

2010, the commanding American general in Afghanistan lost his job after publically questioning President Obama's Afghanistan policies.

Even outside the context of ongoing warfare, differences between civilian and military leaders can lead to tensions. Opinion surveys consistently show that U.S. military officers, on average, maintain different opinions than civilians on issues such as the use of force as a tool of leverage. Scholars have begun to study why this gap between civilians and the military has developed and its implications for American foreign policy.

Similar tensions exist in other democracies. In Turkey, tensions have grown between the Islamic government and its military. Historically, Turkey's military has intervened numerous times to take control from elected leaders when military officers felt the government was threatening the secular nature of Turkey. Recently, however, the civilian government has been aggressive at arresting officers who they believe may be plotting a coup. These actions have led to a fragile situation in that country. In the 2011 Arab Spring, the Egyptian military refused to fire on protesters, yet in 2013 it deposed Egypt's Islamist president and assumed control of the government.

Overall, states face complex choices regarding the configuration of their military forces. Despite the threat of conflict or war and the importance of security concerns, trade, money, and business are playing more and more powerful roles in international relations. In the next chapter, we move to a discussion of the politics of international economic activities, the world monetary system, and the role of private companies as nonstate actors in the world economy.

Chapter Review

Summary

- Wars vary greatly in size and character, from guerrilla wars and raids to hegemonic war for leadership of the international system. Currently, 15 wars are in progress, mostly small to intermediate in size, all pitting a regular state army against local rebels or militias.

- Many theories have been offered as general explanations of the causes of war, but political scientists cannot reliably predict the outbreak of war.

- Ethnic conflicts, especially when linked with territorial disputes, are very difficult to resolve because of psychological biases.

- Fundamentalist religious movements pose a broad challenge to the rules of the international system in general and to state sovereignty in particular.

- Territorial disputes are among the most serious international conflicts because states place great value on territorial integrity. With a few exceptions, however, almost all the world's borders are now firmly fixed and internationally recognized.

- Military spending tends to stimulate economic growth in the short term but reduce growth over the long term. In the 1990s, military forces and expenditures of the great powers—especially Russia—were reduced and restructured. Since then, U.S. defense spending has risen back to Cold War–era levels.

- Control of territory is fundamental to state sovereignty and is accomplished primarily with ground forces.

- Air war, using precision-guided bombs against battlefield targets, proved extremely effective in the U.S. campaigns in Iraq in 1991, Serbia in 1999, Afghanistan in 2001, and Iraq in 2003.

- A "revolution in military affairs" uses new information technologies to enhance the power of small units.

- The 2001 attacks on the United States differed from earlier terrorism in both their scale of destruction and the long reach of the global al Qaeda terrorist network.

- The production of nuclear weapons is technically within the means of many states and some nonstate actors, but the necessary fissionable material (uranium-235 or plutonium) is very difficult to obtain. Most industrialized states, and many poor ones, have refrained voluntarily from acquiring nuclear weapons.

- Slowing the proliferation of ballistic missiles and weapons of mass destruction in the global South is a central concern of the great powers.

- The United States is testing systems to defend against ballistic missile attack, although none has yet proven feasible, and withdrew from the ABM Treaty with Russia to pursue this program.

- The United States and Russia have arsenals of thousands of nuclear weapons; China, Britain, and France have hundreds; Israel, India, and Pakistan each have scores.

- North Korea apparently has six nuclear weapons and has tested three, one each in 2006, 2009, and 2013. Iran has a nuclear program which it will reduce after an agreement with the great powers in 2015.

Key Terms

hegemonic war 116
total war 118
limited war 118
civil war 118
guerrilla war 118
truth commissions 120
conflict 120
nationalism 123
ethnic groups 125
genocide 126
ethnocentrism 127

secular 130
Islam 130
Muslims 130
Islamist 130
irredentism 140
ethnic cleansing 141
territorial waters 144
airspace 145
counterinsurgency 149
landmines 150
power projection 151

electronic warfare 155
state-sponsored
    terrorism 158
weapons of mass destruction
    (WMDs) 160
fissionable material 161
ballistic missiles 162
intercontinental
    ballistic missiles
    (ICBMs) 162
cruise missile 162

Critical Thinking Questions

1. How many of the six types of international conflict discussed in this chapter can you connect with the phenomenon of nationalism discussed on pages 123–124? What are the connections in each case?

2. The rise of fundamentalism among the world's major religions challenges traditional notions of state sovereignty. How might this trend strengthen, or weaken, the United Nations and other attempts to create supranational authority (which also challenge state sovereignty)?

3. Most of the great powers are reconfiguring their military forces in the post–Cold War era. What kinds of capabilities do you think your own country needs in this period? Why?

Chapter 5
Trade and Finance

WORLD'S LARGEST CONTAINER SHIP DOCKS IN GREAT BRITAIN, 2015.

 Learning Objectives

5.1 Describe three policies that interfere with the free trade of goods and services in international markets.

5.2 Identify at least one factor behind the current impasse in World Trade Organization (WTO) negotiations in the Doha Round.

5.3   Describe at least two ways in which countries or individual citizens resist global trade.

5.4   Summarize the three types of exchange rate systems adopted by states.

5.5   Explain three reasons why states go into debt.

5.6   Identify two risks to firms who engage in foreign direct investment and two risks to countries who host foreign direct investment.

Theories of Trade

5.1   **Describe three policies that interfere with the free trade of goods and services in international markets.**

International trade amounts to about one-sixth of the total economic activity in the world. Around $19 trillion worth of goods and services cross international borders each year. This is a very large number, about 11 times the world's military spending. The great volume of international trade reflects the fact that trade is profitable.

The role of trade in the economy varies somewhat from one nation to another, but overall, it is at least as important in the global South as in the industrialized North. The global South accounts for a relatively small part of all trade in the world economy, but this is because its economic activity is only 45 percent of the world total (see p. 22).

Trade is not only an economic issue but a highly political one. It crosses state-defined borders, is regulated by states that are pressured by interest groups, and occurs within trade regimes maintained and negotiated among states.

Scholars of *international political economy (IPE)* study the politics of international economic activities. The most frequently studied of these activities are trade, monetary relations, and multinational corporations. Most scholars of IPE focus on the industrialized regions of the world, where most of the world's economic activity occurs. However, the global South has received growing attention as globalization integrates parts of the South into the world economy more intensely (see Chapter 7).

The core principles laid out in Chapter 1 and the concepts of power and bargaining developed initially in Chapter 2 apply to IPE. States are the most important actors in IPE, but they are not as important as in international security. Actors in IPE, as in security affairs, tend to act in their own interests. As Brazil's foreign minister explained in 2001, his country shared with the United States the same guiding principle in negotiating a hemisphere-wide free trade area: "What's in it for us?"

Liberalism and Mercantilism

mercantilism An economic theory and a political ideology opposed to free trade; it shares with realism the belief that each state must protect its own interests without seeking mutual gains through international organizations.

Two major approaches within IPE differ on their views of trade. One approach, called **mercantilism**, generally shares with realism the belief that each state must protect its own interests at the expense of others—not relying on international organizations to create a framework for mutual gains. Mercantilists therefore emphasize relative power (as do realists): What matters is not so much a state's absolute amount of well-being as its position relative to rival states.

In addition, mercantilism (like realism) holds that the importance of economic transactions lies in their implications for the military. States worry about relative wealth and trade because these can be translated directly into military power. Although military power is generally not useful in economic negotiations, mercantilists believe that the outcome of economic negotiations matters for military power.

economic liberalism In the context of IPE, an approach that generally shares the assumption of anarchy (the lack of a world government) but does not see this condition as precluding extensive cooperation to realize common gains from economic exchanges. It emphasizes absolute over relative gains and, in practice, a commitment to free trade, free capital flows, and an "open" world economy.

Economic liberalism, an alternative approach, generally shares with liberal internationalism a belief in the possibility of cooperation to realize common gains (see pp. 5–6 and pp. 70–71). It holds that, by building international organizations, institutions, and norms, states can mutually benefit from economic exchanges. It matters little to liberals whether one state gains more or less than another—just whether the state's wealth is increasing in *absolute* terms.

Liberalism and mercantilism are *theories* of economics and also *ideologies* that shape state policies. Liberalism is the dominant approach in Western economics, though more so in *microeconomics* (the study of firms and households) than in *macroeconomics* (the study of national economies). Marxism is often treated as a third theoretical/ideological approach to IPE, along with mercantilism and liberalism (see Chapter 3). Marxist approaches are attuned to economic exploitation as a force that shapes political relations. Chapter 7 explores Marxist theories in depth because they find their greatest explanatory power in North-South relations.

Most international economic exchanges (as well as security relationships) contain some element of mutual interests—joint gains that can be realized through cooperation—and some element of conflicting interests. Game theorists call this a "mixed interest" game. In international trade, even when two states both benefit from a trade (a shared interest), one or the other will benefit more (a conflicting interest). Liberalism emphasizes the shared interests in economic exchanges, whereas mercantilism emphasizes the conflicting interests. For liberals, the most important goal of economic policy is to create a maximum of total wealth by achieving optimal *efficiency* (maximizing output, minimizing waste). For mercantilists, the most important goal is to create the most favorable possible *distribution* of wealth.

Liberalism sees individual households and firms as the key actors in the economy and views government's most useful role as one of noninterference in economics except to regulate markets in order to help them function efficiently (and to create infrastructure such as roads, which also help the economy function efficiently). Politics, in this view, should serve the interests of economic efficiency.

With the hand of government removed from markets, the "invisible hand" of supply and demand can work out the most efficient patterns of production, exchange, and consumption (through the mechanism of prices). Because of the benefits of **free trade** among countries, liberals disdain realists' obsession with international borders because borders constrain the maximum efficiency of exchange.

The distribution of benefits from trade may not be divided equally among participating states. Liberal economists are interested in maximizing the overall (joint) benefits from exchange rather than how total benefits are distributed among the parties (see Figure 5.1).

When two or more states are simultaneously dependent on each other, they are *interdependent*. **Interdependence** is a political and not just an economic phenomenon. States that trade become mutually dependent on each other's *political* cooperation in order to realize economic gains through trade. In IPE, interdependence refers less often to a *bilateral* mutual dependence than to a *multilateral* dependence in which each state depends on the political cooperation of most or all of the others to keep world markets operating efficiently. Trade-based wealth depends on international political cooperation, and violence usually does not work well in pursuing such wealth. Thus, liberals argue that interdependence inherently promotes peace, an idea introduced earlier (pp. 75–76). (Then again, some observers saw similar trends in international interdependence just before World War I, but war occurred anyway.)

free trade The flow of goods and services across national boundaries unimpeded by tariffs or other restrictions; in principle (if not always in practice), free trade was a key aspect of Britain's policy after 1846 and of U.S. policy after 1945.

interdependence A political and economic situation in which two states are simultaneously dependent on each other for their well-being. The degree of interdependence is sometimes designated in terms of "sensitivity" or "vulnerability."

Figure 5.1 Joint and Individual Benefits

Any deal struck, such as at point A, yields certain benefits to each actor (dotted lines). Joint benefits are maximized at the Pareto-optimal frontier, but the distribution of those benefits, as between points B and C (both of which are better than A for both actors), is a matter for bargaining. Liberalism is more concerned with joint benefits, mercantilism more with the relative distribution.

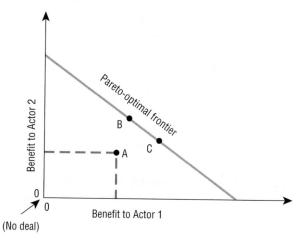

Mercantilists' preferred means of making trade serve a state's political interests—even at the cost of some lost wealth that free markets might have created—is to create a favorable balance of trade. The **balance of trade** is the value of a state's imports relative to its exports. A state that exports more than it imports has a *positive balance of trade,* or *trade surplus.* A state that imports more than it exports has a *negative balance of trade* (*trade deficit*). A trade deficit is different from a budget deficit in government spending. Since the late 1990s, the U.S. trade deficit has grown steadily to hundreds of billions of dollars per year, exceeding $750 billion in 2014, with about a quarter (and more each year) accounted for by China and another quarter by oil imports. China has run a large trade surplus for years, nearing $400 billion in 2014 (see Figure 5.2).

Figure 5.2 China's Growing Trade Surplus

Source: Chinese National Statistical Bureau.

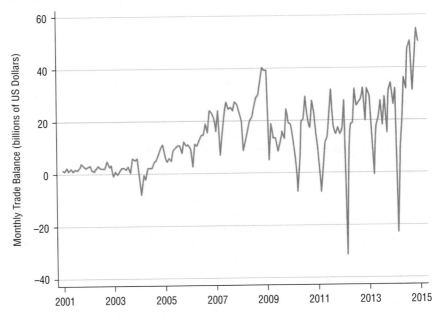

States must ultimately reconcile the balance of trade. It is tracked financially through the system of national accounts (see pp. 211–212). In the short term, a state can trade for a few years at a deficit and then for a few years at a surplus. The imbalances are carried on the national accounts as a kind of loan. But a trade deficit that persists for years becomes a problem. In recent years, to balance its trade deficit, the United States has "exported" currency (dollars) to China, Japan, Europe, and other countries, which use the dollars to buy things such as shares of U.S. companies, U.S. Treasury bills, or U.S. real estate. Economists worry that if foreigners lose their taste for investments in the United States, the U.S. economy could suffer.

This is one reason why mercantilists favor national economic policies to create a trade surplus. Then, rather than being unable to find the money it might need to cope with a crisis or fight a war, the state sits on a pile of money representing potential power. Historically, mercantilism literally meant stockpiling gold (gained from running a trade surplus) as a fungible form of power (see Figure 5.3). Such a strategy is attuned to realism's emphasis on relative power. For one state to have a trade surplus, another must have a deficit.

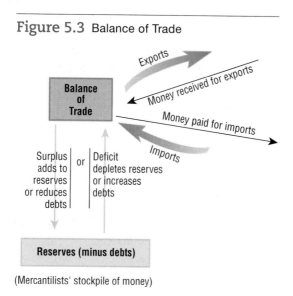

Figure 5.3 Balance of Trade

(Mercantilists' stockpile of money)

Comparative Advantage

The overall success of liberal economics is due to the substantial gains that can be realized through trade. These gains result from the **comparative advantage** that different states enjoy in producing different goods (a concept pioneered by economists Adam Smith and David Ricardo 200 years ago). States differ in their abilities to produce certain goods because of differences in natural resources, labor force characteristics, technology, and other such factors. To maximize the overall creation of wealth, each state should specialize in producing the goods for which it has a comparative advantage and then trade for goods that another state produces best. Of course, the costs of transportation and of processing the information in the trade (called *transaction costs*) must be included in the costs of producing an item. But increasingly, as globalization proceeds, both of these are low relative to the differences in the cost of producing items in different locations.

comparative advantage The principle that says states should specialize in trading goods that they produce with the greatest relative efficiency and at the lowest relative cost (relative, that is, to other goods produced by the same state).

Two commodities of great importance in the world are oil and cars. It is much cheaper to produce oil (or another energy source) in Saudi Arabia than in Japan, and much cheaper to produce cars in Japan than in Saudi Arabia. Japan needs oil to run its industry (including its car industry), and Saudi Arabia needs cars to travel its vast territory (including reaching its remote oil wells). Even with shipping and transaction costs, shipping Japanese cars to Saudi Arabia and Saudi oil to Japan saves a huge amount of money compared to the costs if each tried to be self-reliant.

A state need not have an absolute advantage (that is, be the most efficient producer in the world) in producing one kind of good to make specialization pay. It need only specialize in producing goods that are relatively lower in cost than other goods. Imagine that Japan discovered a way to produce synthetic oil using the same mix of labor and capital that it now uses to produce cars; also imagine that this synthetic oil could be produced a bit more cheaply than what it costs Saudi Arabia to produce oil but that Japan could still produce cars *much* more cheaply than could Saudi Arabia. It might seem intuitive that Japan should produce synthetic oil rather than pay extra for Saudi oil. But this is wrong. From a strictly economic point of view, Japan should keep producing cars (where it has a huge comparative advantage) and not divert capital and labor to make synthetic oil (where it has only a slight advantage). The extra profits Japan would make from exporting more cars would more than compensate for the slightly higher price it would pay to import oil.

Thus, international trade allocates global resources to states that have the greatest comparative advantage in producing each kind of commodity. As a result, prices are both lower overall and more consistent worldwide. Increasingly, production is oriented to the world market.

The economic benefits of trade, however, come with some political drawbacks. First, long-term benefits may incur short-term costs. When a state begins to import goods that it had been producing domestically, its economy may be disrupted; workers may need to retrain and find new jobs, and capital may not be easy to convert to new uses.

Also, the benefits and costs tend to be unevenly distributed *within* a state. Some industries or communities may benefit at the expense of others. For example, if a U.S. manufacturing company moves its factory to Mexico to take advantage of cheaper labor there and exports its goods back to the United States, the workers at the old U.S. factory lose their jobs, but U.S. consumers enjoy cheaper goods. The costs of such a move fall heavily on a few workers, but the benefits are spread thinly across many consumers. This kind of unequal distribution of costs and benefits often creates political problems for free trade even when the *overall* economic benefits outweigh the costs. Worker or industry interest groups (see pp. 191–193) will form against the concentrated costs (losing jobs) far more often than consumer groups will form against the diffuse losses (such as a $20 increase for many).

Political Interference in Markets

A free and efficient market requires many buyers and sellers with fairly complete information about the market. Also, the willingness of participants to deal with each other should not be distorted by personal (or political) preferences but should be governed only by price and quality considerations. Deviation from these conditions, called *market imperfections,* reduces efficiency.

International trade occurs more often at world market prices than does *domestic* economic exchange. No world government owns industries, provides subsidies, or regulates prices. Nonetheless, world markets are often affected by politics. When states are the principal actors in international economic affairs, the number of participants is often small. When there is just one supplier of an item—a *monopoly*—the supplier can set the price quite high. An *oligopoly* is a monopoly shared by just a few large sellers—often allowing for tacit or explicit coordination to force the price up. To the extent that companies band together along national lines, monopolies and oligopolies are more likely.

Another common market imperfection in international trade is *corruption;* individuals may receive payoffs to trade at nonmarket prices. The government or company involved may lose some of the benefits being distributed, but the individual government official or company negotiator gets increased benefits (see pp. 309–310). Politics provides a *legal framework* for markets—ensuring that participants keep their commitments, buyers pay for goods that they purchase, counterfeit money is not used, and so forth. As in security affairs, rules can be codified in international treaties, but enforcement depends on practical reciprocity (see pp. 259–260).

Taxation is another political influence on markets. Taxes generate revenue for the government and regulate economic activity by incentives. For instance, a government may keep taxes low on foreign companies in hopes of attracting them to locate and invest in the country. Taxes applied to international trade itself, called *tariffs,* are a frequent source of international conflict (see p. 183).

SANCTIONS Political interference in free markets is most explicit when governments apply sanctions against economic interactions of certain kinds or between certain actors. Political power then prohibits an economic exchange that would otherwise have been mutually beneficial. In 2015, the United States had trade restrictions on 11 states in response to those states' political actions, such as human rights violations.

Enforcing sanctions is always a difficult task because participants have a financial incentive to break the sanctions through black markets or other means. Without

SANCTIONS BITE Economic sanctions, such as the current international restrictions on trade and business with Iran, are among the most obvious ways that politics interferes in markets. Sanctions are hard to enforce, especially when not all countries participate, because doing business is profitable. Once Europe and the United States coordinated tough sanctions on Iran, they caused major economic disruption there, triggering a decline in Iran's currency by about half. Here, a street vendor offers banknotes on a Tehran street, 2013.

broad, multilateral support for international sanctions, they generally fail. For instance, in 2012, India—Iran's top oil customer—sent a trade delegation to Iran to take advantage of openings created by Western sanctions. One concern with the 2015 nuclear deal between Western powers and Iran (which removed sanctions in exchange for limits on Iran's nuclear program) is that, if Iran cheated, the sanctions would be nearly impossible to impose again on Iran because of the difficulty of international cooperation.

AUTARKY One obvious way to avoid becoming dependent on other states, especially for a weak state whose trading partners would tend to be more powerful, is to avoid trading and instead try to produce everything it needs by itself. Such a strategy is called self-reliance or **autarky**. As the theory of comparative advantage suggests, such a policy has proven ineffective. A self-reliant state pays a very high cost to produce goods for which it does not have a comparative advantage. As other states cooperate among themselves to maximize their joint creation of wealth, the relative power of the autarkic state in the international system tends to fall.

China's experience illustrates the problems with autarky. China's economic isolation in the 1950s and 1960s, resulting from an economic embargo imposed by the United States and its allies, deepened during its Cultural Revolution in the late 1960s when it broke ties with the Soviet Union as well. In that period, China rejected all things foreign. When China opened up to the world economy in the 1980s, the pattern reversed. The rapid expansion of trade, along with some market-oriented reforms in its domestic economy, resulted in rapid economic growth.

autarky A policy of self-reliance, avoiding or minimizing trade and trying to produce everything one needs (or the most vital things) by oneself.

Protectionism

Although few states pursue strategies of autarky, many states try to manipulate international trade to strengthen one or more domestic industries and shelter them from world markets. Such policies are broadly known as **protectionism**— protection of domestic industries from international competition. Although this term encompasses a variety of trade policies arising from various motivations, all are contrary to liberalism because they seek to distort free markets to gain an advantage for the state (or for substate actors within it), generally by discouraging imports of competing goods or services.

A state's motivation to protect domestic industry can arise from several sources. Often governments simply cater to the political demands of important domestic industries and interests, regardless of the overall national interest. An industry may lobby or give campaign contributions in order to win special tax breaks, subsidies, or restrictions on competing imports (see pp. 215–218). Sometimes, states attempt to protect an *infant industry* as it starts up in the state for the first time and until it can compete on world markets. Another motivation for protection is to give a domestic industry breathing room when market conditions shift or new competitors arrive on the scene.

protectionism The protection of domestic industries against international competition, by trade tariffs and other means.

Governments also protect industries considered vital to national security. In the 1980s, U.S. officials sought to protect the U.S. electronics and computer industries against being driven out of business by Japanese competitors because those industries were considered crucial to military production. The government sponsored a consortium of U.S. computer chip companies to promote the U.S. capability to produce chips cheaply (ordinarily the government would discourage such a consortium as an antitrust violation). Autarky may not pay in most economic activities, but for military goods, states will sacrifice some economic efficiency for the sake of self-sufficiency to reduce vulnerability in the event of war.

Finally, protection may be motivated by a defensive effort to ward off predatory practices by foreign companies or states. *Predatory* generally refers to efforts to capture unfairly a large share of world markets, or even a near-monopoly, so that eventually the predator can raise prices without fearing competition. Most often these efforts entail **dumping** products in foreign markets at prices below the minimum necessary to make a profit. Great disagreements occur about whether a given price level is predatory or merely competitive. These conflicts now generally are resolved through the WTO (see pp. 185–187).

dumping The sale of products in foreign markets at prices below the minimum level necessary to make a profit (or below cost).

Just as there are several motivations for protectionism, so too governments use several tools to implement this policy. The simplest is a **tariff** (or *duty*)—a tax imposed on certain types of imported goods, usually as a percentage of their value, as they enter the country. Tariffs not only restrict imports but can also be an important source of state revenues. If a state is to engage in protectionism, international norms favor tariffs as the preferred method of protection because they are straightforward and not hidden (see pp. 185–187). Most states maintain a long, complex list of tariffs on thousands of categories of goods.

tariff A duty or tax levied on certain types of imports (usually as a percentage of their value) as they enter a country.

Other means to discourage imports are **nontariff barriers** to trade. Imports can be limited by a *quota*. Quotas are ceilings on how many goods of a certain kind can be imported; they are imposed to restrict the growth of such imports. The extreme version is a flat prohibition against importing a certain type of good (or goods from a certain country). The U.S. government used quotas to restrict the number of Japanese-made cars that could enter the United States in the 1980s, when the U.S. automobile industry was losing ground rapidly to Japanese imports. Most of those quotas were *voluntary* in that Japan and the United States negotiated a level that both could live with.

nontariff barriers Forms of restricting imports other than tariffs, such as quotas (ceilings on how many goods of a certain kind can be imported).

The two nontariff barriers that are the most fought about in the WTO are subsidies and regulation. *Subsidies* are payments to a domestic industry that allow it to lower its prices without losing money. Such subsidies are extensive in, but not limited to, state-owned industries. Subsidies to an industry struggling to get established or facing strong foreign competition include *tax breaks, loans* (or guaranteed private loans) on favorable terms, and high *guaranteed prices* paid by governments. Subsidies to farmers have been the major sticking point between rich and poor countries in the Doha Round trade talks. In 2010, the United States

KING COTTON Protectionism uses various means to keep foreign imports from competing with domestic products. Agricultural producers in the global South complain that subsidies and other protectionist measures in Europe and the United States prevent poor farmers in developing countries from exporting to world markets. Here, cotton awaits processing in Mali, where low prices for cotton, the country's most important cash crop, have hurt farmers badly (2006).

and Brazil settled a WTO case over American subsidies to cotton growers. Prior to the settlement, Brazil was set to begin imposing nearly $830 million in sanctions against the United States.

Subsidies are also a frequent source of U.S.-European conflict, often involving EU policies regarding the Common Agricultural Policy (see p. 247). Subsidies outside the agricultural sector can also be sensitive politically. A European aerospace company that receives EU subsidies now actively bids on American defense department projects. American manufacturers complain that the subsidies given to the EU-based company make it difficult for them to compete because the subsidies allow the European company to place a lower bid. Thus, subsidies have moved from an issue in trade policy to the security area as well.

Imports can also be restricted by *regulations* that make it hard to distribute and market a product even when it can be imported. In marketing U.S. products in Japan, U.S. manufacturers complain of complex bureaucratic regulations and a tight system of corporate alliances funneling the supply of parts from Japanese suppliers to Japanese manufacturers. Environmental and labor regulations can function as nontariff barriers as well. This has caused great controversy in the WTO, such as when Europe banned genetically modified crops that happened to come mostly from the United States. Finally, when a state nationalizes an entire industry, such as oil production or banking, foreign competition is shut out.

Sometimes a country's culture, rather than state action, discourages imports. Citizens may (with or without government encouragement) follow a philosophy of *economic nationalism*—use of economics to influence international power and relative standing in the international system (a form of mercantilism). For example, U.S. citizens sometimes ignore the advice of liberal economists to buy the best product at the best price and instead "buy American" even if it means paying a bit more for an equivalent product. Although such a bias reduces the overall efficiency of world production, it does benefit U.S. workers.

Protectionism has both positive and negative effects on an economy, most often helping producers but hurting consumers. Another problem with protectionism is that domestic industry may use protection to avoid needed improvements and may therefore remain inefficient and uncompetitive—especially if protection continues over many years.

Trade Regimes

5.2   **Identify at least one factor behind the current impasse in World Trade Organization (WTO) negotiations in the Doha Round.**

As information technologies link the world across space, a global integration process based on free trade is shaping the international economic agenda. The World Trade Organization plays the central role in this process.

The World Trade Organization

The **World Trade Organization (WTO)** is a global, multilateral intergovernmental organization (IGO) that promotes, monitors, and adjudicates international trade. Together with the regional and bilateral arrangements to be described shortly, the WTO shapes the overall expectations and practices of states regarding international trade. The WTO is the successor organization to the **General Agreement on Tariffs and Trade (GATT)**, which was created in 1947 to facilitate freer trade on a multilateral basis. The GATT was more of a negotiating framework than an administrative institution. It did not actually regulate trade. Before the GATT, proposals for a stronger institutional agency had been rejected because of U.S. fears that overregulation would stifle free trade. In addition to its main role as a negotiating forum, the GATT helped arbitrate trade disputes, clarifying the rules and helping states observe them.

In 1995, the GATT became the WTO, which incorporated the GATT agreements on manufactured goods and extended the agenda to include trade in services and intellectual property. The WTO has some powers of enforcement and an international bureaucracy (600 people) that monitors trade policies and practices in each member state and adjudicates disputes among members. The WTO wields some power over states but, as with many international institutions, this power is limited. An ongoing public backlash against free trade (see pp. 199–200) reflects uneasiness about the potential power of a foreign and secretive organization to force changes in democratically passed national laws. But the WTO is the central international institution governing trade and therefore one that almost all countries want to participate in and develop.

Over time, the membership of the WTO has grown. By 2016, 161 countries—including all of the world's major trading states—had joined the WTO. Russia's membership bid succeeded in 2011 after 17 years, when neighboring Georgia agreed not to block it (a consensus of all members is needed). Politically unstable Yemen joined in 2014. More than 20 states are seeking admission, the most important of which are Iran and Iraq. After more than a decade of contentious negotiations, China joined in 2001. The United States and other countries usually demand, as a condition of membership, liberalization of the trading practices of would-be members. These new practices have affected China's economic and political development (see pp. 302–304).

World Trade Organization (WTO) An organization begun in 1995 that expanded the GATT's traditional focus on manufactured goods and created monitoring and enforcement mechanisms.

General Agreement on Tariffs and Trade (GATT) A world organization established in 1947 to work for freer trade on a multilateral basis; the GATT was more of a negotiating framework than an administrative institution. It became the World Trade Organization (WTO) in 1995.

most-favored nation (MFN) A principle by which one state, by granting another state MFN status, promises to give it the same treatment given to the first state's most-favored trading partner.

Generalized System of Preferences (GSP) A mechanism by which some industrialized states began in the 1970s to give tariff concessions to poorer states on certain imports; an exception to the most-favored nation (MFN) principle.

The WTO framework rests on the principle of reciprocity—matching states' lowering of trade barriers to one another. It also uses the concept of nondiscrimination, embodied in the **most-favored nation (MFN)** concept, which says that trade restrictions imposed by a WTO member on its most-favored trading partner must be applied equally to all WTO members. If Australia applies a 20 percent tariff on auto parts imported from France, it must not apply a 40 percent tariff on auto parts imported from the United States. Thus, the WTO does not get rid of barriers to trade altogether but equalizes them in a global framework to create a level playing field for all member states. States are not prevented from protecting their own industries, but they cannot play favorites among their trading partners. States may also extend MFN status to others that are not WTO members, as the United States did with China before it joined the WTO.

An exception to the MFN system is the **Generalized System of Preferences (GSP)**, by which rich states give trade concessions to poor ones to help their economic development. Preferences amount to a promise by rich states to allow imports from poor ones under lower tariffs than those imposed under MFN.

The WTO continues the GATT's role as a negotiating forum for multilateral trade agreements that lower trade barriers on a fair and reciprocal basis. These detailed and complex agreements specify commitments to lower certain trade barriers by certain amounts on fixed schedules. Almost every commitment entails domestic political costs because domestic industries lose protection against foreign competition. Even when other states agree to make similar commitments in other areas, lowering trade barriers is often hard for national governments.

As a result, negotiations on these multilateral agreements are long and difficult, typically stretching on for years in a *round of negotiations*. Among the five rounds of GATT negotiations from 1947 to 1995, the most important was the *Uruguay Round*, which started in 1986 in Uruguay. Although the rough outlines of a new GATT agreement emerged after a few years, closure eluded five successive G7 summit meetings in 1990–1994. A successful conclusion to the round would add more than $100 billion to the world economy annually. But that money was a collective good, to be enjoyed both by states that made concessions in the final negotiations and by those that did not. Agreement was finally reached in late 1994.

From 1947, the GATT encouraged states to use import tariffs rather than nontariff barriers to protect industries, and to lower those tariffs over time. The GATT concentrated on manufactured goods and succeeded in substantially reducing the average tariffs, from 40 percent of the goods' value decades ago to 3 percent by 2002 (under the Uruguay Round agreement). Tariff rates in the global South are much higher, around 30 percent (reflecting the greater protection that industry there apparently needs).

Agricultural trade is politically more sensitive than trade in manufactured goods and came into play only in the Uruguay Round. Trade in services, such as banking and insurance, is another current major focus of the WTO. Such trade exceeded one-fifth of the total value of world trade in 2015. Trade in telecommunications is a related area of interest. In 1997, 70 states negotiating through the WTO agreed on a treaty to allow telecommunications companies to enter each other's markets.

The problems in expanding into these and other sensitive areas became obvious at a 1999 Seattle WTO conference, where trade ministers had hoped to launch a new post-Uruguay round of trade negotiations. Representatives of poor countries argued that they needed trade to raise incomes and could not meet the standards of industrialized countries (which, after all, had allowed low wages, harsh working conditions, and environmental destruction when *they* began industrializing). Environmental and labor activists, joined by window-smashing anarchists, staged street protests that delayed the conference opening by a day. The meeting ended in failure.

Recovering from Seattle, in 2001, trade ministers meeting in Doha, Qatar, agreed to launch a new round of trade negotiations, the **Doha Round**. The issues under negotiation included agriculture, services, industrial products, intellectual property, WTO rules (including how to handle antidumping cases), dispute settlement, and some trade and environmental questions. The main obstacle remains the resistance of the industrialized West to cut agricultural subsidies as demanded by countries in the global South.

Smaller agreements within the WTO negotiations have kept hope alive that the Doha round will end with a new global trade agreement. A deal between the United States and India in 2014 concerning agricultural subsidies for the stockpiling of food brought renewed hopes of a breakthrough, but significant disagreements still remained between countries of the global South and global North.

In general, states continue to participate in the WTO because the benefits, in terms of global wealth creation, outweigh the costs, in terms of harm to domestic industries and painful adjustments in national economies. States try to change the rules in their favor during negotiations, and between rounds, they may evade the rules in minor ways. But the overall benefits are too great to jeopardize by nonparticipation.

Doha Round A series of negotiations under the World Trade Organization that began in Doha, Qatar, in 2001. It followed the *Uruguay Round* and has focused on agricultural subsidies, intellectual property, and other issues.

Bilateral and Regional Agreements

Although the WTO provides an overall framework for multilateral trade in a worldwide market, most international trade also takes place in more specific international agreements—bilateral trade agreements and regional free-trade areas.

BILATERAL AGREEMENTS   Bilateral treaties covering trade are reciprocal arrangements to lower barriers to trade between two states. Usually they are very specific. For instance, one country may reduce its prohibition on imports on product X (which the second country exports at competitive prices) while the second country lowers its tariff on product Y (which the first country exports). A sweeping agreement, such as that between Canada and India in 2007, generally contains mind-numbing levels of detail concerning specific industries and products. As with most agreements based on the reciprocity principle, trade treaties involve great complexity and constant monitoring. U.S. free trade deals with South Korea, Panama, and Colombia took effect in 2011.

Part of the idea behind the GATT/WTO was to strip away the maze of bilateral agreements on trade and simplify the system of tariffs and preferences. This effort has only partially succeeded. Bilateral trade agreements continue to play an important role. They have the advantages of reducing the collective goods problem inherent in multilateral negotiations and facilitating reciprocity as a means to achieve cooperation. When WTO negotiations bog down, bilateral agreements can keep trade momentum going. The number of bilateral agreements has grown substantially in the past decade, and their numbers far overwhelm all other types of agreements combined.

FREE TRADE AREAS   Regional free-trade areas also matter in the structure of world trade. In such areas, groups of neighboring states agree to remove most or all trade barriers within their area. Beyond free trade areas, states may reduce trade barriers and adopt a common tariff toward states that are not members of the agreement. This is known as a customs union. If members of a customs union decide to coordinate other policies such as monetary exchange, the customs union becomes a common market. The creation of a regional trade agreement (of any type) allows a group of states to cooperate in increasing their wealth without waiting for the rest of the world.

The most important free trade area is in Europe; it is connected with the European Union but has a somewhat larger membership. Europe contains a number of small industrialized states living close together, so the creation of a single integrated market allows these states to gain the economic advantages that come inherently to a large state such as the United States. The European free trade experiment has been a great success overall, contributing to Europe's accumulation of wealth (see Chapter 6).

North American Free Trade Agreement (NAFTA) A free trade zone encompassing the United States, Canada, and Mexico since 1994.

The United States, Canada, and Mexico signed the **North American Free Trade Agreement (NAFTA)** in 1994, following a U.S.-Canadian free trade agreement in 1988. In NAFTA's first decade, U.S. imports from both Mexico and Canada more than doubled, then fell back somewhat (after 1999). Canada and Mexico were the largest and third-largest U.S. trading partners, respectively (Japan was second). Over 15 years, neither the great benefits predicted by NAFTA supporters nor the disasters predicted by opponents have materialized.

Politicians in North and South America have long spoken of creating a single free trade area in the Western hemisphere, from Alaska to Argentina—the *Free Trade Area of the Americas (FTAA)*. FTAA negotiations began in 2003 with a target date of 2005. But the 2001 recession and post–September 11 security measures reduced trade, China provided U.S. companies with a better source of cheap labor, and left-leaning governments came to power in most of the Latin American countries. Those countries cared most about tariff-free trade, while the U.S. position emphasized a range of other issues such as services, intellectual property, and financial openness. Currently, the FTAA talks remain in hibernation, although the United States reached free trade agreements with several Latin American countries.

In 2007, the ten Association of South East Asian Nations (ASEAN) countries met with China, Japan, India, Australia, and New Zealand to begin negotiating an East Asian free trade area. The group, unlike some other Asia-Pacific IGOs, does not include the United States, but it does include half the world's population and some of its most dynamic economies. The negotiations between ASEAN states and China were successful, and in 2010, a free trade area went into effect between these countries. The ASEAN-China free trade agreement (FTA) is the world's third-largest free trade area, after the EU and NAFTA.

In the wake of the failed FTAA talks, however, the United States has entered negotiations to explore the formation of what are being called "mega-FTAs." EU and U.S. officials are negotiating the Transatlantic Trade and Investment Partnership (*T-TIP*), which would provide lower tariffs and lower barriers to investment between the United States and the EU. In addition, the United States has negotiated the Trans-Pacific Partnership (*TPP*), which would bring together economies as diverse as Japan, Chile, New Zealand, Vietnam, Canada, Malaysia, Singapore, and others. TPP negotiations concluded in 2015, but Congress must still approve the agreement, which will be controversial. The fact that the United States is pursuing these larger trade agreements could be a sign that the Doha Round is in trouble.

Latin America has followed a winding path toward free trade. The Southern Cone Common Market (MERCOSUR) began in the early 1990s with Brazil, Argentina, Uruguay, and Paraguay, which opposed letting Venezuela in. After Paraguay's president was hastily impeached in 2012, Brazil engineered Paraguay's suspension from MERCOSUR for ten months, during which Venezuela was admitted. Chile, Bolivia, Colombia, Ecuador, and Peru have joined as associate members. MERCOSUR members trade more with the United States than they do with each other, but they played a leading role in blocking a proposed free trade area of North and South America. In 2002, the countries agreed to allow their 250 million citizens free movement and residency across countries. A Caribbean common market (CARICOM) was created in 1973, but the area is neither large nor rich enough to make regional free trade a very important accelerator of economic growth. In 1969, Colombia, Ecuador, Peru, and Bolivia created a group now known as the Andean Community of Nations, which had modest successes and counts the MERCOSUR members as associate members. Finally, in 2008, a single continent-wide Union of South American Nations (UNASUR) began taking shape, to merge MERCOSUR and the Andean Community in an effort to follow the example of the European Union. UNASUR came into being in 2010 with the ratification by Uruguay.

If regional free-trade areas such as those in Europe and North America gain strength and new ones arise, the WTO may be weakened. The more that states meet the political requirements of economic growth through bilateral and regional agreements, the less they may depend on the worldwide agreements developed through the WTO.

Cartels

cartel An association of producers or consumers (or both) of a certain product, formed for the purpose of manipulating its price on the world market.

A **cartel** is an association of producers or consumers, or both, of a certain product and is formed to manipulate its price on the world market. It is an unusual but interesting form of trade regime. Most often producers and not consumers form cartels because there are usually fewer producers than consumers, and it seems possible for them to coordinate to keep prices high. Cartels can use a variety of means to affect prices; the most effective is to coordinate limits on production by each member and thus lower the supply, relative to demand, of the good.

Organization of Petroleum Exporting Countries (OPEC) The most prominent cartel in the international economy; its members control about half the world's total oil exports, enough to affect the world price of oil significantly.

The most prominent cartel in the international economy is the **Organization of Petroleum Exporting Countries (OPEC)**. Its member states together control hundreds of billions of dollars in oil exports annually—about 40 percent of the world total and enough to affect the price significantly. (A cartel need not hold a monopoly on production of a good to affect its price.) At OPEC's peak of strength in the 1970s, the proportion was even higher. OPEC maintains a headquarters in Vienna, Austria, and holds negotiations several times a year to set quotas for each country's production of oil in order to keep world oil prices in a target range. Saudi Arabia is by far the largest oil exporter (although the United States is the largest oil producer) and therefore occupies a unique position in the world economy (see Table 5.1).

Table 5.1 OPEC Members and Oil Production, 2014

Member State	Millions of Barrels/Day
Saudi Arabia	9.7
Iran	3.1
Venezuela	2.7
Iraq	3.1
Kuwait	2.9
United Arab Emirates	2.8
Nigeria	1.8
Angola	1.7
Libya	0.5
Algeria	1.2
Qatar	0.7
Ecuador[a]	0.6
Total OPEC	30.7
Percent of World	40%

[a]Ecuador re-joined OPEC in 2007 after suspending its membership in 1992.

Note: Major oil exporters not in OPEC include Russia, Kazakhstan, Mexico, China, Britain, and Norway. Gabon left OPEC in 1995. The United States, until several decades ago a major oil exporter, is now a major importer.

Source: Data adapted from: OPEC Annual Statistical Bulletin.

OPEC illustrates the potential that a cartel creates for collective goods problems. Individual members of OPEC can cheat by exceeding their production quotas while still enjoying the collective good of high oil prices. The collective good breaks down when too many members exceed their quotas, as has happened repeatedly to OPEC. Then world oil prices drop. (Iraq's accusations that fellow OPEC member Kuwait was exceeding production quotas and driving oil prices down was one factor in Iraq's invasion of Kuwait in 1990.)

OPEC may work as well as it does only because one member, Saudi Arabia, has enough oil to manipulate supply enough unilaterally to drive prices up or down—a form of hegemonic stability (see p. 5) within the cartel. Saudi Arabia can take up the slack from some cheating in OPEC (cutting back its own production) and keep prices up. Or if too many OPEC members are cheating on their quotas, it can punish them by flooding the market with oil and driving prices down until the other OPEC members collectively come to their senses.

In general, the idea of cartels runs counter to liberal economics because cartels deliberately distort free markets. Cartels usually are not as powerful as market forces in determining overall world price levels: Too many producers and suppliers exist, and too many substitute goods can replace ones that become too expensive, for a cartel to corner the market.

Industries and Interest Groups

Industries and other domestic political actors often seek to influence a state's foreign economic policies (see pp. 78–79). These pressures do not always favor protectionism. Industries that are advanced and competitive in world markets try to influence their governments to adopt free trade policies. This strategy promotes a global free-trade system in which such industries can prosper. By contrast, industries that lag behind their global competitors tend to seek government protection.

Means to influence foreign economic policy include lobbying, forming interest groups, paying bribes, and even encouraging coups. Actors include industry-sponsored groups, companies, labor unions, and individuals. Within an industry, such efforts usually work in a common direction because, despite competition among companies and between management and labor, all share common interests regarding the trade policies. However, a different industry may be pushing in a different direction. For instance, some U.S. industries support NAFTA; others oppose it.

Interest groups not organized along industry lines also have particular interests in state trade policies. U.S. environmentalists, for example, do not want U.S. companies to use NAFTA to avoid pollution controls by relocating to Mexico (where environmental laws are less strict). U.S. labor unions do not want companies to use NAFTA to avoid paying high wages. However, Mexican American citizens' groups in the United States tend to support NAFTA because it strengthens ties to relatives in Mexico.

Several industries are particularly important in trade negotiations currently. Atop the list is the agricultural sector. Traditionally, agriculture has been protected because self-sufficiency in food reduces national vulnerability (especially in time of war). Although such security concerns have now faded somewhat, farmers are well-organized and powerful domestic political actors in Europe, the United States, Japan, and other countries. In the Doha Round of WTO negotiations that began in 2001, agricultural subsidies were a key sticking point. The talks collapsed in 2003 in Cancun, Mexico, over the subsidies but were revived the next year after U.S. promised to cut farm subsidies 20 percent. At the 2005 Hong Kong talks, wealthy countries agreed to end all farm export subsidies. Unfortunately, export subsidies are only a small part of agricultural subsidies used in those countries.

A second important focus in recent years has been the textile and garment sector. As of 2005, textile quotas worldwide were dropped as part of previously negotiated WTO deals. At the same time, China began dominating world clothing exports, with whole cities specializing in one type of garment produced for mass export to giant retailers. With vast pools of cheap and disciplined labor, China threatened to drive U.S. textile and clothing producers out of business and give stiff new competition to exporters such as Pakistan and Bangladesh, where textiles make up 70 percent of exports. Later in 2005, the European Union and the United States each reached bilateral agreements with China to reimpose textile quotas for a few years. Now, countries such as Vietnam have begun to take textile business away from China by providing even lower production costs.

intellectual property rights The legal protection of the original works of inventors, authors, creators, and performers under patent, copyright, and trademark law. Such rights became a contentious area of trade negotiations in the 1990s.

Intellectual property rights are a third contentious area of trade negotiations. Intellectual property rights are the rights of creators of books, films, computer software, and similar products to receive royalties when their products are sold. The United States has a major conflict with some states in the global South over piracy of computer software, music, films, and other creative works—products in which the United States has a strong comparative advantage globally. It is technically easy and cheap to copy such works and sell them in violation of the copyright, patent, or trademark. Because U.S. laws cannot be enforced in foreign countries, the U.S. government wants foreign governments to prevent and punish such violations. Countries that reportedly pirate large amounts of computer software, music, and entertainment products include China, Taiwan, India, Thailand, Brazil, and

HEAP OF TROUBLE Intellectual property rights have been an important focus of recent trade negotiations. In many countries, pirated copies of videos, music, and software sell cheaply on the street with no royalty payments. Here, Chinese officials watch over illegal DVDs and CDs about to be destroyed in a campaign against piracy, 2015.

the former Soviet republics. The worldwide piracy rate was estimated at 42 percent in 2015. Infringement of intellectual property rights is widespread in many countries of the global South on products such as DVDs and prescription drugs.

In response, the international community has developed an extensive IGO with 184 member states, the World Intellectual Property Organization (WIPO), which tries to regularize patent and copyright law across borders. The WTO oversees the world's most important multilateral agreement on intellectual property, called Trade-Related Aspects of Intellectual Property Rights (TRIPS). The 2001 WTO meeting at Doha led to a declaration that states could exempt certain drugs from TRIPS rules to deal with serious domestic health crises, such as an HIV/AIDS epidemic. (The U.S. government supported this move after it had threatened to take over production of a powerful antibiotic drug, Cipro, during the post-9/11 anthrax scare.) Although procedures were established for these exceptions, only a few developing countries have used them. For several years, these disputes slowed the effective distribution of medicines to millions of Africans with AIDS, though progress picked up after 2004.

A fourth key trade issue is the openness of countries to trade in the **service sector** of the economy. This sector includes many services, especially those concerning information, but the key focus in international trade negotiations is on banking, insurance, and related financial services. In general, as telecommunications becomes cheaper and more pervasive, services offered by companies in one country can be used efficiently by consumers in other countries. U.S. consumers phoning customer service at U.S. companies and connecting to India or another English-speaking developing country engage in a long-distance trade in services.

service sector The part of an economy that concerns services (as opposed to the production of tangible goods); the key focus in international trade negotiations is on banking, insurance, and related financial services.

Another especially important industry in international trade is the arms trade, which operates largely outside the framework of normal commercial transactions because of its national security implications. Governments in industrialized countries want to protect their domestic arms industries rather than rely on imports to meet their weapons needs. And those domestic arms industries become stronger and more economically viable by exporting their products (as well as supplying their own governments). Governments usually participate actively in the military-industrial sector of the economy, even in countries such as the United States that lack industrial policy in other economic sectors. For example, fighter jets are a product in which the United States enjoys a global comparative advantage. The Middle East has been the leading arms-importing region of the global South, with India and China increasing recently.

A different problem is presented by the "industry" of illicit trade, or *smuggling*. Illicit trade often creates conflicts of interest among states and leads to complex political bargaining among governments, each looking after its own interests.

Enforcement of Trade Rules

As with international law generally, economic agreements among states depend strongly on reciprocity for enforcement (see pp. 5–6 and pp. 259–260). If one state protects its industries or puts tariffs on the goods of other states or violates the copyright on works produced in other countries, the main resort that other states have is to apply similar measures against the offending state.

Enforcement of equal terms of trade is complicated by differing interpretations of what is "fair." States generally decide which practices of other states they consider unfair (often prodded by affected domestic industries) and then take (or threaten) retaliatory actions to punish those practices. A U.S. law, the Super 301 provision, mandates retaliation against states that restrict access to their markets. One disadvantage of reciprocity is that it can lead to a downward spiral of noncooperation, popularly called a trade war. Third-party arbitration can help resolve trade disputes. Currently, the World Trade Organization (see pp. 185–187) hears complaints and sets levels of acceptable retaliation. In some cases, regional trade agreements establish mechanisms to hear and resolve complaints as well.

Retaliation for unfair trade practices usually tries to match the violation in type and extent. Under WTO rules, a state may impose retaliatory tariffs equivalent to the losses caused by another state's unfair trade practices (as determined by WTO hearings). But the retaliatory measures do not necessarily need to stay in the same sector. For instance, in 2013, Antigua and Barbuda received permission to punish the United States for blocking its online gambling sites, costing the tiny Caribbean country $21 million a year. (Because various forms of gambling are widely available domestically, the U.S. government failed to show why its citizens should be protected from "imported" gambling online.) The WTO said Antigua and Barbuda could steal $21 million annually in U.S. intellectual property by, for example, putting movies and TV shows online without paying for U.S. copyrights.

In cases of dumping, retaliation aims to offset the advantage enjoyed from goods imported at prices below the world market. Retaliatory tariffs raise the price back to market levels. In 2001, the weakened U.S. steel industry pleaded for U.S. government protection from cheap foreign steel, under an antidumping rationale. Before such tariffs are imposed, a U.S. government agency, the International Trade Commission (ITC), decides whether the low-priced imports have actually hurt the U.S. industry. The ITC ruled that U.S. steelmakers had indeed been hurt, and the U.S. government imposed 30 percent tariffs in 2002. But the WTO ruled against the United States in 2003 and gave other countries the right to impose $2 billion in retaliatory tariffs against the United States. As Europeans drew up their list of tariffs, targeting maximum damage to swing electoral states in 2004, President Bush backed down and abolished the steel tariffs (declaring them successful and no longer needed). By making the cost of tariffs higher than the benefits, the WTO effectively changed U.S. policy—an indication of the WTO's growing power.

Trade disputes and retaliatory measures are common. States keep close track of the exact terms of trade. Large bureaucracies monitor international economic transactions (prices relative to world market levels, tariffs, etc.) and

countries. The subsequent fall in consumer demand for goods led to declines in global trade of 9 percent—the largest decline since World War II.

Resistance to Trade

The globalization of the world economy has fueled a countercurrent of growing nationalism in several world regions where people believe their identities and communities to be threatened by the penetration of foreign influences. In addition, the material dislocations caused by globalization directly affect the self-interests of certain segments of countries' populations.

Workers in industrialized countries in industries that face increasing competition from low-wage countries in the global South—such as steel, automobiles, electronics, and clothing—are among the most adversely affected by free trade. The competition from low-wage countries holds down wages in those industries in the industrialized countries. It also creates pressures to relax standards of labor regulation, such as those protecting worker safety, and it can lead to job losses if manufacturers close down plants in high-wage countries and move operations to the global South. Not surprisingly, labor unions have been among the strongest political opponents of unfettered trade expansion. (Although the United States stands at the center of these debates, other industrialized countries face similar issues.)

Human rights nongovernmental organizations (NGOs) have joined labor unions in pushing for trade agreements to include requirements for low-wage countries to improve working conditions such as minimum wages, child labor, and worker safety. The United States bans imports of goods (mostly rugs) made by South Asia's 15 million indentured (slave) child laborers. Companies stung by criticism of conditions in their Asian factories have adopted voluntary measures to end the worst abuses, as Apple Computer did in 2012 after its Chinese supplier Foxconn faced worker protests and media attention over working conditions. More than 200 million children under age 14 work in the global South, more than half in hazardous labor, according to the International Labor Organization. In Ivory Coast, the world's largest exporter of cocoa (for chocolate consumed in the global North), tens of thousands of children work for low wages, or even as slaves, on cocoa plantations.

COSTLY LABOR Labor, environmental, and human rights organizations have all criticized unrestricted free trade. They argue that free trade agreements encourage multinational corporations (MNCs) to produce goods under unfair and unhealthy conditions, including the use of child labor. Here, a woman grieves over a missing family member at the site of the eight-story garment factory that collapsed in Bangladesh in 2013. The collapse killed an estimated 1,100 workers.

Environmental groups have also actively opposed the unrestricted expansion of trade, which they see as undermining environmental laws in industrialized countries and promoting environmentally harmful practices worldwide (see pp. 340–341). For example, U.S. regulations require commercial shrimp boats to use devices that prevent endangered species of sea turtles from drowning in shrimp nets. Indonesia, Malaysia, Thailand, and Pakistan, whose shrimp exports to the United States were blocked because they do not require the use of such devices, won a ruling from the World Trade Organization that the U.S. regulation unfairly discriminated against them. Sea turtles thus became a symbol of environmentalist opposition to the WTO. (In 2001, the WTO ruled the U.S. law acceptable after changes had made application of the law more even-handed.)

Labor, environmental, and consumer groups all portray the WTO as a secretive bureaucracy outside democratic control that serves the interests of big corporations at the expense of ordinary people in both the global North and South. More fundamentally, these critics distrust the corporate-driven globalization of which the WTO is just one aspect.

Recent U.S. surveys show a drop in the belief that trade is good for the economy. According to a 2014 survey, 68 percent believe trade is good for the United States, while 28 percent say it is not—up several percentage points from just five years earlier. In similar surveys, Americans' support for NAFTA has also declined: 56 percent say it should be renegotiated while only 16 percent support the agreement as it currently stands. Globally, however, public opinion supports trade: The same 2014 poll found that majorities in all 43 countries surveyed saw international trade as a good thing, despite concerns about negative cultural and environmental effects. Support was especially high in export-dependent economies—above 90 percent in Vietnam, Israel, South Korea, and Germany, for example.

The benefits of free trade are much more diffuse than the costs. U.S. consumers enjoy lower prices on goods imported from low-wage countries. Consumers may therefore spend more money on other products and services, eventually employing more U.S. workers. Cheap imports also help keep inflation low, which benefits citizens and politicians. However, the costs of free trade fall disproportionately on smaller groups (for example, steelworkers) who are likely to put up resistance.

Globalization, Financial Markets, and the Currency System

5.4 Summarize the three types of exchange rate systems adopted by states.

Globalization has led to momentous changes in many areas of international relations. So far, we have discussed how globalization has influenced global security and international trade relations. Globalization has had its most profound influence in the way states, businesses, and individuals deal with financial markets.

Today, global financial markets are as integrated as they have ever been. Investors in one country buy and sell assets or exchange currency with a few clicks of a mouse. Banks' investment portfolios often contain millions of dollars in assets (real estate, land, stocks) located in other countries. Nearly $1.5 trillion each day is exchanged on currency markets because investors need various currencies to do business in other countries and also to bet on the rise and fall of currencies, which we discuss momentarily.

This financial integration has tremendous advantages. It offers investors and businesses access to overseas markets to spur economic growth. It allows for the possibility of better returns on investments for individuals investing for college tuition or retirement. But as we have witnessed in the past two years, financial integration also carries risks. An economic crisis in one state can quickly spread to another, then another. The spread of economic difficulties can quickly lead to a global economic crisis affecting small and large economies alike.

Such was the case in 2008. As an economic downturn began in the United States, many Americans who had taken out loans on their homes found themselves unable to pay back these loans. At the same time, the value of their homes began to fall so that even if banks were to reclaim them, the banks could not recover the money they had loaned. Moreover, these loans had been resold by the banks to other businesses as investments, often in other countries. Several large U.S. banks then announced that they were on the verge of failing because they had too much money tied up in these bad home loans. This was a problem not only for the banks and the individuals who could not pay for their homes but also for those businesses who had purchased these loans as investments.

Given the global integration of financial markets, this housing crisis led quickly to a global banking crisis. Several British banks then announced they were near bankruptcy. The U.S. government responded with a rescue package of $800 billion to help shore up failing banks. Britain also created a rescue package of nearly $450 billion. The entire banking sector of Iceland was taken over by the government, and Iceland, a prosperous country, needed a loan from the IMF to rescue the government from bankruptcy.

Global stock markets tumbled dramatically as a result of this financial crisis. Unemployment increased worldwide. What began as trouble in the U.S. housing market ended as a global financial meltdown. The remainder of this chapter investigates two central pillars of our global financial markets: the politics of the world monetary system and the role of private companies as nonstate actors in the world economy.

The world economy recovered after 2008, but it soon faced the ripple effects of a debt crisis in Europe. It began in Greece and spread to Spain, Portugal, and Italy, threatening the European Union as a whole while holding back growth in the United States and China. The crisis illustrated dramatically the financial interdependence of today's world.

The Currency System

Nearly every state prints its own money. Because of the nature of state sovereignty, the international economy is based on national currencies, not a world currency. One of the main powers of a national government is to create its own currency as the sole legal currency in the territory it controls. The national currencies are of no inherent value in another country, but one can be exchanged for another.

For centuries, the European state system used precious metals as a global currency, valued in all countries. Gold was most important, and silver was second. These metals had inherent value because they looked pretty and were easily molded into jewelry or similar objects. They were relatively rare, and the mining of new gold and silver was relatively slow. These metals lasted a long time, and they were difficult to dilute or counterfeit.

Over time, gold and silver became valuable *because* they were a world currency—because other people around the world trusted that the metals could be exchanged for future goods—and this overshadowed any inherent functional value of gold or silver. Bars of gold were held by states as a kind of bank account denominated in an international currency.

gold standard A system in international monetary relations, prominent for a century before the 1970s, in which the value of national currencies was pegged to the value of gold or other precious metals.

In recent years the world has not used such a **gold standard** but has developed an international monetary system divorced from any tangible medium such as precious metals. Even today, some private investors buy stocks of gold or silver at times of political instability as a haven that would reliably have future value. But gold and silver have now become basically like other commodities, with unpredictable fluctuations in price. The change in the world economy away from bars of gold to purely abstract money makes international economics more efficient; the only drawback is that, without tangible backing in gold, currencies may seem less worthy of people's confidence.

Today, national currencies are valued against each other, not against gold or silver. Each state's currency can be exchanged for a different state's currency according to an **exchange rate**. These exchange rates affect almost every international economic transaction. In particular, currency policies affect trade issues directly, but they are not governed by the WTO regime.

exchange rate The rate at which one state's currency can be exchanged for the currency of another state. Since 1973, the international monetary system has depended mainly on floating rather than fixed exchange rates.

International Currency Exchange

Most exchange rates are expressed in terms of the world's most important currencies—the U.S. dollar, the Japanese yen, and the EU euro. Thus, the rate for exchanging Danish kroner for Brazilian reals depends on the value of each relative to these world currencies. Exchange rates that most affect the world economy are those *within* the large economic states—U.S. dollars, euros, yen, British pounds, and Canadian dollars.

The relative values of currencies at a given point in time are arbitrary; only the *changes* in values over time are meaningful. For instance, the euro happens to be fairly close to the U.S. dollar in value, whereas the Japanese yen is denominated in units closer to the U.S. penny. In itself this says nothing about the desirability of these currencies or the financial positions of their states. However, when the value of the euro rises (or falls) *relative* to the dollar because euros are considered more (or less) valuable than before, the euro is said to be strong (or weak).

Some states do not have *convertible* currencies. The holder of such money has no guarantee of being able to trade it for another currency. Such is the case in states cut off from the world capitalist economy, such as the former Soviet Union. In practice, even nonconvertible currency can often be sold, in black markets or by dealing directly with the government issuing the currency, but the price may be extremely low.

Some currencies are practically nonconvertible because they are inflating so rapidly that holding them for even a short period means losing money. The industrialized West has kept inflation relatively low—mostly below 5 percent annually—since 1980. Inflation in the global South is lower than two decades ago (see Table 5.2). Latin America brought inflation from 750 percent to below 15 percent, while China and South Asia got inflation rates below 5 percent. Most dramatically, in Russia and other former Soviet republics, inflation rates of more than 1,000 percent came down to less than 8 percent. Extremely high, uncontrolled inflation—more than 50 percent per month, or 13,000 percent per year—is called **hyperinflation**. The 100-trillion-dollar notes introduced by Zimbabwe in 2009 quickly lost most of their initial value (about $30 U.S.) under hyperinflation exceeding 200 million percent per year. Even just moderately high inflation causes money to lose value weekly, making it hard to conduct business.

hyperinflation An extremely rapid, uncontrolled rise in prices, such as occurred in Germany in the 1920s and some poor countries more recently.

Table 5.2 Inflation Rates by Region, 1993–2014

Region	Inflation Rate (percent per year)		
	1993	2006	2014[a]
Industrialized West	3	2	1
Russia/CIS	1,400	10	8
China	15	1	2
Middle East	27	10	3
Latin America	750	5	10
South Asia	6	7	9
Africa	112	6	6

[a]Data are estimates based on partial data for 2014.

Note: Regions are not identical to those used elsewhere in this book.

Source: Adapted from United Nations. *World Economic Situation and Prospects 2015*. United Nations, 2015.

By contrast with nonconvertible currency, **hard currency** is money that can be readily converted to leading world currencies (which now have relatively low inflation). For example, a Chinese computer producer can export its products and receive payment in dollars, euros, or another hard currency, which it can use to pay for components it needs to import from abroad. But a Chinese

hard currency Money that can be converted readily to leading world currencies.

farmer paid in Chinese currency for rice could not simply take that currency to buy imported goods. Rather, the exchange for foreign currency would be controlled by the Chinese government at rates the government set.

States maintain **reserves** of hard currency. These are the equivalent of the stockpiles of gold in centuries past. National currencies are now backed by hard-currency reserves, not gold. Some states continue to maintain gold reserves as well. In 2010, Saudi Arabia disclosed that it maintained over 300 tons of gold in reserve, worth more than $10 billion. China's gold reserves were three times larger. The industrialized countries have financial reserves roughly in proportion to the size of their economies.

reserves Hard-currency stockpiles kept by states.

One form of currency exchange uses **fixed exchange rates**. Here governments decide, individually or jointly, to establish official rates of exchange for their currencies. The Canadian and U.S. dollars were for many years equal in value; a fixed rate of one-to-one was maintained (this is no longer true). States have various means for trying to maintain, or modify, such fixed rates in the face of changing economic conditions (see pp. 299–307).

fixed exchange rates The official rates of exchange for currencies set by governments; not a dominant mechanism in the international monetary system since 1973.

Floating exchange rates are now more common and are used for the world's major currencies. Rates are determined by global currency markets in which private investors and governments alike buy and sell currencies. There is a supply and demand for each state's currency, with prices constantly adjusting in response to market conditions. Just as investors might buy shares of Apple or Wal-Mart stock if they expected its value to rise, so they would buy a pile of Japanese yen if they expected that currency's value to rise in the future. Through short-term speculative trading in international currencies, exchange rates adjust to changes in the longer-term supply and demand for currencies.

floating exchange rates The rates determined by global currency markets in which private investors and governments alike buy and sell currencies.

Major international currency markets operate in a handful of cities—the most important being New York, London, Zurich (Switzerland), Tokyo, and Hong Kong—linked by instantaneous computerized communications. These markets are driven in the short term by one question: What will a state's currency be worth in the future relative to what it is worth today? These international currency markets involve huge amounts of money—$1.5 trillion every day—moving around the world (of course, only the computerized information actually moves). They are private markets, not as strongly regulated by governments as are stock markets.

National governments periodically intervene in financial markets, buying and selling currencies in order to manipulate their value. (These interventions may also involve changing interest rates paid by the government; see pp. 211–213.) Such government intervention to manage the otherwise free-floating currency rates is called a **managed float** system. The leading industrialized states often, but not always, work together in such interventions. If the price of the U.S. dollar, for instance, goes down too much relative to other important currencies (a political judgment), governments step into the currency markets, side by side with private investors, and buy dollars. With this higher demand for dollars, the price may then stabilize and perhaps rise again. (If the price gets too high,

managed float A system of occasional multinational government interventions in currency markets to manage otherwise free-floating currency rates.

governments step in to sell dollars, increasing supply and driving the price down.) Such interventions usually happen quickly and may be repeated several times in order to have the desired effect. In their interventions in international currency markets, governments are at a disadvantage because even acting together, they control only a small fraction of the money moving on such markets; most of it is privately owned.

A successful intervention can make money for governments at the expense of private speculators. If, for example, the Group of Twenty (G20) governments step in to raise the price of U.S. dollars by buying them around the world (selling other hard currencies), and if they succeed, the governments can then sell again and pocket a profit. If the intervention fails and the price of dollars keeps falling, however, the governments *lose* money and may have to keep buying and buying in order to stop the slide. In fact, if investors become aware of such

WHAT'S IT WORTH TO YOU? Money has value only because people trust its worth. Inflation erodes a currency's value if governments print too much money or if political instability erodes public confidence. Constant minor adjustments set currencies' values; this Ukrainian exchange in 2015 reacts to increased violence in the eastern portion of that country, further eroding the value of its currency.

moves, they may interpret this action as a signal that the currency being bought is weak, which could depress the price even further. In extreme cases, the governments may run out of their stockpiles of hard currencies before then and have to absorb a huge loss. Thus, governments must be realistic about the limited effects they can have on currency prices.

These limits were well illustrated in the 2001 Argentine financial collapse. Argentina in the 1990s had pegged the value of its currency at a fixed rate to the U.S. dollar—a wonderfully effective way to stop the runaway inflation that had recently wreaked devastation on Argentina's economy. Tying the peso to the dollar, however, represented a loss of sovereignty over monetary policy, one of the key levers to control an economy. Argentina accumulated $132 billion in foreign loans and could not service its debts. IMF assistance in restructuring debt was contingent on a tight financial policy of tax increases and spending cuts—a mistake during a major multiyear recession, according to critics. In 2001, as the United States and the IMF stood by, Argentina's economy collapsed; two presidents resigned in short order; and a populist took power, defaulted on foreign debts, and devalued the peso to create jobs—an embarrassing chapter for the IMF and a painful one for Argentina. In 2003, Argentina defaulted on a $3 billion payment to the IMF, the largest default in IMF history. Its economy turned around and it paid the IMF in 2006.

Another Latin American case, Venezuela, demonstrates the harmful effects of poor currency policy choices. Beginning in 2003, Venezuela imposed a differentiated exchange rate—the official exchange rate varied depending on what was being bought and sold. Because some imported goods were bought at a more favorable exchange rate, certain "expensive" goods became very cheap (luxury cars and liquor), while staple goods (milk) became expensive. By 2015, the Venezuelan economy was near to experiencing hyperinflation.

More recently, pressures built up in a vastly more important case—China's currency. As in Argentina in 2001, the current policy of pegging China's currency to the dollar did not adjust to different economic conditions in the two countries. China runs a big trade surplus and the United States a big trade deficit—over $300 billion with China alone in 2012 and over $500 billion in total. Critics charge that the dollar–yuan ratio is held artificially high, making China's exports to the United States cheaper and contributing to the trade imbalance and the loss of U.S. manufacturing jobs—an issue in U.S. domestic politics. As the economic position of the United States has worsened in the past three years, pressure on China to reform its currency has grown. Yet China is concerned about domestic stability—for employment to stay high, China must export goods. China's undervalued currency keeps exports cheap and workers employed. China has only slowly allowed its currency to appreciate in value modestly and will not allow it to float freely.

In 2006, China, Japan, and South Korea announced plans to work toward coordinating their currency policies. In 2013, South Korea extended a currency exchange agreement, worth over $50 billion, with China to run until 2017. Along with the ASEAN countries, South Korea is also studying the creation of an Asian currency unit that would track the aggregate value of the region's currencies. Both measures are possible early steps toward the eventual creation of an Asian currency like the euro. But such a major move is in the early stages at best.

Why Currencies Rise or Fall

In the short term, exchange rates depend on speculation about the future value of currencies. But over the long term, the value of a state's currency tends to rise or fall relative to others because of changes in the long-term supply and demand for the currency. *Supply* is determined by the amount of money a government prints. Printing money is a quick way to generate revenue for the government, but the more money printed, the lower its price. *Demand* for a currency depends on the state's economic health and political stability. People do not want the currency of an unstable country because political instability leads to the breakdown of economic efficiency and of trust in the currency.

A *strong* currency increases its value relative to other currencies—not just in day-to-day fluctuations on currency markets but in a longer-term perspective. A weak currency is the opposite. The strength of a state's currency tends to reflect that state's monetary policy and economic growth rate. Investors seek a currency that will not be watered down by inflation and that can be profitably invested in a growing economy.

Policy Perspectives
President of China, Xi Jinping

PROBLEM *How do you balance international political pressures with domestic economics?*

BACKGROUND Imagine that you are the president of China. The Chinese economy has grown rapidly in the past decade. Growth rates continue to run near 9 percent, exceeding nearly all countries in the developing world. After economic slowdowns during the 2008 global financial crisis, growth has returned. Chinese exports fell during the crisis, but they have surged back, leading to yearly trade surpluses.

Your position in the international economy is unique because China's currency, the yuan, does not float freely and was pegged to the U.S. dollar (and then to a basket of currencies) for more than a decade. Although your predecessor let the currency rise by 40 percent, many economists consider it still substantially undervalued.

Many feel that your fixed currency is one explanation for your country's tremendous economic growth and trade surplus. The demand for the yuan is high (to pay for your exports), but the fixed rate keeps the yuan low. The result is that Chinese exports are much cheaper on the world market.

DOMESTIC CONSIDERATIONS Economic growth is important for your country. Given the country's large population, increases in jobs are important to keep unemployment low. Higher wages help ensure low birthrates (through the demographic transition; see p. 354). Exports are a key part of this picture, contributing heavily to your economic growth, generating hard currency for your economy, and creating jobs.

Recently, however, two dangers have appeared on the horizon. The first is economic. Since 2010, your country has experienced labor unrest from workers unhappy with their low pay. Responses to these protests could include higher wages, raising the costs of goods produced and potentially lowering exports. Stock market instability in 2015 created further tensions and unrest. The second danger is political. Both Europe and the United States have complained bitterly about your exchange rate and trade surplus. The United States has blamed the undervalued yuan for costing it 1.5 million jobs.

SCENARIO Now imagine that the United States offers the possibility of awarding the next presidency of the World Bank to China (until now the World Bank president has always been an American). The condition is that you allow the yuan to float freely on international currency markets. Such a move would be very popular internationally and would lessen the chances that your own economy will become inflationary. In addition, leading the World Bank would provide great prestige.

Of course, there are also dangers in this course of action. If the yuan rises rapidly in value, your exports will be less competitive internationally, risking a stall in a key engine of your economy. You also become more vulnerable to international currency shocks, such as the 1997 Asian economic crisis, which you avoided in large part because of your fixed exchange rate.

CHOOSE YOUR POLICY Do you allow the yuan to float freely on international currency markets? If yes, how do you make sure your economy stays on a high-growth path and your exports stay competitive? If no, how do you deal with the political pressure arising from your existing currency policy? Can you also run the risk that your economy will grow too fast, risking inflation and domestic discontent?

To some extent, states have *common* interests—opposed to those of private investors—in maintaining stable currency exchange rates. Despite these shared interests, states also experience conflicts over currency exchange. States often prefer a low value for their own currency relative to others because a low value promotes exports and helps turn trade deficits into surpluses—as mercantilists especially favor (see pp. 176–179).

Exchange rates and trade surpluses or deficits tend to adjust automatically toward equilibrium (the preferred outcome for liberals). An *overvalued* currency is one whose exchange rate is too high, resulting in a chronic trade deficit. The deficit can be covered by printing more money, which in turn waters down the currency's value and brings down the exchange rate (if it floats freely). Because they see adjustments as harmless, liberals do not mind exchange rate changes, which they view as mechanisms for the world economy to work out inefficiencies and maximize growth.

devaluation A unilateral move to reduce the value of a currency by changing a fixed or official exchange rate.

A unilateral move to reduce the value of one's own currency by changing a fixed or official exchange rate is called a **devaluation**. Generally, devaluation is a quick fix for financial problems in the short term, but it can create new problems. It causes losses to foreigners who hold one's currency (which suddenly loses value). This reduces the trust people place in the currency. As a result, demand for the currency drops, even at the new lower rate. Investors become wary of future devaluations, and indeed such devaluations often follow one after another in unstable economies. In the first three weeks of 2009, Russia devalued its ruble six times, after the price of its main export, oil, plummeted. A currency may be devalued by being allowed to float freely after a period of fixed exchange rates, often bringing a single sharp drop in values.

States also share an interest in the integrity of their currencies against counterfeiting, but so-called rogue states may feel otherwise. In 2006, the United States accused North Korea of passing off tens of millions of dollars in extremely realistic counterfeit $100 bills—a direct gain for the North Korean regime at the expense of the U.S. Treasury.

In recent years, a new phenomenon known as electronic currencies have gained attention around the world. None of these currencies exist in physical form. The most widely used of these currencies, bitcoin, is

PRICES SUBJECT TO CHANGE Changes in the value of the dollar—reflecting underlying trends in U.S. and foreign economies as well as governments' monetary policies—directly affect the prices of imported goods such as gasoline, here rising in California in 2015.

now accepted by many businesses worldwide. These currencies may be traded for traditional currencies on a number of web-based trading firms. Bitcoin, worth as little as $0.05 at its creation, traded for nearly $1,000 in the summer of 2014, settling back to around $300 by 2015. What makes electronic currencies unique is that they are not issued by states, yet individuals use them to buy and sell goods (initially, mostly illegal goods on international markets). Whether these new currencies will play a bigger role in global commerce remains to be seen.

Central Banks

Governments control the printing of money. In some states, the politicians or generals who control the government directly control the amounts of money printed. It is not surprising that inflation tends to be high in those states because political problems can often be solved by printing more money. But in most industrialized countries, politicians know they cannot trust themselves with day-to-day decisions about printing money. To enforce self-discipline and enhance public trust in the value of money, these decisions are turned over to a **central bank**.

central bank An institution common in industrialized countries whose major tasks are to maintain the value of the state's currency and to control inflation.

The economists and technical experts who run the central bank seek to maintain the value of the state's currency by limiting the amount of money printed and not allowing high inflation. Politicians appoint the people who run the bank, but generally for long terms that do not coincide with those of the politicians. Thus, central bank managers try to run the bank in the national interest, a step removed from partisan politics. If a state leader orders a military intervention, the generals obey, but if the leader orders an intervention in currency markets, the central bank does not have to comply. In practice, the autonomy of central banks varies.

In the United States, the central bank is the *Federal Reserve,* or the Fed. The Fed can affect the economy by releasing or hoarding its money. Internationally, it does this by intervening in currency markets as described earlier. Multilateral interventions are usually coordinated by the heads of central banks and treasury (finance) ministries in the leading countries. The long-term, relatively nonpartisan perspective of central bankers makes it easier for states to achieve the collective good of a stable world monetary system.

Domestically, the Fed exercises its power mainly by setting the **discount rate**—the interest rate that the government charges when it loans money to private banks. In effect, this rate controls how fast money is injected into the economy. If the Fed sets too low a discount rate, too much money will enter into circulation and inflation will result. If the rate is set too high, too little money will circulate, and consumers and businesses will find it hard to borrow as much or as cheaply from private banks; economic growth will be depressed.

discount rate The interest rate charged by governments when they lend money to private banks. The discount rate is set by countries' central banks.

Although central banks control sizable reserves of currency, they are constrained by the limited share of world money they own. Most wealth is controlled by private banks and corporations. As economic actors, states do not drive the direction of the world economy; in many ways, they follow it, at least over the long run. Yet as we have seen in the recent global economic crises, states still play a key role in the global economy. In the short run, states can adopt massive financial stimulus packages, rescue private banks and corporations that teeter on bankruptcy, and prosecute individuals that act illegally to cause economic hardship.

The World Bank and the IMF

Because of the importance of international cooperation for a stable world monetary system and because of the need to overcome collective goods problems, international regimes and institutions have developed around norms of behavior in monetary relations. Just as the UN institutionally supports regimes based on norms of behavior in international security affairs, the same is true in the world monetary regime.

As in security affairs, the main international economic institutions were created near the end of World War II. The **Bretton Woods system** was adopted at a conference of the winning states in 1944 (at Bretton Woods, New Hampshire). It established the *International Bank for Reconstruction and Development (IBRD)*, more commonly called the **World Bank**, as a source of loans to reconstruct the European economies after the war and to help states through future financial difficulties. (Later, the main borrowers were developing countries and, in the 1990s, Eastern European ones.) Closely linked with the World Bank is the **International Monetary Fund (IMF)**. The IMF coordinates international currency exchange, the balance of international payments, and national accounts (discussed shortly). The World Bank and the IMF continue to be the pillars of the international financial system. (The roles of the World Bank and the IMF in international development are taken up in Chapter 7.)

To replace gold as a world standard after 1971, the IMF created a new world currency, the **Special Drawing Right (SDR)**. The SDR has been called "paper gold" because it is created in limited amounts by the IMF, is held as a hard-currency reserve by states' central banks, and can be exchanged for various international currencies. The SDR is today the closest thing to a world currency that exists, but it cannot buy goods—only currencies. And it is owned only by states (central banks), not by individuals or companies. SDRs are linked in value to a basket of several key international currencies. Since the 1970s, the major national currencies have been governed by the managed float system. Transition from the dollar–gold regime to the managed float regime was difficult. States had to bargain politically over the targets for currency exchange rates in the meetings known as Group of Six (G6) summits. The G6 was later expanded to the G8 with

Bretton Woods system A post–World War II arrangement for managing the world economy, established at a meeting in Bretton Woods, New Hampshire, in 1944. Its main institutional components are the World Bank and the International Monetary Fund (IMF).

World Bank Formally the International Bank for Reconstruction and Development (IBRD), an organization that was established in 1944 as a source of loans to help reconstruct the European economies. Later, the main borrowers were developing countries and, in the 1990s, Eastern European ones.

International Monetary Fund (IMF) An intergovernmental organization (IGO) that coordinates international currency exchange, the balance of international payments, and national accounts. Along with the World Bank, it is a pillar of the international financial system.

the addition of Canada (in 1976) and Russia (in 1997). (Russia's membership was suspended in 2014, after its annexation of Crimea.) In 2009, it was announced that the G20, including far more developed and developing countries, would begin to replace the G8 in undertaking major financial deliberations.

The technical mechanisms of the IMF are based on each member state's depositing financial reserves with the IMF, based on the size and strength of a state's economy. A state can then borrow to stabilize its economy in difficult times and repay the IMF in subsequent years. In 2009, world leaders pledged an additional $1 trillion to be paid to the IMF so it could help developing countries cope with the global financial crisis.

Unlike the WTO or UN General Assembly, the IMF and the World Bank use a *weighted voting system*—each state has a vote equal to its deposits. Thus, the advanced economies control the IMF, although nearly all the world's states are members. The United States has the single largest vote (17 percent), and its capital city (Washington, DC) is headquarters for both the IMF and the World Bank. In 2006 and 2008, the IMF adjusted the voting formula, increasing modestly the voting power of China (from about 3 to 3.7 percent of the total) along with other developing countries.

Since 1944, the IMF and the World Bank have tried to accomplish three major missions. First, they sought to provide stability and access to capital for states ravaged by World War II, especially Japan and the states of Western Europe. This mission was a great success, leading to growth and prosperity in those states. Then, especially in the 1970s and 1980s, the World Bank and the IMF have tried to promote economic development. That mission was far less successful—as seen in the lingering poverty in much of the global South (see Chapter 7). The third mission, in the 1990s, was the integration of Eastern Europe and Russia into the world capitalist economy. This effort posted a mixed record but has had general success overall.

Special Drawing Right (SDR) A world currency created by the International Monetary Fund (IMF) to replace gold as a world standard. Valued by a "basket" of national currencies, the SDR has been called "paper gold."

State Financial Positions

5.5 Explain three reasons why states go into debt.

As currency rates change and state economies grow, the overall positions of states relative to each other shift.

National Accounts

The IMF maintains a system of *national accounts* statistics to keep track of the overall monetary position of each state. A state's **balance of payments** is like the financial statement of a company: It summarizes all the flows of money into and out of the country. The system itself is technical and not political in nature. Essentially, three types of international transactions go into the balance of payments.

The *current account* is basically the balance of trade discussed earlier. *Capital flows* are foreign investments in, and by, a country. *Changes in foreign exchange*

balance of payments A summary of all the flows of money into and out of a country. It includes three types of international transactions: the current account (including the merchandise trade balance), flows of capital, and changes in reserves.

reserves make the national accounts balance. Any difference between the inflows and outflows of money is made up by an equal but opposite change in the state's reserves (purchases and sales of SDRs, gold, and hard currencies other than its own, and changes in its deposits with the IMF). Thus, national accounts always balance in the end.

International Debt

In one sense, an economy is constantly in motion, as money moves through the processes of production, trade, and consumption. But economies also contain *standing wealth*. The hard-currency reserves owned by governments are one form of standing wealth, but they are not the most important. Most standing wealth is in the form of homes and cars, farms and factories, ports and railroads. In particular, *capital* goods (such as factories) are products that can be used as inputs for further production. Nothing lasts forever, but standing wealth lasts for enough years to be treated differently from goods that are quickly consumed. The main difference is that capital can be used to create more wealth: Factories produce goods, railroads support commerce, and so forth. Standing wealth creates new wealth, so the economy tends to grow over time. As it grows, more standing wealth is created. In a capitalist economy, money makes more money.

If the state's economy is healthy, it can borrow money from foreign governments, banks, or companies and create enough new wealth to repay the debts a few years later. But states, like businesses, sometimes operate at a loss; then their debts mount up. In a vicious circle, more and more of the income they generate goes to paying interest, and more money must be borrowed to keep the state in operation.

Why do states go into debt? One major reason is a trade deficit. In the balance of payments, a trade deficit must be made up somehow. It is common to borrow money to pay for a trade deficit. A second reason is the income and consumption pattern among households and businesses. If people and firms spend more than they take in, they must borrow to pay their bills. The credit card they use may be from a local bank, but that bank may be getting the money it lends to them from foreign lenders.

A third reason for national debt is government spending relative to taxation.

DEBATING DEBT Failure to make payments on international debt, called a default, is a very serious action because it can cut off a country's access to future investment and loans. Nonetheless, several states have defaulted on debts rather than inflict painful budget cuts that would hurt the population. In 2011–2012, Greece narrowly averted defaulting on its huge debts, accepting EU bailouts. Here, Greece's new prime minister, Alexis Tsipras, watches a debate about adopting austerity measures to help pay off Greek debts, 2015.

Under the principles of **Keynesian economics** (named for economist John Maynard Keynes), governments sometimes spend more on programs than they accrue in tax revenue—*deficit spending*—to stimulate economic growth. This was the strategy adopted by many countries, especially the United States, in the 2008–2009 financial crisis. If the strategy works, increased economic growth eventually generates higher tax revenues to make up the deficit. If it does not, a state finds itself with a poor economy and even deeper in debt.

Government decisions about spending and taxation are called **fiscal policy**; decisions about printing and circulating money are called **monetary policy**. These are the two main tools available for a government to manage an economy. There is no free lunch: High taxation chokes off economic growth, printing excess money causes inflation, and borrowing to cover a deficit places a mortgage on the state's standing wealth. This is why, for all the complexities of governmental economic policies and international economic transactions, a state's wealth and power ultimately depend more than anything on the underlying health of its economy—the education and training of its labor force, the amount and modernity of its capital goods, the morale of its population, and the skill of its managers. In the long run, international debt reflects these underlying realities.

Multinational Business

5.6   **Identify two risks to firms who engage in foreign direct investment and two risks to countries who host foreign direct investment.**

Although states are the main rule makers for currency exchange and other international economic transactions, those transactions are carried out mainly by private firms and individuals, not governments. Most important among these private actors are multinational corporations.

Multinational Corporations

Multinational corporations (MNCs) are companies based in one state with affiliated branches or subsidiaries operating in other states. There is no exact definition, but the clearest case of an MNC is a large corporation that operates on a worldwide basis in many countries simultaneously, with fixed facilities and employees in each. There is also no exact count of the total number of MNCs, but most estimates are in the tens of thousands worldwide.

Most important are *industrial corporations,* which make goods in factories in various countries and sell them to businesses and consumers in various countries. The automobile, oil, and electronics industries have the largest MNCs. Almost all of the largest MNCs are based in Organization for Economic Co-operation and Development (OECD) states. *Financial corporations* (the most important being banks) also operate multinationally—though often with more restrictions than industrial MNCs do. Money moves across borders at the rate of $1.5 trillion per

Keynesian economics The principles articulated by British economist John Maynard Keynes, used successfully in the Great Depression of the 1930s, including the view that governments should sometimes use deficit spending to stimulate economic growth.

fiscal policy A government's decisions about spending and taxation, and one of the two major tools of macroeconomic policy making (the other being monetary policy).

monetary policy A government's decisions about printing and circulating money, and one of the two major tools of macroeconomic policy making (the other being fiscal policy).

multinational corporation (MNC) A company based in one state with affiliated branches or subsidiaries operating in other states.

DOING BUSINESS WORLDWIDE Multinational corporations (MNCs) play important roles in international relations and are powerful actors with considerable resources in negotiating with governments. Here, Airbus, a division of a European MNC, shows off its new super-jumbo jet at the Singapore Airshow, 2008.

day. In this context, financial corporations are becoming more internationalized. Some MNCs sell *services.* The McDonald's fast-food chain and American Telephone and Telegraph (AT&T) are good examples.

Some scholars see MNCs almost as being agents of their home national governments. This view resonates with mercantilism, in which economic activity ultimately serves political authorities; thus, MNCs have clear national identities and act as members of their national society under state authority. A variant of this theme (from a more revolutionary worldview) considers national governments to be agents of their MNCs; state interventions (economic and military) serve private, monied interests.

Others see MNCs as citizens of the world beholden to no government. The head of Dow Chemical once said that he dreamed of buying an island beyond any state's territory and putting Dow's world headquarters there. In such a view, MNCs act globally in the interests of their (international) stockholders and owe loyalty to no state. In any case, MNCs are motivated by the need to maximize profits. Only in the case of state-owned MNCs—an important exception but a small minority of the total companies worldwide—do MNC actions reflect state interests. Even then, managers of state-owned MNCs have won greater autonomy to pursue profit in recent years (as part of the economic reforms instituted in many countries), and in many cases state-owned enterprises are being sold off (privatized).

As independent actors in the international arena, MNCs are increasingly powerful. Dozens of industrial MNCs have annual sales of tens of billions of dollars each (hundreds of billions for the top corporations). Only 26 states had more economic activity per year (GDP) in 2014 than did the largest MNC, Wal-Mart, at nearly $500 billion. However, the largest *government* (the United States) has government revenues above $2 *trillion*—about six times that of Wal-Mart. Thus the power of MNCs does not rival that of the largest states but exceeds that of many poorer states (see pp. 310–312).

Giant MNCs contribute to global interdependence. They are so deeply entwined in so many states that they have a profound interest in the stable operation of the international system—in security affairs as well as in trade and monetary relations. MNCs prosper in a stable international atmosphere that permits freedom of trade, of movement, and of capital flows (investments)—all governed by market forces with minimal government interference. Thus MNCs are, overall, a strong force for liberalism in the world economy, despite the fact that particular MNCs in particular industries push for certain mercantilist policies to protect their own interests.

Foreign Direct Investment (FDI)

MNCs do not just operate in foreign countries, they also own capital there—buildings, factories, cars, and so forth. For instance, U.S. and German MNCs own some of the capital located in Japan, and Japanese MNCs own capital located in the United States and Germany. Investments in foreign countries are among the most important, and politically sensitive, activities of MNCs. Figure 5.5 illustrates the growth of foreign direct investment.

Figure 5.5 Foreign Direct Investment, World Total, 1970–2013

Source: World Bank data.

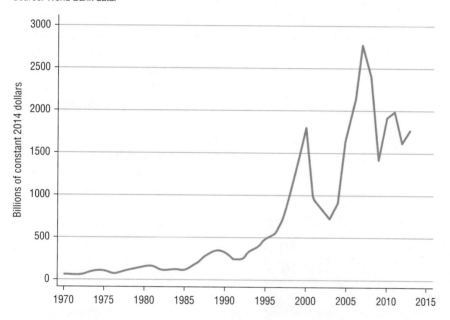

Unlike portfolio investment (on paper), *foreign direct investment* involves tangible goods such as factories and office buildings (including ownership of a sizable fraction of a company's total stock, as opposed to a portfolio with little bits of many companies). Paper can be traded on a global market relatively freely, but direct investments cannot be moved freely from one state to another when conditions change. Direct investment is long term, and it is more visible than portfolio investment. Investments in the manufacturing sector usually entail the greatest investment in fixed facilities and in training workers and managers. Investments in the service sector tend to be less expensive and easier to walk away from if conditions change.

Mercantilists tend to view foreign investments in their own country suspiciously. In developing countries, foreign direct investment often evokes concerns about a loss of sovereignty because governments may be less powerful than the MNCs that invest in their country. These fears also reflect the historical fact that most foreign investment in the global South once came from colonizers. Although such investments create jobs, they also bring dislocations of traditional ways of life and cultures. Many poor and transitional states desperately need capital from any source to stimulate economic growth, so foreign direct investment is generally welcomed and encouraged despite the fears of economic nationalists (on North-South investment, see pp. 310–312). Most foreign direct investment (like most portfolio investment) is not in the global South, however, but in industrialized countries.

Host and Home Government Relations

A state in which a foreign MNC operates is called the *host country;* the state where the MNC has its headquarters is called its *home country.* Because host governments can regulate activities on their own territories, an MNC cannot operate in a state against the wishes of the host country's government. Conversely, because MNCs have many states to choose from, a host government cannot generally force an MNC to do business in the country against the MNC's wishes. Both the MNC and the host government benefit—the MNC from profits, the government directly by taxation and indirectly through economic growth (generating future taxes and political support).

However, conflicts also arise in the relationship. One obvious conflict concerns the distribution of new wealth between the MNC and the host government. This distribution depends on the rate at which MNC activities or profits are taxed, as well as on the ground rules for MNC operations. Before an MNC invests or opens a subsidiary in a host country, it sits down with the government to negotiate these issues. Threats of violent leverage are largely irrelevant. Rather, the government's main leverage is to promise a favorable climate for doing business and making money; the MNC's main leverage is to threaten to take its capital elsewhere.

Governments can offer a variety of incentives to MNCs to invest. Special terms of taxation and of regulation are common. National and local governments may offer to provide business infrastructure—such as roads, airports, or phone lines—at the government's expense.

MNC relations with host governments contain several sources of potential conflict. One is the potential for governments to break agreements with MNCs regarding taxes, regulations, or other conditions. In the

IT'S A JOB Foreign direct investment is often sought by host governments because it stimulates employment and economic growth, though at wages that home countries would not tolerate. Here, Muslim women in Indonesia assemble Barbies at a Mattel factory. Note that along with investment, a host country imports certain cultural trappings of the MNC's activity—such as Mattel's rendition of femininity in its doll. (This is a literal case of what postmodern feminists call the social construction of gender roles.)

extreme case, nationalization, a host government takes ownership of MNC facilities and assets in the host country (with or without compensation). However, governments hesitate to break their word with MNCs because other MNCs may not invest there in the future. Nationalization of foreign assets is rare now.

Another source of conflict is the trade policies of the host government. Government restrictions on trade seldom help foreign MNCs; more often they help the host country's own industries—which often compete directly with foreign MNCs. Ironically, although they favor global free trade, MNCs may funnel direct investment to states that restrict imports because MNCs can avoid the import restrictions by producing goods in the host country (rather than exporting from the home country).

Monetary policy also leads to conflicts between MNCs and host governments. When a state's currency is devalued, imports suddenly become more expensive. A foreign MNC selling an imported product (or a product assembled from imported parts) in the host country can be devastated by such a change. Therefore, an MNC making a long-term investment in a host country wants the country's currency to be reasonably stable.

Finally, MNCs may conflict with host governments on issues of international security as well as domestic political stability. When an MNC invests in a country, it assumes that its facilities there will operate profitably over a number of years. If a war or revolution takes away the MNC's facility, the company loses not just income but capital—the standing wealth embodied in that facility. In 2003, ethnic violence in Nigeria led to a costly, weeks-long shutdown of oil production there by ChevronTexaco, Shell, and TotalFinaElf.

In negotiating over these different sources of conflict, MNCs use a variety of means to influence host governments. They hire lobbyists, use advertisements to influence public opinion, and offer incentives to host-country politicians (such as locating facilities in their districts). Such activities are politically sensitive because host-country citizens and politicians may resent foreigners' trying to influence them. Corruption is another means of influence over host governments. Nobody knows the full extent to which MNCs use payoffs, kickbacks, gifts, and similar methods to win the approval of individual government officials for policies favorable to the MNC.

MNCs have a range of conflicts with their home governments as well. Taxation is an important one, as are trade policies. A recurrent complaint of MNCs against home governments is that policies adopted to punish political adversaries—economic sanctions and less extreme restrictions—end up harming the home-country MNCs more than the intended target. Unless ordered to do so, MNCs tend to go on doing business wherever it is profitable, with little regard for the political preferences of their governments.

The location of an MNC's headquarters determines its home nationality. The shareholders and top executives of an MNC are mostly from its home country. But as the world economy becomes more integrated, this is becoming less true. Just as MNCs are increasingly doing business all over the world and assembling products from parts made in many countries, so are shareholders and managers becoming more international in composition.

All business activity takes place in an environment shaped by politics. The international business environment most conducive to the creation of wealth by MNCs is one of stable international security. It is difficult and risky to make money in a situation of international conflict, especially one that threatens to degenerate into violence and war. War destroys wealth, reduces the supply of labor, and distorts markets in many ways. Certainly some businesses profit from international instability and the threat of war—such as arms merchants and smugglers—but these are the exceptions.

Beyond these international security concerns, MNCs favor political stability in the broader rules of the game governing international business. In monetary policy, international business benefits from the stability of rates that the managed float system tries to achieve. In trade policy, business benefits from the stability of tariff levels in the slowly shifting WTO framework. In norms of international law, business benefits from the traditions holding governments responsible for their predecessors' debts and requiring compensation for nationalized foreign assets.

We do not yet live in a world without national borders—not by a long shot—but the international activities of MNCs are moving us in that direction. The next chapter considers first the United Nations and its limited supranational role; then the European Union, the most highly developed intergovernmental organization; and finally the structure and norms governing international law and how they are changing the nature of the world order.

Chapter Review

Summary

- The volume of world trade is very large—about one-sixth of global economic activity—and is concentrated heavily in the states of the industrialized West (Western Europe, North America, and Japan) and China.

- Liberal economics emphasizes international cooperation—especially through worldwide free trade—to increase the total creation of wealth (regardless of its distribution among states).

- Mercantilism emphasizes the use of economic policy to increase state power relative to other states. It mirrors realism in many ways.

- Trade creates wealth by allowing states to specialize in producing goods and services for which they have a comparative advantage (and importing other needed goods).

- The distribution of benefits from an exchange is determined by the price of the goods exchanged. With many buyers and sellers, prices are generally determined by market equilibrium (supply and demand).

- Politics interferes in international markets in many ways, including the use of economic sanctions as political leverage on a target state. However, sanctions are difficult to enforce unless all major economic actors agree to abide by them.

- States that have reduced their dependence on others by pursuing self-sufficient autarky have failed to generate new wealth to increase their well-being. Self-reliance, like central planning, has been largely discredited as a viable economic strategy.

- Through protectionist policies, many states try to protect certain domestic industries from international competition. Such policies tend to slow down the global creation of wealth but do help the particular industry in question.

- The World Trade Organization (WTO), formerly the GATT, is the most important multilateral global trade agreement. The GATT was revised in 1995 with the creation of the WTO, which expanded the focus on manufactured goods to consider agriculture and services. Intellectual property is another recent focus.

- In successive rounds of GATT negotiations over 50 years, states have lowered overall tariff rates (especially on manufactured goods). The Uruguay Round of the GATT, completed in 1994, added hundreds of billions of dollars to the global creation of wealth. The Doha Round began in 2003, and textile tariffs were dropped worldwide in 2005.

- Although the WTO provides a global framework, states continue to operate under thousands of other trade agreements specifying the rules for trade in specific products between specific countries, such as regional free-trade areas (with few if any tariffs or nontariff barriers) that have been created in Europe, North America, South America, Asia, and Africa.

- International cartels are occasionally used by leading producers (sometimes in conjunction with leading consumers) to control and stabilize prices for a commodity on world markets. The most visible example in recent decades has been the oil producers' cartel, OPEC, whose members control more than half the world's exports of a vital commodity, oil.

- Because there is no world government to enforce rules of trade, such enforcement depends on reciprocity and state power. In particular, states reciprocate each other's cooperation in opening markets (or punish each other's refusal to let in foreign products). Although it leads to trade wars on occasion, reciprocity has achieved substantial cooperation in trade.

- The world economy has generated wealth at an accelerating pace in the past two centuries and is integrated on a global scale, although with huge inequalities.

- Free trade agreements have led to a backlash from politically active interest groups adversely affected by globalization; these include labor unions, environmental and human rights NGOs, and certain consumers.

- Each state uses its own currency (except 19 states share the euro). These currencies have no inherent value but depend on people's belief that they can be traded for future goods and services.

- Gold and silver were once used as world currencies that had value in different countries. Today's system is more abstract: National currencies are valued against each other through exchange rates.

- The most important currencies—against which most other states' currencies are compared—are the U.S. dollar, the euro, and the Japanese yen.

- Inflation, most often resulting from the printing of currency faster than the creation of new goods and services, causes the value of a currency to fall relative to other currencies. Inflation rates vary widely but are generally much higher in the global South and former Soviet bloc than in the industrialized West.

- States maintain reserves of hard currency and gold. These reserves back a national currency and cover short-term imbalances in international financial flows.

- Fixed exchange rates can be used to set the relative value of currencies, but more often states use floating exchange rates driven by supply and demand on world currency markets.

- Over the long term, the relative values of national currencies are determined by the underlying health of the national economies and by the monetary policies of governments (how much money they print). To ensure discipline in printing money—and to avoid inflation—industrialized states turn monetary policy over to semiautonomous central banks, such as the U.S. Federal Reserve.

- The World Bank and the International Monetary Fund (IMF) work with states' central banks to maintain stable international monetary relations. Since 1971, the system has used Special Drawing Rights (SDRs)—a kind of world currency controlled by the IMF—rather than gold.

- The IMF operates a system of national accounts to keep track of the flow of money into and out of states. The balance of trade (exports minus imports) must be balanced by capital flows (investments and loans) and changes in reserves.

- International debt results from a protracted imbalance in capital flows—a state borrowing more than it lends—usually in order to cover a chronic trade deficit or government budget deficit.

- Multinational corporations (MNCs) do business in more than one state simultaneously. The largest are based in the leading industrialized states, and most are privately owned. MNCs are increasingly powerful in international economic affairs.

- MNCs try to influence the international political policies of both their headquarters state and the other states in which they operate. Generally, MNCs promote policies favorable to business—low taxes, light regulation, stable currencies, and free trade. They also support stable international security relations because war generally disrupts business.

Key Terms

mercantilism 176
economic liberalism 176
free trade 177
interdependence 177
balance of trade 178
comparative advantage 179
autarky 182
protectionism 182
dumping 183
tariff 183

nontariff barriers 183
World Trade Organization (WTO) 185
General Agreement on Tariffs and Trade (GATT) 185
most-favored nation (MFN) 186
Generalized System of Preferences (GSP) 186
Doha Round 187

North American Free Trade Agreement (NAFTA) 188
cartel 190
Organization of Petroleum Exporting Countries (OPEC) 190
intellectual property rights 192
service sector 193
industrialization 195

Critical Thinking Questions

1. Suppose your state had a chance to reach a major trade agreement by making substantial concessions. The agreement would produce $5 billion in new wealth for your state, as well as $10 billion for each of the other states involved (which are political allies but economic rivals). What advice would a mercantilist give your state's leaders about making such a deal? What arguments would support the advice? How would liberal advice and arguments differ?

2. China seems to have made a successful transition to market economics and is growing rapidly. It is emerging as the world's second-largest economy. Do you think this is a good thing or a bad thing for your state? Does your reasoning reflect mercantilist or liberal assumptions?

3. If you were representing an MNC such as Toyota in negotiations over building an automobile factory in a foreign country, what kinds of concessions would you ask the host government for? What would you offer as incentives? In your report to Toyota's top management regarding the deal, which points would you emphasize as most important? If instead you were representing the host state in the negotiations and reporting to top state leaders, what would be your negotiating goals and the focus of your report?

Chapter 6
International Organization, Law, and Human Rights

CHINESE PEACEKEEPERS ARRIVE IN SOUTH SUDAN, 2015.

 Learning Objectives

6.1 Identify the contradictory forces faced by all international organizations.

6.2 Describe the structure and rules of the UN Security Council, including identification of the five permanent members.

6.3 Describe the growth of the European Union (EU) in terms of the number of members and identify two challenges arising from the increase in membership.

6.4 Evaluate the arguments over the effectiveness or ineffectiveness of international law in restraining state behavior.

6.5 Contrast the effectiveness of international law, nongovernmental organizations (NGOs), and states in advancing the cause of human rights around the globe.

Globalization and Integration

6.1 **Identify the contradictory forces faced by all international organizations.**

Common to most discussions of globalization is a sense that there are forces in the world bringing us all closer together. Some of these forces are the result of state decisions—as we discussed in Chapter 5, states have attempted to integrate their economies through free trade agreements. Still other forces are factors such as technological changes that influence how states, nonstate actors, and even individual citizens function on a day-to-day basis.

This chapter discusses this "coming together." We focus on state decisions to cooperate in order to create international organizations that are **supranational**— they subsume a number of states and their functions within a larger whole. The UN has some supranational aspects, although they are limited by the UN Charter, which is based on state sovereignty. On a regional level, the European Union (EU) is a more supranational entity than the UN; other regional organizations have tried to follow Europe's path as well but with only limited success. These international organizations (IOs) all contain a struggle between the contradictory forces of *nationalism* and *supranationalism*—between state sovereignty and the higher authority of supranational structures.

In addition to formal intergovernmental organizations (IGOs) such as the UN and the EU, people are also becoming connected across international borders through the meshing of ideas, including norms, rules, and international laws. Whether the sources of this connection are from states or nonstate actors, the process of integration always involves transnational actors or issues. *Transnational actors* (for example, multinational corporations [MNCs] and NGOs) bridge national borders, creating new avenues of interdependence among states. *Transnational issues* (for example, global warming or the spread of information technology) are processes that force states to work together because they cannot solve or manage the issues alone.

The rules that govern most interactions in international relations (IR) are rooted in norms. **International norms** are the expectations that actors hold about normal international relations. The attempt to define international norms

supranational
Larger institutions and groupings such as the European Union to which state authority or national identity is subordinated.

international norms
The expectations held by participants about normal relations among states.

follows a centuries-long philosophical tradition. Philosophers such as Kant argued that it was natural for autonomous individuals (or states) to cooperate for mutual benefit because they could see that pursuing their narrow individual interests would end up hurting all. Thus, sovereign states could work together through structures and organizations that would respect each member's autonomy and not create a world government over them. In the nineteenth century, such ideas were embodied in practical organizations in which states participated to manage specific issues such as control of traffic on European rivers.

Agreed norms of behavior, institutionalized through such organizations, become *habitual* over time and gain *legitimacy*. State leaders become used to behaving in a normal way and stop calculating whether violating norms would pay off. For example, at the turn of the nineteenth century, U.S. war planners had active war plans for the possibility of a major naval conflict between the United States and Great Britain. Today, such plans seem ridiculous. Over time, states refrain from behavior not just for cost-benefit reasons (as emphasized by realists and liberals) but for normative reasons having little to do with material calculations (as emphasized by constructivists). Legitimacy and habit explain why international norms can be effective even when they are not codified and enforced.

The power of international norms and standards of morality may vary, however, when different states or world regions hold different expectations of what is normal. To the United States, it was a moral imperative to remove Saddam Hussein from power. But from the perspective of Arab populations, the U.S. invasion was an unjust violation of territorial sovereignty. In cases of diverging norms, morality can be a factor for misunderstanding and conflict rather than a force of stability. Realists point to examples such as these to suggest that international norms do not hold much sway on important matters of IR. Rather, realists point out, many of the accepted norms were shaped by the powerful states in the system (the dominance principle), and these same powerful states are often responsible for their interpretation. Yet constructivist scholars point out that, even if international norms are violated, states (even the United States) go to tremendous lengths to justify behaviors that violate the norm. This suggests that strong norms do exist and are recognized by even the most powerful states.

international organizations (IOs) Intergovernmental organizations (IGOs) such as the UN and nongovernmental organizations (NGOs) such as the International Committee of the Red Cross (ICRC).

Roles of International Organizations

International organizations (IOs) include *intergovernmental organizations (IGOs),* such as the UN, and *nongovernmental organizations (NGOs),* such as the International Committee of the Red Cross. The number of IOs has grown more than fivefold since 1945, to about 350 independent IGOs and tens of thousands of NGOs (depending somewhat on definitions). Figure 6.1 illustrates this growth. This weaving together of people across national boundaries through specialized groups reflects world interdependence (see p. 177).

Figure 6.1 States and IGOs in the World, 1815–2015

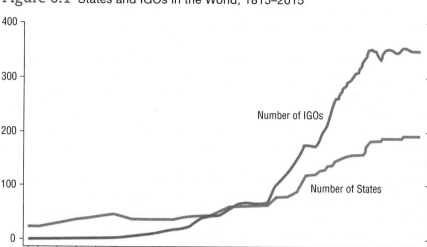

NOT THE NORM International norms are evolving in such areas as humanitarian intervention and human rights. These norms help define the roles of international organizations. One of their areas of concern is the use of child soldiers, like this ten-year-old Libyan rebel in 2011. Another concern, the protection of civilians from slaughter, inspired NATO intervention in the Libya conflict.

Some IGOs are global in scope; others are regional or just bilateral (having only two states as members). Some are general in their purposes; others have specific functional purposes. Overall, the success of these IGOs has been mixed; the regional ones have had more success than the global ones, and those with specific functional or technical purposes have worked better than those with broad purposes. IGOs hold together because they promote the national interests (or enhance the leverage) of their member states—not because of vague ideals.

Among *regional* IGOs, the European Union encompasses some of the most important organizations, but it is not the only example. Other important regional IGOs are the Association of South East Asian Nations (ASEAN), the Southern Cone Common Market (MERCOSUR), and the African Union (AU).

Global IGOs (aside from the UN) usually have functional purposes involving coordinating actions of some set of states around the world. The IGO called Intelsat, for example, is a consortium of governments and private businesses that operates communications satellites. Members of the Organization of Petroleum Exporting Countries (OPEC) are major oil producers who meet periodically in Vienna to set production quotas for members in an effort to keep world oil prices high and stable.

NGOs tend to be more specialized in function than IGOs. Many NGOs have economic or business-related functions. For example, the International Air Transport Association coordinates the work of airline companies. Other NGOs have global political purposes—for example, Amnesty International for human rights and Planned Parenthood for reproductive rights and family planning. Still other NGOs have cultural purposes—for example, the International Olympic Committee.

Religious groups are among the largest NGOs—their memberships often span many countries. Both in today's world and historically, sects of Christianity, Islam, Buddhism, Judaism, Hinduism, and other world religions have organized themselves across state borders, often in the face of hostility from one or more national governments. Missionaries have deliberately built and nurtured these transnational links. The Roman Catholic Church historically held a special position in the European international system, especially before the seventeenth century. NGOs with broad purposes and geographical scope often maintain observer status in the UN so that they can participate in UN meetings about issues of concern.

A web of international organizations of various sizes and types now connects people in all countries. The rapid growth of this network, and the increasingly intense communications and interactions that occur within it, indicate rising international interdependence. These organizations in turn provide the institutional mesh to hold together some kind of world order, even when leaders and contexts come and go and even when norms are undermined by sudden changes in power relations. At the center of that web of connection stands the most important international organization today, the United Nations.

The United Nations

6.2   Describe the structure and rules of the UN Security Council, including identification of the five permanent members.

The UN and other international organizations have both strengths and weaknesses in the anarchic international system. State sovereignty creates a real need for such organizations on a practical level because no central world government performs the function of coordinating the actions of states for mutual benefit. However, state sovereignty also severely limits the power of the UN and other IOs because governments reserve power to themselves and are stingy in delegating it to the UN or to anyone else. The UN has had a mixed record with these strengths and weaknesses—in some ways providing remarkable global-level management and in other ways appearing helpless against the sovereignty of even modest-sized states (not to mention great powers).

The UN System

The UN is a relatively new institution, just 70 years old. Even newer is the more prominent role that the UN has played in international security affairs since the end of the Cold War. Despite this new prominence, the main purposes of the UN are the same now as when it was founded after World War II.

PURPOSES OF THE UN   The UN is the closest thing to a world government that has ever existed, but it is not a world government. Its members are sovereign states that have not empowered the UN to enforce its will within states' territories except with the consent of those states' governments. Thus, although the UN strengthens world order, its design acknowledges the realities of international anarchy and the unwillingness of states to surrender their sovereignty. Within these limits, the basic purpose of the UN is to provide a global institutional structure through which states can sometimes settle conflicts with less reliance on the use of force.

The **UN Charter** is based on the principles that states are *equal* under international law, have full *sovereignty* over their own affairs, should have full *independence* and *territorial integrity,* and should carry out their international *obligations*—such as respecting diplomatic privileges, refraining from committing aggression, and observing the terms of treaties they sign. The Charter also lays out the structure of the UN and the methods by which it operates.

The UN exists not because it has power to force its will on the world's states; it exists because states have created it to serve their needs. A state's membership in the UN is essentially a form of indirect leverage. States gain leverage by using the UN to seek more beneficial outcomes in conflicts. The cost of this leverage is modest—UN dues and the expenses of diplomatic representatives, in addition to the agreement to behave in accordance with the Charter (most of the time).

States get several benefits from the UN. Foremost among these is the international stability (especially in security affairs) that the UN tries to safeguard; this allows states to realize gains from trade and other forms of exchange. The UN is a *symbol* of international order and even of global identity. It is

UN Charter The founding document of the United Nations; it is based on the principles that states are equal, have sovereignty over their own affairs, enjoy independence and territorial integrity, and must fulfill international obligations. The Charter also lays out the structure and methods of the UN.

WATCHFUL EYE The United Nations has very limited powers and resources, yet the world places some of the most important tasks on the UN, including peacekeeping between former belligerents. Here, UN peacekeepers from an observer force on the Golan Heights, between Syria and Israel, watch fighting on the Syrian side of the border, 2014.

also a *forum* where states promote their views and bring their disputes. And it is a *mechanism* for conflict resolution in international security affairs. The UN also promotes and coordinates development assistance (see Chapter 7) and other programs of economic and social development in the global South. These programs reflect the belief that economic and social problems—above all, poverty—are an important source of international conflict and war. Finally, the UN is a coordinating system for *information* and planning by hundreds of internal and external agencies and programs, and for the publication of international data.

Despite its heavy tasks, the UN is still a small and fragile institution. Compare, for instance, what states spend on two types of leverage for settling conflicts: military forces and the UN. Every year, the world spends almost $2 trillion on the military, and about $5 billion on the UN regular budget. The whole budget of UN operations, peacekeeping, programs, and agencies combined is less than 3 percent of world military spending. That proportion is even more extreme in the United States: more than 100 to 1. Each U.S. citizen pays (on average) about $2,000 a year for U.S. military spending but only about $15 a year for U.S. payments of UN dues, assessments, and voluntary contributions to UN programs and agencies combined.

Sometimes the UN succeeds, and sometimes it fails. The UN deals with the issues that are perhaps the most difficult in the world. If groups of states could easily solve problems such as ethnic conflicts, human rights, refugees, and world hunger themselves, they most likely would have done so. Instead, states turn many of these difficult problems over to the UN and hope it can take care of them.

STRUCTURE OF THE UN   The UN's structure (see Figure 6.2) centers on the **UN General Assembly**, where representatives of all states sit together in a huge room, listen to speeches, and pass resolutions. The General Assembly coordinates a variety of development programs and other autonomous agencies through the Economic and Social Council (ECOSOC). Parallel to the General Assembly is the **UN Security Council**, in which five great powers and ten rotating member states make decisions about international peace and security. The Security Council has responsibility for the dispatch of peacekeeping forces to trouble spots. The administration of the UN takes place through the **UN Secretariat** (executive branch), led by the Secretary General of the UN. The World Court (International Court of Justice, discussed below) is a judicial arm of the UN.

National delegations to the UN, headed by ambassadors from each member state, work and meet together at UN headquarters in New York City. They have diplomatic status in the United States, which as host country also assumes certain other obligations to facilitate the UN's functioning. For example, the U.S. government has permitted people such as Fidel Castro—normally barred from entry to the United States—to visit New York long enough to address the UN.

A major strength of the UN structure is the *universality of its membership*. The UN had 193 members in 2016. Almost every territory in the world is either a UN

UN General Assembly A body composed of representatives of all states that allocates UN funds, passes nonbinding resolutions, and coordinates economic development programs and various autonomous agencies through the Economic and Social Council (ECOSOC).

UN Security Council A body of five great powers (which can veto resolutions) and ten rotating member states that makes decisions about international peace and security, including the dispatch of UN peacekeeping forces.

Figure 6.2 The United Nations

Source: United Nations

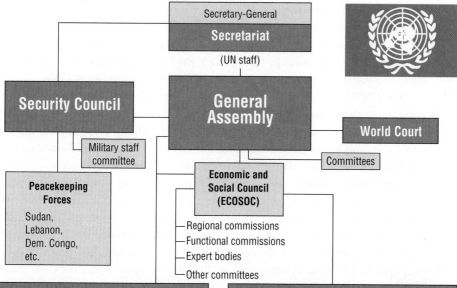

UN Programs	
UNEP	UN Environment Program
UNICEF	UN Children's Fund
UNDRO	Office of the UN Disaster Relief Coordinator
UNHCR	Office of the UN High Commissioner for Refugees
UNRWA*	UN Relief Works Agency [for Palestinian Refugees]
UNDP	UN Development Program
UNITAR*	UN Institute for Training and Research
UNIFEM	UN Development Fund for Women
INSTRAW	UN International Research and Training Institute [for women]
UNCTAD	UN Conference on Trade and Development
WFP	World Food Program
WFC	World Food Council
UNCHS	Human Settlements (Habitat)
UNFPA	UN Population Fund
UNU	UN University
UNDCP	Drug Control Program
ITC	International Trade Center

* Does not report to ECOSOC.

Autonomous Agencies	
IAEA*	International Atomic Energy Agency (Vienna)
WHO	World Health Organization (Geneva)
FAO	Food and Agriculture Organization (Rome)
IFAD	International Fund for Agricultural Development (Rome)
ILO	International Labor Organization (Geneva)
UNESCO	UN Educational, Scientific, and Cultural Organization (Paris)
UNIDO	UN Industrial Development Organization (Vienna)
ITU	International Telecommunications Union (Geneva)
IPU	International Postal Union (Berne)
ICAO	International Civil Aviation Organization (Montreal)
IMO	International Maritime Organization (London)
WIPO	World Intellectual Property Organization (Geneva)
WMO	World Meteorological Organization (Geneva)
MIGA	Multilateral Investment Guarantee Agency
IMF	International Monetary Fund (Washington)
IBRD	International Bank for Reconstruction and Development [World Bank] (Washington)
IDA	International Development Association (Washington)
IFC	International Finance Corporation (Washington)
WTO*	World Trade Organization (Geneva)

* Does not report to ECOSOC.

UN Secretariat The UN's executive branch, led by the Secretary General.

member or formally a province or colony of one. (Taiwan is considered part of China; Switzerland, traditionally neutral, joined in 2003; and Palestine became a nonmember observer state in 2012.) Agreement on the Charter, even if sometimes breached, commits all states to basic rules governing their relations.

One way the UN induced all the great powers to join was to reassure them that their participation in the UN would not harm their national interests. Recognizing the role of power in world order, the UN Charter gave five great powers each a veto over substantive decisions of the Security Council.

The UN Charter establishes a mechanism for *collective security*—the banding together of the world's states to stop an aggressor. Chapter 7 of the Charter explicitly authorizes the Security Council to use military force against aggression if the nonviolent means called for in Chapter 6 have failed. Because of the great power veto, however, the UN cannot effectively stop aggression by (or supported by) a great power. As often happens with the dominance principle, this structure creates resentments by smaller powers. In 2006, Iran's president asked the General Assembly, "If the governments of the United States or the United Kingdom commit atrocities or violate international law, which of the organizations in the United Nations can take them to account?" (None of them, of course, is the answer.) Chapter 7 was used only once during the Cold War—in the Korean War when the Soviet delegation unwisely boycotted the proceedings (and when China's seat was held by the nationalists in Taiwan).

HISTORY OF THE UN   The UN was founded in 1945 in San Francisco by 51 states. It was the successor to the League of Nations, which had failed to counter aggression effectively in the 1930s. Like the League, the UN was founded to increase international order and the rule of law to prevent another world war. A certain tension has long existed between the UN and the United States as the world's most powerful state. (The United States had not joined the League, and it was partly to ensure U.S. interest that the UN headquarters was placed in New York.)

In the 1950s and 1960s, the UN's membership more than doubled as colonies in Asia and Africa won independence. This changed the character of the General Assembly, in which each state has one vote regardless of size. The new members had different concerns from those of the Western industrialized countries and in many cases resented having been colonized by Westerners. Many states in the global South believed that the United States enjoyed too much power in the UN.

Until 1971, China's seat on the Security Council (and in the General Assembly) was occupied by the nationalist government on the island of Taiwan, which had lost power in mainland China in 1949. In 1971, the Chinese seat was taken from the nationalists and given to the communist government. Today, Taiwan—which functions autonomously in many international matters despite its formal status as a Chinese province—is not a member of the UN. But it is the only important nonmember.

Throughout the Cold War, the UN had few successes in international security because the U.S.-Soviet conflict prevented consensus. The UN appeared somewhat irrelevant in a world order structured by two opposing alliance blocs. The General Assembly, with its predominantly third world membership, concentrated on the economic and social problems of poor countries, and these became the main work of the UN. States in the global South also used the UN as a forum to criticize rich countries in general and the United States in particular. By the 1980s, the U.S. government showed its displeasure with this trend by withholding U.S. dues to the UN (eventually more than $1 billion), paying up only years later after UN reforms.

After the Cold War, the great powers could finally agree on measures regarding international security. The UN had several major successes in the late 1980s in ending violent regional conflicts (in Central America and the Iran-Iraq War) while introducing peacekeepers to monitor the cease-fires. Between 1987 and 1993, Security Council resolutions increased from 15 to 78, peacekeeping missions increased from 5 to 17, peacekeepers increased from 12,000 to 78,000, and countries sending troops increased from 26 to 76.

The new missions ran into serious problems, however. Inadequate funding and management problems undermined peacekeeping efforts in Angola, Somalia, and Cambodia. In the former Yugoslavia in 1993–1995, the UN undertook a large peacekeeping mission before a cease-fire was in place—"peacekeeping where there is no peace to keep." In response to these problems (and because of the unpaid U.S. dues), the UN scaled back peacekeeping operations (from 78,000 to 19,000 troops) in 1995–1997 and carried out reductions and reforms in the UN Secretariat and UN programs.

The 2003 Iraq War triggered serious divisions among the great powers that sidelined the UN. After reaching consensus to insist on Iraqi disarmament and send back UN weapons inspectors, the Security Council split on whether to authorize force against Iraq—the United States and Britain in favor; France, Russia, and China against. A U.S.-British coalition toppled the Iraqi government without explicit UN backing. UN Secretary General Kofi Annan later called the war "illegal." The UN sent a team to Iraq to help with reconstruction, but suicide truck bombers destroyed it, killing the chief of the mission and dozens of others. The UN withdrew its staff from Iraq in 2003 and found itself largely sidelined in the world's most prominent international conflict.

To aggravate U.S.-UN tensions further, documents recovered during the Iraq War showed that high-ranking UN, French, Chinese, and Russian officials (and American oil companies) illegally profited from the UN's $64 billion oil-for-food program for Iraq, which was supposed to ease the civilian suffering caused by economic sanctions in the 1990s. In 2005, an independent investigation found the program corrupt and heavily criticized the UN for mismanagement and poor oversight of the program.

Currently, the UN follows a principle of "three pillars"—security, economic development, and human rights—which are considered mutually necessary for any one of the pillars to succeed. In a postwar conflict situation, in particular, the three pillars reinforce each other. In the past decade, the UN has attempted to deal with conflicts in Libya, Syria, and Ukraine.

The UN is in some ways just beginning to work as it was originally intended to, through a concert of great powers and universal recognition of the Charter. In the coming years, the UN must continue to grapple with the challenges of its evolving role in a unipolar world, the limitations of its budget, and the strength of state sovereignty.

The Security Council

The Security Council is responsible for maintaining international peace and security and for restoring peace when it breaks down. Its decisions are *binding* on all UN member states. The Security Council has tremendous power to *define* the existence and nature of a security threat, to *structure* the response to such a threat, and to *enforce* its decisions through mandatory directives to UN members (such as to halt trade with an aggressor). Since 1945, the Council has passed more than 2,230 resolutions, with new ones added by the week. These resolutions represent the great powers' blueprints for resolving the world's various security disputes, especially in regional conflicts.

The five *permanent members* of the Council—the United States, Britain, France, Russia, and China—are the most important. What they can agree on, generally the world must go along with. Issues on which they disagree can quickly become contentious. In 2008, after the Council failed to decide whether the Serbian province of Kosovo should be independent, Kosovars unilaterally declared their independence from Serbia. Kosovo was quickly recognized by some Security Council members (the United States, France, and Britain) but not others (China and Russia). Angry Serbians rejected Kosovo's declaration. In 2010, the World Court held Kosovo's *declaration* to be legal, but its substantive status remains bitterly disputed. As of 2015, 108 UN members have recognized Kosovo's independence.

COUNCIL OF POWER Collective security rests with the UN Security Council, which has authorized such military interventions as the Gulf War and the 2001 campaign in Afghanistan. Military actions not approved by the Council—such as the 1999 bombing of Serbia and the 2003 U.S.-British invasion of Iraq—tend to be controversial. Here, Serbia's president (left end of table) objects to Kosovo's claim of independence from Serbia, 2008. With the permanent members split on the issue—Russia and China backed Serbia while the United States, Britain, and France recognized Kosovo—the Council did not take action.

Substantive Security Council resolutions require 9 votes from among the 15 members. But a no vote by any permanent member defeats the resolution—the *veto* power. Many resolutions have been vetoed by the permanent members, and many more have never been proposed because they would have faced certain veto. In the past twenty years, however, the use of the veto has dropped abruptly, to just 25 vetoes—14 by the United States and 7 each by Russia and China (multiple states can veto the same resolution).

The Council's ten *nonpermanent members* rotate onto the Council for two-year terms. Nonpermanent members are elected (five each year) by the General Assembly from a list prepared by informal regional caucuses. Usually there is a mix of regions and country sizes, though not by any strict formula. Often, countries lobby vigorously for a seat on the Council, producing books, advertisements, and memos to gain votes from other members of the regional caucuses. In 2014, Saudi Arabia won a coveted Security Council seat but then refused to accept it. They became the first state to refuse a seat on the Council. This high-profile protest came after the Saudis heavily criticized what they considered weak responses by the UN to the conflict in Syria and negotiations with Iran over that country's nuclear program.

Table 6.1 shows the recent rotations of members onto the Security Council. The system of nomination by regional caucuses has kept the regional balance on the Council fairly constant, as individual states come and go. Major regional actors, including those mentioned as candidates for possible new permanent seats, tend to rotate onto the Council more often than do smaller states.

Table 6.1 Regional Representation on the UN Security Council

Region	Permanent Members[a]	Nonpermanent Members[b]			Possible Contenders for New Permanent Seats[c]
		2015	2014	2013	
North America	United States				
W. Europe	Britain France	Spain Lithuania	Luxembourg Lithuania	Luxembourg	Germany
Japan/Pacific		New Zealand Malaysia	South Korea Australia	Australia South Korea	Japan
Russia/CIS	Russia			Azerbaijan	
China	China				
Middle East		Jordan	Jordan	Morocco	Egypt?
Latin America		Venezuela Chile	Argentina Chile	Argentina Guatemala	Brazil, Mexico?
South Asia				Pakistan	India, Indonesia?
Africa		Angola Nigeria Chad	Chad Nigeria Rwanda	Rwanda Togo	Nigeria? South Africa?

[a]The five permanent members hold veto power.
[b]Nonpermanent members are elected for two-year terms by the General Assembly, based on nominations by regional caucuses.
[c]Possible new permanent seats might have fewer if any veto powers.

The Security Council's power is limited in two major ways; both reflect the strength of state sovereignty in the international system. First, the Council's decisions depend entirely on the interests of its member states (see Figure 6.3). The ambassadors who represent those states cannot change a Council resolution without authorization from their governments. Second, although Security Council resolutions in theory bind all UN members, member states in practice often try to evade or soften their effect. For instance, trade sanctions are difficult to enforce. A Security Council resolution can be enforced in practice only if enough powerful states care about it. Even when the Security Council cannot agree on means of enforcement, however, its resolutions shape the way disputes are seen and ultimately how they are resolved.

Figure 6.3 Divergent Interests on the UN Security Council

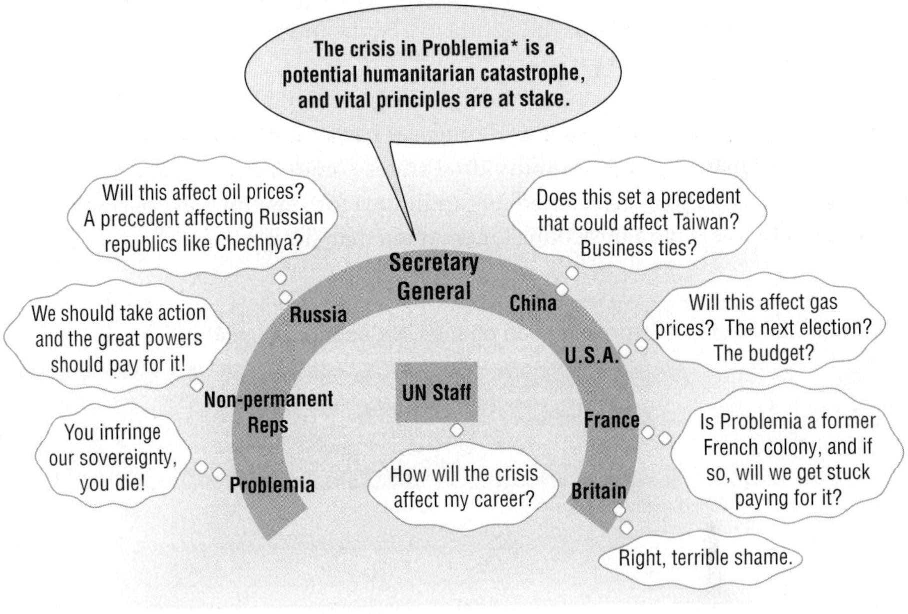

*Problemia could be Kurdish Iraq in 1991 or Darfur, Sudan, in 2007.

PROPOSED CHANGES   The structure of the Security Council is not without problems. Japan and Germany are great powers that contribute substantial UN dues (based on economic size) and make large contributions to UN programs and peacekeeping operations. Yet they have exactly the same formal representation in the UN as tiny states: one vote in the General Assembly and the chance to rotate onto the Security Council (in practice they rotate onto the Council more often than others). As global trading powers, Japan and Germany have huge stakes in the ground rules for international security affairs and would like seats at the table.

But including Japan and Germany as permanent Security Council members would not be simple. If Germany joined, three of the seven permanent members would be European, giving that region unfair weight. The three European seats could be combined into one (a rotating seat or one representing the European Union), but this would water down the power of Britain and France, which can veto any such change in the Charter. Japan's bid for a seat faces Chinese opposition. Also, if Japan or Germany got a seat, then what about India, with 20 percent of the world's population? And what about an Islamic country such as Indonesia? Finally, what about Latin America and Africa? Possible new permanent members could include Germany, Japan, India, Brazil, Egypt, and either Nigeria or South Africa. None of these plans has made much progress. Any overhaul of the Security Council would reduce the power of the current five permanent members, any of which could veto the change.

Peacekeeping Forces

Peacekeeping forces are not mentioned in the UN Charter. The Charter requires member states to place military forces at the disposal of the UN, but such forces were envisioned as being used in response to aggression (under collective security). In practice, when the UN has authorized force to reverse aggression—as in the Gulf War in 1990—the forces involved have been *national* forces not under UN command.

The UN's *own* forces—borrowed from armies of member states but under the flag and command of the UN—have been *peacekeeping* forces to calm regional conflicts, playing a neutral role between warring forces. These forces won the Nobel Peace Prize in 1988 in recognition of their growing importance and success. However, such neutral forces do not succeed well in a situation in which the Security Council has identified one side as the aggressor.

PEACEKEEPING MISSIONS   The Secretary General assembles a peacekeeping force for each mission, usually from a few states totally uninvolved in the conflict, and puts it under a single commander. The soldiers are called blue helmets. Peacekeeping forces serve at the invitation of a host government and must leave if that government orders them out.

Authority for peacekeeping forces is granted by the Security Council, usually for a period of three to six months that may be renewed—in some cases for decades. *Funds* must be voted on by the General Assembly, and lack of funds is today the single greatest constraint on the use of peacekeeping forces. Special assessments against member states pay for peacekeeping operations. With the expansion of peacekeeping, these expenses far exceed the rest of the UN budget, coming to over $8 billion in 2015.

RECENT MISSIONS   At the beginning of 2016, the UN maintained more than 100,000 international personnel (including troops, military observers, police, and administrators) in 16 peacekeeping or observing missions, spanning five world regions, using military personnel from 128 countries (see Table 6.2).

Table 6.2 UN Peacekeeping Missions as of September 2015

Location	Region	Personnel	Annual Cost (million $)	Role	Since
Democratic	Congo Africa	21,000	$1,400	Enforce cease-fire; protect civilians	2010
Sudan/Darfur	Africa	16,500	1,150	Protect civilians	2007
Sudan/South Sudan	Africa	12,000	1,100	Support peace agreement	2011
Lebanon	Middle East	10,500	500	Monitor cease-fire on Israeli border	1978
Mali	Africa	10,000	830	Protect civilians for elections	2013
Central African Rep.	Africa	9,100	650	Protect civilians; demobilization	2014
Ivory Coast	Africa	8,000	500	Help implement peace agreement	2004
Haiti	Latin America	7,000	500	Assist transitional govt.	2004
Liberia	Africa	6,500	400	Assist transitional govt.	2003
Sudan/Abyei	Africa	4,100	300	Monitor disputed town on border	2011
Syria (Golan Heights)	Middle East	1,000	60	Monitor Israel-Syria cease-fire	1974
Cyprus	Middle East	900	60	Monitor Greek-Turkish cease-fire	1964
Western Sahara	Africa	300	55	Organize referendum in territory	1991
Israel	Middle East	250	75	Observe Arab-Israeli truce	1948
Kosovo	Europe	150	45	Civil administration; relief	1999
India/Pakistan	South Asia	60	20	Observe India-Pakistan cease-fire	1949
Total		110,000	8,500		

Note: Size indicates total international personnel (mostly troops but some civilian administrators and police).

Source: United Nations

The two largest peacekeeping missions in 2015 were in the Darfur region of Sudan and Democratic Congo. In the Congo mission, over 20,000 peacekeepers monitored a cease-fire and protected civilians after a civil war. In 2012, these UN peacekeepers proved weak when a rebel movement in the unstable east of the country went on the attack, displacing civilians. A decade after the main war ended, such recurrent attacks proved vexing for UN forces. Additional troops were added in 2013–2014 to help confront local rebels.

In 2007, the Security Council approved a nearly 20,000-troop peacekeeping force for the Darfur region in Sudan, after several years of resistance from the Sudanese government. As of 2015, a force of over 15,000 troops and police personnel is still being maintained. The UN troops joined an already-deployed (but small) African Union (AU) contingent. It took several more years for all of the authorized troops to arrive because of numerous objections from Sudan, and attacks on civilians continued despite their presence. In 2012, fighting between government and rebel forces drove 25,000 civilians out of one refugee camp. The Darfur mission is in addition to over 10,000 UN troops enforcing a cease-fire between Sudan and newly independent South Sudan, focused on the disputed town of Abyei.

The UN's other largest peacekeeping operations were in Liberia (maintaining a cease-fire after a civil war), Ivory Coast and Burundi (stabilizing peace agreements), Lebanon (following the 2006 Israeli-Hezbollah war), and Mali (trying to maintain stability during a government transition). The largest recent missions reflect the resurgence of UN peacekeeping after a shakeout in the mid-1990s.

North Atlantic Treaty Organization (NATO)–led forces largely replaced UN peacekeepers in Bosnia in the late 1990s (and later took military control of Kosovo). UN operations in these countries focus on civilian governmental functions, leaving security matters largely to UN-authorized but independently commanded international forces. The same approach was used in East Timor with an Australian-led force.

In the 1990s, the UN had several spectacular failures in peacekeeping, in the former Yugoslavia, Rwanda, Angola, and Somalia. Less newsworthy were the successful missions in that period. In Cambodia, 15,000 peacekeepers worked with a large force of UN administrators who nearly took over the Cambodian government after a long and devastating civil war. The lessons learned in Cambodia helped the UN accomplish a similar mission more easily in Mozambique. Missions in El Salvador and Namibia were also early successes for post–Cold War UN peacekeeping. These experiences helped the UN respond effectively after civil wars in Sierra Leone, Ivory Coast, and Liberia in 2002–2003. But problems with sex-related crimes in UN peacekeeping operations, and the importance of women in postwar societies, spurred the Security Council to pass Resolution 1325 in 2000 to focus attention on gender issues in UN peacekeeping and reconstruction.

As UN peacekeeping has become more intensive in recent years, new missions have expanded the range of what are now broadly called *peace operations*. These operations include not only traditional peacekeeping but also the use of force to protect civilians (as in Democratic Congo), the supervision of elections (as in Liberia), and even running the government while a society gets back on its feet (as in Cambodia, East Timor, and Kosovo). These expanded operations after conflicts are called **peacebuilding**. In an effort to provide longer-term support after wars, in 2005 the UN created a Peacebuilding Commission to coordinate reconstruction, institution building, and economic recovery efforts after peacekeeping missions end.

peacebuilding The use of military peacekeepers, civilian administrators, police trainers, and similar efforts to sustain peace agreements and build stable, democratic governments in societies recovering from civil wars. Since 2005 a UN Peacebuilding Commission has coordinated and supported these activities.

OBSERVING AND PEACEKEEPING "Peacekeepers" actually perform two different functions: observing and peacekeeping. Observers are unarmed military officers sent to a conflict area in small numbers simply to watch what happens and report back to the UN. With the UN watching, the parties to a conflict are often less likely to break a cease-fire. Observers can monitor various aspects of a country's situation—cease-fires, elections, respect for human rights, and other issues.

The function of *peacekeeping* is carried out by lightly armed soldiers (in armored vehicles with automatic rifles but without artillery, tanks, and other heavy weapons). Such forces play several roles. They can *interpose* themselves physically between warring parties to keep them apart (more accurately, to make them attack the UN forces in order to get to their enemy). UN peacekeepers often try to *negotiate* with military officers on both sides. This channel of communication can bring about tactical actions and understandings that support a cease-fire. But the UN forces in a war zone cannot easily get from one side's positions to those of the other to conduct negotiations. Peacekeeping is much more difficult if one side sees the UN forces as being biased toward the other side. When cease-fires break down, UN troops get caught in the middle. More than 3,300 have been killed over the years.

Many countries contribute their national military forces to UN peacekeeping missions. In 2014, the five leading contributors (with troop and police numbers) were Bangladesh (over 9,000), Pakistan (over 8,000), India (8,000), Ethiopia (nearly 8,000), and Rwanda (5,500). Reasons for troop contributions to UN peacekeeping vary. Some states feel that, by contributing to a common good, they are advancing the interest of peace while simultaneously projecting the image of a strong military power. In this way, states may serve to increase their soft power. Alternatively, some states find contributing to these missions financially beneficial because peacekeeping forces are paid for with UN contributions. In a few countries such as Nepal and Sierra Leone, sending military forces out of the country for peacekeeping is useful for domestic political stability after a civil war.

In some conflicts, peacekeepers organized outside the UN framework have been used instead of UN-commanded forces. Some 3,500 French peacekeepers—not under UN command—serve in Ivory Coast alongside 11,000 UN peacekeepers monitoring a 2003 cease-fire. When government airstrikes killed nine French soldiers in 2004, the French forces retaliated robustly, destroying the government's air force. In 2011, after the incumbent president lost an election but refused to leave, UN and French troops helped the winner dislodge him by force.

Peacekeeping forces have generally been unable to make peace, only to keep it. To go into a shooting war and suppress hostilities requires military forces far beyond those of past UN peacekeeping missions. Thus, peacekeepers are usually not sent until a cease-fire has been arranged, has taken effect, and has held up for some time. Often dozens of cease-fires are broken before one sticks and the UN gets its chance.

In the late 1990s, seven countries—Denmark, Norway, Sweden, Poland, the Netherlands, Austria, and Canada—formed a 4,000-troop UN Standby High Readiness Brigade. Headquartered in Denmark and available to deploy to conflict areas in two to four weeks rather than in months, as traditional forces now require, the brigade is controlled by the Security Council. It participated in the UN mission to Ethiopia-Eritrea in 2000–2001. In 2005, the brigade deployed to Sudan to support a peace agreement between northern and southern regions after a long civil war.

The Secretariat

The Secretary General of the UN is the closest thing to a "president of the world" that exists. But the Secretary General represents member states—not the world's 7 billion people. The Secretary General is nominated by the Security Council—requiring the consent of all five permanent members—and must be approved by the General Assembly. The term of office is five years and may be renewed. Secretaries General have come from various regions of the world but never from a great power.

Secretary General Ban Ki-moon, a former foreign minister of South Korea, began his term in 2007 focused on UN reform, economic development, human rights, terrorism, proliferation, environmental problems, and HIV/AIDS. His second term began in 2012. His predecessor, Kofi Annan, from Ghana, served ten years and helped reinvigorate the UN, winning the one-hundredth-anniversary Nobel Peace Prize for his efforts.

ACTION HEROES The UN Secretary General has a lofty mission but limited power and resources. Here, Ban Ki-moon meets with actor Daniel Craig to discuss landmines. The Secretary General must attempt to persuade member states to take action in a number of issue areas including development, human rights, and peace and security.

The Secretariat of the UN is its executive branch, headed by the Secretary General. It is a bureaucracy for administering UN policy and programs. In security matters, the Secretary General personally works with the Security Council; development programs in poor countries are coordinated by a second-in-command, the director-general for Development and International Economic Cooperation. The Secretariat is divided into functional areas, with undersecretaries-general and assistant secretaries-general. The UN staff in these areas includes administrative personnel as well as technical experts and economic advisers working on various programs and projects in the member countries. The staff numbers about 43,000 people, and the total number of employees in the UN system (including the World Bank and the International Monetary Fund [IMF]) is about 75,000.

One purpose of the UN Secretariat is to develop an *international civil service* of diplomats and bureaucrats whose loyalties lie at the global level, not with their states of origin. The UN Charter sets the Secretary General and staff apart from the authority of national governments and calls on member states to respect the staff members' "exclusively international character." The UN has been fairly successful in this regard; the Secretary General is most often seen as an independent diplomat thinking about the whole world's interests, not as a pawn of any state. But in the early 1990s, the UN bureaucracy came under increasing criticism for both inefficiency and corruption. These criticisms, coming especially from the United States, which saw itself as bearing an unfair share of the costs, led to a reform program. By the late 1990s, UN staff was reduced by one-quarter compared to a decade earlier, and budgets were scaled back year by year.

The Secretary General is more than a bureaucratic manager. He (it has not yet been a she) is a visible public figure whose personal attention to a regional conflict can move it toward resolution. The Charter allows the Secretary General to use the UN's "good offices" to serve as a neutral mediator in international conflicts—to bring hostile parties together in negotiations.

The Secretary General also works to bring together the great power consensus on which Security Council action depends. The Secretary General has the power under the Charter to bring to the Security Council any matter that might threaten international peace and security, and so to play a major role in setting the UN's agenda in international security affairs. Still, the Secretary General experiences tensions with the Security Council. When the Secretary General asks for authority for a peacekeeping mission for six months, the Security Council is likely to say three months. If the Secretary General asks for $10 million, he might get $5 million. Thus the Secretary General remains, like the entire UN system, constrained by state sovereignty.

The General Assembly

The General Assembly is made up of all 193 member states of the UN, each with one vote. It usually meets every year, from late September through January, in *plenary session*. State leaders or foreign ministers, including the U.S. president, generally come through one by one to address this assemblage. This global town hall is a unique institution and provides a powerful medium for states to put forward their ideas and arguments. Presiding over it is a president elected by the Assembly—a post without much power.

The Assembly convenes for *special sessions* every few years on general topics such as economic cooperation or disarmament. The Assembly has met in *emergency session* in the past to deal with an immediate threat to international peace and security, but this has happened only nine times and has now become uncommon.

The General Assembly has the power to accredit national delegations as members of the UN (through its Credentials Committee). For instance, in 1971 the delegation of the People's Republic of China was given China's seat in the UN (including on the Security Council) in place of the nationalists in Taiwan. Some political entities that fall short of state status send *permanent observer missions* to the UN, which participate without a vote in the General Assembly; these include the Vatican (Holy See) and the Palestinian Authority.

The General Assembly's main power lies in its control of finances for UN programs and operations, including peacekeeping. It can also pass resolutions on various matters, but these are purely advisory and at times have served largely to vent frustrations of the majority. The Assembly also elects members of certain UN agencies and programs. Finally, the Assembly coordinates UN programs and agencies through its own system of committees, commissions, and councils.

Many of the activities associated with the UN do not take place under tight control of either the General Assembly or the Security Council. They occur in functional agencies and programs that have various amounts of autonomy from UN control.

UN Programs

Through the Economic and Social Council, the General Assembly oversees more than a dozen major programs to advance economic development and social stability in poor states of the global South. Through its programs, the UN helps manage global North-South relations: it organizes a flow of resources and skills from the richer parts of the world to support development in the poorer parts.

The programs are funded partly by General Assembly allocations and partly by contributions that the programs raise directly from member states, businesses, or private charitable contributors. The degree of General Assembly funding, and of operational autonomy from the Assembly, varies from one program to another. Each UN program has a staff, a headquarters, and various operations in the field, where it works with host governments in member states.

The *UN Environment Program (UNEP)* became more prominent in the 1990s as the economic development of the global South and the growing economies of the industrialized world took a toll on the world environment (see Chapter 8). The UNEP grapples with global environmental strategies. It provides technical assistance to member states, monitors environmental conditions globally, develops standards, and recommends alternative energy sources.

UNICEF is the UN Children's Fund, which gives technical and financial assistance to poor countries for programs benefiting children. Unfortunately, the needs of children in many countries are still urgent, and UNICEF is kept busy. Financed by voluntary contributions, UNICEF has for decades organized U.S. children in an annual Halloween fund drive (Trick-or-Treat Drive for UNICEF) on behalf of their counterparts in poorer countries.

HELPING WHERE NEEDED An array of UN programs, operating under the General Assembly, aim to help countries in the global South to overcome social and economic problems. These programs play a crucial role in the international assistance after disasters and wars. This girl displaced by ethnic violence in Kyrgyzstan in 2010 receives help from UNICEF.

The *Office of the UN High Commissioner for Refugees (UNHCR)* is also busy. It coordinates efforts to protect, assist, and eventually repatriate the many refugees who flee across international borders each year to escape war and political violence. (The longer-standing problem of Palestinian refugees is handled by a different program, the *UN Relief Works Agency [UNRWA]*.)

The *UN Development Program (UNDP)*, funded by voluntary contributions, coordinates all UN efforts related to development in poor countries. With about 5,000 projects operating simultaneously around the world, UNDP is the world's largest international agency for technical development assistance. The UN also runs several development-related agencies for training and for promoting women's role in development.

Many poor countries depend on export revenues to finance economic development, making them vulnerable to fluctuations in commodity prices and other international trade problems. The **UN Conference on Trade and Development (UNCTAD)** negotiates international trade agreements to stabilize commodity prices and promote development. Because countries of the global South do not have much power in the international economy, however, UNCTAD has little leverage to promote their interests in trade (see p. 317). The World Trade Organization has become the main organization dealing with trade issues (see pp. 185–186).

In 2006, the UN created a new Human Rights Council, replacing a Human Rights Commission notorious for including human rights abusers as member states. The new council has expanded powers and more selective membership (47 states). On more than one occasion, a state with a questionable human rights record (e.g., Sudan and Syria) has been left off the Council ballot to prevent them from serving. Other UN programs manage problems such as disaster relief, food aid, housing, and population issues. Throughout the poorer countries, the UN maintains an active presence.

UN Conference on Trade and Development (UNCTAD) A structure established in 1964 to promote development in the global South through various trade proposals.

Autonomous Agencies

In addition to its own programs, the UN General Assembly maintains formal ties with about 20 autonomous international agencies not under its control. Most are specialized technical organizations through which states pool their efforts to address problems such as health care and labor conditions. The only such agency in international security affairs is the *International Atomic Energy Agency (IAEA)*, headquartered in Vienna, Austria. It was established under the UN but is formally autonomous. Although the IAEA has an economic role in helping develop civilian nuclear power, it mainly works to prevent nuclear proliferation (see p. 166). The IAEA was responsible for inspections in Iraq in 2002–2003, which found no evidence of a secret nuclear weapons program. It is involved in monitoring Iran's nuclear program to the extent Iran allows. The IAEA won the 2005 Nobel Peace Prize.

In the area of health care, the Geneva-based **World Health Organization (WHO)** provides assistance to improve conditions and conduct major

World Health Organization (WHO) An organization based in Geneva that provides technical assistance to improve health conditions in the developing world and conducts major immunization campaigns.

immunization campaigns in poor countries. In the 1960s and 1970s, WHO led one of the great public health victories of all time—the worldwide eradication of smallpox. Today, WHO is a leading player in the worldwide fight to control AIDS (see pp. 357–359).

In agriculture, the Food and Agriculture Organization (FAO) is the lead agency. In labor standards, it is the International Labor Organization (ILO). UNESCO—the UN Educational, Scientific, and Cultural Organization—facilitates international communication and scientific collaboration. The UN Industrial Development Organization (UNIDO) promotes industrialization in the global South.

The longest-established IOs, with some of the most successful records, are specialized agencies dealing with technical aspects of international coordination. For instance, the *International Telecommunications Union (ITU)* allocates radio frequencies. The *Universal Postal Union (UPU)* sets standards for international mail. The *International Civil Aviation Organization (ICAO)* sets binding standards for international air traffic. The *International Maritime Organization (IMO)* facilitates international cooperation on shipping at sea. The *World Intellectual Property Organization (WIPO)* seeks world compliance with copyrights and patents and promotes development and technology transfer within a legal framework that protects such intellectual property. The *World Meteorological Organization (WMO)* promotes the exchange of weather information.

The major coordinating agencies of the world economy (discussed in Chapters 5 and 7) are also UN-affiliated agencies. The World Bank and the IMF give loans, grants, and technical assistance for economic development (and the IMF manages international balance-of-payments accounting). The World Trade Organization (WTO) sets rules for international trade.

Overall, the density of connections across national borders, both in the UN system and through other IOs, is increasing year by year. These interconnections are furthest developed in the European Union.

The European Union

6.3 **Describe the growth of the European Union (EU) in terms of the number of members and identify two challenges arising from the increase in membership.**

Like the UN, the **European Union (EU)** was created after World War II and has developed since. But whereas the UN structure has changed little since its Charter was adopted, the EU has gone through several waves of expansion in its scope, membership, and mission over the past 50 years. The EU today has nearly 500 million citizens and surpasses the U.S. economy in gross domestic product (GDP).

European Union (EU) The official term for the European Community (formerly the European Economic Community) and associated treaty organizations. The EU has 28 member states and is negotiating with other states that have applied for membership.

Integration Theory

The theory of international integration attempts to explain why states choose supranationalism, which challenges once again the foundations of realism (state sovereignty and territorial integrity). **International integration** refers to the process by which supranational institutions replace national ones—the gradual shifting upward of sovereignty from state to regional or global structures. The ultimate expression of integration would be the merger of several (or many) states into a single state—or ultimately into a single world government. Such a shift in sovereignty to the supranational level would probably entail some version of federalism, in which states or other political units recognize the sovereignty of a central government while retaining certain powers for themselves. This is the form of government adopted in the U.S. Constitution.

international integration The process by which supranational institutions come to replace national ones; the gradual shifting upward of some sovereignty from the state to regional or global structures.

In practice, the process of integration has never gone beyond a partial and uneasy sharing of power between state and supranational levels. States have been unwilling to give up their exclusive claim to sovereignty and have severely limited the power and authority of supranational institutions. The most successful example of the process of integration by far—though even that success is only partial—is the European Union. The regional coordination now occurring in Western Europe is a new historical phenomenon.

Until 50 years ago, the European continent was the embodiment of national sovereignty, state rivalry, and war. For 500 years until 1945, the states of Europe were locked in chronic intermittent warfare; in the twentieth century alone, two world wars left the continent in ruins. The European states have historical and present-day religious, ethnic, and cultural differences. The 28 members of the EU in 2016 spoke 24 different official languages. If ever there were a candidate for the failure of integration, Europe would appear to be it. Even more surprising, European integration began with the cooperation of Europe's two bitterest enemies over the previous 100 years, enemies in three major wars since 1870—France and Germany.

CROSSING THE BORDER Integration processes in Europe and elsewhere are making state borders more permeable to people, goods, and ideas—increasing interdependence. The European Union is deepening economic integration while expanding eastward. Here, in 2006, the Tour de France crosses into Germany, passing only a road sign where in centuries past, great armies faced off across massive fortifications.

That Western European states began forming supranational institutions and creating an economic community to promote free trade and coordinate economic policies caught the attention of IR scholars, who used the term *integration* to describe what they observed. Seemingly, integration challenged the realist assumption that states were strictly autonomous and would never yield power or sovereignty. These scholars proposed that European moves toward integration could be explained by *functionalism*—growth of specialized technical organizations that cross national borders. According to functionalists, technological and economic development lead to more and more supranational structures as states seek practical means to fulfill necessary *functions* such as delivering mail from one country to another or coordinating the use of rivers that cross borders. As these connections became denser and the flows faster, functionalism predicted that states would be drawn together into stronger international economic structures.

The European experience, however, went beyond the creation of specialized agencies to include the development of more general, more political supranational bodies, such as the European Parliament. **Neofunctionalism** is a modification of functional theory by IR scholars to explain these developments. Neofunctionalists argue that economic integration (functionalism) generates a *political* dynamic that drives integration further. Closer economic ties require more political coordination in order to operate effectively and eventually lead to political integration as well—a process called *spillover*.

neofunctionalism A theory that holds that economic integration (functionalism) generates a "spillover" effect, resulting in increased political integration.

Some scholars focused on the less-tangible *sense of community* ("we" feeling) that began to develop among Europeans, running contrary to nationalist feelings that still existed as well. The low expectation of violence among the states of Western Europe created a **security community** in which such feelings could grow. This is a prime example of the identity principle in IR.

security community A situation in which low expectations of interstate violence permit a high degree of political cooperation—as, for example, among NATO members.

COSTS OF INTEGRATION   The new wave of integration in Europe and elsewhere is encountering limits and setbacks. Integration can mean greater centralization at a time when individuals, local groups, and national populations demand more say over their own affairs. The centralization of political authority, information, and culture as a result of integration can threaten both individual and group freedom. Ethnic groups want to safeguard their own cultures, languages, and institutions against the bland homogeneity that a global or regional melting pot would create. As a result, many states and citizens, in Europe and elsewhere, responded to the new wave of integration with resurgent nationalism over the past decade.

Indeed, these forces have set in motion a wave of *disintegration* of states running counter to (though simultaneous with) the integrating tendencies in today's world. The wave of disintegration in some ways began with the decolonization of former European empires after World War II. After the Cold War, disintegration centered on Russia and Eastern Europe—especially in the former Soviet Union and former Yugoslavia. States in other regions—Somalia, Democratic Congo, and Iraq—appear in danger of breaking into pieces, in practice if not formally. A challenge to integration theorists in the future will be to account for these new trends running counter to integration.

Throughout the successful and unsuccessful efforts at integration runs a common thread—the tension between nationalism and supranational loyalties (regionalism or globalism). In the less successful integration attempts, nationalism stands almost unchallenged, and even in the most successful cases, nationalism remains a potent force locked in continual struggle with supranationalism. This struggle is a central theme even in the most successful case of integration—the European Union.

The Vision of a United Europe

Europe in 1945 was decimated by war. Most of the next decade was spent recovering with help from the United States through the Marshall Plan. But already two French leaders, Jean Monnet and Robert Schuman, were developing a plan to implement the idea of functionalism in Europe—that future wars could be prevented by creating economic linkages that would eventually bind states together politically.

In 1950, Schuman, as French foreign minister, proposed a first modest step—the merger of the French and German steel (iron) and coal industries into a single framework that could use most efficiently the two states' coal resources and steel mills. Coal and steel were key to European recovery and growth. The Schuman plan gave birth in 1952 to the *European Coal and Steel Community (ECSC),* in which France and Germany were joined by Italy (the third large industrial country of continental Europe) and by three smaller countries—Belgium, the Netherlands, and Luxembourg (together called the *Benelux countries*). These six states worked through the ECSC to reduce trade barriers in coal and steel and to coordinate their coal and steel policies. The ECSC also established a High Authority that to some extent could bypass governments and deal directly with companies, labor unions, and individuals. Britain, however, did not join.

If coal and steel sound like fairly boring topics, that was exactly the idea of functionalists. The issues involved were matters for engineers and technical experts and did not threaten politicians. (Of course, coal and steel were not chosen by accident; both were essential to make war.) If German and French steel experts had more in common than German and French politicians, this is even truer of scientists. Today the European scientific community is one of the most internationally integrated areas of society. For example, the EU operates the European Space Agency and the European Molecular Biology Laboratory.

Although technical cooperation succeeded in 1952, political and military cooperation proved much more difficult. In line with the vision of a united Europe, the six ECSC states signed a second treaty in 1952 to create a European Defense Community to work toward integrating Europe's military forces under one budget and command. But the French parliament failed to ratify the treaty, and Britain refused to join such a force. The ECSC states also discussed formation of a European Political Community in 1953, but they could not agree on its terms. Thus, in economic cooperation, the supranational institutions succeeded, but in political and military affairs, state sovereignty prevailed.

The Treaty of Rome

In the **Treaty of Rome** in 1957, the same six states (France, Germany, Italy, Belgium, the Netherlands, and Luxembourg) created two new organizations. One extended the coal-and-steel idea into a new realm, atomic energy. **Euratom**, the European Atomic Energy Community, was formed to coordinate nuclear power development by pooling research, investment, and management. It continues to operate today with an expanded membership. The second organization was the *European Economic Community (EEC)*, later renamed the *European Community (EC)*.

As discussed briefly in Chapter 5, there are important differences between *free trade areas, customs unions,* and *common markets.* Creating a **free trade area** meant lifting tariffs and restrictions on the movement of goods across (EEC) borders, as was done shortly after 1957. Today, the *European Free Trade Association (EFTA)* is an extended free trade area associated with the European Union; its members are Norway, Iceland, Liechtenstein, and Switzerland.

In a **customs union**, participating states adopt a unified set of tariffs on goods coming in from outside the free trade area. Without this, each type of good could be imported into the state with the lowest tariff and then reexported (tariff free) to the other states in the free trade area. The Treaty of Rome committed the six states to creating a customs union by 1969. A customs union creates free and open trade within its member states, bringing great economic benefits. Thus, the customs union remains the heart of the EU and the one aspect widely copied elsewhere in the world.

A **common market** means that, in addition to the customs union, member states allow labor and capital (as well as goods) to flow freely across borders. For instance, a Belgian financier can invest in Germany on the same terms as a German investor. Although the Treaty of Rome adopted the goal of a common market, even today it has been only partially achieved.

One key aspect of a common market was achieved, at least in theory, in the 1960s when the EU (then the EC) adopted a **Common Agricultural Policy (CAP)**. In practice, the CAP has led to recurrent conflicts among member states and tensions between nationalism and regionalism (see pp. 78–79). To promote national self-sufficiency in food, many governments give subsidies to farmers. The CAP was based on the principle that a subsidy extended to farmers in any member state should be extended to farmers in all EU countries. That way, no member government was forced to alienate politically powerful farmers by removing subsidies, yet the overall policy would be equalized throughout the community in line with the common market principle. As a result, subsidies to farmers today absorb about 40 percent of the total EU budget, with France as the main beneficiary, and are the single greatest source of trade friction between Europe and the United States (see pp. 183–184).

The next step in the plan for European integration, after a free trade area, customs union, and common market, was an *economic and monetary union (EMU)*

Treaty of Rome (1957) The founding document of the European Economic Community (EEC) or Common Market, now subsumed by the European Union.

Euratom An organization created by the Treaty of Rome in 1957 to coordinate nuclear power development by pooling research, investment, and management.

free trade area A zone in which there are no tariffs or other restrictions on the movement of goods and services across borders.

customs union A common external tariff adopted by members of a free trade area; that is, participating states adopt a unified set of tariffs with regard to goods coming in from outside.

common market A zone in which labor and capital (as well as goods) flow freely across borders.

Common Agricultural Policy (CAP) A European Union policy based on the principle that a subsidy extended to farmers in any member country should be extended to farmers in all member countries.

in which the overall economic policies of the member states would be coordinated for greatest efficiency and stability. In this step, a single currency would replace separate national currencies (see p. 252). A possible future step could be the supranational coordination of economic policies such as budgets and taxes.

To reduce state leaders' fears of losing sovereignty, the Treaty of Rome provides that changes in its provisions must be approved by all member states. For example, France vetoed Britain's application for membership in the EEC in 1963 and 1967. In 1973, however, Britain did finally join, along with Ireland and Denmark. This expanded the organization's membership to nine, including the largest and richest countries in the region.

In 1981, Greece was admitted, and in 1986, Portugal and Spain joined. Inclusion of these poorer countries with less industry and lower standards of living created difficulties in effectively integrating Europe's economies that persist today, as the rich European states give substantial aid to the poorer ones in hopes of strengthening the weak links. Yet, by 2015, the debt problems of these countries had led to wealthier member states spending billions in bailout funds, while continuing economic turmoil threatened the stability of the wider European economy.

Structure of the European Union

The structure of the EU reflects its roots in technical and economic cooperation. The coal and steel experts have been joined by experts on trade, agriculture, and finance at the heart of the community. The EU headquarters and staff have the reputation of colorless bureaucrats—sometimes called *Eurocrats*—who care more about technical problem solving than about politics. These supranational bureaucrats are balanced in the EU structure by provisions that uphold the power of states and state leaders.

Although the rule of Eurocrats follows the functionalist plan, it has created problems as the EU has progressed. Politicians in member states have qualms about losing power to the Eurocrats. Citizens in some states have become uncomfortable with the growing power of faceless Eurocrats over their lives. Citizens can throw their own political leaders out of office in national elections, but the Eurocrats seem less accountable.

European Commission A European Union body whose members, while appointed by states, are supposed to represent EU interests. Supported by a multinational civil service in Brussels, the commission's role is to identify problems and propose solutions to the Council of the European Union.

The EU's structure is illustrated in Figure 6.4. The Eurocrats consist of a staff of 34,000, organized under the **European Commission** at EU headquarters in Brussels, Belgium. The Commission has 28 individual members—one from each member state—who are chosen for four-year renewable terms. Their role is to identify problems and propose solutions to the Council of the European Union. They select one of their members as the Commission president. These individuals are supposed to represent the interests of Europe as a whole (supranational interests), not their own states, but this goal has been only imperfectly met.

The European Commission lacks formal autonomous power except for day-to-day EU operations. Formally, the Commission reports to, and implements

Figure 6.4 Structure of the European Union (EU)

Source: European Commission in the European Union.

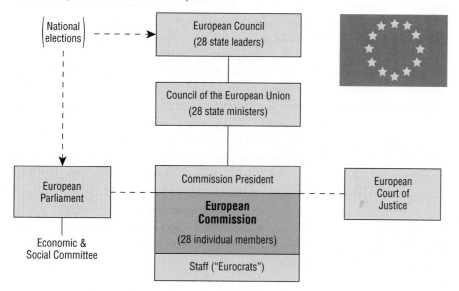

policies of, the **Council of the European Union**. The Council is a meeting of the relevant ministers (foreign, economic, agriculture, finance, etc.) of each member state—politicians who control the bureaucrats (or who try to). This formal structure reflects states' resistance to yielding sovereignty. It also means that the individuals making up the Council of the European Union vary from one meeting to the next and that technical issues receive priority over political ones. The arrangement thus gives some advantage back to the Commission staff. Recall the similar tension between politicians and career bureaucrats in national foreign policy making (see pp. 77–78).

The Council of the European Union in theory has functioned using weighted voting based on each state's population, but in practice it operates by consensus on major policy issues (all members must agree). After adoption of the Lisbon Treaty (see p. 255), nearly all issues are now decided by qualified majority voting. The Treaty's definition of qualified majority voting is that at least 55 percent of EU members, representing 65 percent of EU citizens, must vote in favor to secure passage. The Council has a rotating presidency (with limited power). The Council of the European Union must approve the policies of the European Commission and give it general directions.

In the 1970s, state leaders (prime ministers or presidents) created a special place for themselves in the EC, to oversee the direction of the community; this structure again shows state leaders' resistance to being governed by any supranational body. This *European Council* of the 28 state leaders meets with the Commission president twice a year. They are the ones with the power to get things done in their respective national governments (which still control most of the money and power in Europe).

Council of the European Union A European Union institution in which the relevant ministers (foreign, economic, agriculture, finance, etc.) of each member state meet to enact legislation and reconcile national interests. Formerly known as the Council of Ministers. When the meeting takes place among the state leaders, it is called the "European Council."

European Parliament
A quasi-legislative body of the European Union that operates as a watchdog over the European Commission and has limited legislative power.

There is a **European Parliament**, which falls somewhat short of a true legislature passing laws for all of Europe. The proposed European constitution would have strengthened it. At present, it operates partly as a watchdog over the Commission, but with some power to legislate. It must approve the Commission's budget but cannot control it item by item. The parliament shares power with the Council under a "co-decision procedure" in areas such as migration, employment, health, and consumer protection. It also serves as a debating forum and a symbol of European unity. The recent Lisbon Treaty significantly expanded the areas in which the co-decision procedure applies. In 1999, an independent commission created by the parliament found waste and fraud in the Commission, leading all 20 commissioners to resign. Since 1979, voters throughout Europe have directly elected their representatives according to population—750 members representing nearly 500 million citizens. Political parties are organized across national lines.

The *Economic and Social Committee* discusses continent-wide issues that affect particular industries or constituencies. This committee is purely advisory; it lobbies the Commission on matters it deems important. It is designed as a forum in which companies, labor unions, and interest groups can bargain transnationally.

European Court of Justice A judicial arm of the European Union, based in Luxembourg. The court has actively established its jurisdiction and its right to overrule national law when it conflicts with EU law.

The **European Court of Justice** in Luxembourg adjudicates disputes on matters covered by the Treaty of Rome—which covers many issues. Unlike the World Court (see pp. 260–261), the European Court has actively established its jurisdiction and not merely served as a mechanism of international mediation. The Court can overrule national laws that conflict with EU law—giving it unique powers among international courts. It hears cases brought by individuals, not just governments. In hundreds of cases, the Court has ruled on matters such as discrimination in the workplace and the pensions of Commission staff members.

The Single European Act

European integration has proceeded in a step-by-step process that produces tangible successes, reduces politicians' fears of losing sovereignty, and creates pressures to continue the process. Often major steps forward are followed by periods of stagnation or even reversals in integration. The first major revision of the Treaty of Rome—the 1985 *Single European Act*—began a new phase of accelerated integration. The EU set a target date of the end of 1992 for the creation of a true common market in Europe. This comprehensive set of changes was nicknamed *Europe 1992* and centered on about 300 directives from the European Commission, aimed at eliminating nontariff barriers to free trade in goods, services, labor, and capital within the EC. The issues tended to be complex and technical. For example, a dispute raged for decades over the definition of chocolate because Belgium—famous for its chocolates—required the exclusive use of cocoa butter, but Britain allowed substitution of other vegetable oils.

Thus, economic integration sets in motion changes that reach into every corner of society and affect the daily lives of millions of people. The Commission bureaucrats worked to smooth out such inconsistencies and create a uniform set of standards. Each national government had to pass laws to implement these measures.

The 1992 process also deepened a trend toward the EU's dealing directly with provinces rather than the states they belong to—thus beginning to "hollow out" the state from below (stronger provincial governments) as well as from above (stronger Europe-wide government). However, Europe 1992 continued to put aside for the future the difficult problems of political and military integration.

The Maastricht Treaty

The **Maastricht Treaty**, signed in the Dutch city of Maastricht in 1992, renamed the EC as the EU and committed it to further progress in three main areas. The first was monetary union (discussed shortly), in which the existing national currencies were to be abolished and replaced by a single European currency. A second set of changes, regarding justice and home affairs, created a European police agency and responded to the new reality that borders were opening to immigrants, criminals, and contraband. It also expanded the idea of citizenship so that, for example, a French citizen living in Germany can vote in local elections there. A third goal of Maastricht—political and military integration—was even more controversial. The treaty commits European states to work toward a common foreign policy with a goal of eventually establishing a joint military force.

Maastricht Treaty A treaty signed in the Dutch city of Maastricht and ratified in 1992; it commits the European Union to monetary union (a single currency and European Central Bank) and to a common foreign policy.

Some citizens of Europe began to react strongly against the loss of national identity and sovereignty implicit in the Maastricht Treaty. In the end, the EU implemented the Maastricht Treaty, although more slowly and with fewer participating countries than originally hoped. Economic and technical integration, including the monetary union among 12 initial members, maintained momentum.

Europe's economic integration has begun to reshape political economy at a global level. The EU now sets the rules for access to one of the world's largest markets, for a vast production and technology network, and for the world's strongest currency. Europe's new power is illustrated in its environmental initiatives. The U.S. chemical industry operated under U.S. regulations that exempt 80 percent of chemicals. But the EU adopted stricter chemical regulations, requiring tests of health effects of all chemicals used in products, and mandating efforts to substitute for toxic chemicals in everyday products. Similarly, Japanese car manufacturers adapted production processes to meet the EU's requirement that new cars consist of 85 percent recyclable components by 2006 (and 95 percent in 2015). Political and military integration are a bigger problem. The struggle between nationalism and supranationalism seems precariously balanced; the transition to supranationalism has not yet been accomplished in the realms of sovereignty and foreign policy. Even after 50 years of preparation, spillover from economic to political issues is elusive.

Monetary Union

euro Also called the ECU (European currency unit); a single European currency used by 19 members of the European Union (EU).

A European currency, the **euro**, has replaced national currencies in 19 EU member states. After several years as an abstract unit like the IMF's Special Drawing Right (SDR) (see p. 210), the euro came into full circulation in 2002, and the national currencies ceased to exist. The European Central Bank took over the functions of states' central banks.

Monetary union is difficult for both economic and political reasons. In participating states, fundamental economic and financial conditions must be equalized. One state cannot stimulate its economy with low interest rates (for example, because of a recession) while another cools inflation with high interest rates (because of high economic growth). For example, in 2015, the unemployment rate was over 24 percent in Spain but only 5 percent in Britain. In an integrated economy that is also politically centralized, the central government can reallocate resources, as the United States might do if Texas were booming and Maine were in recession. But the EU does not have centralized powers of taxation or control of national budgets.

One solution is to work toward equalizing Europe's economies. For example, to reduce the disparity between rich and poor EU states, the Maastricht Treaty increased the EU budget by $25 billion annually to provide economic assistance to the poorer members. But the richer EU members pay the cost for this aid—in effect carrying the poor countries as free riders on the collective good of EU integration. Partly for this reason, $25 billion annually was far too small to equalize the rich and poor countries.

The main solution adopted at Maastricht was to restrict membership in the monetary union, at least in the first round, to only those countries with enough financial stability not to jeopardize the union. To join the unified currency, a state had to achieve a budget deficit of less than 3 percent of GDP, a national debt of less than 60 percent of GDP, an inflation rate no more than 1.5 percentage points above the

MASS UNEMPLOYMENT The Maastricht Treaty called for a monetary union with a common currency. In 2002, the euro currency came into effect smoothly in 12 (now 19) countries and emerged as a world currency that rivals the U.S. dollar. But the 2008 recession exposed underlying problems that triggered a eurozone debt crisis and second recession in 2012, especially in weaker members. These workers in hard-hit Spain, where unemployment passed 25 percent, protest against government austerity policies in a so-called March of Dignity, 2015.

average of the three lowest-inflation EU members, and stable interest rates and national currency values.

This meant hard choices by governments in France, Spain, Italy, and other countries to cut budgets and benefits and to take other politically unpopular moves. Governments fell to opposition parties in several countries, but the new leaders generally kept to the same course. As a result of their newfound fiscal discipline, all 12 EU members that wanted to participate in the euro ultimately qualified. Slovenia joined in 2007, Cyprus and Malta in 2008, Slovakia in 2009, Estonia in 2011, Latvia in 2014, and Lithuania in 2015. Britain, Denmark, and Sweden opted to retain their national currencies.

Money is more political than steel tariffs or chocolate ingredients. A monetary union infringes on a core prerogative of states—the right to print currency. Because citizens use money every day, the euro could deepen citizens' sense of identification with Europe—a victory for supranationalism over nationalism. When the euro went into circulation in 2002, people for the first time could "put Europe in their pocket." Precisely for this reason, however, some state leaders and citizens resisted the idea of giving up the symbolic value of their national currencies.

Conflicts have arisen within the eurozone. In 2004, the European Commission challenged the EU member states for voting to let France and Germany break the euro rules by running high budget deficits. And Latvia's government lost power within six months of the country's joining the EU, under pressure of unpopular budget cuts needed to meet the euro rules within four years.

In 2010, new challenges to the euro arose. Greece, which had previously admitted to falsifying economic data in order to be admitted to the eurozone, had for years borrowed more than it could repay and needed a European bailout to survive the global financial crisis. Because Greece used the euro, its troubles affected global investors' impressions of all euro states.

Worse, the debt problems soon spread beyond Greece. In fact, in 2010, only two states in the EU (Finland and Luxembourg) actually met the EU targets for debt levels. Greece, Spain, Portugal, Ireland, and Italy all undertook large-scale economic reforms, and governments lost power in Greece, Italy, and other EU states. Germany and France fought over who would help bail out the euro states in trouble. After Germany's economic minister stated that Germany "would not offer Greece a cent," cooler heads prevailed and the EU countries banded together to support one another's economies. Soon Ireland also needed, and received, a massive bailout.

By 2012, the EU had patched together a bailout system backed by more than $1 trillion and capable of propping up its members' economies when needed. But the EU's decision process remained cumbersome, and citizens took to the streets frequently in countries such as Greece and Spain that had to implement harsh austerity budgets in exchange for bailouts. The austerity measures not only drove up unemployment, around 25 percent in the case of Spain in 2015 (50 percent unemployment for those under age 25), but also slowed economic activity in the whole eurozone. In 2014, fed up with austerity measures, Greece elected a new leftist government on the promise of negotiating less harsh conditions from the EU.

Despite these recent problems in the eurozone, the creation of a European currency is arguably the largest financial overhaul ever attempted in history, and in its first 17 years it has been mostly successful.

Expanding the European Union

The EU's success has attracted neighboring states to join. In 1995, Austria, Sweden, and Finland joined the EU, bringing the total number of members to 15. The EU has expanded from 15 members to 28 in 2013, with potentially far-reaching changes in how the EU operates.

The EU's current expansion is guided by the 2000 Treaty of Nice, which came into effect in 2003 after Irish voters reversed an earlier vote and approved it. Ten new members joined in 2004: Poland, Czech Republic, Slovakia, Hungary, Slovenia, Estonia, Latvia, Lithuania, Malta, and Cyprus. The European Commission expanded to 25 members, without the five largest having two seats, and with new voting rules that move away from a requirement for consensus. Romania's and Bulgaria's entry in 2007, and Croatia's in 2013, brought the EU membership to 28.

Turkey continues to seek membership. Although it rebuffed Turkey in 2002, the EU later agreed to begin formal entry negotiations with Turkey in 2005—the start of a years-long process. Proponents of Turkish membership note that Turkey has made major economic and political changes, including abolishing the death penalty and improving human rights, to try to win EU membership. Granting full membership would reward these changes, keeping an implicit promise to reciprocate Turkey's actions. Turkey's GDP, growing rapidly in recent years, would add about 5 percent to the EU's economy. And Turkish workers could help alleviate a labor shortage in Western Europe. Supporters also argue that Turkey as an EU member would serve as a bridge between Europe and the important but unstable Middle East region, and as an example of secular democracy to other Middle Eastern countries.

Opponents note that Turkey would be the only Muslim country in the EU yet would be the second most populous EU member after Germany. With 2 million Turks already living in Germany, opponents argue that EU membership would open the floodgates for immigration from a large, poor country, overwhelming the smaller and richer EU members. In economic terms, Turkey would be the poorest member (see Figure 6.5). Costs to subsidize Turkish farmers and expand social programs could reach tens of billions of euros. Finally, opponents want Turkey to remove its military forces from EU member Cyprus, where a Greek-Turkish partition has endured for decades. In 2010–2015, the financial crisis in the eurozone pushed aside the question of admitting Turkey or other new members.

The EU in the last decade has shown signs of dividing into "inner" and "outer" layers—with states such as France and Germany joining a currency union and deepening their integration, and those such as Britain and perhaps the new members operating at the edges of the EU with more autonomy. Still, in

Figure 6.5 Income Levels of Old and New EU Members, 2014

Source: World Bank data.

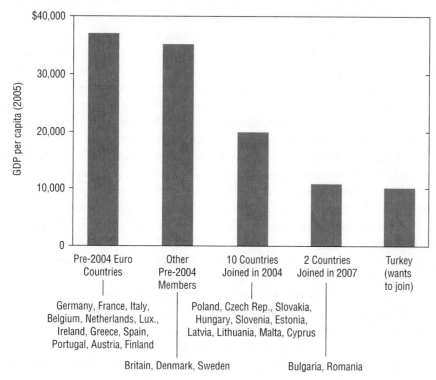

some areas, there have been consistent strides toward integration. Since 1995, the EU has established and gradually expanded a zone, called the *Schengen area,* in which border controls have been abolished. Goods and people move freely within the zone without stopping at borders. The agreement also strengthens police cooperation among the member countries. The Schengen countries include the major EU states (except Britain, by its choice). Norway, Iceland, and Switzerland also belong, although they are not EU members.

The Lisbon Treaty

To grapple with the implications of an expanding EU, the 25 leaders signed an EU constitution in 2004, and the European Parliament gave it a strong vote of support in 2005. To take effect, it was to be ratified by all 25 states, including several requiring referenda. The constitution would establish a stronger president of the EU, as well as a foreign minister, and would replace the requirement for consensus in EU decision making with majority voting in more cases. It also guaranteed fundamental rights to all EU citizens. But voters in France and the Netherlands rejected the constitution, and the process halted. In 2007, the EU moved forward with another new proposed constitution, the Lisbon Treaty. The treaty was similar to the previous constitution but faced a popular referendum only in Ireland. (Lisbon did not require more state-level votes because it only amended previous EU treaties rather than replacing them as the constitution proposed to do.) In 2008, Ireland rejected the new treaty, but it voted again in 2009, approving the treaty, after several concessions to Ireland were made. The treaty came into force in 2009.

The treaty creates numerous changes in both the structure and the day-to-day operations of the EU. Some of those changes promote more supranational decision making. For example, a charter of human rights was made legally binding on all member states. A new position called the High Commissioner on Foreign Affairs and Security Policy was created to better coordinate foreign policy among member states. (This position immediately became controversial when a relatively unknown British lord was chosen to fill the position.)

On the other hand, some changes allow state members and individual citizens to place more checks on EU power. Now, national parliaments can have more say in who is admitted to the EU (likely bad news for Turkey). National parliaments will now also receive draft legislation to evaluate and respond to before it is enacted in Brussels. The Treaty also attempts to increase transparency by requiring European Council meetings to be held in public. And in an attempt to engage EU citizens directly, the Commission must now take up any proposal or petition that receives 1 million signatures.

Despite these new checks, deep political divisions emerged in the EU in 2015 when thousands of refugees, fleeing conflicts in the Middle East, immigrated to eastern Europe. The EU responded by approving a plan to resettle many of the refugees, despite objections from the Czech Republic, Slovakia, Hungary, and Romania. This plan strained relations between Germany and newer eastern European members.

Beyond the EU itself, Europe is a patchwork of overlapping structures with varying memberships (see Figure 6.6). Despite the Single European Act, there are still many Europes. Within the EU are the "inner six," and the new arrivals, each with its own concerns. Around the edges are the EFTA states participating in the European Economic Area. NATO membership overlaps partly with the EU. Russia and even the United States are European actors in some respects. One truly universal intergovernmental organization exists in Europe—the *Organization for Security and Cooperation in Europe (OSCE)*. Operating by consensus, with a large universal membership of 56 states, the OSCE has little power except to act as a forum for discussions of security issues. In the late 1990s, the OSCE shifted into new tasks such as running elections and helping political parties.

Thus, international integration is not a matter of a single group or organization but more a mosaic of structures tying states together. These various structures of the European political system, centered on the EU, are IGOs composed of states as members. IOs impinge on state sovereignty by creating new structures (both supranational and transnational) for regulating relations across borders. International law and international norms limit state sovereignty in another way. They create principles for governing international relations that compete with the core realist principles of sovereignty and anarchy.

Figure 6.6 Overlapping Memberships of European States

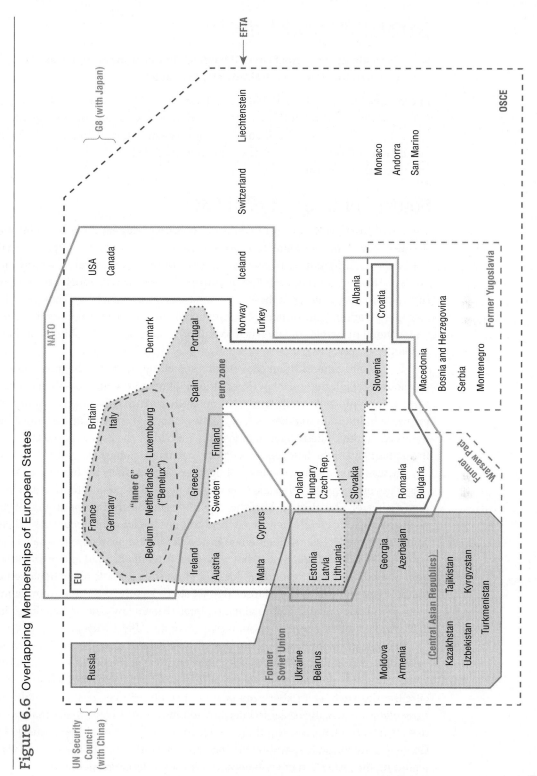

International Law

6.4 Evaluate the arguments over the effectiveness or ineffectiveness of international law in restraining state behavior.

International law, unlike national laws, derives not from actions of a legislative branch or other central authority but from tradition and agreements signed by states. It also differs in the difficulty of enforcement, which depends not on the power and authority of central government but on reciprocity, collective action, and international norms.

Sources of International Law

Laws within states come from central authorities—legislatures or dictators. Because states are sovereign and recognize no central authority, international law rests on a different basis. The declarations of the UN General Assembly are not laws, and most do not bind the members. The Security Council can compel certain actions by states, but these are commands rather than laws: They are specific to a situation. Four sources of international law are recognized: treaties, custom, general principles of law (such as equity), and legal scholarship (including past judicial decisions).

Treaties and other written conventions signed by states are the most important sources of international law. International treaties now fill more than a thousand thick volumes, with tens of thousands of individual agreements. A principle in international law is that treaties, once signed and ratified, must be observed. In the United States, treaties duly ratified by the Senate are considered the highest law of the land, equal with acts passed by Congress.

Treaties and other international obligations such as debts are binding on successor governments whether the new government takes power through an election, a coup, or a revolution. After the revolutions in Eastern Europe around 1990, newly democratic governments were held responsible for debts incurred by their communist predecessors. Even when the Soviet Union broke up, Russia as the successor state had to guarantee that Soviet debts would be paid and Soviet treaties honored. Although revolution does not free a state from its obligations, some treaties have built-in escape clauses that let states legally withdraw from them, after giving due notice, without violating international law. The United States in 2001 invoked the six-month opt-out provision of the ABM treaty.

Because of the universal commitment by all states to respect certain basic principles of international law, the UN Charter is one of the world's most important treaties. Its implications are broad and far-reaching, in contrast to more specific treaties such as a fishery management treaty. However, the specialized agreements are usually easier to interpret and more enforceable than broad treaties such as the Charter. Another key treaty in international law is the 1949 Geneva Convention (expanding an 1864 convention) defining the laws of war regarding the protection of civilians and prisoners, among related issues.

Custom is the second major source of international law. If states behave toward each other in a certain way for long enough, their behavior may become generally accepted practice with the status of law. Western international law (though not Islamic law) tends to be *positivist* in this regard—it draws on actual customs, the practical realities of self-interest, and the need for consent rather than on an abstract concept of divine or natural law.

General principles of law also serve as a source of international law. Actions such as theft and assault recognized in most national legal systems as crimes tend to have the same meaning in an international context.

The fourth source of international law, recognized by the World Court as subsidiary to the others, is *legal scholarship*—the written arguments of judges and lawyers around the world on the issues in question. Only the writings of the most highly qualified and respected legal figures can be taken into account, and then only to resolve points not resolved by the first three sources of international law.

Often international law lags behind changes in norms; law is quite tradition-bound. Certain activities such as espionage are technically illegal but are so widely condoned that they do not violate international norms. Other activities are still legal but have come to be frowned upon and seen as abnormal. For example, China's shooting of student demonstrators in 1989 violated international norms but not international law.

Enforcement of International Law

Although these sources of international law distinguish it from national law, an even greater difference exists as to the *enforcement* of the two types of law. International law is much more difficult to enforce. There is no world police force. Enforcement of international law depends on the power of states themselves, individually or collectively, to punish transgressors.

Enforcement of international law depends heavily on the reciprocity principle (see p. 71). States follow international law most of the time because they want other states to do so. The reason neither side in World War II used chemical weapons was not that anyone could *enforce* the treaty banning use of such weapons. It was that the other side would probably respond by using chemical weapons, too, and the costs would be high to both sides. International law recognizes in certain circumstances the legitimacy of *reprisals:* actions that would have been illegal under international law may sometimes be legal if taken in response to the illegal actions of another state.

A state that breaks international law may face a collective response by a group of states, such as the imposition of *sanctions*—agreements among other states to stop trading with the violator, or to stop some particular commodity trade (most often, military goods) as punishment for its violation. Over time, a sanctioned state can become a pariah in the community of nations, cut off from normal relations with others. This is very costly in today's world. Libya suffered for decades from its isolated status in the international community, and it decided in 2003 to make a clean break and regain normal status. Libya admitted responsibility for past terrorism; began to compensate victims; and agreed to disclose and dismantle its nuclear, chemical, and biological weapons programs.

Even the world's superpower constrains its behavior, at least some of the time, to adhere to international law. For example, in late 2002 a North Korean freighter was caught en route to Yemen with a hidden load of 15 Scud missiles. The United States, fighting the war on terrorism, had an evident national interest in preventing such proliferation and had the power to prevent it. But when U.S. government lawyers determined that the shipment did not violate international law, the United States backed off and let the delivery continue.

International law enforcement through reciprocity and collective response depends entirely on national power. Reciprocity works only if the aggrieved state has the power to inflict costs on the violator. If international law extends only as far as power reaches, what good is it? Without common expectations regarding the rules of the game and adherence to those rules most of the time by most actors, power alone would create great instability in the anarchic international system. International law, even without perfect enforcement, creates expectations about what constitutes legal behavior by states. In most cases, although power continues to reside in states, international law establishes workable rules for those states to follow. The resulting stability is so beneficial that usually the costs of breaking the rules outweigh the short-term benefits that could be gained from such violations.

The World Court

World Court (International Court of Justice) The judicial arm of the UN; located in The Hague, it hears only cases between states.

As international law has developed, a general world legal framework in which states can pursue grievances against each other has begun to take shape. The rudiments of such a system now exist in the **World Court** (formally called the **International Court of Justice**), although its jurisdiction is limited and its caseload light. The World Court is a branch of the UN. Only states, not individuals or businesses, can sue or be sued in the World Court. When a state has a grievance against another, it can take the case to the World Court for an impartial hearing. The Security Council or General Assembly may also request advisory Court opinions on matters of international law.

The World Court has 15 judges elected for nine-year terms (five judges every three years) by a majority of both the Security Council and General Assembly. The Court meets in The Hague, the Netherlands. Permanent members of the Security Council customarily have one of their nationals as a judge at all times. Ad hoc judges may be added to the 15 if a party to a case does not already have one of its nationals as a judge.

The great weakness of the World Court is that states have not agreed in a comprehensive way to subject themselves to its jurisdiction or to obey its decisions. Almost all states have signed the treaty creating the Court, but only about a third have signed the *optional clause* in the treaty agreeing to give the Court jurisdiction in certain cases—and even many of those signatories have added their own stipulations reserving their rights and limiting the degree to which the Court can infringe on national sovereignty. For example, Colombia withdrew in 2012 after the Court awarded disputed territorial waters to Nicaragua. In such cases, the Court may hear cases anyway and usually rules in favor of the participating side—but it has no means to enforce the ruling. Justice can also move slowly. In 2007, the Court issued a ruling against Bosnia's case accusing Serbia of genocide, after 14 years of preliminary maneuvering.

In 2002, the World Court settled a long-standing and sometimes violent dispute over an oil-rich peninsula on the Cameroon-Nigeria border. It gave ownership to Cameroon, and Nigeria (which is more powerful) pulled troops out in 2006.

A main use of the World Court now is to arbitrate issues of secondary importance between countries with friendly relations overall. The United States has settled commercial disputes with Canada and with Italy through the Court. Because security interests are not at stake and because the overall friendly relations are more important than the particular issue, states have been willing to submit to the Court's jurisdiction. In 2004, the court ordered the United States to review death sentences of Mexican nationals to see if their lack of access to Mexican officials had harmed their legal case. Figure 6.7 illustrates one of the Court's recent cases, a dispute between Argentina and Uruguay.

Because of the difficulty of winning enforceable agreements on major conflicts through the World Court, states have used the Court infrequently over the years—a dozen or fewer cases per year (about 150 judgments and advisory opinions since 1947).

International Cases in National Courts

Most legal cases concerning international matters—whether brought by governments or by private individuals or companies—remain entirely within the legal systems of one or more states. National courts hear cases brought under national laws and can enforce judgments by collecting damages (in civil suits) or imposing punishments (in criminal ones).

A party with a dispute that crosses national boundaries gains several advantages by pursuing the matter through the national courts of one or more of the relevant states rather than through international channels. First, judgments are enforceable. The party that wins a lawsuit in a national court can collect from the other party's assets within the state. Second, individuals and companies can pursue legal complaints through national courts (as can subnational governmental bodies), whereas in most areas of international law, states must themselves bring suits on behalf of their citizens. (Even national governments pursue most of their legal actions against each other through national courts.)

Figure 6.7 World Court Case of Argentina v. Uruguay

Source: The International Court of Justice aka the World Court

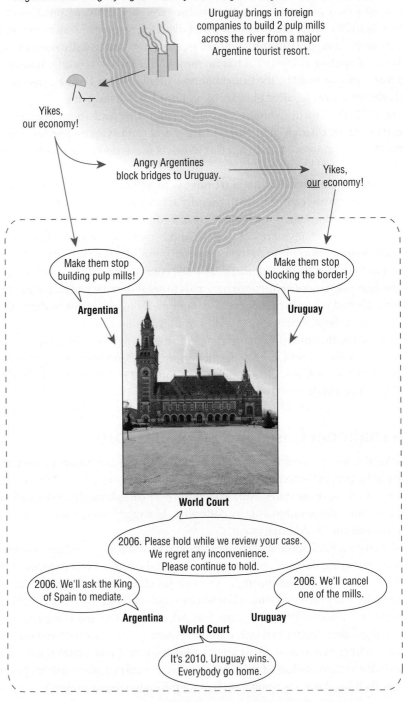

Third, there is often a choice of more than one state within which a case could legally be heard; one can pick the legal system most favorable to one's case. Each state's court system must decide whether it has *jurisdiction* in a case (the right to hear it), and courts tend to extend their own authority with a broad interpretation. Traditionally, a national court may hear cases concerning any activity on its national territory, any actions of its own citizens anywhere in the world, and actions taken toward its citizens elsewhere in the world. Noncitizens can use the national courts to enforce damages against citizens because the national court has authority to impose fines and, if necessary, to seize bank accounts and property.

The United States is a favorite jurisdiction within which to bring cases for two reasons. First, U.S. juries have a reputation for awarding bigger settlements in lawsuits than juries elsewhere in the world (if only because the United States is a rich country). Second, because many people and governments do business in the United States, it is often possible to collect damages awarded by a U.S. court.

There are important limits to the use of national courts to resolve international disputes, however. Most important is that the authority of national courts stops at the state's borders, where sovereignty ends. To bring a person outside a state's territory to trial, the state's government must ask a second government to arrest the person on the second state's territory and hand him or her over for trial. Called *extradition,* this is a matter of international law because it is a legal treaty arrangement between states. If no such treaty exists, the individual generally remains immune from a state's courts by staying off its territory.

Gray areas exist in the jurisdiction of national courts over foreigners. If a government can lure a suspect onto the high seas, it can nab the person without violating another country's territoriality. More troublesome are cases in which a government obtains a foreign citizen from a foreign country for trial without going through extradition procedures.

The principle of territoriality also governs *immigration law.* When people cross a border into a new country, the decision about whether they can remain there, and under what conditions, is up to the new state. The state of origin cannot compel their return. National laws establish conditions for foreigners to travel and visit a state's territory, to work there, and sometimes to become citizens (*naturalization*). Many other legal issues are raised by people traveling or living outside their own country—passports and visas, babies born in foreign countries, marriages to foreign nationals, bank accounts, businesses, taxes, and so forth. Practices vary from country to country, but the general principle is that national laws prevail on the territory of a state.

Despite the continued importance of national court systems in international legal affairs and the lack of enforcement powers of the World Court, it would be wrong to conclude that state sovereignty is supreme and international law impotent. Rather, there is a balance of sovereignty and law in international interactions. The remainder of this chapter discusses particular areas of international law, from the most firmly rooted and widely respected to newer and less-established areas. In each area, the influence of law and norms runs counter to the unimpeded exercise of state sovereignty. This struggle becomes more intense as one moves from long-standing traditions of diplomatic law to recent norms governing human rights.

diplomatic recognition The process by which the status of embassies and that of an ambassador as an official state representative are explicitly defined.

Laws of Diplomacy

The bedrock of international law is respect for the rights of diplomats. The ability to conduct diplomacy is necessary for all other kinds of relations among states, except perhaps all-out war. Since the rise of the international system five centuries ago, it has been considered unjustifiable to harm an emissary sent from another state as a means of influencing the other state.

The status of embassies and of an ambassador as an official state representative is explicitly defined in the process of **diplomatic recognition**. Diplomats are *accredited* to each other's governments (they present "credentials"), and thereafter the individuals so defined enjoy certain rights and protections as foreign diplomats in the host country. Diplomats have the right to occupy an *embassy* in the host country, within which the host country's laws may not be enforced without the consent of the embassy's country. For this reason, embassies occasionally shelter dissidents who take refuge there from their own governments.

Diplomats enjoy **diplomatic immunity** even when they leave the embassy grounds. The right to travel varies from one country to another; diplomats may be restricted to one city or they may be free to roam about the countryside. Alone among all foreign nationals, diplomats are beyond enforcement of the host country's national courts. If they commit crimes, they may be shielded from arrest. All the host country can do is take away a diplomat's accreditation and expel the person from the host country. However, strong countries sometimes pressure weaker ones to lift immunity so that a diplomat may face trial for a crime.

Because of diplomatic immunity, espionage activities are commonly conducted through the diplomatic corps, out of an embassy. Spies are often posted to low-level positions in embassies, such as cultural attaché, press liaison, or military attaché. If the host country catches them spying, it cannot prosecute them, so it merely expels them.

OUT OF REACH International law prohibits attacks on diplomats and embassies. This fundamental principle, like others in international law, is ultimately enforced through reciprocity. When the founder of Wikileaks took refuge in the Ecuadorian embassy in London to avoid extradition to Sweden, the British government considered coming in and taking him, but thought better of it. Here, after six months in residency, he delivers a speech from the embassy balcony, 2012.

Diplomatic norms (though not law) call for politeness when expelling spies; the standard reason given is "for activities not consistent with his or her diplomatic status." If a spy operates under cover of being a businessperson or tourist, then no immunity applies; the person can be arrested and prosecuted under the host country's laws.

diplomatic immunity A privilege under which diplomats' activities fall outside the jurisdiction of the host country's national courts.

To *break diplomatic relations* means to withdraw one's diplomats from a state and expel its diplomats from one's own state. This tactic is used to show displeasure with another government; it is a refusal to do business as usual. When two countries lack diplomatic relations, they often do business through a third country. This is called an *interests section* in the third country's embassy. Thus, the practical needs of diplomacy can overcome a formal lack of relations between states. For instance, during their long period of mutual nonrecognition, U.S. interests were represented by the Swiss embassy in Cuba, and Cuban interests were represented by the Swiss embassy in the United States. In practice, these interests sections are located in the former U.S. and Cuban embassies and are staffed with U.S. and Cuban diplomats.

States register lower levels of displeasure by *recalling their ambassadors* home for some period of time; diplomatic norms call for a trip home "for consultations" even when everyone knows the purpose is to signal annoyance. Milder still is the expression of displeasure by a *formal complaint.*

The law of diplomacy is repeatedly violated in one context—terrorism (see pp. 156–159). Because states care so much about the sanctity of diplomats, diplomats make a tempting target for terrorists, and because terrorist groups do not enjoy the benefits of diplomatic law (as states do), they are willing to break diplomatic norms and laws. An attack on diplomats or embassies is an attack on the territory of the state itself—yet can be carried out far from the state's home territory. Many diplomats have been killed in recent decades.

Just-War Doctrine

After the law of diplomacy, international law regarding war is one of the most developed areas of international law. Laws concerning war are divided into two areas—laws *of* war (when war is permissible) and laws *in* war (how wars are fought). To begin with the laws of war, international law distinguishes **just wars** (which are legal) from wars of aggression (which are illegal). (We discuss laws in war later in the context of human rights.) This area of law grows out of centuries-old religious writings about just wars (which once could be enforced by threats to excommunicate individuals from the church). Today, the legality of war is defined by the UN Charter, which outlaws aggression. Above and beyond its legal standing, just-war doctrine has become a strong international norm, not one that all states follow but an important part of the modern intellectual tradition governing matters of war and peace that evolved in Europe.

just wars A category in international law and political theory that defines when wars can be justly started (*jus ad bellum*) and how they can be justly fought (*jus in bello*).

The idea of aggression, around which the doctrine of just war evolved, is based on a violation of the sovereignty and territorial integrity of states.

Aggression refers to a state's use of force, or an imminent threat to do so, against another state's territory or sovereignty—unless the use of force is in response to aggression. Tanks swarming across the border constitute aggression, but so do tanks massing at the border if their state has threatened to invade. The lines are somewhat fuzzy. But for a threat to constitute aggression (and justify the use of force in response), it must be a clear threat of using force, not just a hostile policy or general rivalry.

States have the right to respond to aggression in the only manner thought to be reliable—military force. Just-war doctrine is thus not based on nonviolence. Responses can include both *repelling* the attack itself and *punishing* the aggressor. Responses can be made by the victim of aggression or by other states not directly affected—as a way of maintaining the norm of nonaggression in the international system. Response to aggression is the only allowable use of military force according to just-war doctrine. The just-war approach thus explicitly rules out war as an instrument to change another state's government or policies, or in ethnic and religious conflicts. In fact, the UN Charter makes no provision for "war" but rather for "international police actions" against aggressors. For a war to be morally just, it must be more than a response to aggression; it must be waged for the *purpose* of responding to aggression. The *intent* must be just. A state may not take advantage of another's aggression to wage a war that is essentially aggressive.

Just-war doctrine has been undermined by the changing nature of warfare. In civil wars and low-intensity conflicts, it can be hard to identify an aggressor, because the belligerents can range from poorly organized militias to national armies, and the battleground is often a patchwork of enclaves and positions with no clear front lines (much less borders). It is harder to identify an aggressor in such situations, and it is harder to balance the relative merits of peace and justice.

Human Rights

6.5 **Contrast the effectiveness of international law, nongovernmental organizations (NGOs), and states in advancing the cause of human rights around the globe.**

human rights The rights of all people to be free from abuses such as torture or imprisonment for their political beliefs (political and civil rights), and to enjoy certain minimum economic and social protections (economic and social rights).

One of the newest areas of international law concerns **human rights**—the rights of human beings against certain abuses of their *own* governments.

Individual Rights Versus Sovereignty

The very idea of human rights flies in the face of the sovereignty and territorial integrity of states. Sovereignty gives states the right to do as they please in their own territory: Nobody can tell them how to treat their own citizens.

Thus, a consensus on the most important human rights is difficult to reach. One approach to human rights argues that rights are *universal*. No matter where a person resides; no matter his or her ethnic nationality; and no matter his or her local religious, ethnic, or clan traditions, that person has certain rights that must be respected. The other approach to human rights is often labeled *relativism*. According to this idea, local traditions and histories should be given due respect, even if this means limiting rights that others outside that local context find important. Efforts to promote human rights are routinely criticized by governments with poor human rights records by Western standards (including China and Russia) as "interference in our internal affairs." This charge puts human rights law on shaky ground and reflects a relativist stance.

The concept of human rights arises from three sources. The first is religion. Nearly every major world religion has at its foundation the idea that humans were created in an image of a higher power and that therefore all humans are to be afforded the dignity and respect that are due that higher power.

Second, political and legal philosophy has discussed for centuries the idea of natural law and natural rights. From Aristotle to John Locke, to Immanuel Kant, to Jean-Jacques Rousseau, political philosophers have developed the idea that a natural law exists that grants all humans the right to life, liberty, property, and happiness.

Finally, political revolutions in the eighteenth century, such as the American and French Revolutions, translated the theory of natural law and natural rights into practice. In the United States, the Declaration of Independence, and in France, the Declaration of the Rights of Man and Citizen, created laws that solidified the idea that humans have certain rights that no state or other individuals can take away.

Of course, criticisms of these ideas of human rights exist, on both a theoretical and a practical level. Theoretically, relativists point out that much of the origin and development of human rights ideas (at least two of the three sources discussed) are Western in origin. Non-Western societies have different philosophical traditions and may choose to emphasize group or family rights, for example, over individual ones. At a practical level, many (especially non-Western) critics are quick to point out that even after the eighteenth-century revolutions in Europe and America, rights were still not universal. Women, children, and usually nonwhites were not assumed to enjoy the same rights as landholding white males, making the very idea of universal rights misleading.

Partially because of this controversy, there are no globally agreed-upon definitions of the essential human rights. Rights are often divided into two broad types: civil-political and economic-social. Civil-political rights are sometimes referred to as "negative rights" and include what are considered traditional Western rights such as free speech, freedom of religion, equal protection under the law, and freedom from arbitrary imprisonment. These are rights generally thought to be best guaranteed by limiting the power of governments over their people. Economic-social rights are referred to as "positive rights" and include rights to good living conditions, food, health care, social security, and education. These rights are often thought to be best promoted by the expansion of governments to provide minimal standards to their people.

No state has a perfect record on any type of human rights, and states differ as to which areas they respect or violate. When the United States criticizes China for prohibiting free speech, using prison labor, and torturing political dissidents (civil-political rights), China notes that the United States has 40 million poor people, the highest ratio of prison inmates in the world, and a history of racism and violence (economic-social rights). During the Cold War, the United States and its allies consistently criticized the Soviet Union and China for violations of civil-political rights yet refused to endorse treaties championing economic-social rights. Likewise, communist states encouraged the development of the latter rights while ignoring calls for the former. Overall, despite the poor record of the world's states on some points, progress has been made on others. For example, slavery—once considered normal worldwide—has mostly been abandoned in the past 150 years.

Human Rights Institutions

Universal Declaration of Human Rights (UDHR) (1948) The core UN document on human rights; although it lacks the force of international law, it sets forth international norms regarding behavior by governments toward their own citizens and foreigners alike.

In 1948, the UN General Assembly adopted what is considered the core international document concerning human rights: the **Universal Declaration of Human Rights (UDHR)**. The UDHR does not have the force of international law, but it sets forth (hoped-for) international norms regarding behavior by governments toward their own citizens and foreigners alike. The declaration roots itself in the principle that violations of human rights upset international order (causing outrage, sparking rebellion, etc.) and in the fact that the UN Charter commits states to respect fundamental freedoms. The declaration proclaims that "all human beings are born free and equal" without regard to race, sex, language, religion, political affiliation, or the status of the territory in which they were born. It goes on to promote norms in a wide variety of areas, including banning torture, guaranteeing religious and political freedom, and ensuring the right of economic well-being.

Since the adoption of the UDHR, the UN has opened eight treaties for state signature to further define protections of human rights (see Table 6.3). Unlike the UDHR, these treaties are legally binding contracts signed by states. Of course, international law is only as good as the enforcement mechanisms behind it. Yet these treaties are important in outlining the basic protections for individuals expected by the international community.

Two key treaties are the *International Covenant on Civil and Political Rights* and the *International Covenant on Economic, Social, and Cultural Rights*. These two treaties, both of which entered into force in 1976, codify the promises of the UDHR while dividing the list of rights in the UDHR into civil-political and economic-social rights, respectively. These two covenants, along with the UDHR, are often referred to as the International Bill of Human Rights.

The remaining treaties each deal with a particular group that the international community considers vulnerable. The International Convention on the Elimination of All Forms of Racial Discrimination (ICERD), enacted in 1969,

Table 6.3 Ratification Status of Seven Core UN Human Rights Treaties, 2016

Treaty	Date in Force	Number of Parties	Key Non-Members
Convention on the Elimination of All Forms of Racial Discrimination (CERD)	January 4, 1969	177	Bhutan, Burma, Malaysia, North Korea
Covenant on Economic, Social and Cultural Rights (CESCR)	January 3, 1976	164	Cuba, Saudi Arabia, U.S.
Covenant on Civil and Political Rights (CCPR)	March 23, 1976	168	Burma, China, Cuba, Saudi Arabia
Convention on the Elimination of Discrimination Against Women (CEDAW)	September 3, 1981	189	Iran, Somalia, Sudan, U.S.
Convention Against Torture (CAT)	June 26, 1987	158	Angola, Burma, India, Iran, Sudan
Convention on the Rights of the Child (CRC)	September 2, 1990	200	U.S.
Convention on the Protection of the Rights of all Migrant Workers (CMW)	July 1, 2003	48	France, Great Britain, China, Russia, U.S.
Convention on the Rights of Persons with Disabilities	May 3, 2008	159	Chad, Ireland, Finland, Netherlands, U.S.

Source: United Nations

bans discrimination against individuals based on race, ethnicity, religion, or national origin. The ICERD does not include language concerning gender discrimination. The Convention on the Elimination of All Forms of Discrimination against Women (CEDAW), however, fills this void by banning discrimination against women. CEDAW entered into force in 1981.

The Convention against Torture (CAT), which entered into effect in 1987, bans dehumanizing, degrading, and inhumane treatment of individuals even in times of war. The Convention on the Rights of the Child (CRC), which came into force in 1990, promotes children's health, education, and physical well-being (every country in the world except the United States has approved the CRC). The International Convention on the Protection of the Rights of All Migrant Workers and Members of Their Families (CMW) entered into force in 2003. The CMW attempts to protect the political, labor, and social rights of the nearly 100 million migrant workers around the globe. Finally, the most recent UN human rights treaty is the Convention on the Rights of Persons with Disabilities (CRPD), which entered into force in 2008. This treaty promotes dignity, equality of legal protection, and reasonable accommodation for disabled persons.

Equally important as these UN treaties themselves are the *optional protocols* that are attached to several of the treaties. These protocols can be thought of as addendums to the treaties because they contain additional protections not included in the original treaties. In general, far fewer states sign these optional protocols because the protections contained in them were too controversial for the original document. In addition, some of the optional protocols contain stronger enforcement mechanisms, such as giving individuals in signatory states the right to go to the UN monitoring bodies without the approval of their governments. States that are not party to the original treaty may sign them, as is the case with the United States, which has not signed the CRC but *has* signed its two optional protocols.

Besides the UN-related human rights treaties, several regional IOs have promoted the protection of human rights. Nowhere is this more true than in Europe, where the European Union, the Council of Europe, and the European Court of Human Rights all work to ensure that human rights are respected by all states in the region. In Latin America as well, the *Inter-American Court of Human Rights* has had some success in promoting human rights, yet it has also been limited by state refusal to abide by its decisions. Finally, the African Union helps support the African Human Rights Commission, but the Commission has been hampered by its lack of monetary and political support from African states.

In the past decade, developed states have begun to use other international organizations to pressure developing states to improve human rights conditions. Free trade agreements (see Chapter 5) frequently contain provisions that condition trade benefits on the respect for human rights, especially workers' rights. Because these treaties provide policies beneficial to the developing states, they create a ready mechanism to punish countries who abuse their citizens. Others argue, however, that limiting economic benefits to countries harms their economic development, which is likely only to make the human rights situation worse.

Today, NGOs play a key role in efforts to win basic political rights in authoritarian countries—including a halt to the torture, execution, and imprisonment of those expressing political or religious beliefs. The leading organization pressing this struggle is **Amnesty International**, an NGO that operates globally to monitor and try to rectify glaring abuses of human rights. Amnesty International has a reputation for impartiality and has criticized abuses in many countries, including the United States. Other groups, such as Human Rights Watch, work in a similar way but often with a more regional or national focus. NGOs often provide information and advocacy for UN and other regional organizations. They essentially serve as a bridge between the global or regional organizations and efforts to promote human rights "on the ground."

Enforcing norms of human rights is difficult because it involves interfering in a state's internal affairs. Cutting off trade or contact with a government that violates human rights tends to hurt the citizens whose rights are being violated. Yet such measures keep those suffering from human rights abuses in the global spotlight, drawing more attention to their plight. And governments shy away from humanitarian interventions using military force to overcome armed resistance by local authorities or warlords and to bring help to civilian victims of wars and disasters. However, international norms have increasingly shifted against sovereignty and toward protecting endangered civilians. A major summit of world leaders in 2005 enshrined the concept of the **responsibility to protect (R2P)**, which holds that governments worldwide must act to save civilians

Amnesty International An influential nongovernmental organization that operates globally to monitor and try to rectify glaring abuses of political (not economic or social) human rights.

responsibility to protect (R2P) Principle adopted by world leaders in 2005 holding governments responsible for protecting civilians from genocide and crimes against humanity perpetrated within a sovereign state.

from genocide or crimes against humanity perpetrated or allowed by their own governments. The people of Syria did not get protection in 2011–2015, however, as tens of thousands were slaughtered by their government and, starting in 2014, also by Islamic State in Iraq and Syria (ISIS) rebels.

The U.S. State Department has actively pursued human rights since the late 1970s. An annual U.S. government report assesses human rights in states around the world. In states where abuses are severe or becoming worse, U.S. foreign aid has been withheld. (But in other cases, Central Intelligence Agency [CIA] funding has supported the abusers.) Currently, human rights is one of the two main areas of conflict (along with Taiwan) in China's relationship with the United States. Several practices draw criticism, including imprisoning political opponents of the government, the use of prison labor, and a criminal justice system prone to abuses. According to Amnesty International, China executes more people than the rest of the world combined—thousands each year—sometimes within days of the crime and sometimes for relatively minor crimes.

war crimes Violations of the law governing the conduct of warfare, such as by mistreating prisoners of war or unnecessarily targeting civilians.

crimes against humanity A category of legal offenses created at the Nuremberg trials after World War II to encompass genocide and other acts committed by the political and military leaders of the Third Reich (Nazi Germany).

War Crimes

Large-scale abuses of human rights often occur during war. Serious violations of this kind are considered **war crimes**. In wartime, international law is especially difficult to enforce, but extensive norms of legal conduct in war are widely followed. After a war, losers can be punished for violations of the laws of war, as Germans were in the Nuremberg trials after World War II. Because the Nazi murders of civilians did not violate German law, the Nuremberg Tribunal treated them as **crimes against humanity**, conceived as inhumane acts and persecutions against civilians on a vast scale in the pursuit of unjust ends.

In the 1990s, for the first time since World War II, the UN Security Council authorized an international war crimes tribunal, directed against war crimes in the former Yugoslavia. Similar tribunals were later established for genocide in Rwanda and Sierra Leone. The tribunal on the former Yugoslavia, headquartered in The Hague, the Netherlands, indicted Serbian strongman Slobodan Milosevic in 1999. After Milosevic lost power, the new Serbian government turned him over to the tribunal in 2001. His trial continued until his death in 2006. By 2011, no Bosnia war criminals

REMAINS OF WAR CRIMES War crimes include unnecessary targeting of civilians and mistreatment of prisoners of war (POWs). The most notorious war crime in Europe in recent decades was the massacre of more than 7,000 men and boys by Serbian forces who overran the UN "safe area" of Srebrenica, Bosnia, in 1995. Here, a mass grave there is excavated in 2007.

remained at large, and at the end of 2012, the Rwanda tribunal also completed all of its 71 cases.

Following the civil war in Sierra Leone, the government there ran a war crimes tribunal jointly with the UN. In 2003, it indicted the sitting state leader in next-door Liberia, Charles Taylor, for his role in the war's extreme brutality. He fled to Nigeria shortly afterward but was captured there, turned over to the tribunal for trial in 2006, and convicted in 2012.

International Criminal Court (ICC) A permanent tribunal for war crimes and crimes against humanity.

Following up on the UN tribunals for former Yugoslavia and Rwanda, in 1998 most of the world's states signed a treaty to create a permanent **International Criminal Court (ICC)**. It hears cases of genocide, war crimes, and crimes against humanity from anywhere in the world. The ICC opened for business in 2003 in The Hague, with 18 judges sworn in from around the world (but not the United States). In 2008, the ICC began its first trial, of a militia leader from Democratic Congo accused of drafting children under the age of 15 and killing civilians. He was convicted in 2012.

The United States has refused to ratify the ICC agreement and shows little interest in doing so. The United States has pressured many ICC member states to sign immunity agreements (known as Bilateral Immunity Agreements [BIAs]) to protect American soldiers serving in those countries from prosecution. In 2005, after several ICC members refused to sign a BIA, Congress voted to cut foreign aid to those states. U.S. leaders are concerned that American soldiers serving in peacekeeping missions or in NATO allies will fall under the jurisdiction of the ICC rather than the American military's own justice system.

War crimes in Darfur, Sudan—which a UN commission found grave but short of "genocide"—have also been referred to the ICC after the United States dropped its objections in 2005 (when exemptions for U.S. soldiers serving in peacekeeping operations were restored). The Darfur case is a difficult challenge for the ICC. In 2009, the ICC indicted the sitting Sudanese president, Omar al-Bashir, on charges of war crimes and crimes against humanity, and issued a warrant for his arrest. The indictment angered the Sudanese government, which then expelled humanitarian organizations from Darfur. In 2010, al-Bashir left Sudan for the first time, but his destination country of Chad refused to arrest him, citing bias in the ICC (all ICC prosecutions have been in Africa). The ICC faces a difficult balance in holding officials in Sudan accountable yet being sensitive to efforts to end the violence in Darfur (see p. 126). In 2011, the ICC quickly indicted Libya's dictator and several others, but he was killed before he had to face justice.

The most important principle in the laws of war is the effort to limit warfare to the combatants and to protect civilians when possible. It is illegal to target civilians in a war. It is not illegal, however, to target military forces knowing civilians will be killed. Even then, the amount of force used must be *proportional* to the military gain, and only the *necessary* amount of force can be used.

To help separate combatants from civilians, soldiers must wear uniforms and insignia, such as a shoulder patch with a national flag. This provision is

Policy Perspectives
International Criminal Court Chief Prosecutor, Fatou Bensouda

PROBLEM *How do you balance respect for international legal principles and national interests?*

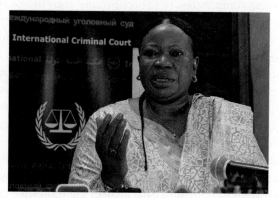

BACKGROUND For six years, fighting has raged in the western Sudanese province of Darfur. This conflict has been labeled genocide by many observers. It is estimated that 2.7 million people have been forced from their homes and perhaps 300,000 have died. While some of the violence in Darfur is between warring rebel groups, the Sudanese government has been accused of arming one set of militias and encouraging the violence.

You are the chief prosecutor for the International Criminal Court (ICC). Sudan is not a member of the ICC, but because the Security Council referred the Darfur case to the ICC, you may choose to begin a case against anyone in the Sudan. The ICC has already issued two arrest warrants for war crimes related to Darfur. In 2009, your predecessor obtained an indictment and arrest warrant against Sudan's president, Omar al-Bashir, on charges of war crimes and crimes against humanity. Such a move to prosecute a sitting president of a country in the middle of a civil war was unprecedented.

DOMESTIC CONSIDERATIONS While human rights groups applauded the decision to pursue criminal charges against the Sudanese president, many countries opposed the move. China and Russia, both of which maintain diplomatic ties with Sudan, have expressed disapproval and pressed the ICC to stop prosecutions. Many African Union (AU) countries, which currently deploy peacekeepers in Darfur, have opposed the move, warning that it could lead to a breakdown of the peace process. In fact, after the ICC announced plans to indict al-Bashir, violence did increase in Darfur, including attacks against AU peacekeepers, and after the indictment was announced, Sudan expelled humanitarian NGOs from Darfur, gravely imperiling the population there. The AU has called for the ICC to suspend all ICC proceedings relating to Darfur, and the Arab League has condemned the indictment of al-Bashir.

The United States and the major European countries support efforts to bring members of the Sudanese government to justice. And while Russia and China have suggested revoking ICC authority to prosecute cases related to Darfur, the United States, France, or Britain could use their Security Council veto to stop such an effort. Supporters of the ICC have argued that Darfur represents a crucial case for the future of the legitimacy of the Court. This case will set important precedents related to the power of this relatively new body.

SCENARIO Imagine that the Chinese government approaches you and asks you to suspend the indictment of al-Bashir. In return, China agrees to press Sudan both to end violence in Darfur and to allow for more peacekeepers to be deployed there. China has no direct control over Sudan, however, so China's promises may bring little change in behavior on the part of Sudan. On the other hand, China does have some pull with the Sudanese leadership. The United States and its allies would be likely to support such a move if it resulted in a stable cease-fire.

CHOOSE YOUR POLICY Do you suspend the ICC's efforts to prosecute the Sudanese leadership, especially the Sudanese president, for war crimes? How do you balance the demands of competing great powers? How do you balance your desire to bring justice to the victims of the conflict in Darfur with the reality of the peace process, which hangs in the balance? Can justice be delayed to save lives in the short term? If justice is delayed, will it ever be achieved?

frequently violated in guerrilla warfare, making that form of warfare particularly brutal and destructive of civilian life. If one cannot tell the difference between a bystander and a combatant, one is likely to kill both when in doubt.

In recent years, the unprecedented rise in the use of private military forces in wars, especially in Iraq, has challenged the laws of war. Because these private forces are not members of a country's military, the international laws of war do not necessarily apply to them (only states, not corporations, sign the Geneva Conventions). In Iraq, the U.S. government had granted a waiver to these companies to ensure that they could not be prosecuted for violations of international law, only local law. But because there was no formal Iraqi government, no one could enforce violations of domestic law committed by these companies. Several high-profile incidents (including abuses at the Abu Ghraib prison and several shootings of civilians) led Congress, the UN, and Iraq to hold private forces accountable. A 2008 Iraqi-U.S. agreement on the status of American military forces ended the legal waiver for private contractors beginning in 2009.

Soldiers have the right under the laws of war to surrender, which is to abandon their status as combatants and become *prisoners of war (POWs)*. They give up their weapons and their right to fight, and earn instead the right (like civilians) not to be targeted. POWs may not be killed, mistreated, or forced to disclose information beyond their name, rank, and serial number.

International Committee of the Red Cross (ICRC) A nongovernmental organization (NGO) that provides practical support, such as medical care, food, and letters from home, to civilians caught in wars and to prisoners of war (POWs). Exchanges of POWs are usually negotiated through the ICRC.

The laws of war reserve a special role for the **International Committee of the Red Cross (ICRC)**. The ICRC provides practical support—such as medical care, food, and letters from home—to civilians caught in wars and to POWs. Exchanges of POWs are usually negotiated through the ICRC. Armed forces must respect the neutrality of the Red Cross, and usually they do (again, guerrilla war is problematical). In the war on terrorism, the United States does not consider the "enemy combatants" it detains as POWs, but it has granted the ICRC access to most (though not all) of them. More controversial is the U.S. policy of "extraordinary rendition," which lets terrorist suspects captured overseas be transferred to other countries, including some that use torture, for questioning.

The laws of warfare impose moral responsibility on individuals, as well as on states, in wartime. The Nuremberg Tribunal established that participants can be held accountable for war crimes they commit. German officers defended their actions as "just following orders," but this was rejected; the officers were punished, and some were executed.

CHANGING CONTEXT The laws of warfare have been undermined by the changing nature of war. Conventional wars by defined armed forces on defined battlegrounds are giving way to irregular and "low-intensity" wars fought by guerrillas and death squads in cities or jungles. The lines between civilians and soldiers blur in these situations, and war crimes become more commonplace. In the Vietnam War, one of the largest problems faced by the United States was an enemy that seemed to be everywhere and nowhere. This led frustrated U.S.

forces to attack civilian villages seen as supporting the guerrillas. In one infamous case, a U.S. officer was court-martialed for ordering his soldiers to massacre hundreds of unarmed civilians in the village of My Lai in 1968 (he was convicted but given a light sentence). In today's irregular warfare, frequently inflamed by ethnic and religious conflicts, the laws of war are increasingly difficult to uphold.

Another factor undermining laws of war is that states rarely issue a *declaration of war* setting out whom they are warring against and the cause of their action. Ironically, such declarations are historically the exception, not the rule. This trend continues today because declarations of war bring little benefit to the state declaring war and incur obligations under international law.

These new norms still remain unsettled. New expectations are emerging in areas such as human rights, UN peacekeeping, humanitarian interventions, Russia's and China's roles as great powers, and the U.S. role as a superpower. These changes will play out in a world increasingly marked by the gap between rich and poor countries—the subject of Chapter 7.

Chapter Review

Summary

- Supranational processes bring states together in larger structures and identities. These processes generally lead to an ongoing struggle between nationalism and supranationalism.

- The UN embodies a tension between state sovereignty and supranational authority. The UN has made sovereignty the more important principle, limiting the UN's power.

- The UN has attracted nearly universal membership of the world's states, including all the great powers.

- Each of the 193 UN member states has one vote in the General Assembly.

- The Security Council has ten rotating member states and five permanent members: the United States, Russia, China, Britain, and France.

- The UN is administered by international civil servants in the Secretariat, which is headed by the Secretary General.

- UN peacekeeping forces are deployed in regional conflicts in five world regions. Their main role is to monitor compliance with agreements such as cease-fires, disarmament plans, and fair election rules. UN peacekeepers operate under the UN flag and command. Sometimes national troops operate under their own flag and command to carry out UN resolutions.

- International integration partially shifts sovereignty from the state toward supranational institutions.

- The European Union (EU) is the most advanced case of integration. Its 28 member states have given considerable power to the EU in economic decision making. However, national power still outweighs supranational power, even in the EU.

- The most important and most successful element in the EU is its customs union (and free trade area). Goods can cross borders of member states freely, and the members adopt unified tariffs on goods entering from outside the EU.

- The EU's Common Agricultural Policy (CAP) equalizes subsidies to farmers within the community. Carrying out the CAP consumes 40 percent of the EU's budget.

- The EU has a monetary union with a single currency (the euro) in 19 of the 28 EU states. It is the biggest experiment with money in history and had great success in its first years, but it hit a crisis in 2010–2015 over some members' debts.

- In structure, the EU revolves around the permanent staff of so-called Eurocrats under the European Commission. However, member states have power over the Commission.

- The European Parliament has members directly elected by citizens in EU states, but it cannot legislate the rules for the community. The European Court of Justice has extended its jurisdiction more successfully than any other international court and can overrule national laws.

- Thirteen new members, mostly Eastern European, joined the EU in 2004, 2007, and 2013. The EU's structures and procedures are being adapted as it moves from 15 to 28 members. To some extent, the broadening of membership conflicts with the deepening of ties among the existing members.

- International law, the formal body of rules for state relations, derives from treaties (most important), custom, general principles, and legal scholarship—not from legislation passed by any government.

- International law is difficult to enforce but is enforced in practice by national power, international coalitions, and reciprocity.

- The World Court hears grievances of one state against another but cannot infringe on state sovereignty in most cases.

- A permanent International Criminal Court (ICC) began operations in 2003. It hears cases of genocide, war crimes, and crimes against humanity, including war crimes in Sudan.

- Laws of war distinguish combatants from civilians, giving each certain rights and responsibilities. Guerrilla wars and ethnic conflicts have blurred these distinctions.

- International norms concerning human rights are becoming stronger and more widely accepted. However, human rights law is problematic because it entails interference by one state in another's internal affairs.

Key Terms

supranational 223
international norms 223
international organizations (IOs) 224
UN Charter 227
UN General Assembly 228

UN Security Council 228
UN Secretariat 230
peacebuilding 237
UN Conference on Trade and Development (UNCTAD) 242

World Health Organization (WHO) 242
European Union (EU) 243
international integration 244
neofunctionalism 245
security community 245

Critical Thinking Questions

1. Suppose you were asked to recommend changes in the structure of the UN Security Council (especially in permanent membership and the veto). What changes would you recommend, if any? Based on what logic?

2. Functional economic ties among European states have contributed to the emergence of a supranational political structure, the EU, which has considerable though not unlimited power. Do you think the same thing could happen in North America? Could the U.S.-Canadian-Mexican NAFTA develop into a future North American Union like the EU? What problems would it be likely to face, given the experience of the EU?

3. Although international norms concerning human rights are becoming stronger, China and many other states continue to consider human rights an internal affair over which the state has sovereignty within its territory. Do you think human rights are a legitimate subject for one state to raise with another? If so, how do you reconcile the tensions between state autonomy and universal rights? What practical steps could be taken to get sovereign states to acknowledge universal human rights?

Chapter 7
North-South Relations

AFRICAN MIGRANTS BOARDING SHIP, ITALY, 2015.

∨ Learning Objectives

7.1 Identify at least four basic human needs and describe how at least one region in the global South is meeting those needs.

7.2 Identify examples of states that world-system theorists would identify as members of the core, semiperiphery, and periphery.

7.3 Compare three different effects of colonialism and explain how these effects have led to problems with economic development in the global South.

7.4 Compare and contrast the experiences of China and India in achieving economic development.

7.5 Identify and evaluate two different strategies that developing states have used in attempting to achieve economic growth.

7.6 Describe three reasons why countries might provide foreign aid to countries of the global South.

The State of the South

7.1 **Identify at least four basic human needs and describe how at least one region in the global South is meeting those needs.**

This chapter concerns the world's poor regions—the global South—where most people live. States in these regions are called by various names, which are used interchangeably: *third world countries, less-developed countries* (LDCs), *underdeveloped countries* (UDCs), or **developing countries**. The chapter first discusses the gap in wealth between the industrialized regions (the North) and the rest of the world (the South), and develops the theories of imperialism introduced in Chapter 3 (pp. 96–99) that try to explain this gap in terms of historical colonization of the South by the North. It then considers international aspects of economic development in the South.

IR scholars do not agree on the causes or implications of poverty in the global South, nor do they agree on solutions (if any) to the problem. Thus, they also disagree about the nature of relations between rich and poor states (North-South relations). Everyone agrees, however, that much of the global South is poor, and some of it extremely poor.

In all, about 1 billion people live in abject poverty, without access to basic nutrition or health care. They are concentrated in Africa, where income levels have lagged for decades. Two decades ago the concentration was as strong in South Asia, but economic growth there has greatly reduced extreme poverty. Still, the average income per person in South Asia—home to 2 billion people—is only $4,800 per year, and in Africa, it's $3,200 (even after adjusting for the lower costs of living in these regions compared to richer ones). Although billions of people are rising out of poverty, the number of very poor people nonetheless remains about the same because of population growth.

The bottom line is that every ten seconds, somewhere in the world, a child dies as a result of malnutrition—not eating enough food or eating the right food

developing countries States in the global South, the poorest regions of the world—also called third world countries, less-developed countries, and undeveloped countries.

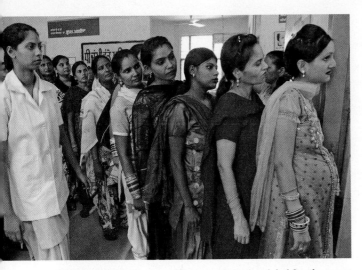

BABY BOOST Nearly a billion people in the global South—most of them in Africa and South Asia—live in abject poverty, lacking safe water, housing, food, and the ability to read. Natural disasters, droughts, and wars can displace subsistence farmers from their land and make matters worse. But sustained advances in health care, such as the prenatal checkup given these women in India in 2013, are bringing dramatic improvements.

to resist diseases. That is over 3 million every year. The world produces enough food to nourish these children and enough income to afford to nourish them, but their own families or states do not have enough income. They die, ultimately, from poverty. Meanwhile, in that same ten seconds, the world spends over $500,000 on military forces, a thousandth of which could save the child's life and more. Likewise, people lack water, shelter, health care, and other necessities because they cannot afford them. The widespread, grinding poverty of people who cannot afford necessities is less visible than the dramatic examples of starvation triggered by war or drought, but it affects many more people.

The UN in 2000 adopted the **Millennium Development Goals (MDG)**, which set targets for basic needs measures to be achieved by 2015 and measured against 1990 data. The first of the eight goals is to

Millennium Development Goals UN targets for basic needs measures, such as reducing poverty and hunger, adopted in 2000.

cut in half the proportion of the world's population living in "extreme poverty," defined as income of less than $1.25 per day. This goal was met ahead of schedule in 2010, although Africa lagged far behind Asia in cutting poverty. Since 1990, 2 billion people have gained access to improved drinking water, but 1 billion remain hungry around the world.

The five regions of the global South differ not only on poverty reduction but also on income level and growth. As Figure 7.1 shows, the regions experiencing the fastest growth—China and South Asia—are neither the highest- nor the lowest-income regions. The Middle East is about as developed as China in terms of gross domestic product (GDP) per capita, but it is growing at only half the rate. Later in this chapter, we will explore the reasons for these differences in economic growth, but here we note simply that the world's regions vary on both income and growth, with the two dimensions not correlated.

According to the World Bank, between 1990 and 2013, incomes per person (adjusted for inflation, in today's dollars) in the global South as a whole rose from about $3,000 to about $8,000 (figures expressed in 2015 dollars). In the global North, they rose from about $20,000 to about $40,000. Does this indicate a slow closing of the gap because the ratio fell from about 6.7 to 5.0 as the result of a higher rate of growth in the South? Or does it indicate a widening of the gap between a person in the North and one in the South because in absolute terms, it increased from $17,000 to over $32,000? Each has some truth.

Figure 7.1 Income Level and Growth Rate by World Region

Source: World Bank.

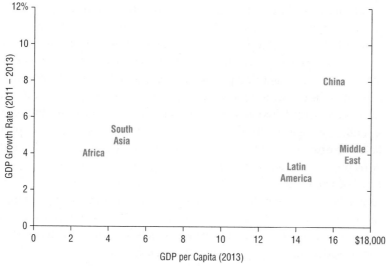

Note: For the global North overall, GDP per capita is $40,000.

Basic Human Needs

Some countries in the global South have made rapid progress in raising incomes, but others are caught in a cycle of poverty. To put economic growth on a firm foundation, the **basic human needs** of most of the population must be met. People need food, shelter, and other necessities of daily life in order to feel secure. Furthermore, as long as people in the global South blame imperialism for a lack of basic needs, extreme poverty fuels revolution, terrorism, and anti-Western sentiments.

Children are central to meeting a population's basic needs. In particular, education allows a new generation to meet other basic needs and move through the demographic transition (see Chapter 8). Literacy—which UNESCO defines as the ability to read and write a simple sentence—is the key component of education. A person who can read and write can obtain a wealth of information about farming, health care, birth control, and so forth. Some poor countries have raised literacy rates substantially; others lag behind.

Great variation also exists in schooling. Primary-school enrollment in 2013 was more than 90 percent in most world regions, though only 77 percent for Africa. Secondary education—middle and high school—is another matter. In the North, about 90 percent of secondary-school-age children are enrolled, but in most of the global South, those numbers are significantly smaller. College is available to only a small fraction of the population.

In 2013 in the global South, according to UNICEF, one in four children suffered from malnutrition, one in seven lacked access to health care, and one in

basic human needs The fundamental needs of people for adequate food, shelter, health care, sanitation, and education. Meeting such needs may be thought of as both a moral imperative and a form of investment in "human capital" essential for economic growth.

seven had no safe drinking water. The AIDS epidemic is undoing progress made over decades in reducing child mortality and increasing education.

Figure 7.2 shows the variation across regions in two key indicators of children's well-being at different stages—immunizations and secondary-school enrollments. In both cases, achievement of these basic needs for children roughly correlates with the regions' respective income levels. Effective health care in poor countries is not expensive—less than $5 per person per year for primary care. Since 1990, despite the daunting problems of war and the HIV/AIDS epidemic, public health in the global South has registered some important gains. Infant tetanus deaths were halved, and access to safe water was extended to a billion more people. Polio was nearly eliminated, but resistance to vaccination in parts of Nigeria let the disease begin to spread again, with three countries having indigenous virus populations as of 2016 (Pakistan, Afghanistan, and Nigeria—and the virus traveled from Pakistan to Egyptian sewage in 2013; Ukraine officials feared an outbreak in 2016 after polio reappeared there). In eight African countries in 2006, following successful trials in several other countries, authorities combined the distribution of insecticide-treated mosquito nets for malaria with measles and polio vaccines, deworming pills, vitamin A supplements, and educational materials—a combined approach proven to work. In the past 25 years, the number of children immunized in developing countries has risen from 5 percent to more than 50 percent. In 2014, deaths of children under five worldwide hit a record low, well below 7 million, declining by half since 1990. Measles deaths dropped by three-quarters in just ten years, 2000–2010, an enormous success.

Figure 7.2 Basic Needs Indicators by Region (2013)

Source: World Bank data. Regions do not exactly match those used elsewhere in this book.

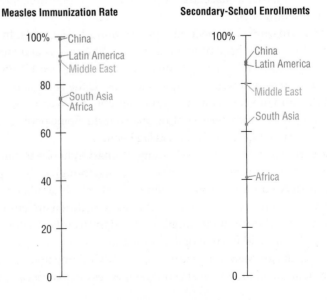

Still, the global disparities in access to health care are striking. The 75 percent of the world's people living in the global South have about 30 percent of the world's doctors and nurses. In medical research, less than 5 percent of world expenditures are directed at problems in developing countries, according to the World Health Organization (WHO). The biggest killers are AIDS, acute respiratory infections, diarrhea, tuberculosis (TB), malaria, and hepatitis. More than 600 million people are infected with tropical diseases—300 to 500 million with malaria alone. But because the people with such diseases are poor, there is often not a large enough market for drug companies (multinational corporations [MNCs]) in the industrialized world to invest in medicines for them. And when poor countries need medicines developed for rich markets, the drugs may be prohibitively expensive (see pp. 358–359).

DO THE MATH Children are a main focus of efforts to provide basic human needs in the global South. Education is critical to both economic development and the demographic transition. Girls worldwide receive less education than boys, and in Afghanistan under the Taliban, they were banned from schools altogether. This math class in Kandahar, Afghanistan, in 2002 followed the Taliban's fall.

Safe water is another essential element of meeting basic human needs. In many rural locations, people must walk miles every day to fetch water. Access to water does not mean running water in every house, but a clean well or faucet for a village. In 1990–2010, the number without access fell by half, meeting the MDG target early, but one in six people worldwide still lack safe drinking water. And many among those with safe drinking water lack sanitation facilities (such as sewers and sanitary latrines). Some 2.5 billion people, a third of the world's population, do not have access to sanitation. The result is recurrent epidemics and widespread diarrhea, which kill millions of children each year. Rural areas are worse than cities. Poor sanitation in Haiti allowed a cholera epidemic (ironically introduced by visiting Nepalese peacekeepers sent to help Haiti) to kill thousands in 2010–2013. Despite the tremendous progress the world has made in improving water and sanitation, with population growth there are still about 1 billion people lacking safe water and more than 2 billion without adequate sanitation.

Shelter is another key basic need. Of the world's 7 billion people, about one in six lives in substandard housing or is homeless altogether. For indicator after indicator, we find about 1 billion people left behind with nothing. The different indicators do not overlap perfectly, but basically, the bottom 1 billion of humanity, most living in rural areas, are in desperate poverty. The most important factors keeping these people in desperate poverty appear to be civil war, corruption, the "resource curse" (see pp. 296–298), and landlocked locations without ready access to trade.

War in the global South—both international and civil war—is a leading obstacle to the provision of basic needs. War causes much greater damage to society than merely the direct deaths and injuries it inflicts. In war zones, economic infrastructure such as transportation is disrupted, as are government services such as health care and education. Wars drastically reduce the confidence in economic and political stability on which investment and trade depend.

Figure 7.3 maps the rates of access to safe water and food. The worldwide pattern somewhat resembles the map of wars in progress on page 117. If indeed there is a relationship between recent or present warfare and a lack of basic

Figure 7.3 Rates of Access to Water and Food, 2005

Source: United Nations.

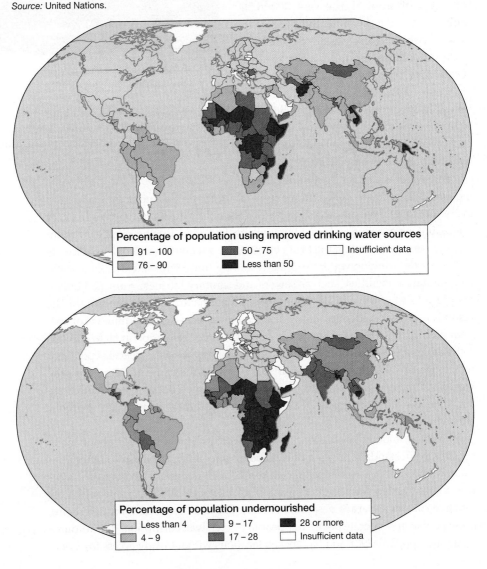

Percentage of population using improved drinking water sources
- 91 – 100
- 76 – 90
- 50 – 75
- Less than 50
- Insufficient data

Percentage of population undernourished
- Less than 4
- 4 – 9
- 9 – 17
- 17 – 28
- 28 or more
- Insufficient data

The number of international refugees in the world was over 15 million in 2014. In addition, about 30 million more people were displaced within their own countries. Three-fourths of these internally displaced persons (IDPs) resided in Colombia, Congo, Somalia, Sudan, Iraq, Afghanistan, and Syria. An additional 5 million Palestinian refugees fall under the responsibility of the UN Relief and Works Agency (UNRWA). The majority of refugees and IDPs have been displaced by wars (see Table 7.2), most recently in the civil war in Syria, which by 2015 had generated 3 million refugees in Turkey, Lebanon, Iraq, and Jordan, and 6.5 million internally displaced persons, all fleeing violence in general and sexual violence in particular.

Table 7.2 Refugee Populations, 2013

Region	Millions	Main Concentrations
Middle East and Asia	21	Afghanistan, Iraq, Pakistan, Thailand, Iran
Palestinians under UNRWA	5	Palestine, Jordan, Lebanon, Syria
Africa	13	Somalia, Uganda, Sudan, D.R. Congo
Latin America	6	Colombia
Europe	5	Germany
World Total	50	

Source: UN High Commissioner for Refugees (UNHCR). Includes refugees, asylum seekers, returned refugees, and internally displaced people.

The political impact of refugees has been demonstrated repeatedly. The most politicized refugee problem for decades has been that of Palestinians displaced in the 1948 and 1967 Arab-Israeli wars (and their children and grandchildren). They live in "camps" in Jordan, Lebanon, and the Palestinian territories of Gaza and the West Bank. The question of Palestinian refugees' right to return to what is now Israel has challenged every attempt at a comprehensive peace settlement for years.

It is not always easy to distinguish a refugee fleeing war or political persecution from a migrant seeking economic opportunity. Illegal immigrants may claim to be refugees in order to be allowed to stay when really they are seeking better economic opportunities. In recent decades, this issue has become a major one throughout the North. In Germany, France, Austria,

ON THE MOVE Refugees are both a result of international conflict and a source of conflict. In addition to those fleeing war and repression and those seeking economic opportunity, hundreds of thousands of people each year cross borders as sex and labor slaves. These refugees crossing from war-torn Libya into Tunisia in 2011 show their Bangladesh passports.

Hungary, and elsewhere, resentment of foreign immigrants has fueled upsurges of right-wing nationalism in domestic politics. In 2015, European Union countries enacted a plan to distribute thousands of refugees across member states as individuals fled the Middle East and northern Africa. Tensions in the EU rose when some central European countries objected to the plan, but the EU approved it anyway. These refugees arrived at a time when Europe was already nervous about its economic situation, leading to heated debates about the best response to the wave of immigrants, many from Syria.

remittances Money sent home by migrant workers to individuals (usually relatives) in their country of origin.

REMITTANCES   A crucial aspect of migration and immigration is **remittances**—money sent home by migrants to relatives in their country of origin. They are an important source of income for many poor countries. Remittances are important for states in many regions of the world. In 2014, worldwide remittances neared $600 billion, after tripling in a decade, and were three times as large as global foreign aid, according to the World Bank (which notes the true figure may be even higher).

Remittances are becoming an increasingly important part of the global economy (see Figure 7.4). Unlike foreign direct investment (FDI), remittances are not transferred between companies or wealthy individuals but usually between

Figure 7.4 Global Flows of Remittances, 1970–2014

Source: World Bank calculations.

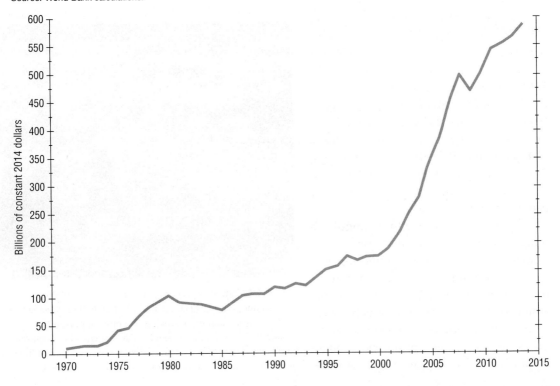

families. Thus, remittances cannot be withdrawn from a recipient economy. They are also not handed out by governments and thus are not subject to corruption or governmental waste. Also, unlike foreign aid, remittances are not subject to conditions from donors. They are given freely from family to family. These characteristics of remittances (as well as their growing size) make them important yet also difficult to study.

Remittances help states in the global South. They give poorer households more disposable income. They have helped some poorer states, such as the Philippines and Bangladesh, improve their investment ratings and sell bonds, luring more foreign direct investment. However, remittance levels are very vulnerable to economic downturns in wealthy countries. Remittances also continue the cycle of dependency of poor states on wealthy ones. Should wealthy states close their borders or expel migrant populations, this would create hardships for individual families as well as the economies of developing countries.

TRAFFICKING   In addition to migration and refugees, a growing number of people—estimated at about 700,000 annually—are trafficked across international borders against their will. They include both sex slaves and labor slaves, with each category including females and males, adults and children. Perhaps 20,000 of these people are trafficked to the United States annually. In 2014, the U.S. State Department listed 23 countries making insufficient efforts to stop human trafficking, including friends such as Kuwait, Malaysia, Thailand, and Saudi Arabia.

In general, South-North migration of all types creates problems for the industrialized states that can be solved, it seems, only by addressing the problems of the South itself.

Theories of Accumulation

7.2   Identify examples of states that world-system theorists would identify as members of the core, semiperiphery, and periphery.

How do we explain the enormous gap between income levels in the world's industrialized regions and those in the global South? What are the implications of that gap for international politics? There are several very different approaches to these questions; we will concentrate on two contrasting theories of wealth accumulation, based on more liberal and more revolutionary perspectives.

Economic Accumulation

A view of the problem from the perspective of capitalism is based on liberal economics—stressing overall efficiency in maximizing *economic growth*. This view sees the global South as merely lagging behind the industrialized North. More wealth creation in the North is a good thing, as is wealth creation in the South—the two are not in conflict.

A different view of things, from the perspective of socialism, is concerned with the distribution of wealth as much as the absolute creation of wealth. It sees the North-South divide as more of a zero-sum game in which the creation of wealth in the North most often comes at the expense of the South. It also gives politics (the state) more of a role in redistributing wealth and managing the economy than does capitalism. Socialism thus parallels mercantilism in some ways. But socialists see economic classes rather than states as the main actors in the political bargaining over the distribution of the world's wealth. And mercantilism promotes the idea of concentrating wealth (as a power element), whereas socialism promotes the broader distribution of wealth.

Capitalist and socialist approaches are rather incompatible in their language and assumptions about the problem of third world poverty and its international implications. The next few sections somewhat favor socialist approaches, focusing on the history of imperialism and on revolutionary strategies and massive redistribution of wealth as solutions, whereas the sections concluding the chapter lean toward capitalist approaches. In Latin America, in recent years, several states have elected leftist presidents committed to changing course away from free market capitalism and toward a socialist philosophy with more state-owned industries.

The World-System

world-system A view of the world in terms of regional class divisions, with industrialized countries as the core, poorest countries as the periphery, and other areas (for example, some of the newly industrializing countries) as the semiperiphery.

The global system of regional class divisions has been seen by some IR scholars as a **world-system** or a *capitalist world economy*. This view is Marxist in orientation (focusing on economic classes; see Chapter 3) and relies on a global level of analysis. In the world-system, class divisions are regionalized. Regions in the global South mostly extract raw materials (including agriculture)—work that uses much labor and little capital, and pays low wages. Industrialized regions mostly manufacture goods—work that uses more capital, requires more skilled labor, and pays workers higher wages. The manufacturing regions are called the *core* (or *center*) of the world-system; the extraction regions are called the *periphery*.

The most important class struggle today, in this view, is that between the core and periphery of the world-system. The core uses its power (derived from its wealth) to concentrate surplus from the periphery, as it has done for about 500 years. Conflicts among great powers, including the two world wars and the Cold War, basically result from competition among core states over the right to exploit the periphery.

In world-system theory, the semiperiphery is an area in which some manufacturing occurs and some capital concentrates, but not to the extent of the most advanced areas in the core. Eastern Europe and Russia are commonly considered semiperipheral, as are some of the newly industrializing countries (see pp. 300–302) such as Taiwan and Singapore. The semiperiphery acts as a kind of political buffer between the core and periphery because poor states can aspire to join the semiperiphery instead of aspiring to rebel against domination by the core. Over time, membership in the core, the semiperiphery, and the periphery changes somewhat, but the overall global system of class relations remains.

Semiperiphery regions, which export manufactured products, are just those—China and South Asia—that have been growing very rapidly in recent years (see Figure 7.1). The three periphery regions that engage with the globalizing world economy primarily as raw-material exporters (Africa, the Middle East, and Latin America) are growing more slowly.

Having exportable natural resources would seem a big plus for an economy, but in fact the problems of basing economic growth on resource exports have been called the resource curse (see p. 297). Even in a middle-income country, Chile, the quadrupling of the price of its main export commodity, copper, in 2003–2006 was a mixed blessing. Protesters demanded that the billions of dollars be spent on social services for the poor, but the president (although a socialist) warned against spending what could be a temporary windfall. Meanwhile the high export earnings strengthened Chile's currency, making it harder for other industries to export their products. Then, in late 2008, the global recession caused a crash in copper prices, drastically cutting Chile's income.

Imperialism

7.3 Compare three different effects of colonialism and explain how these effects have led to problems with economic development in the global South.

Both the disparities in wealth between the global North and South and the specialization in regions' exports have long histories. In Chapter 3 we discussed Marxist theories of imperialism, which give a particular kind of explanation for how the North-South gap evolved. Here we review how imperialism affected the South over the centuries and how its aftereffects are still felt around the world. Imperialism, especially in the sixteenth to mid-twentieth centuries, structured world order starkly around the dominance principle, with masters and slaves, conquerors and conquered peoples with their land, labor, and treasures. At the same time, imperialism depended on the identity principle to unite the global North around a common racial identity that defined nonwhite people as an out-group. (Although identity issues today are more complex, racism still affects North-South relations.)

European imperialism got its start in the fifteenth century with the development of oceangoing sailing ships in which a small crew could transport a sizable cargo over a long distance. Portugal pioneered the first voyages of exploration beyond Europe. Spain, France, and Britain soon followed. With superior military technology, Europeans gained control of coastal cities and of resupply outposts along major trade routes. Gradually this control extended farther inland, first in Latin America, then in North America, and later throughout Asia and Africa (see Figure 7.5).

Figure 7.5 Conquest of the World

Former colonial territories of European states.

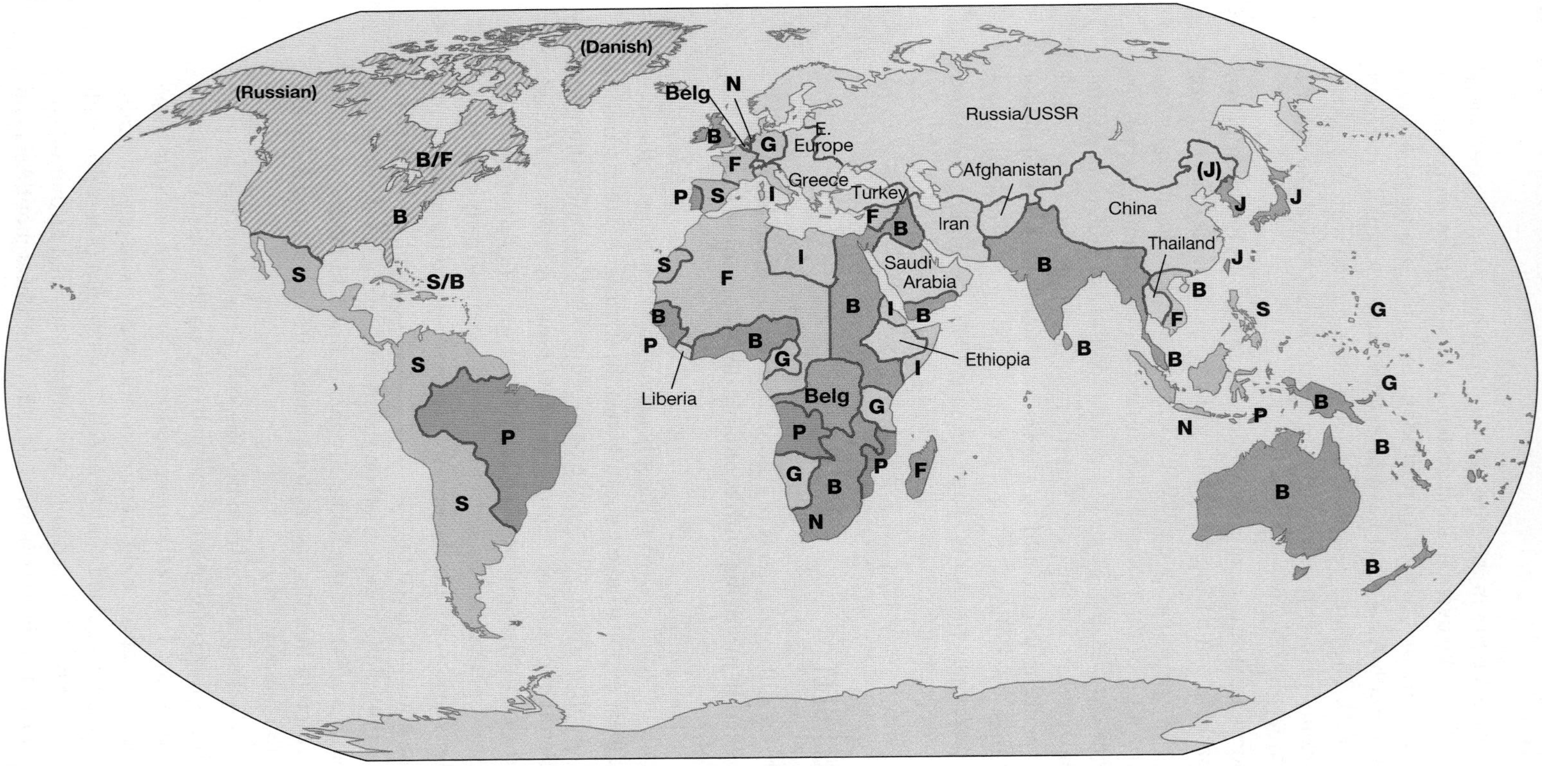

B	=	British	G	=	German	N	=	Netherlands
Belg	=	Belgian	I	=	Italian	P	=	Portuguese
F	=	French	J	=	Japanese	S	=	Spanish

These empires decimated indigenous populations and cultures, causing immense suffering. Over time, the economies of colonies developed with the creation of basic transportation and communication infrastructure, factories, and so forth. But these economies were often molded to the needs of the colonizers, not the local populations.

In the twentieth century, the world regions formerly dominated by Europe gained independence, with their own sovereign states participating in the international system. Independence came earlier in the Americas (around 1800). Decolonization continued through the mid-1970s until almost no European colonies remained. Most of the newly independent states have faced tremendous challenges and difficulties in the postcolonial era because of their colonial histories.

Effects of Colonialism

For most states in the global South, the history of having been colonized by Europeans is central to their national identity, foreign policy, and place in the world. For these states—and especially for those within them who favor socialist perspectives—international relations (IR) revolves around their asymmetrical power relationships with industrialized states.

Being colonized has a devastating effect on a people and culture. Foreigners overrun a territory with force and take it over. They install their own government, staffed by their own nationals. The inhabitants are forced to speak the language of the colonizers, to adopt their cultural practices, and to be educated at schools run under their guidance. The inhabitants are told that they are racially inferior to the foreigners.

White Europeans in third world colonies in Africa and Asia were greatly outnumbered by native inhabitants but maintained power by a combination of force and (more important) psychological conditioning. After generations under colonialism, most native inhabitants either saw white domination as normal or believed that nothing could be done about it. The whites often lived in a bubble world separated from the lives of the local inhabitants.

Colonialism also had certain negative *economic* implications. The most easily accessible minerals were dug up and shipped away. The best farmland was planted in export crops rather than subsistence crops. The infrastructure that was built served the purposes of imperialism rather than the local population—for instance, railroads going straight from mining areas to ports. The education and skills needed to run the economy were largely limited to whites.

The economic effects were not all negative, however. Colonialism often fostered local economic accumulation (although controlled by whites). Cities grew. Mines were dug and farms established. Much of the infrastructure that exists today in many developing countries was created by colonizers. In some cases (though not all), colonization combined disparate communities into a cohesive political unit with a common religion, language, and culture, thus creating more opportunities for economic accumulation. In some cases, the local political cultures replaced by colonialism had been oppressive to the majority of the people.

Wherever there were colonizers, there were anticolonial movements. Independence movements throughout Africa and Asia gained momentum during and after World War II, when the European powers were weakened. Through the 1960s, a wave of successful independence movements swept from one country to the next, as people stopped accepting imperialism as normal or inevitable. Within a few decades, nearly all of Africa overthrew white rule (see Figure 7.6).

Figure 7.6 Areas of White Minority Rule in Africa, 1952–1994

Formal colonialism was swept away over 40 years. However, postcolonial dependency lingers on in many former colonies.

Source: Adapted from Andrew Boyd, *An Atlas of World Affairs*. 9th ed. NY: Routledge, 1992, p. 91.

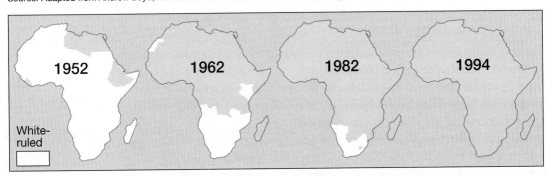

Although many developing countries gained independence around the same time, the methods by which they did so varied. In India, the most important colony of the largest empire (Britain), Gandhi led a movement based on nonviolent resistance to British rule (see p. 101). However, nonviolence broke down in the subsequent Hindu-Muslim civil war, which split India into two states—India mostly with Hindus, and Pakistan (including what is now Bangladesh) mostly with Muslims. Some colonies—for example, Algeria and Vietnam—won independence through warfare to oust their European masters; others won it peacefully by negotiating a transfer of power with weary Europeans.

Postcolonial Dependency

If imperialism concentrated the accumulation of wealth in the core and drained economic surplus from the periphery, one might expect that accumulation in the global South would take off once colonialism was overthrown. Generally, however, this was not the case. A few states, such as Singapore, have accumulated capital successfully since becoming independent. But others, including many African states, seem to be going backward, with little new capital accumulating to replace the old colonial infrastructure. Most former colonies are making only slow progress in accumulation. Political independence has not been a cure-all for poor countries.

One reason for these problems is that under colonialism, the training and experience needed to manage the economy were often limited to white Europeans, leaving a huge gap in technical and administrative skills after independence. Another problem faced by many newly independent states was that their economies rested on the export of one or two products. For Zambia, it was copper ore; for El Salvador, coffee; for Botswana, diamonds. Such a narrow export economy would seem well suited to use the state's comparative advantage to specialize in one niche of the world economy. And having exportable natural resources might seem a big plus for an economy. But in fact, the problems of basing economic growth on resource exports have been called the **resource curse**. Dependence on exporting resources distorts an economy, facilitates corruption, and leaves a country vulnerable to price swings. The liberal free trade regime based around the World Trade Organization (WTO) corrected only partially for the North's superior bargaining position in North-South trade. And the WTO has allowed agriculture (exported by the periphery) to remain protected in core states while promoting liberalization of trade in manufactured goods exported by the core (see pp. 292–293).

resource curse The difficulties faced by resource-rich developing countries, including dependence on exporting one or a few commodities whose prices fluctuate, as well as potentials for corruption and inequality.

The newly independent states inherited borders that were drawn in European capitals by foreign officers looking at maps. As a result, and especially in Africa, the internal rivalries of ethnic groups and regions made it very difficult for the new states to implement coherent economic plans. In a number of cases, ethnic conflicts within former colonies led to civil wars, which halted or reversed capital accumulation.

Finally, governments of many postcolonial states did not function very effectively, creating another obstacle to accumulation. In some cases, corruption became much worse after independence (see pp. 309–310). In other cases, governments tried to impose central control and planning on their national economy, based on nationalism, mercantilism, or socialism.

In sum, liberation from colonial control did not transform underlying economic realities. The main trading partners of newly independent countries were usually their former colonial masters. The main products were usually those developed under colonialism. The administrative units and territorial borders were those created by

MY DOLL, MY SELF European colonialism worldwide promoted values and norms implying that the colonizer's culture was superior to the indigenous culture. Lingering effects remain in postcolonial societies. This girl displaced by violence in Kenya, a former British colony, plays with a light-skinned doll, 2008.

Europeans. The state continued to occupy the same peripheral position in the world-system after independence as it had before. And in some cases it continued to rely on its former colonizer for security.

For these reasons, the period after independence is sometimes called **neocolonialism**—the continuation of colonial exploitation without formal political control. This concept also covers the relationship of the global South with the United States, which (with a few exceptions) was not a formal colonizer. And it covers the North-South international relations of Latin American states, independent for almost two centuries.

neocolonialism The continuation, in a former colony, of colonial exploitation without formal political control.

DEPENDENCY Marxist IR scholars have developed **dependency theory** to explain the lack of accumulation in the global South. These scholars define dependency as a situation in which accumulation of capital cannot sustain itself internally. A dependent country must borrow capital to produce goods; the debt payments then reduce the accumulation of surplus.

dependency theory A Marxist-oriented theory that explains the lack of capital accumulation in poor countries as a result of the interplay between domestic class relations and the forces of foreign capital.

Dependency theorists focus not on the overall structure of the world-system (center and periphery) but on how a peripheral state's own internal class relationships play out. The development (or lack of development) of a poor country depends on its local conditions and history, though it is affected by the same global conditions as other countries located in the periphery.

One historically important configuration of dependency is the **enclave economy**, in which foreign capital is invested in a third world country to extract a particular raw material in a particular place—usually a mine, oil well, or plantation. A different historical pattern is that of nationally controlled production, in which a local capitalist class controls a cycle of accumulation based on producing export products. The cycle still depends on foreign markets, but the profits accrue to the local capitalists, building up a powerful class of rich owners within the country—the local bourgeoisie. After World War II, a third form of dependency became more common—penetration of national economies by MNCs. Here the capital is provided externally (as with enclaves), but production is for local markets. For instance, a General Motors (GM) factory in Brazil would produce cars mostly for sale within Brazil. To create local markets for such manufactured goods, income must be concentrated enough to create a middle class. This sharpens disparities of income within the country (most people remain poor).

enclave economy A historically important form of dependency in which foreign capital is invested in a developing country to extract a particular raw material in a particular place—usually a mine, oil well, or plantation.

According to dependency theory, the particular constellation of forces within a country determines which coalitions form among the state, the military, big landowners, local capitalists, foreign capitalists (that is, MNCs), foreign governments, and middle classes. On the other side, peasants, workers, and sometimes students and the church form alliances to work for more equal distribution of income, human and political rights, and local control of the economy. These class alliances and the resulting social relationships are not determined by any general rule but by concrete conditions and historical developments in each country. Like other Marxist theories, dependency theory pays special attention to class struggle as a source of social change. Some people think that under conditions of dependency, economic development is almost impossible. Others think that development is possible under dependency despite certain difficulties. We will return to these possibilities later in the chapter.

Overall, North-South relations show how difficult it has become to separate political economy from international security. The original political relations contained in European imperialism led to economic conditions in the South—such as high population growth, urbanization, and concentrations of wealth—that in turn led to political movements for independence, and later to revolutions. The various aspects of the North-South gap considered in the first half of this chapter—including hunger, refugees, and the structure of commodity exports—all contain both economic and political-military aspects. The remainder of the chapter turns to the question of how economies in the South can develop the accumulation process and what role the North can play in that process.

Development Experiences

7.4 Compare and contrast the experiences of China and India in achieving economic development.

Economic development refers to the combined processes of capital accumulation, rising per capita incomes (with consequent falling birthrates), increasing skills in the population, adoption of new technological styles, and other related social and economic changes. The most central aspect is the accumulation of capital (with its ongoing wealth-generating potential). The concept of development has a subjective side that cannot be measured statistically—the judgment of whether a certain pattern of wealth creation and distribution is good for a state and its people. But one simple measure of economic development is the per capita GDP—the amount of economic activity per person. This measure was the horizontal axis in Figure 7.1 (p. 281), and change in this measure was on the vertical axis.

By this measure, we can trace the successes and failures of the South as a whole and, more important, its regions and countries. The latter is more important because it contains the seeds of possible lessons and strategies that could build on the South's successes in the future. Most of the global South made progress on economic development in the 1970s, but real per capita GDP decreased in the 1980s in Latin America, Africa, and the Middle East, with only China growing robustly. In the 1990s, real economic growth returned across much of the South—about 5–6 percent annual growth for the South as a whole, compared to 2–3 percent in the global North. China stood out among the regions of the South as making rapid progress toward economic development.

In the new century, growth has accelerated in the South and now outpaces the North (see Figure 7.7). This growth is uneven. South Asia (6–7 percent a year) has joined China (8–9 percent a year) in achieving rapid growth. Because China and South Asia together contain the majority of the population in the

economic development The combined processes of capital accumulation, rising per capita incomes (with consequent falling birthrates), the increasing of skills in the population, the adoption of new technological styles, and other related social and economic changes.

global South, this development is very important. Even in Africa, according to the World Bank, economies grew by more than 4 percent annually from 2011 to 2013 (led by, but not limited to, oil- and mineral-exporting nations). While the 2008–2009 global economic crisis threatened the developing world, most states in the global South have emerged more quickly than their wealthy counterparts in the global North, a noteworthy trend.

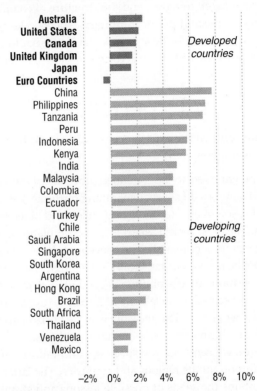

Figure 7.7 Real GDP Growth of Selected Countries, 2013

Source: World Bank, *World Development Indicators.*

newly industrializing countries (NICS) Countries in the global South that have achieved self-sustaining capital accumulation, with impressive economic growth. The most successful are the "four tigers" or "four dragons" of East Asia: South Korea, Taiwan, Hong Kong, and Singapore.

Today, much attention is given to a group of countries known as the BRICS (Brazil, Russia, India, China, and South Africa). While there are important economic differences between these states, each of them have large economies and populations. They are considered an important group of countries that provide a strong voice to developing states, often in negotiation with wealthier North American and European states.

The Newly Industrializing Countries

Before China took off, a handful of poor states—called the **newly industrializing countries (NICs)**—achieved self-sustaining capital accumulation, with impressive economic growth. These semiperiphery states, which export light manufactured goods, posted strong economic growth in the 1980s and early 1990s (see The World-System on pp. 292–293). They suffered a setback in the late 1990s because growth had been too fast, with overly idealistic loans, speculative investments, and corrupt deals (see pp. 309–310). Notwithstanding these setbacks, the NICs resumed growth and have developed much faster than most of the global South.

The most successful NICs are the **"four tigers" or "four dragons"** of East Asia: South Korea, Taiwan, Hong Kong, and Singapore. Each succeeded in developing particular sectors and industries that were competitive on world markets. These sectors and industries can create enough capital accumulation within the country to raise income levels not just among the small elite but across the population more broadly. Scholars do not know whether the NICs are just the lucky few that have moved from the periphery to the semiperiphery of the world-system or whether their success can eventually be replicated throughout the world. This growth, however, shows that it is possible to rise out of poverty to relative prosperity. South Korea did so, followed by China, and India appears to be starting on the same curve (see Figure 7.8).

South Korea, with iron and coal resources, developed competitive steel and automobile industries that export globally, creating a trade surplus (see pp. 178–189). Taiwan also used a strong state industrial policy, specializing in the

"four tigers"/"four dragons" The most successful newly industrialized areas of East Asia: South Korea, Taiwan, Hong Kong, and Singapore.

Figure 7.8 Per Capita GDP of South Korea, China, India, and Ghana, 1960–2011

Source: Based on Penn World Tables, World Bank, and IMF data.

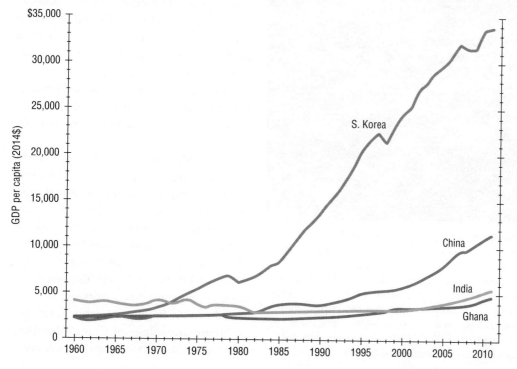

electronics and computer industries, and in other light manufacturing. Hong Kong—controlled by China since 1997—also has world-competitive electronics and other light industries, but its greatest strengths are in banking and trade. Singapore is a trading city located at the tip of the Malaysian peninsula—convenient to the South China Sea, the Indian Ocean, and Australia.

For different reasons, each of these states holds a somewhat unusual political status in the international system. South Korea and Taiwan were hot spots of international conflict that came under the U.S. security umbrella during the Cold War. Both were militarized, authoritarian states intolerant of dissent that later became democratic.

Hong Kong and Singapore have a different political profile. They are both former British colonies. They are more city-states than nation-states, and their cities are trading ports and financial centers. Although not as repressive or as militarized as South Korea and Taiwan during the Cold War era, Hong Kong and Singapore were not democracies either. Hong Kong was ruled by a British governor, and Singapore by a dominant individual.

Beyond the four tigers, other Southeast Asian countries have tried, since the 1980s, to follow in their footsteps. These countries include Thailand, Malaysia, and Indonesia. Because their experiences vary, they are discussed below with other Asian economies (see pp. 306–307).

CAR CULTURE China's rapid economic growth has raised incomes dramatically, especially for a growing middle class. These successes followed China's opening to the world economy and adoption of market-oriented reforms. China is also attempting to develop its domestic market and grow consumer spending rather than relying so heavily on exports to fuel growth. Here, Chinese consumers do their part as they mob the Beijing auto show in 2014, hoping to get in on China's growing infatuation with that ultimate big-ticket consumer item, the automobile.

The Chinese Experience

If there was ever a doubt that the successes of the NICs could be replicated elsewhere and on a larger scale, China ended those doubts. China has over 1.3 billion people, and this size alone makes China's efforts to generate self-sustaining accumulation worthy of study. But China has also had the world's fastest-growing economy over the past two decades.

After Mao died in 1976, China under Deng Xiaoping instituted economic reforms and transformed its southern coastal provinces into *free economic zones* open to foreign investment and run on capitalist principles. Peasants worked their own fields, instead of collective farms, and got rich (by Chinese standards) if they did well. Entrepreneurs started companies, hired workers, and generated profits. Foreign investment flooded in, taking advantage of China's location, cheap labor, and relative political stability.

However, China has also re-created some of the features of capitalism that Mao's revolutionaries had overturned. New class disparities emerged, with rich entrepreneurs driving fancy imported cars while poor workers found themselves unemployed. Social problems such as prostitution returned, as did economic problems such as inflation (since largely tamed). Most frustrating for ordinary Chinese is the widespread official corruption accompanying the get-rich atmosphere.

Popular resentment over problems such as inflation and corruption led industrial workers and even government officials to join students in antigovernment protests at Beijing's Tiananmen Square in 1989. Authorities used the military to suppress the protests violently, killing hundreds of people and signaling the government's determination to maintain tight political control while economic reform proceeded. Foreign investors returned quickly after the political disruption of 1989, however, and economic growth roared ahead. Chinese exports grew to over $2.3 trillion in 2014, making China the world's largest exporter.

In 2012, a new generation of Chinese leaders took charge, led by President Xi Jinping. China had sustained its rapid economic growth (generally 10 percent annually) year after year, even after the 2008 global economic downturn hurt Chinese exports, with the help of large government infrastructure expenditures. But growing inequality and widespread corruption threatened the legitimacy of the Communist Party. An exposé by the *New York Times* in 2012 showed that family members of China's outgoing prime minister had amassed $3 billion of private wealth while he held power. Despite efforts to clamp down on political expression, many Chinese citizens expressed their views not only in strikes and demonstrations but also on wildly popular microblogging sites, China's version of Twitter. In rural villages, peasants openly protested land seizures, taxes, pollution, and corruption by local officials. President Xi declared the battle against corruption a top priority while continuing to discourage protests and writings that target party officials engaging in corrupt practices.

With China now in the WTO and its citizens wired to the Internet, the economy gains great advantages, but citizens can also bypass government-controlled information. Some observers expect economic integration in an information era to open up China's political system inexorably and lead to democratization, whereas others think that as long as Chinese leaders deliver economic growth, the population will have little appetite for political change.

China's economic success has given it both more prestige in the international system and a more global perspective on international relations far from China's borders. In 2007, China announced $3 billion in preferential loans to Africa, which, China emphasized, "carry no political conditions" (unlike Western loans, which often demand policies such as respect for human rights or fighting corruption). In 2013, President Xi visited Africa and promised to continue economic assistance. He also attended a BRICS meeting where leaders from each of those countries promised to cooperate with

African states in economic development. China's rising international standing was also reflected in its selection to host the 2008 Olympics, which were enormously successful.

China's economic miracle did hit a bump in the 2008–2009 economic crisis. China's investments in the United States, made with the trade surpluses China had accumulated over the years, lost a substantial fraction of their value in the financial meltdown of late 2008. Chinese leaders announced a major stimulus package aimed at spurring domestic consumption in China, but this faced problems in the short term, including the cultural problem of getting people with a history of poverty to spend instead of save, and the economic problem of reorienting an export-driven economy to produce for domestic markets. Yet despite these dangers and risks, China's economy has forged ahead out of the economic crisis. For example, Chinese exports quickly returned to pre-recession levels after a drop in 2009 and kept growing.

China's economy appears to have hit a second bump in the new millennium. Throughout 2015, China's stock markets dropped very significantly, leading many to question China's economic stability. China also undertook two surprise currency devaluations, lowered official interest rates, and increased public spending to stave off what could be a coming recession. And while many aspects of China's economy still remain strong, the bumps of 2015 did lead some experts to question how long China could continue its high rates of economic growth.

For years it appeared that China's huge population would supply limitless cheap labor to foreign investors making goods in China. In recent years, however, China's growth has begun to squeeze the available labor force and push wages up somewhat. Labor unrest has become more common throughout China as workers demand higher wages and better working conditions. MNCs have begun to move some light manufacturing to other Asian countries with even cheaper labor, such as Vietnam.

It is unclear what lessons China's economic success over the past decade holds for the rest of the global South. The shift away from central planning and toward private ownership was clearly a key factor in its success, yet the state continues to play a central role in overseeing the economy (even more than in the NICs). These topics are being debated vigorously as China navigates its new era of rising prosperity and rising expectations, finds its way in the newly turbulent world economy, and other poor states look to China's experience for lessons.

India Takes Off

India, like China, deserves special attention because of its size and recent robust growth. From 1996 to 2013, India's average annual growth rate exceeded 5 percent. India's decade of success still does not compare to China's nearly three decades, and India's GDP per person is still not much more than half of China's.

But India's success has started it toward what could be, in the coming years, a repetition of China's rise out of poverty.

India's economy was for decades based loosely on socialism and state control of large industries but on private capitalism in agriculture and consumer goods. The state subsidizes basic goods and gives special treatment to farmers. Unlike China, India has a democratic government, but a fractious one, with various autonomy movements and ethnic conflicts. India's government has suffered from corruption, although this has improved in recent years.

In the era of globalization, India's niche in the globalized world economy is in the service and information sectors. Whereas South Korea specializes in exporting heavy manufactured goods and China in light manufactured goods, India specializes in exporting information products such as software and telephone call center services. Each country uses its labor force to add value to products that could be exported

AT YOUR SERVICE India has grown rapidly in recent years, using its large, well-educated, English speaking population to generate export revenues in the service sector—software companies, call centers serving American customers, and professional services in such areas as accounting, architecture, engineering, and medicine. This radiologist in Bangalore, India's technology capital, reads body scans from a U.S. hospital sent via the Internet and discusses the results by phone with the patient's doctor in Connecticut, 2004.

worldwide, especially to the large American market. In India's case, the labor force is well educated and speaks English. India can also use its location to advantage by working during the nighttime hours in North America. Software companies can hand off projects daily for the India shift to work on overnight, and American hospitals can send medical notes for overnight transcription. MNCs widely use India's labor force to answer phone calls from around the world, such as technical support calls for the company's products.

India's future success or failure will bear strongly on several competing theories about economic development. In particular, China has had success under a harsh, centralized political system, whereas India has a free-wheeling democracy. If India cannot sustain growth, then maybe authoritarian government helps development, and democracy should wait until a later stage (an argument we discuss shortly). If India continues to succeed, however, then clearly authoritarian government is not a precondition.

Figure 7.9 compares China's and India's progress on two key indicators—infant mortality (a good overall measure of public health) and the fertility rate (see pp. 355–356). In both cases, China was able to make dramatic improvements very quickly because of its authoritarian government, whose control (in theory) extended to every village and every bedroom. In the 1950s, after taking power, China ordered mass campaigns in which citizens exterminated pests and set up

Figure 7.9 Comparing Chinese and Indian Development

Source: World Bank.

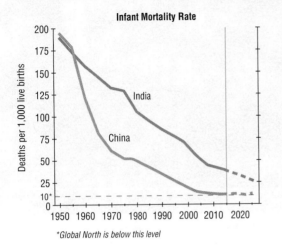

Infant Mortality Rate

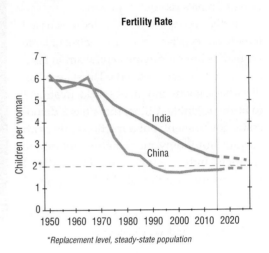

Fertility Rate

*Global North is below this level

*Replacement level, steady-state population

sanitation facilities. As a result, in the 1960s, China's rates of epidemic diseases such as cholera and plague dropped, and so did the infant mortality rate. In the 1970s, with its heavy-handed one-child policy, China forced down the fertility rate. Women who objected could be forcibly sterilized. Thus, China relied on the dominance principle to force individuals to take actions that were in society's interest. Its successes in improving public health and lowering fertility provided a foundation for China's subsequent economic success, although obviously at a cost to individual freedom.

India, by contrast, has relied more on the identity principle, getting people to change their preferences and *want* to have fewer children and help improve public health. Without a dictatorship to force compliance, India's progress has been slower. Over time, however, India is moving toward the same results as China, albeit decades later, and doing so without giving up its own national identity as a democracy.

Other Experiments

Other sizable developing countries have pursued various development strategies, with mixed successes and failures. The best results have come from Asia. Figure 7.10 shows the income levels and growth rates of the 16 largest countries by population in the global South. The graph parallels that for world regions in Figure 7.1. Clearly the large countries of the South vary widely in income level. The five highest-income countries (Turkey, Iran, Thailand, Mexico, and Brazil) come from three of the four regions and vary from −5 to 4 percent growth rates. The fastest-growing countries (Bangladesh, Philippines, Ethiopia, and Democratic Congo), at 7–9 percent, are at the lower end of the income scale. Over the past decade, China has developed faster than the other 15 large countries of the

Figure 7.10 Largest Countries' Income Levels and Growth Rates, 2013

Source: World Bank, *World Development Indicators*.

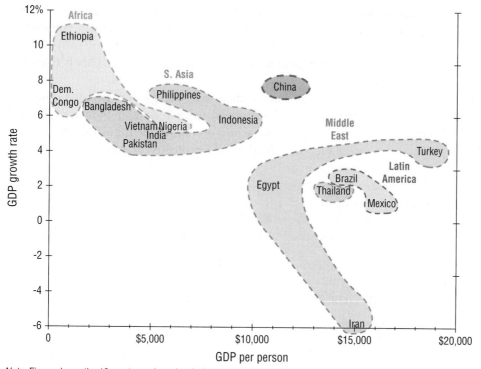

Note: Figure shows the 16 most populous developing countries. Iran's low growth was a result of economic sanctions.

global South, and with these growth rates, China will soon become one of the five highest-income countries in this group. Clearly, too, regional location makes a difference. The fact that the five regions of the global South can be mapped onto single contiguous zones in this figure shows that whole regions are moving together in distinct patterns.

The largest developing countries are following somewhat different strategies with somewhat different results. But several common themes recur. These themes concern trade, the concentration of capital, authoritarianism, and corruption.

Import Substitution and Export-Led Growth

Throughout the global South, states are trying to use international trade as the basis of accumulation. For the reasons discussed in Chapter 5, a policy of self-reliance or autarky is at best an extremely slow way to build up wealth. But through the creation of a trade surplus, a state can accumulate hard currency and build industry and infrastructure.

One way to try to create a trade surplus, used frequently a few decades ago, is through **import substitution**—the development of local industries to

import substitution
A strategy of developing local industries, often conducted behind protectionist barriers, to produce items that a country had been importing.

produce items that a country had been importing. These industries may receive state subsidies or tariff protection. This might seem to be a good policy for reducing dependency—especially on the former colonial master—while shrinking a trade deficit or building a trade surplus. But it is against the principle of comparative advantage and has not proven effective in most cases. Some scholars think that import substitution is a useful policy only at a very early phase of economic development, after which it is counterproductive. Others think it is never useful.

export-led growth
An economic development strategy that seeks to develop industries capable of competing in specific niches in the world economy.

More and more states have shifted to a strategy of **export-led growth**, a strategy used by the NICs. This strategy seeks to develop industries that can compete in specific niches in the world economy. The industries may receive special treatment such as subsidies and protected access to local markets. Exports from these industries generate hard currency and create a favorable trade balance. The state can then spend part of its money on imports of commodities produced more cheaply elsewhere. Such a strategy has risks, however, especially when a state specializes in the export of a few raw materials (see pp. 296–298). It leaves poor countries vulnerable to sudden price fluctuations for their exports.

Concentrating Capital for Manufacturing

Manufacturing emerges as a key factor in both export-led growth and self-sustaining industrialization (home production for home markets). To invest in manufacturing, these countries must *concentrate* what surplus their economies produce. Money spent building factories cannot be spent subsidizing food prices or building better schools. Thus, the concentration of capital for manufacturing can sharpen disparities in income. And because manufacturing industries in poor countries are not immediately competitive on world markets, one common strategy is first to build up the industry with sales to the home market (protected by tariffs and subsidies). But home markets for manufactured goods do not come from poor peasants in the countryside or the unemployed youth in city slums. Rather, wealth must be concentrated in a *middle class* that has the income to buy manufactured goods. These disparities may result in crowds rioting in the streets or guerrillas taking over the countryside.

Capital for manufacturing can come instead from foreign investment or foreign loans, but this reduces the amount of surplus (profit) available to the state in the long term. Another way to minimize capital needs is to start out in low-capital industries. These industries can begin generating capital, which can then be used to move into somewhat more technologically demanding and capital-intensive kinds of manufacturing. A favorite starter industry is *textiles*. The industry is fairly labor-intensive, giving an advantage to countries with cheap labor, and does not require huge investments of capital to get started. In 2005, textile tariffs were removed worldwide, so textile exporters in developing countries gained access to Western markets but faced intensified competition from China.

A related approach to capitalization in very poor countries, growing in popularity in recent years, is **microcredit** (or *microlending*). Based on a successful model in Bangladesh (the Grameen Bank, which won the 2006 Nobel Peace Prize, and now operates more than 2,400 branch offices), microcredit uses small loans to poor people, especially women, to support economic self-sufficiency. The borrowers are organized into small groups and take responsibility for each other's success, including repaying the loans. Repayment rates have been high, and the idea has spread rapidly in several regions. In one popular application, village women used small loans to start businesses renting cell phone time. Rural farmers used the phone time to find out market conditions before making a long trek to sell their products. Thus, bringing the information revolution to isolated villages raised incomes for farmers and the entrepreneurial women alike, and the bank got its loans repaid. Microcredit is now being applied on a macro scale. Tens of millions of families have received loans from thousands of institutions worldwide. Microcredit is the opposite of a trickle-down approach—it injects capital at the bottom of the economic hierarchy. A loan to buy a goat or cell phone may do more good, dollar for dollar, than a loan to build a dam.

> **microcredit** The use of very small loans to small groups of individuals, often women, to stimulate economic development.

The World Bank reviewed evidence on the effect of income inequality on economic growth, and concluded that inequality holds back growth by wasting human potential. The World Bank recommends extending access to health care, education, and jobs—as well as to political power—to the poorest people in societies of the global South in order to spur faster economic growth.

Corruption

Corruption is an important negative factor in economic development in many states. Corruption centers on the government as the central actor in economic development, especially in its international aspects. Through foreign policy, the government mediates the national economy's relationship to the world economy. It regulates the conditions under which MNCs operate in the country. It enforces worker discipline—calling out the army if necessary to break strikes or suppress revolutions. It sets tax rates and wields other macroeconomic levers of control over the economy. And in most developing countries, it owns a sizable stake in major industries—a monopoly in some cases.

State officials decide whether to let an MNC into the country, which MNC to give leases or contracts to, and what terms to insist on. Corruption adds another player, the corrupt official, to share the benefits. In 2003, an ExxonMobil Oil executive was indicted for paying $78 million to two senior officials in Kazakhstan—with a kickback of $2 million for himself—to secure ExxonMobil's billion-dollar stake in a huge oil field there.

Corruption is by no means limited to the global South. But for several reasons, corruption has a deeper effect in poor countries. First, there is simply less surplus to keep economic growth going; accumulation is fragile. And in developing countries dependent on exporting a few products, the revenue arrives in a

CLEAN IT UP! Corruption is a major impediment to economic development in both rich and poor countries but is more devastating to economies in the global South and to transitional former communist economies. In India, widespread corruption has held back economic development and equality for years. These Delhi supporters of hunger-striking anti-corruption activist Anna Hazare hold a "key" to corrupt officials' Swiss bank locker, 2012.

very concentrated form—large payments in hard currency—presenting a greater opportunity for corruption than in a more diversified economy. This is a major element in the "resource curse" (see pp. 297–298). Furthermore, incomes in developing countries are often so low that corrupt officials are more tempted to accept payments.

Corruption in the global South presents a collective goods problem for states and MNCs in the global North: Individually, MNCs and their home states can profit by clinching a deal with a private payoff; collectively, the MNCs and states of the North lose money by having to make these payoffs. This gives an incentive to clamp down on corruption only if other industrialized states do likewise. A Berlin-based NGO, Transparency International, publishes annual surveys showing the countries that business executives consider most corrupt. The top five on the list in 2014 were Somalia, North Korea, Afghanistan, Sudan, and South Sudan. In 1997, the world's 29 leading industrialized states agreed to forbid their companies from bribing foreign officials. And the Extractive Industries Transparency Initiative, a coalition of states, NGOs, and MNCs launched by Britain in 2002, fights corruption in the especially vulnerable oil, gas, and mineral sectors worldwide by getting companies to release information on payments they make to developing countries.

North-South Capital Flows

7.5 **Identify and evaluate two different strategies that developing states have used in attempting to achieve economic growth.**

Capital from the global North moves to the South and potentially spurs growth there in several forms—foreign investment, debt, and foreign aid. The rest of this chapter discusses these capital flows from North to South.

Foreign Investment

Poor countries have little money available to invest in new factories, farms, mines, or oil wells. Foreign investment—investment in such capital goods by foreigners (most often MNCs)—is one way to get accumulation started (see p. 215). Foreign investment has been crucial to the success of China and other Asian developing countries. Overall, private capital flows to the global South were over $700 billion in 2014—four times the amount given in official development assistance.

Foreigners who invest in a country then own the facilities; the investor, by virtue of its ownership, can control decisions about how many people to employ, whether to expand or shut down, what products to make, and how to market them. Also, the foreign investor can usually take the profits from the operation out of the country (repatriation of profits). However, the host government can share in the wealth by charging fees and taxes, or by leasing land or drilling rights (see pp. 215–216).

Because of past colonial experiences, many governments in the global South have feared the loss of control that comes with foreign investments by MNCs. Sometimes the presence of MNCs was associated with the painful process of concentrating capital and the sharpening of class disparities in the host state. Although such fears remain, they are counterbalanced by the ability of foreign investors to infuse capital and generate more surplus. By the 1980s and 1990s, as models based on autarky or state ownership were discredited and the NICs gained success, many poor states rushed to embrace foreign investment. China has been the most successful of these by far.

One way in which states have sought to soften the loss of control is through *joint ventures,* companies owned partly by a foreign MNC and partly by a local firm or the host government itself. Sometimes foreign ownership in joint ventures is limited to some percentage (often 49 percent), to ensure that ultimate control rests with the host country. The percentage of ownership is usually proportional to the amount of capital invested; if a host government wants more control, it must put up more money. Joint ventures work well for MNCs because they help ensure the host government's cooperation in reducing bureaucratic hassles and ensuring success (by giving the host government a direct stake in the outcome).

MNCs invest in a country because of some advantage of doing business there. In some cases, it is natural resources. Sometimes it is cheap labor. Some states have better *absorptive capacity* than others—the ability to put investments to productive use—because of developed infrastructure and skilled workers. MNCs also look for a favorable *regulatory environment* in which a host state will facilitate, rather than impede, the MNC's business.

MNC decisions about foreign investment also depend on prospects for *financial stability,* especially prospects for low inflation and stable currency exchange rates. If a currency is not convertible, an MNC will not be able to take profits back to its home state or reinvest them elsewhere. Of equal importance in attracting investment is *political stability* (see p. 217). Banks and MNCs conduct *political risk analyses* to assess the risks of political disturbances in developing countries in which they might invest.

Beyond these financial considerations, a foreign investor producing for local markets wants to know that the host country's *economic growth* will sustain demand for the goods being produced. Similarly, whether producing for local consumption or export, the MNC wants the local labor supply—whether semi-skilled or just cheap—to be stable. Foreign investors often look to international financial institutions, such as the World Bank and the International Monetary Fund (IMF), and to private analyses, to judge a state's economic stability before investing in it.

technology transfer Developing states' acquisition of technology (knowledge, skills, methods, designs, specialized equipment, etc.) from foreign sources, usually in conjunction with direct foreign investment or similar business operations.

Technology transfer refers to a poor state's acquisition of technology (knowledge, skills, methods, designs, and specialized equipment) from foreign sources, usually in conjunction with foreign direct investment or similar business operations. A developing country may allow an MNC to produce certain goods in the country under favorable conditions, provided the MNC shares knowledge of the technology and design behind the product. The state may try to get its own citizens into the management and professional workforce of factories or facilities created by foreign investment. Not only can physical capital accumulate in the country but so can the related technological base for further development. Of course, MNCs may be reluctant to share proprietary technology.

Most poor states seek to build up an educated elite with knowledge and skills to run the national economy. One way to do so is to send students to industrialized states for higher education. This entails some risks, however. Students may enjoy life in the North and fail to return home. The problem of losing skilled workers to richer countries, called the **brain drain**, has impeded economic development in states such as India, Pakistan, and the Philippines (where more nurses emigrated than graduated nursing school in 2000–2004).

brain drain Poor countries' loss of skilled workers to rich countries.

North-South Debt

Borrowing money is an alternative to foreign investment and thus a way of obtaining funds to prime a cycle of economic accumulation. If accumulation succeeds, it produces enough surplus to repay the loan and still make a profit. Borrowing has several advantages. It keeps control in the hands of the state (or other local borrower) and does not impose painful sacrifices on local citizens, at least in the short term.

Debt has disadvantages too. The borrower must service the debt—making regular payments of interest and repaying the principal according to the terms of the loan. *Debt service* is a constant drain on whatever surplus is generated by investment of the money. With foreign direct investment, a money-losing venture is the problem of the foreign MNC; with debt, it is the problem of the borrowing state, which must find the money elsewhere. Often, a debtor must borrow new funds to service old loans, slipping further into debt. Debt service has created a net financial outflow from South to North in recent years because the South has paid billions more in interest to banks and governments in the North than it has received in foreign investment or development aid.

default Failure to make scheduled debt payments.

Failure to make scheduled payments, called a **default**, is considered a drastic action because it destroys lender confidence and results in cutoff of future loans. Rather than defaulting, borrowers usually attempt **debt renegotiation**—reworking the terms on which a loan will be repaid. By renegotiating their debts with lenders, borrowers seek a mutually acceptable payment scheme to keep at least some money flowing to the lender. If interest rates have fallen since a loan was first taken out, the borrower can refinance. Borrowers and lenders can also negotiate to restructure a debt by changing the length of the loan (usually to a longer payback period) or the other terms. Occasionally state-to-state loans are written off altogether—forgiven—for political reasons, as happened with U.S. loans to Egypt after the Gulf War.

North-South debt encompasses several types of lending relationships, all of which are influenced by international politics. The borrower may be a private firm or bank in a developing country, or it may be the government itself. Loans to the government are somewhat more common because lenders consider the government less likely to default than a private borrower. The lender may be a private bank or company, or a state (both are important). Usually banks are more insistent on receiving timely payments and firmer in renegotiating debts than are states. Some state-to-state loans are made on artificially favorable *concessionary* terms, in effect subsidizing economic development in the borrowing state.

Debt renegotiation has become a perennial occupation of developing countries. Such renegotiations are complex international bargaining situations. For lenders, debt renegotiations involve a collective goods problem: All of them have to agree on the conditions of the renegotiation but each really cares only about getting its own money back. To solve this problem, state creditors meet together periodically as the *Paris Club,* and private creditors as the *London Club,* to work out their terms.

Through such renegotiations and the corresponding write-offs of debts by banks, developing countries have largely avoided defaulting on their debts. In 2001, however, Argentina in effect defaulted. By then, financial institutions had adjusted psychologically to the reality that Argentina could not pay its debt, so the default did not cause a wider panic. Indeed, Argentina recovered—its economy growing 9 percent a year since 2001—and in 2005 offered its creditors a take-it-or-leave-it deal for repayment of less than 30 cents on the dollar. Most took it.

In the past decade, these debt problems jumped to the global North as the eurozone grappled with the heavy indebtedness of some of its poorer members—especially Greece as well as Portugal, Spain, and Ireland. By 2015, the European Union is still struggling to confront debt problems in these member states, Greece in particular.

Despite stabilization, developing countries have not yet solved the debt problem. As shown in Table 7.3, the South owes over $5 trillion in foreign debt and pays nearly $2 trillion a year to service that debt. The debt service (in hard currency) absorbs over a third of the entire hard-currency export earnings in Latin America—the region most affected. For the entire global South, it is nearly 25 percent of exports.

debt renegotiation
A reworking of the terms on which a loan will be repaid; frequently negotiated by poor debtor governments in order to avoid default.

Table 7.3 Debt in the Global South, 2014

Region	Foreign Debt		Annual Debt Service	
	Billion $	% of GDP[a]	Billion $	% of Exports
Latin America	1,700	29%	400	35%
Asia	2,200	16	1,000	27
Africa	350	23	60	13
Middle East	800	27	300	16
Total "South"	5,050	24	1,760	23

[a]GDP not calculated at purchasing-power parity.

Source: IMF, World Economic Outlook, October 2015. Regions do not exactly match those used elsewhere in this book. Africa here includes North Africa. Asia includes China.

In recent years, activists and NGOs have called for extensive debt forgiveness for the poorest countries, most of which are in Africa. Critics say such cancellations just put more money in the hands of corrupt, inept governments. But Group of Seven (G7) members in early 2005 agreed on a new plan to eliminate all debts owed by 37 very poor countries to the World Bank and IMF—cutting almost in half the poorest countries' estimated $200 billion in debt. The first $40 billion, owed by 18 countries, began to be written off in 2006. As of 2014, the IMF had forgiven $75 billion of debt in the poorest 36 countries.

IMF Conditionality

The IMF and the World Bank have a large supply of capital from their member states (see pp. 210–211). This capital plays an important role in funding early stages of accumulation in developing countries and in helping them get through short periods of great difficulty. And, as a political entity rather than a bank, the IMF can make funds available on favorable terms.

The IMF scrutinizes developing countries' economic plans and policies, withholding loans until it is satisfied that the right policies are in place. Then it makes loans to help states through the transitional process of implementing the IMF-approved policies. The IMF also sends important signals to private lenders and investors. Its approval of a state's economic plans is a "seal of approval" that bankers and MNCs use to assess the wisdom of investing in that state. Thus, the IMF wields great power to influence the economic policies of developing countries.

IMF conditionality
An agreement to loan IMF funds on the condition that certain government policies are adopted. Dozens of developing countries have entered into such agreements with the IMF in the past two decades.

An agreement to loan IMF funds on the condition that certain government policies are adopted is called an **IMF conditionality** agreement; implementation of these conditions is referred to as a *structural adjustment program*. Dozens of developing countries have entered into such agreements with the IMF in the past two decades. The terms insisted on by the IMF are usually painful for the citizens (and hence for national politicians). The IMF demands that inflation be brought under control, which requires reducing state spending and closing budget deficits. This often spurs unemployment and requires that subsidies of food and basic goods be reduced or eliminated. Short-term consumption is curtailed in favor of longer-term investment. Surplus must be concentrated to service debt and invest in new capital accumulation. The IMF wants to ensure that inflation does not eat away all progress and that the economy is stable enough to attract investment. In addition, it demands steps to curtail corruption.

Because of the pain inflicted by a conditionality agreement—and to some extent by any debt renegotiation agreement—such agreements are often politically unpopular in the global South. On quite a few occasions, a conditionality agreement has brought rioters into the streets demanding the restoration of subsidies. Sometimes governments have backed out of the agreements or have broken their promises under such pressure. Occasionally, governments have been toppled.

MIRACLE OF LOAVES IMF conditionality agreements often call for reducing subsidies for food, transportation, and other basic needs. In Egypt, bread prices are heavily subsidized, forcing the government to use hard currency to import wheat. But public resistance to bread price increases is so strong that the government has not brought itself to cut the subsidy. Here, bread is delivered in Cairo during opposition protests in 2011.

Of course, these IMF conditions have also proved unpopular in developed countries that needed assistance during the 2008–2009 recession. After receiving a $6 billion rescue package from the IMF, Iceland was forced to make fundamental reforms to its banking sector. Greece, which received over $133 billion from the IMF, agreed to eliminate several paid holidays while cutting all wages of all public workers by 3 percent. This led to massive street protests and numerous strikes by workers.

The South in International Economic Regimes

Because of the need for capital and the wealth created by international trade, most states of the global South see their future economic development as resting on a close interconnection with the world economy, not on national autarky or regional economic communities. Thus poor states must play by the rules embedded in international economic regimes, as discussed in Chapter 5.

The WTO trading regime sometimes works against poor states, however, relative to industrialized ones. A free trade regime makes it harder for poor states to protect infant industries in order to build self-sufficient capital accumulation. It forces competition with more technologically advanced states. A poor state can be competitive only in low-wage, low-capital niches—especially those

Policy Perspectives

Prime Minister of Turkey, Recep Tayyip Erdogan

PROBLEM *How do you balance the demands of domestic actors and international financial institutions?*

BACKGROUND Imagine that you are the prime minister of Turkey. Your economy suffered from the recent global recession but has emerged from that crisis in strong shape. GDP growth was more than 4 percent in 2013. Exports comprise a significant portion of your economy and are diverse: Agricultural products, automotive and electronic parts, as well as textiles, are some of your most popular exports.

Your country has undergone extensive privatization over the past decade because you sold ownership in key industries to private investors. Indeed, most major manufacturing industries in your country are now privately owned, a significant change from 20 years ago. Much of this privatization was encouraged by the IMF after a significant economic crisis in 2001.

One area of your economy that has not liberalized as fast as the industrial sector is the financial and banking sector. The financial and banking industries are still protected by extensive regulation that limits foreign ownership. These regulations have discouraged FDI

from wealthy European Union (EU) states, the United States, and Japan.

DOMESTIC CONSIDERATIONS You are an incredibly popular prime minister, having recently won an unprecedented third term in office. Much of your popularity is based, however, on the economic success you have engineered. Voters have continued to support your privatization and economic liberalization efforts, mostly because the Turkish economy has remained strong.

Business elites, however, continue to support strong regulation efforts in the finance and banking sector in order to insulate Turkey from international economic crises. These regulations also protect their own advantageous financial positions within the Turkish economy. International investors, however, would like more freedom to invest in these sectors of your economy.

SCENARIO Now imagine that one of the key sources of capital for your economy, the EU, continues to struggle with debt crisis issues in Greece, Spain, Portugal, and Italy. As a result of these EU struggles, FDI to your country declines precipitously. Moreover, exports fall due to declining economic fortunes in your key trading partners in Europe. The economy that bolstered your popularity and international standing is now becoming a major problem for your administration.

One potential solution to your economic problems would be to loosen the regulatory controls in the finance and banking sector. Western observers and the IMF have suggested that such a policy change would provide a much needed injection of capital into your economy, which could lift the Turkish economy out of its current downturn.

CHOOSE YOUR POLICY Do you loosen your investment rules in order to encourage more FDI? Do you risk the domestic political backlash of this move, which would cause key economic supporters to oppose you? Do you expose Turkey to the possibility of additional economic crises? Or do you wait and hope the EU recovery will happen soon and revive your own economic fortunes? Do you keep Turkey isolated from additional capital flows that could help increase economic growth?

using natural resources that are scarce in the North, such as tropical agriculture, extractive (mining and drilling) industries, and textiles.

Yet those economic sectors in which developing countries have comparative advantages in world markets—agriculture and textiles in particular—were largely excluded from the free trade rules for decades (see pp. 185–187). Instead, world trade deals concentrated on free trade in manufactured goods, in which states in the North have comparative advantages. As a result, developing countries had to open their home markets to foreign products, against which home industries were not competitive, yet see their own export products shut out of foreign markets. Current WTO negotiations are attempting to remedy this inequity but so far without success.

Another criticism leveled at the WTO centers on the trade dispute system, in which states may bring complaints of unfair trading practices. Such legal disputes can cost millions of dollars to litigate, requiring expensive lawyers and a large staff at WTO headquarters in Geneva. Few states in the global South can afford this legal process, and therefore few use it to help their own industries knock down unfair barriers to trade. Recall that even if a state wins a WTO dispute, it gains only the right to place tariffs on the offending country's goods in an equal amount. For small states, this retaliation can inflict as much damage on their own economies as on the economies of the offending states.

To compensate for these inequities and to help developing countries use trade to boost their economic growth, the WTO has a Generalized System of Preferences (GSP). These and other measures—such as the Lomé and Cotonou conventions in which EU states relaxed tariffs on goods from the global South—are exceptions to the overall rules of trade, intended to ensure that participation in world trade advances development. Nonetheless, critics claim that developing countries are the losers in the overall world trading regime.

Countries in the South continue to pursue proposals to restructure world trade to benefit the South through the *UN Conference on Trade and Development (UNCTAD)*, which meets periodically but lacks power to implement major changes in North-South economic relations. Such efforts have left the South dependent on the North.

Foreign Assistance

7.6   Describe three reasons why countries might provide foreign aid to countries of the global South.

Foreign assistance (or *overseas development assistance*) is money or other aid made available to help states speed up economic development or simply meet basic humanitarian needs. It covers a variety of programs—from individual volunteers lending a hand to massive government packages.

Different kinds of development assistance have different purposes, which often overlap. Some are humanitarian, some are political, and others are

foreign assistance
Money or other aid made available to states in the global South to help them speed up economic development or meet humanitarian needs. Most foreign assistance is provided by governments and is called official development assistance (ODA).

intended to create future economic advantages for the giver. The state or organization that gives assistance is called a *donor*; the state or organization receiving the aid is the *recipient*. Foreign assistance creates, or extends, a relationship between donor and recipient that is simultaneously political and cultural as well as economic. Foreign assistance can be a form of power in which the donor seeks to influence the recipient, or it can be a form of interdependence. The remainder of this chapter examines the patterns and types of foreign assistance, the politics involved in providing assistance, and the potential impacts of foreign assistance.

Patterns of Foreign Assistance

Development Assistance Committee (DAC) A committee whose members—consisting of states from Western Europe, North America, and East Asia—provide 90 percent of official development assistance to countries of the global South.

bilateral aid Government assistance that goes directly to governments as state-to-state aid.

multilateral aid Government foreign aid from several states that goes through a third party, such as the UN or another agency.

UN Development Program (UNDP) A program that coordinates the flow of multilateral development assistance and manages 6,000 projects at once around the world (focusing especially on technical development assistance).

Large amounts of foreign assistance come from governments in the North. Of the $130 billion in governmental foreign assistance provided in 2013, almost 90 percent came from members of the **Development Assistance Committee (DAC)**, consisting of states from Western Europe, North America, and East Asia. Several oil-exporting Arab countries provide some foreign development assistance, and in 2003, transition economies became a net "exporter" of financial aid. Three-quarters of the DAC countries' assistance goes directly to governments in the global South as state-to-state **bilateral aid**; the rest goes through the UN or other agencies as **multilateral aid**. The DAC countries have set themselves a goal to contribute 0.7 percent of their gross national products (GNPs) in foreign aid. But overall, they give less than half this amount. Only Norway, Sweden, Denmark, the United Kingdom, and Luxembourg are close to the target. In fact, as shown in Figure 7.11, aid budges declined dramatically in the late 1960s and in the 1990s. And while they have returned to higher levels in the 2000s, they are unlikely to rise in the future given global economic uncertainty.

The United States gives one of the lowest percentages of GNP—about two-tenths of 1 percent—of the 30 states of the industrialized West that make up the Organization for Economic Co-operation and Development (OECD). In total economic aid given (over $31 billion in 2013), the United States holds a lead over Britain (which recently increased foreign aid to nearly $18 billion). Germany, Japan, and France each give about $10–$15 billion. U.S. and other decreases brought the world total in foreign assistance down substantially in the 1990s (see Figure 7.11).

China has become a significant actor in the foreign aid area since 2010. According to Chinese government statistics, the country has provided about $5 billion a year in foreign assistance over the past five years. Much of this is in the form of loans, with about half of the total amount of aid provided to the continent of Africa.

Another major source of foreign assistance is *UN programs*. The place of these programs in the UN structure is described in Chapter 6 (see pp. 241–242). The overall flow of assistance through the UN is coordinated by the **UN Development Program (UNDP)**, which manages 6,000 projects at once around the

Figure 7.11 Foreign Assistance as a Percent of Donor's Income, 2013 and 1960–2013

Source: http://Stats.OBCD.026.QWIDS

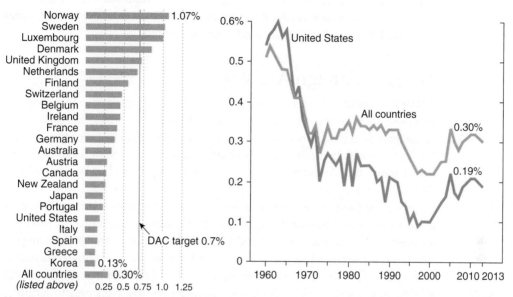

Note: Percent of Gross National Income, which is very close to GDP.

world (focusing especially on technical development assistance). Other UN programs focus on concentrating capital, transferring technology, and developing workforce skills for manufacturing. UN Industrial Development Organization (UNIDO) works on industrialization, United Nations Institute for Training and Research (UNITAR) on training and research. But most UN programs—such as UNICEF, United Nations Population Fund (UNFPA), UNESCO, and WHO—focus on meeting basic needs.

UN programs have three advantages in promoting economic development. One is that governments and citizens tend to perceive the UN as a friend of the global South, not an alien force, a threat to sovereignty, or a reminder of colonialism. Second, UN workers may be more likely to make appropriate decisions because of their backgrounds. UN workers who come from the global South or who have worked in other poor countries in a region may be more sensitive to local conditions and to the pitfalls of development assistance than are aid workers from rich countries. Third, the UN can organize its assistance on a global scale, giving priority to projects and avoiding duplication and the reinvention of the wheel in each state.

A major disadvantage faced by UN development programs is that they are funded largely through voluntary contributions by rich states. Each program has to solicit contributions to carry on its activities, so the contributions can be abruptly cut off if the program displeases a donor government. Also, governments that pledge aid may not follow through. For instance, the UN complained in early 2005 that only 5 percent of the $500 million pledged for southern Sudan by the international community five months earlier had actually been paid. A second major disadvantage of UN programs is their reputation for operating in an inefficient, bureaucratic manner, without the cohesion and the resources that governments and MNCs in the North take for granted.

Types of Foreign Assistance

Bilateral aid takes a variety of forms. *Grants* are funds given free to a recipient state, usually for some stated purpose. *Technical cooperation* refers to grants given in the form of expert assistance in some project rather than just money or goods. *Credits* are grants that can be used to buy certain products from the donor state. For instance, the United States regularly gives credits that can be used to purchase U.S. grain.

Loans are funds given to help in economic development and must be repaid in the future out of the surplus generated by the development process (they too are often tied to the purchase of products from the donor state). Unlike commercial loans, government-to-government development loans are often on concessionary terms, with long repayment times and low interest rates. Although still an obligation for the recipient country, such loans are relatively easy to service.

Loan guarantees, which are used only occasionally, are promises by the donor state to back up commercial loans to the recipient. If the recipient state services such debts and ultimately repays them, there is no cost to the donor. But if the recipient cannot make the payments, the donor has to step in and cover the debts. A loan guarantee allows the recipient state to borrow money at lower interest rates from commercial banks (because the risk to the bank is much lower).

Military aid is not normally included in development assistance, but in a broad sense it belongs there. It is money that flows from North to South, from government to government, and it does bring a certain amount of value into the economies of the global South. If a country is going to have a certain size army with certain weapons, getting them free from a donor state frees up money that can be used elsewhere in the economy. Of all the forms of development assistance, however, military aid is one of the least efficient and most prone to impede rather than help economic development. It is also geared almost exclusively to political alliances rather than development needs.

The main agency dispensing U.S. foreign economic assistance (but not military aid) is the State Department's *Agency for International Development (USAID)*, which works mainly through the U.S. embassy in each recipient country. Major recipients of U.S. foreign aid include Israel, Egypt, Turkey, and Iraq (since 2003)—all important strategic allies in the volatile Middle East.

The U.S. **Peace Corps** provides U.S. volunteers for technical development assistance in developing countries. They work at the request and under the direction of the host state but are paid an allowance by the U.S. government.

Peace Corps An organization started by President John Kennedy in 1961 that provides U.S. volunteers for technical development assistance in poor countries.

Started by President Kennedy in 1961, the Peace Corps now sends about 7,000 volunteers to nearly 70 countries, where they participate in projects affecting about 1 million people.

In foreign aid, the donor must have the permission of the recipient government to operate in the country. This goes back to the principle of national sovereignty and the history of colonialism. National governments have the right to control the distribution of aid and the presence of foreign workers on their soil. Only occasionally is this principle violated, as when the United States and its allies provided assistance to Iraqi Kurds against the wishes of the Iraqi government following the Gulf War. International norms may be starting to change in this regard, with short-term humanitarian assistance starting to be seen as a human right that should not be subject to government veto (see p. 325).

PARTNER IN DEVELOPMENT The Oxfam model of foreign assistance emphasizes support for local groups that can stimulate self-sustaining economic development at a local level. A mutually beneficial North-South partnership is the global goal of such projects. These women show off a mill they purchased with microcredit from an Oxfam-affiliated group in Gambia, 2001.

PRIVATE AID Private donations provide a smaller amount, although sometimes a significant one. For instance, the Bill and Melinda Gates Foundation contributes more than $2 billion annually to world health campaigns. Private aid is an important source of aid for the global South. By 2012, according to the OECD, private aid flows from DAC countries neared $300 billion. This figure was larger than official development assistance given by state governments.

There are many sources of private aid. Individuals in wealthy states may give as individuals (like Bill Gates or George Soros). Individuals may give to charities that send money or food abroad, such as the Red Cross, Doctors without Borders, or their local church. One of the major private charitable groups is **Oxfam America** (one of seven groups worldwide descended from the Oxford Committee for Famine Relief, founded in 1942 in Britain).

Oxfam has developed a unique model of foreign assistance. Originally devoted to short-term aid to famine victims, and still active in that effort, Oxfam America realized that over the longer term, people need not just handouts of food but the means to feed themselves—land, water, seed, tools, and technical training.

The distinctive aspect of the Oxfam model is that it relies on local communities to determine the needs of their own people and to carry out development projects. Oxfam does not operate projects itself but provides funding to local organizations. Nor does Oxfam call itself a donor and these

Oxfam America A private charitable group that works with local communities to determine the needs of their own people and to carry out development projects.

organizations recipients. Rather, it calls both sides "project partners"—working together to accomplish a task. In this model, a little outside money can go a long way toward building sustained local economic development. Furthermore, projects help participants empower themselves by organizing to meet their own needs.

The relationship between North and South—groups such as Oxfam and their project partners—is likened to a good marriage in which decisions are made jointly and dependency does not develop. In this model, economic development is not charity; it is in the interests of people in the rich countries as well as the poor. A cooperative relationship between North and South is essential for a peaceful and prosperous world. Even in a narrow economic sense, development in the global South creates new markets and new products that will enrich the industrialized countries as well. In economics, the creation of wealth is a positive-sum game.

The Oxfam approach seeks to reconceptualize development assistance to focus on long-term development through a bottom-up basic needs strategy and the political empowerment of poor people. The group's philosophy of a "rights-based approach to development" has drawn praise from human rights NGOs. Because of disappointment with the political uses of foreign aid in the past, Oxfam has tried to minimize the role of governments in its projects in both the North and the South. For instance, Oxfam does not accept government funds nor does it make grants to governments.

The general goals of the Oxfam model of foreign aid are consistent with a broader movement in the global South toward grassroots *empowerment.* Efforts such as those of Oxfam partners are organized by poor people to gain some power over their situation and meet their basic needs. The key to success is getting organized, finding information, gaining self-confidence, and obtaining needed resources to implement action plans.

For example, in India, local women's groups using only the power of persuasion and logic have persuaded some landowners to give them land for cooperative income-generating projects such as vegetable farming and raising silkworms. Elsewhere in India, women working as gatherers of wood and other forest products organized to win the legal minimum wage for 250,000 female forest workers—three times what they had been paid before. In this case, government action was necessary, but the pressure for such action came from local organizing. The women took their case to the public and the press, staging protest marches and getting an art exhibit relating to their cause displayed in the provincial capital.

Such examples do not mean that national and foreign governments are unimportant. On the contrary, government policies affect millions of people more quickly and more widely than do grassroots efforts. Indeed, grassroots organizing often has as an ultimate goal the restructuring of national political and social life so that policies reflect the needs of poor people. But the successes of grassroots empowerment show that poor communities can be more than victims of poverty waiting to be saved, or passive bystanders in North-South relations. Nor do poor people need to place their hopes for change in violent revolutions aimed at toppling national governments—revolutions that lead to greater suffering more often than to stable economic development.

The Oxfam model to date has been tested only on a small scale. Although the model may be effective in the local communities it reaches, it would have to be adopted widely and replicated on a much larger scale in order to influence the overall prospects for development.

Indeed, one advantage of private aid giving, like that of Oxfam, is the flexibility with which it can be given. Private aid organizations may also be more efficient (due to their smaller size) and better able to create partnerships with local recipients. Unfortunately, private aid organizations' lack of size and official government status can also be a disadvantage. They can be barred from entering a country (Zimbabwe recently expelled all private NGOs providing assistance), and they may have difficulty providing large-scale relief in times of crisis. They also may promote development policies that are at odds with government policy, putting them in conflict with other donor governments.

The Politics of Foreign Assistance

Many governments and private organizations provide ongoing development assistance in the form of projects in local communities in the South that are administered by agencies from the North to help meet basic needs. Such charitable programs are useful means by which people in the North funnel resources to people in the South, but they may create unanticipated problems. For example, they do not address the causes of poverty, the position of poor countries in the world economy, or local political conditions such as military rule or corruption. For example, photos of a hungry child may stare at the reader from a magazine page while the accompanying text notes that a few cents a day can "save" the child. Although such programs raise awareness in the North of the extent of poverty in the South, at worst they tend to be exploitive and to reinforce racist and paternalistic stereotypes of the helplessness of people in the global South.

Although the motivation for foreign aid is to help those who are less fortunate, donor states have discovered that foreign aid is also an important tool of leverage over recipient states. Many donor states thus try to use some types of foreign aid to create economic and political changes in recipient countries.

Like almost all donor states, the United States uses the promise of foreign aid, or the threat of cutting it off, as leverage in political bargaining with

MOUTHWASH FOR MAURITANIA Sometimes foreign assistance contributes goods to third world economies with little understanding of local needs or longterm strategies. Here, free supplies including cartons of mouthwash are delivered by the U.S. ambassador and the captain of a U.S. Navy ship participating in Project Handclasp, 1989.

recipients. For example, when Pakistan proceeded in the late 1980s with a nuclear weapons program despite U.S. warnings, a sizable flow of U.S. aid was terminated. Then when Pakistan supported U.S. military action in next-door Afghanistan in 2001, U.S. aid was restored.

In 2004, the United States launched the Millennium Challenge Corporation (MCC), which increases U.S. aid but only to governments with certain policies, such as rule of law, control of corruption, investment in education, and sound fiscal management. After potential recipients apply for aid, a board composed of government and private officials reviews the applications. The applicants are then reviewed for their suitability for aid based on a set of criteria established by the MCC. In this way, the United States hopes to reduce the aid lost to corruption and waste.

Of course, foreign assistance is also a complicated domestic political process. For example, in recent years, aid advocates in the United States have fought a U.S. law requiring that food sent to hungry people in Africa be grown in the United States and shipped in U.S. vessels. Instead of this simple handout system, they proposed using U.S. funds to buy food locally in Africa, which would save a lot of money, get aid to the hungry people months faster, and help African farmers. But the proposal was opposed by the so-called Iron Triangle of food aid—U.S. agribusiness that profits from selling the food to the government, U.S. shipping companies that profit from shipping it, and U.S. charities (including CARE and Catholic Relief Services) that fund a healthy fraction of their budgets by selling in Africa some of the grain they ship from the United States. The charities, by becoming international grain merchants and flooding local markets with cheap food (both sold and given away), compete with local farmers and drive down local prices, harming long-term recovery. Yet because of the Iron Triangle's lobbying power, Congress killed off the proposal to allow purchase of local food in Africa.

disaster relief Provision of short-term relief in the form of food, water, shelter, clothing, and other essentials to people facing natural disasters.

The one type of foreign assistance that is the *least* politically motivated is **disaster relief**. The disaster relief model describes the kind of foreign assistance given when poor people are afflicted by famine, drought, earthquakes, flooding, or other such natural disasters. (War is also a disaster.) When disaster strikes a poor state, many people are left with no means of subsistence and often without their homes. Disaster relief is the provision of short-term relief to such people in the form of food, water, shelter, clothing, and other essentials.

Disaster relief is very important because disasters can wipe out years of progress in economic development in a single blow. Generally, the international community tries to respond with enough assistance to get people back on their feet. The costs of such assistance are relatively modest, the benefits visible and dramatic. Having a system of disaster relief in place provides the global South with a kind of insurance against sudden losses that could otherwise destabilize economic accumulation.

Disasters generally occur quickly and without much warning. Rapid response is difficult to coordinate. International disaster relief has become more organized and better coordinated in the past decade, but it is still a complex process that varies somewhat from one situation to the next. Contributions of governments, private charitable organizations, and other groups and agencies are coordinated through the *UN Office of the Disaster Relief Coordinator (UNDRO)* in Geneva. In 2006, the UN set up a $500 million fund to enable it to respond quickly to disasters without waiting to raise funds first each time disaster strikes. Typically, international contributions make up no more than about one-third of the total relief effort, the remainder coming from local communities and national governments in the affected states. The U.S. government's contributions are coordinated by the *Office of Foreign Disaster Assistance (OFDA)*, which is part of USAID.

Disaster relief is something of a collective good because the states of the North do not benefit individually by contributing, yet they benefit in the long run from greater stability in the South. Despite the potential for a collective action problem, disaster relief is generally a positive example of international cooperation to get a job done—and an example of the use of the identity principle to solve a collective goods problem. Food donated by the World Council of Churches may be carried to the scene in U.S. military aircraft and then distributed by the *International Committee of the Red Cross (ICRC)*. Embarrassing failures in the past—of underresponse or overresponse, duplication of efforts, or agencies working at cross-purposes—have been fewer since the 1990s.

The devastating earthquake in Haiti in 2010 showed the progress and the limitations of international relief efforts. Overnight, millions lost family members, homes, possessions, safe drinking water, and ways of life. With no functioning government or medical care system, initial relief efforts were chaotic and international aid was poorly coordinated. Many victims died as planes stacked up over the small airport, unable to deliver supplies. In days, however, U.S. military forces took over the airport, and massive international assistance flowed in. Governments and NGOs pledged billions of dollars to help Haiti get back to its feet under UN guidance.

Both international organizations (IOs) and NGOs quickly mobilized to carry out what has been termed the largest relief effort in human history. The efforts by these organizations were coordinated through a variety of relief agencies, including the ICRC, the International Organization for Migration, the UN High Commissioner for Refugees (UNHCR), and Oxfam. Initially, it appeared as though the United States would coordinate its own relief efforts apart from the UN, but after reconsideration, the United States ceded the lead role in relief to the UN. This somewhat spontaneous coordination of states, IOs, and NGOs seems contrary to the anarchical international system.

The relationship between disasters and economic development is complex, and appropriate responses vary according to location, type and size of disaster, and phase of recovery. Appropriate disaster relief can promote local economic development, whereas inappropriate responses can distort or impede such development. International norms regarding states' legal obligations to assist others in time of natural disaster and to accept such assistance if needed are changing. Some have even suggested extending the idea of the responsibility to protect to the area of disaster relief. This idea became particularly relevant in the wake of Cyclone Nargis, which struck Burma in 2008. An estimated 130,000 people died in that natural disaster, yet the repressive government of Burma delayed or denied efforts of the international community to provide assistance to those affected by the cyclone. While aid did eventually flow into Burma, weeks were wasted while the government denied the needed assistance for coping with the cyclone.

The Impact of Foreign Assistance

There is a danger in providing foreign assistance—especially in large-scale governmental aid programs—that people from the North may provide assistance inappropriate for a developing country's local conditions and culture. This danger is illustrated by an experience in Kenya in the 1970s. Nomadic herders in the area of Lake Turkana near the Sahara desert—the Turkana tribe—were poor and vulnerable to periodic droughts. Western aid donors and the Kenyan government decided that the herders' traditional way of life was not environmentally sustainable and should be replaced by commercial fishing of the abundant tilapia fish in Lake Turkana. Norway, with its long experience in fishing, was asked to teach fishing and boat-building methods to the Turkana. To create a commercially viable local economy, Norwegian consultants recommended marketing frozen fish fillets to Kenya and the world. Thus, in 1981, Norway finished building a $2 million, state-of-the-art fish-freezing plant on the shores of Lake Turkana and a $20 million road connecting the plant to Kenya's transportation system.

There were only three problems. First, with temperatures of 100 degrees outside (a contrast with Norway!), the cost of operating the freezers exceeded the income from the fillets. So after a few days, the freezers were turned off and the facility became a very expensive dried-fish warehouse. Second, Turkana culture viewed fishing as the lowest-status profession, suitable only for those incompetent at herding. Third, every few decades, Lake Turkana shrinks as drought reduces the inflow of water. Such a drought in 1984–1985 eliminated the gulf where the fishing operations were based. The Norwegians might have foreseen these problems by doing more homework instead of just transplanting what worked in Norway. When the drought hit, the 20,000 herders who had been brought to the lake to learn fishing were left in an overcrowded, overgrazed environment in which every tree was cut for firewood and most cattle died. Instead of becoming self-sufficient, the Turkana people became totally dependent on outside aid.

In the past decade, many scholars have undertaken research to understand whether foreign aid is effective at creating economic growth and alleviating poverty in the global South. Heated debates now occur among academics and policy makers about whether aid is effective and therefore whether more or less should be given. On one side, scholars suggest increasing foreign assistance in order to deal with the crushing inequalities between the global North and the global South. Because the global South cannot reliably sustain capital accumulation, assistance from the North is necessary to jump-start economic growth.

Countering this position, however, is research suggesting that aid does not always help poor countries develop. In particular, unless recipient countries possess institutions that practice good government, aid will largely be wasted or fall into the hands of corrupt leaders. This research has been the inspiration for the United States' MCC policies as well as more IMF conditionality.

Other critics of aid suggest that it should be reduced in general. They contend that the flow of aid has allowed leaders in poor states to avoid difficult policy changes that would pave the way for long-term economic growth. They argue that, in some African countries, the massive infusion of foreign assistance after decolonization led to increased poverty and dependence on charity rather than increased wealth and independence.

CONFRONTING THE NORTH-SOUTH GAP The giving and receiving of foreign assistance is political, even if the motivations for giving it are not. Perhaps the most important point is for people in the North to become aware of the tremendous gap between North and South and try to address the problem. Poverty can seem so overwhelming that citizens in rich countries can easily turn their backs and just try to live their own lives.

But in today's interdependent world, this really is not possible. North-South relations have become part of everyday life. The integrated global economy brings to the North products and people from the South. The information revolution puts images of poverty on TV sets in comfortable living rooms. The growing role of the UN brings North and South together in a worldwide community. This global integration is especially evident in the areas of environmental management and technological change, which are discussed in Chapter 8.

Chapter Review

Summary

- Most of the world's people live in poverty in the global South. About 1 billion live in extreme poverty, without access to adequate food, water, and other necessities.

- Moving from poverty to well-being requires the accumulation of capital. Capitalism emphasizes overall growth with considerable concentration of wealth, whereas socialism emphasizes a fair distribution of wealth.

- Most states have a mixed economy with some degree of private ownership of capital and some degree of state ownership. However, state ownership has not been very successful in accumulating wealth.

- Since Lenin's time, many Marxists attribute poverty in the South to the concentration of wealth in the North. In this theory, capitalists in the North exploit the South economically and use the resulting wealth to buy off workers in the North.

- IR scholars in the world-system school argue that the North is a core region specializing in producing manufactured goods and the South is a periphery specializing in extracting raw materials through agriculture and mining. Between these are semiperiphery states with light manufacturing.

- Following independence after World War II, countries of the global South were left with legacies of colonialism, including their basic economic infrastructures, that made wealth accumulation difficult in certain ways. These problems still remain in many countries.

- Wealth accumulation depends on meeting basic human needs such as access to food, water, education, shelter, and health care. Developing countries have had mixed success in meeting their populations' basic needs.

- War has been a major impediment to meeting basic needs, and to wealth accumulation generally, in poor countries.

- Hunger and malnutrition are rampant in the global South. The most important cause is the displacement of subsistence farmers from their land because of war, population pressures, and the conversion of agricultural land into plantations growing export crops to earn hard currency.

- Urbanization is increasing throughout the global South as more people move from the countryside to cities. Huge slums have grown in the cities as poor people arrive and cannot find jobs.

- Women's central role in the process of capital accumulation has begun to be recognized. International agencies based in the North have started taking women's contributions into account in analyzing economic development in the South.

- Poverty in the South has led huge numbers of migrants to seek a better life in the North; this has created international political frictions. War and repression in the South have generated millions of refugees.

- Economic development in the global South has been uneven. In recent years, many poor countries, led by China, have grown robustly. Growth in the global South was strong after the 2008–2009 recession, but these rates have recently slowed.

- Evidence does not support a strong association of economic growth either with internal equality of wealth distribution or with internal inequality.

- The newly industrializing countries (NICs) in Asia—South Korea, Taiwan, Hong Kong, and Singapore—show that it is possible to rise out of poverty into sustained capital accumulation.

- China has registered strong economic growth in the past 30 years of market-oriented economic reforms. Though still quite poor, China is the world's leading success story in economic development.

- Export-led growth has largely replaced import substitution as a development strategy. This reflects the experiences of the NICs and China as well as the theory of comparative advantage.

- Government corruption is a major obstacle to development.

- Given the shortage of local capital in most poor states, foreign investment by MNCs can be a means of stimulating economic growth. MNCs look for favorable local conditions, including political and economic stability, in deciding where to invest.

- Debt, resulting largely from overborrowing in the 1970s and early 1980s, is a major problem in the global South. Despite renegotiations and other debt management efforts, the South remains $5 trillion in debt to the North.

- The IMF makes loans to states in the South conditional on economic and governmental reforms. These conditionality agreements often necessitate politically unpopular measures such as cutting food subsidies.

- The WTO trading regime works against the global South by allowing richer nations to protect sectors in which the global South has advantages—notably agriculture and textiles. The Generalized System of Preferences (GSP) tries to compensate by lowering barriers to exports from the global South.

- Foreign assistance, most of it from governments in the North, plays an important part in the economic development plans of the poorer states of the South.

- Most foreign aid consists of bilateral grants and loans from governments in the North to specific governments in the South. Such aid is often used for political leverage and promotes the export of products from the donor state.

- Donors in the global North use various relief models to distribute aid to the developing world, each with advantages and drawbacks.

Key Terms

Critical Thinking Questions

1. In North and South America, independence from colonialism was won by descendants of the colonists themselves. In Asia and Africa, it was won mainly by local populations with a long history of their own. How do you think this aspect has affected the postcolonial history of one or more specific countries from each group?

2. Currently, incomes in the global North are five times as high, per person, as in the global South. If you could magically redistribute the world's income so that everyone had equal income ($10,000 per person per year), would you? What effects would such a change make in the North and South?

3. Some scholars criticize the IMF for imposing harsh terms in its conditionality agreements with poor states. Others applaud the IMF for demanding serious reforms before providing financial resources. If you were a leader negotiating with the IMF, what kinds of terms would you be willing to agree to and what terms would you resist? Why?

Chapter 8
Environment and Technology

WINDMILL AND NUCLEAR POWER PLANT, BRITAIN, MID-1980S.

 Learning Objectives

8.1 Illustrate the collective action problem facing the international community by focusing on one global environmental issue.

8.2 Evaluate the roadblocks to achieving a successful international agreement to address the problem of global warming.

8.3 Describe three ways in which the need for natural resources can create international conflict.

8.4 Explain the demographic transition and why some states are vulnerable to rapid population growth.

8.5 Explain two ways in which information can be a tool used by governments and two ways in which information can be a tool used against governments.

Interdependence and the Environment

8.1 Illustrate the collective action problem facing the international community by focusing on one global environmental issue.

Global threats to the natural environment are a growing source of interdependence. States' actions regarding pollution, conservation, and natural resources routinely affect other states. Because environmental effects tend to be diffuse and long term and because such effects easily spread from one location to another, international environmental politics creates difficult collective goods problems (see pp. 3–9). A sustainable natural environment is a collective good, and states bargain over how to distribute the costs of providing that good. The collective goods problem arises in each issue area concerning the environment, resources, and population.

For example, the world's major fisheries in international waters are not owned by any state; they are a collective good. The various fishing states must cooperate (partly by regulating nonstate actors such as multinational corporations [MNCs]) to avoid depleting the stocks of fish. If too many states fail to cooperate, the fish population declines and everyone's catch drops. And indeed, in 1997–2007, catches worldwide declined significantly. Further declines are projected for the coming years. Fishers have moved on to new species of seafood after depleting earlier ones, but they have already depleted a third of the species, with the rest projected to go by midcentury. Because the world's states did not solve the collective goods problem of world fisheries, they are paying $20 billion a year in subsidies to bankrupt fishing industries in their respective countries.

This depletion occurred because each additional fishing boat—and the MNC that owns it as well as its state of origin—gains by catching an additional fish. The benefits of that fish go entirely to the one catching it, whereas the eventual costs of depleted stocks will be shared by all who fish there. But what is a state's fair quota of fish? No world government exists to decide such a question, so states must enter into multilateral negotiations, agreements, and regimes.

Such efforts create new avenues for functionalism and international integration but also new potentials for conflict and so-called Prisoner's Dilemmas.

In 1999, a UN-sponsored agreement among all the world's major fishing states set goals to reduce fleet overcapacity. (Four million fishing boats operate worldwide, of which 40,000 are ships larger than 100 tons.) Participating nations are capping the size of fishing fleets and then scaling them back gradually, while reducing subsidies. The pain of unemployment and economic adjustment should thus be shared. However, the agreement is voluntary; its implementation delayed; and its effect on collapsing fisheries probably too little, too late.

This type of collective goods dilemma has been called the **tragedy of the commons**. Centuries ago, the commons were shared grazing land in Britain. As with fisheries, if too many people kept too many sheep, the commons would be overgrazed. Yet adding one more sheep was profitable to that sheep's owner. Britain solved the problem by **enclosure** of the commons—splitting it into privately owned pieces on each of which a single owner would have an incentive to manage resources responsibly. The world's states have taken a similar approach to coastal fisheries by extending territorial waters to put more fish under the control of single states (see p. 352). The *global commons* refers to the shared parts of the earth, such as the oceans and outer space.

TOO MANY COOKS Management of environmental issues is complicated by the large numbers of actors involved, which make collective goods problems hard to resolve (participants may be more tempted to free-ride). Here, many nongovernmental organization (NGO) representatives at the global climate change meeting in Lima discuss responses to last-minute proposals made at the close of the conference, 2014.

tragedy of the commons A collective goods dilemma that is created when common environmental assets (such as the world's fisheries) are depleted or degraded through the failure of states to cooperate effectively.

enclosure The splitting of a common area or good into privately owned pieces, giving individual owners an incentive to manage resources responsibly.

As in other areas of international political economy (IPE), the solution of environmental collective goods problems is based on achieving shared benefits that depend on overcoming conflicting interests. *Regimes* are an important part of the solution (see pp. 72–73), providing rules based on the reciprocity principle to govern bargaining over who gets the benefits and bears the costs of environmental protection. Functional international organizations (IOs) specialize in technical and management aspects of the environment.

These IOs overlap more and more with broader communities of experts from various states that structure the way states manage environmental issues; these have been called *epistemic communities* (knowledge-based communities). For example, the transnational community of experts and policy makers concerned with pollution in the Mediterranean is an epistemic community.

In global environmental politics, it is hard to manage collective goods problems because of the large number of actors. Collective goods are easier to provide in small groups, in which individual actions have more impact on the total picture and cheating is more noticeable. The opposite is true with the environment. The actions of nearly 200 states (albeit some more than others) aggregate to cause indirect but serious consequences throughout the world.

Sustainable Development

Sustainable development refers to economic growth that does not deplete resources and destroy ecosystems so quickly that the basis of that economic growth is itself undermined. The concept applies to both the industrialized regions and the global South.

The 1992 Earth Summit produced an overall plan whereby large states in the global South promise to industrialize along cleaner lines (at a certain cost to economic growth), and industrialized states promise to funnel aid and technology to them to assist in that process. The summit also established the *Commission on Sustainable Development,* which monitors states' compliance with the promises they made at the Earth Summit and hears evidence from environmental nongovernmental organizations (NGOs) such as Greenpeace. But it lacks powers of enforcement over national governments—again reflecting the preeminence of state sovereignty over supranational authority (see pp. 223–226). The commission has 54 member states. But progress has been slow.

China and other developing countries in Asia stand at the center of the debate over sustainable development. In the drive for rapid economic growth, these countries have created serious pollution and other environmental problems. In early 2013, Beijing's smog far exceeded dangerous levels, and residents who ventured outside suffered burning lungs and stinging eyes. Because of China's size, any success in developing its economy along Western industrialized lines (for example, with mass ownership of automobiles) could create shocks to the global environment. In recent years, China has also been scouring the planet for raw materials—such as imports of 200 million tons of iron a year—to fuel its extraordinary growth. At the same time, it has also become a leader in the development of green technology, often surpassing efforts by American and European corporations. For example, China now dominates the production of solar panels. In 2014, it pledged to work with the United States to cut greenhouse gas emissions. But China's growth is still powered in large part by dirty, coal-burning power plants.

Managing the Environment

8.2 **Evaluate the roadblocks to achieving a successful international agreement to address the problem of global warming.**

Most global environmental problems are those that involve collective goods for all states and people in the world.

The Atmosphere

Preserving the health of the earth's atmosphere is a benefit that affects people throughout the world, without regard for their own state's contribution to the problem or its solution. Two problems of the atmosphere have become major international issues: global warming and depletion of the ozone layer.

GLOBAL WARMING   Global climate change, or **global warming**, is a long-term rise in the average world temperature. Growing and compelling evidence shows that global warming is a real problem, that it is caused by the emission of carbon dioxide and other gases, and that it will get much worse. The issue of global warming has risen high on the political agenda in the past decade because of massive melt-offs of Arctic ice; freakish weather; and devastating hurricanes, including Katrina in New Orleans in 2005 and Sandy in New York and New Jersey in 2012. Unfortunately, the international community has had little success solving the problem.

> **global warming** A slow, long-term rise in the average world temperature caused by the emission of greenhouse gases produced by burning fossil fuels—oil, coal, and natural gas.

Over the coming decades, according to most estimates, global temperatures may rise by between 3 and 10 degrees Fahrenheit if nothing is done. Possibly within a few decades, the polar ice caps will begin to melt and cause the sea level to rise by as much as a few feet. Studies in 2012 confirmed that the warming trend is accelerating faster than what had been seen as worst-case scenarios. In fact, nine of the ten warmest years on record have happened since 2000, with 2014 as the warmest year ever recorded. Global warming could flood coastal cities and devastate low-lying areas such as the heavily populated coast of Bangladesh. Urgent calls for action come from island states in the Pacific that will likely disappear this century. Indeed, reflecting an all-too-realistic lack of faith in international action, the low-lying state of the Maldives created a fund to buy land in another country to move its 300,000 residents as its territory disappears.

Global climate change has begun to alter weather patterns in many regions, causing droughts, floods, freezes, and widespread disruption of natural ecosystems. It is also possible that climate changes could benefit some regions and make agriculture more productive. Melting of polar ice is opening new shipping routes north of Canada and Russia that could potentially cut weeks off the transit time from northern Europe or America to Asia (see Figure 8.1), a huge savings for global business. Furthermore, the Arctic seas hold large deposits of oil and gas, which will become commercially accessible as the ice melts (and, ironically, contribute to even more global warming).

The **UN Environment Program (UNEP)**, whose main function is to monitor environmental conditions, works with the World Meteorological Organization to measure changes in global climate from year to year. Since 1989, the UN-sponsored *Intergovernmental Panel on Climate Change* (IPCC) has served as a negotiating forum for this issue. In 2007, the IPCC issued a report from scientists around the world, approved by more than 100 countries, calling global warming "unequivocal" and expressing "very high confidence" that humans are the main cause.

> **UN Environment Program (UNEP)** A program that monitors environmental conditions and, among other activities, works with the World Meteorological Organization to measure changes in global climate.

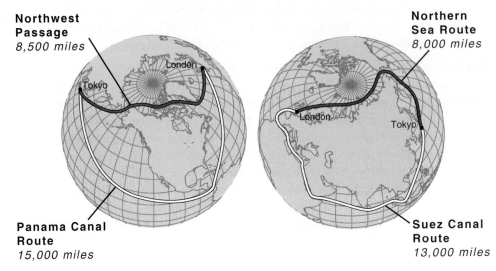

Figure 8.1 Potential Arctic Shipping Routes

Source: United Nations Environment Program

Northwest Passage
8,500 miles

Northern Sea Route
8,000 miles

Panama Canal Route
15,000 miles

Suez Canal Route
13,000 miles

greenhouse gases
Carbon dioxide and other gases that, when concentrated in the atmosphere, act like the glass in a greenhouse, holding energy in and leading to global warming.

It is costly to reduce the emissions of gases—mainly carbon dioxide—that cause global warming. These gases result from the broad spectrum of activities that drive an industrial economy. They are a by-product of burning *fossil fuels*—oil, coal, and natural gas—to run cars, tractors, furnaces, factories, and so forth. These activities create **greenhouse gases**—so named because when concentrated in the atmosphere, these gases act like the glass in a greenhouse: They let energy in as short-wavelength solar radiation but reflect it back when it tries to exit again as longer-wavelength heat waves. The greenhouse gases are *carbon dioxide* (responsible for two-thirds of the effect), *methane gas, chlorofluorocarbons* (CFCs), and *nitrous oxide.* Particulate matter from diesel engines (in the global North) and dirty cookstoves (in the South) are also major contributors. Ironically, data stored in "the cloud," seemingly free from earthly concerns, actually lives in data centers that use vast amounts of electricity and run large diesel generators, contributing to global warming.

Thus, reducing the greenhouse effect means curbing economic growth or shifting it onto entirely new technological paths, both of which are extremely expensive. The political costs of such actions—which would likely increase unemployment, reduce corporate profits, and lower personal incomes—could be severe. If Arctic sea ice melts, polar bears may go extinct, but they do not have a seat at the table in international climate negotiations. Neither do today's children, who cannot vote but will live with the long-term consequences of their elders' actions.

For individual states, the costs of reducing greenhouse emissions are almost unrelated to the benefits of a solution. If one state reduces its industrial production or makes expensive investments in new technologies, this will have little effect on the long-term outcome unless other states do likewise. And if most states took such steps, a free rider that did not go along would save money and still benefit from the solution.

Global warming thus presents states with a triple dilemma. First, there is the dilemma of short-term (and predictable) costs to gain long-term (and less predictable) benefits. Second, specific constituencies such as oil companies and industrial workers pay the costs, whereas the benefits are distributed more generally across domestic society and internationally. Third, there is the collective goods dilemma among states: Benefits are shared globally but costs must be extracted from each state individually.

This third dilemma is complicated by the North-South divide. How can the industrialization of today's poor countries (China and India in particular) take place without pushing greenhouse emissions to unacceptable levels? Greenhouse gases are produced by each state roughly in proportion to its industrial activity. Eighty percent of greenhouse gases now come from the industrialized countries. Half of all greenhouse emissions come from the United States and China. U.S. carbon dioxide emissions, 18 tons per person annually, are twice the European rate and three times China's (although China's aggregate emissions now exceed those of the United States and Canada combined). Yet the most severe impacts of global warming are likely to be felt in the global South. In densely populated countries such as Bangladesh, hundreds of millions of people stand to lose their homes and farmland under a rising sea. Offsetting these North-South divisions, however, is the emerging realization that global climate change could cause environmental catastrophes across both North and South.

All of these elements make for a difficult multilateral bargaining situation, one not yet resolved. The *Framework Convention on Climate Change* adopted at the 1992 Earth Summit set a nonbinding goal to limit greenhouse emissions to 1990 levels by the year 2000. That goal was not met. Western Europe and Japan have been more willing to regulate greenhouse emissions than has the United States (which burns more fossil fuel per person).

The 1997 **Kyoto Protocol** adopted a complex formula for reducing greenhouse emissions to 1990 levels in the global North over about a decade. Countries in the global South received preferential treatment because their levels (per capita) were much lower. Yet China's fast-growing, coal-burning economy is a major factor in global warming (see Figure 8.2). India is another large source of carbon dioxide. The United States signed the treaty, but Congress would not ratify it.

Moving forward without U.S. support, 160 countries in 2001 agreed to implement Kyoto. The agreement called for 40 industrialized countries to reduce emissions to 5 percent below 1990 levels, by 2012, with binding penalties for failure. The European Union (EU) pledged $400 million per year to help the global South reduce its emissions. After enough ratifications, the treaty came into effect in 2005, and mandatory carbon cuts began in 2008, but they are falling short of targets.

Kyoto Protocol (1997) The main international treaty on global warming, which entered into effect in 2005 and mandates cuts in carbon emissions. Almost all the world's major countries, except the United States, are participants.

Figure 8.2 Projected U.S. and Chinese Carbon Dioxide Emissions, 1990–2030

Source: International Energy Agency.

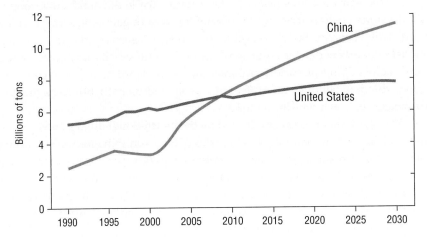

The European Union established markets to trade carbon emission credits among 11,000 industrial facilities across Europe, and in 2012 linked it to Australia's market. However, the economic slowdown in Europe led to a drastic price drop for carbon credits in 2011. Those prices stayed very low through 2014, leading some to question the future of the European emissions trading market. At the same time, however, other countries created similar emissions trading schemes, including South Korea, China, and Japan. All these carbon markets use free market principles to make reduction in carbon emissions more efficient. For example, a venture in Brazil earned carbon credits by burning methane gas from a garbage dump (to generate electricity) instead of venting it as a strong greenhouse gas. European investors bought the credits and could then sell them to a polluting factory in Eastern Europe.

With the Kyoto agreement set to expire after 2012, 180 states negotiated for years about what to do next. The United States rejoined these talks. In late 2011, a meeting in Durban (South Africa) agreed to extend the Kyoto framework to 2013–2017. At a meeting late in 2014 in Peru, participants agreed on the principle that all states—rich and poor—should commit to limit greenhouse emissions. More countries have also agreed to contribute to the Green Climate Fund, which disperses millions to developing countries to help them adapt.

Meanwhile, the United States and China agreed in late 2014 that both countries would accelerate their efforts to reduce emissions. The United States agreed to reduce its emissions by over 25 percent (below 2005 levels) by 2025, while China agreed to continue its shift away from coal plants toward alternative energy sources. Even before this agreement, both countries have shown movement toward these goals. By 2013, the United States was 10 percent below 2005 emission levels and, that same year, China's use of coal declined for the first time in a century.

In addition, about half the states of the United States (notably California), and a number of cities, began taking steps to limit greenhouse emissions. Yet none of these moves are enough, or soon enough, to reverse the direction of climate change decisively. The dilemma of global warming remains fundamentally unsolved, and with weak enforcement mechanisms, even the states that signed the Kyoto Protocol did not meet their targets by 2012. Indeed, even European states, which have adopted the most aggressive policies to lower emissions, have yet to see declines in carbon dioxide.

The Paris climate talks of 2015 were a key meeting in global climate politics. Expectations were high for the meeting, with all sides simultaneously hoping for a strong agreement, yet an agreement that meets their approval. Such agreements are hard to achieve given the public goods nature of climate change. If the Paris meetings come to be viewed as a failure, it is likely that many states will follow the path of the United States and China, making smaller, separate agreements in the absence of a larger, global one.

OZONE DEPLETION A second major atmospheric problem negotiated by the world's governments is the depletion of the world's **ozone layer**. Ozone high in the atmosphere screens out harmful ultraviolet rays from the sun. Certain chemicals expelled by industrial economies float to the top of the atmosphere and interact with ozone in a way that breaks it down. The chief culprits are CFCs, until recently widely used in refrigeration and in aerosol sprays. (Unfortunately, ozone produced by burning fossil fuels does not replace the high-level ozone but only pollutes the lower atmosphere.) As the ozone layer thins, more ultraviolet radiation reaches the earth's surface. Over Antarctica, a seasonal hole in the ozone grew larger year by year. If ozone levels had kept rising, the increased radiation could eventually kill off vegetation, reduce agricultural yields, and disrupt ecosystems.

Clearly, this is another collective goods problem in that one state benefits from allowing the use of CFCs in its economy, provided that most other states prohibit their use. But the costs of replacing CFCs are much lower than the costs of addressing global warming: CFCs can be replaced at modest cost. Furthermore, the consequences of ozone depletion are better understood and more immediate than those of global warming.

ozone layer The part of the atmosphere that screens out harmful ultraviolet rays from the sun. Certain chemicals used in industrial economies break down the ozone layer.

GLIMPSE OF THE FUTURE International treaties have been much more successful at addressing ozone depletion than global warming, mostly because of costs. The 1997 Kyoto Protocol, extended in 2012, set modest goals for industrialized countries to reduce their output of carbon dioxide and related gases, but progress has fallen short. Extreme weather in 2012 offered an early warning sign. Here flooding hits the capital of Indonesia, 2013. If global warming melts polar ice caps in the coming decades, sea levels could rise and devastate many cities.

Montreal Protocol (1987) An agreement on protection of the ozone layer in which states pledged to reduce and then eliminate use of chlorofluorocarbons (CFCs). It is the most successful environmental treaty to date.

Perhaps because of these cost issues, states had much more success in negotiating agreements and developing regimes to manage ozone depletion than global warming. In the 1987 **Montreal Protocol**, 22 states agreed to reduce CFCs by 50 percent by 1998. In 1990, the timetable was accelerated and the number of signatories increased: Eighty-one states agreed to eliminate all CFCs by 2000. In 1992, as evidence of ozone depletion mounted, the schedule was again accelerated, with major industrial states phasing out CFCs by 1995. The signatories agreed in principle to establish a fund to help developing countries pay for alternative refrigeration technologies not based on CFCs. Without such an effort, the states of the global South would be tempted to free-ride and could ultimately undermine the effort. These countries were also given many years to phase out production. The Montreal Protocol was revised and strengthened again in 1997 and 1999. Rich countries stopped making CFCs in 1996 and have contributed about $3 billion to the fund. This money, supporting thousands of projects in more than 100 countries, has helped the global South reduce emissions over the past decade. The ozone hole is projected to shrink back slowly over the coming 50 years if current arrangements continue.

The Montreal Protocol on CFCs is the most important success yet achieved in international negotiations to preserve the global environment. Indeed, UN Secretary General Kofi Annan called it "perhaps the single most successful international agreement to date." It showed that states can agree to take action on urgent environmental threats, agree on targets and measures to counter such threats, and allocate the costs of such measures in a mutually acceptable way and actually pay up when the bill comes. But the international cooperation on the ozone problem has not been widely repeated on other environmental issues.

Biodiversity

biodiversity The tremendous diversity of plant and animal species making up the earth's (global, regional, and local) ecosystems.

Biodiversity refers to the tremendous diversity of plant and animal species making up the earth's (global, regional, and local) ecosystems. Because of humans' destruction of ecosystems, large numbers of species are already *extinct*. Extinction results from overhunting, overfishing, and introducing non-native species that crowd out previous inhabitants. But the most important cause is *loss of habitat*—the destruction of rain forests, pollution of lakes and streams, and loss of agricultural lands to urban sprawl. Because ecosystems are based on complex interrelationships among species, the extinction of a few species can cause deeper changes in the environment. For example, the loss of native microorganisms can lead to chronic pollution of rivers or to the transformation of arable land into deserts.

Because ecosystems are so complex, it is usually impossible to predict the consequences of a species' extinction or of the loss of a habitat or ecosystem. Generally, the activities that lead to habitat loss are economically profitable, so real costs are associated with limiting such activities. Species preservation is thus a collective good resembling global warming; the costs are immediate and substantial but the benefits are long term and ill defined.

It has been difficult to reach international agreement on sharing the costs of preserving biodiversity. A UN convention on trade in endangered species has reduced but not eliminated such trade. At the 1992 Earth Summit, a treaty on biodiversity committed signatories to preserving habitats and got rich states to pay poor ones for the rights to use commercially profitable biological products extracted from rare species in protected habitats (such as medicines from rain forest trees). As of 2016 the treaty had 195 member states. However, because of fears that the treaty could limit U.S. patent rights in biotechnology, the United States never ratified it. The United States does participate, however, in other biological treaties, such as a 1971 wetlands convention and the 1973 Convention on International Trade in Endangered Species (CITES).

International regimes to protect whales and dolphins have had limited success. The **International Whaling Commission** (an intergovernmental organization [IGO]) sets quotas for hunting certain whale species, but participation is voluntary, and governments are not bound by decisions they object to.

The *Inter-American Tropical Tuna Commission* (another IGO) regulates methods used to fish for tuna, with the aim of minimizing dolphin losses. The United States, which consumes half the world's tuna catch, has gone further and unilaterally requires—in the Marine Mammal Protection Act—that dolphin-safe methods be used for tuna sold in U.S. territory. Other countries have challenged the act through international trade organizations as an unfair restriction on tuna exports to the United States. Such conflicts portend future battles between environmentalists and free trade advocates. Free traders argue that states must not use domestic legislation to seek global environmental goals.

Thus, unilateral approaches to biodiversity issues are problematic because they disrupt free trade; multilateral approaches are problematic because of the collective goods problem. It is not surprising that the international response has been fairly ineffective to date.

> **International Whaling Commission**
> An intergovernmental organization (IGO) that sets quotas for hunting certain whale species; states' participation is voluntary.

Forests and Oceans

Two types of habitat—tropical rain forests and oceans—are especially important to biodiversity *and* the atmosphere. Both are also reservoirs of commercially profitable resources such as fish and wood. They differ in that forests are located almost entirely within state territory, but oceans are largely beyond any state territory, in the global commons.

RAIN FORESTS   As many as half the world's total species live in *rain forests,* which replenish oxygen and reduce carbon dioxide in the atmosphere—slowing down global warming. Rain forests thus benefit all the world's states; they are collective goods.

International bargaining on the preservation of rain forests has made considerable progress, probably because most rain forests belong to only a few states. These few states have the power to speed up or slow down the destruction of forests—and international bargaining amounts to agreements to shift costs from those few states onto the broader group of states benefiting from the rain forests.

Although some rich states (including the United States) have large forests, most of the largest rain forests are in poor states such as Brazil, Indonesia, Malaysia, and Madagascar. Such states can benefit economically from exploiting the forests—freely cutting lumber, clearing land for agriculture, and mining. Until recently (and still to an extent), leaders of rich states have been most interested in encouraging maximum economic growth in poor states so that foreign debts could be paid—with little regard for environmental damage.

Now that rich states have an interest in protecting rain forests, they are using development assistance as leverage to induce poorer states to protect their forests rather than exploit them. In some developing countries burdened by large foreign debts, environmentalists and bankers from rich countries have worked out "debt-for-nature swaps" that cancel debts in exchange for a state's agreement to preserve forests. In 2006, for example, the U.S. government and NGOs helped Guatemala cancel more than $20 million in debts in exchange for expanded conservation programs. In 2014, Liberia and Peru agreed to end deforestation in exchange for a significant foreign aid pledge from Norway. In 2008, Brazil announced that it planned to end deforestation by 2015. Environmentalists thought the plan was overly optimistic and Brazil now says it hopes to slow deforestation by 2020.

OCEANS   The *oceans,* covering 70 percent of the earth's surface, are (like the rain forests) a key to regulating climate and preserving biodiversity. Oceans, like forests, are attractive targets for short-term economic uses that cause long-term environmental damage. Such uses include overfishing, dumping toxic and nuclear waste (and other garbage), and long-distance oil shipments with their recurrent spills. Unlike rain forests, oceans belong to no state but are a global commons. This makes the collective goods problem more difficult because no authority exists to enforce regulations. Preserving the oceans depends on the cooperation of more than 100 states and thousands of nonstate actors. Free riders have great opportunities to profit. For example, *drift nets* are huge fishing nets, miles long, that scoop up everything in their path. They are very profitable, but they are destructive of a sustainable ocean environment. Most states have now banned their use (under pressure from the environmental movement). However, no state has the authority to go onto the **high seas** (nonterritorial waters) and stop illegal use of these nets.

high seas The portion of the oceans considered common territory, not under any kind of exclusive state jurisdiction.

One solution that states have pursued involves "enclosing" more of the ocean. Territorial waters have expanded to hundreds of miles off the coast (and around islands), so that state sovereignty encloses substantial resources such as fisheries and offshore oil and mineral deposits. This solution has been pursued in the context of larger multilateral negotiations on ocean management.

The **UN Convention on the Law of the Sea (UNCLOS)**, negotiated from 1973 to 1982, governs the uses of the oceans. After more than a decade's delay and renegotiation of some of the deep-sea mining aspects, the United States signed UNCLOS in 1994 but has yet to ratify the treaty. The UNCLOS treaty established rules on territorial waters—12 miles for shipping and a 200-mile exclusive economic zone (EEZ) for economic activities, such as fishing and mining. The 200-mile limit placed a substantial share of the economically profitable ocean resources in the control of about a dozen states (see Figure 8.3).

Varying interpretations leave economic rights in dispute in a number of locations. In the South China Sea, China, the Philippines, Malaysia, Taiwan, Brunei, and Vietnam all claim small islands and reefs. The islands and reefs are near oil reserves that would be extremely valuable to the state granted the claim. In 2014, it was discovered through satellite photos that China had been building platforms that included military equipment on some of their claimed reefs.

UNCLOS also developed the general principle that the oceans are a common heritage of humankind. A mechanism was created, through an International Sea-Bed Authority, for sharing some of the wealth that rich states might gain from extracting minerals on the ocean floor (beyond 200 miles).

ANTARCTICA   Like the oceans, *Antarctica* belongs to no state. The continent's strategic and commercial values are limited, however, and not many states care about it. Historically, states have been successful in reaching agreements on Antarctica because the costs were low and the players few. The **Antarctic Treaty of 1959**—one of the first multilateral treaties concerning the environment—forbids military activity as well as the presence of nuclear weapons or the dumping of nuclear waste. It sets aside territorial claims on the continent for future resolution and establishes a regime under which various states conduct scientific research in Antarctica. The treaty was signed by all states with interests in the area, including both superpowers. By 1991, Greenpeace had persuaded the treaty signatories to turn the continent into a "world park." Antarctica is largely a success story in international environmental politics.

Pollution

Pollution generally creates a collective goods problem, but one that is not often global in scale. Pollution is more often a regional or bilateral issue. With some exceptions—such as dumping at sea—the effects of pollution are limited to the state where it occurs and its close neighbors; U.S. industrial smokestack emissions cause acid rain in Canada but do not directly affect distant states. China's terrible air pollution kills nearly half a million Chinese a year but few foreigners. Even when pollution crosses state borders, it often has its strongest effects closest to the source. This makes it a somewhat less intractable collective goods problem because a polluting state can seldom free-ride, and few actors are involved.

UN Convention on the Law of the Sea (UNCLOS) A world treaty (1982) governing use of the oceans. The UNCLOS treaty established rules on territorial waters and a 200-mile exclusive economic zone (EEZ).

Antarctic Treaty of 1959 One of the first multilateral environmental treaties. It forbids military activity, sets aside territorial claims for future resolution, and establishes a regime under which various states conduct scientific research in Antarctica.

Figure 8.3 State-Controlled Waters

Overfishing and similar problems of managing the "commons" of world oceans have been addressed by enclosing the most important ocean areas under the exclusive control of states. Shaded areas are within the 200-mile economic zones controlled by states under terms of the UNCLOS treaty.

Source: Based on Andrew Boyd, *An Atlas of World Affairs*, 9th ed. New York: Routledge, 1992.

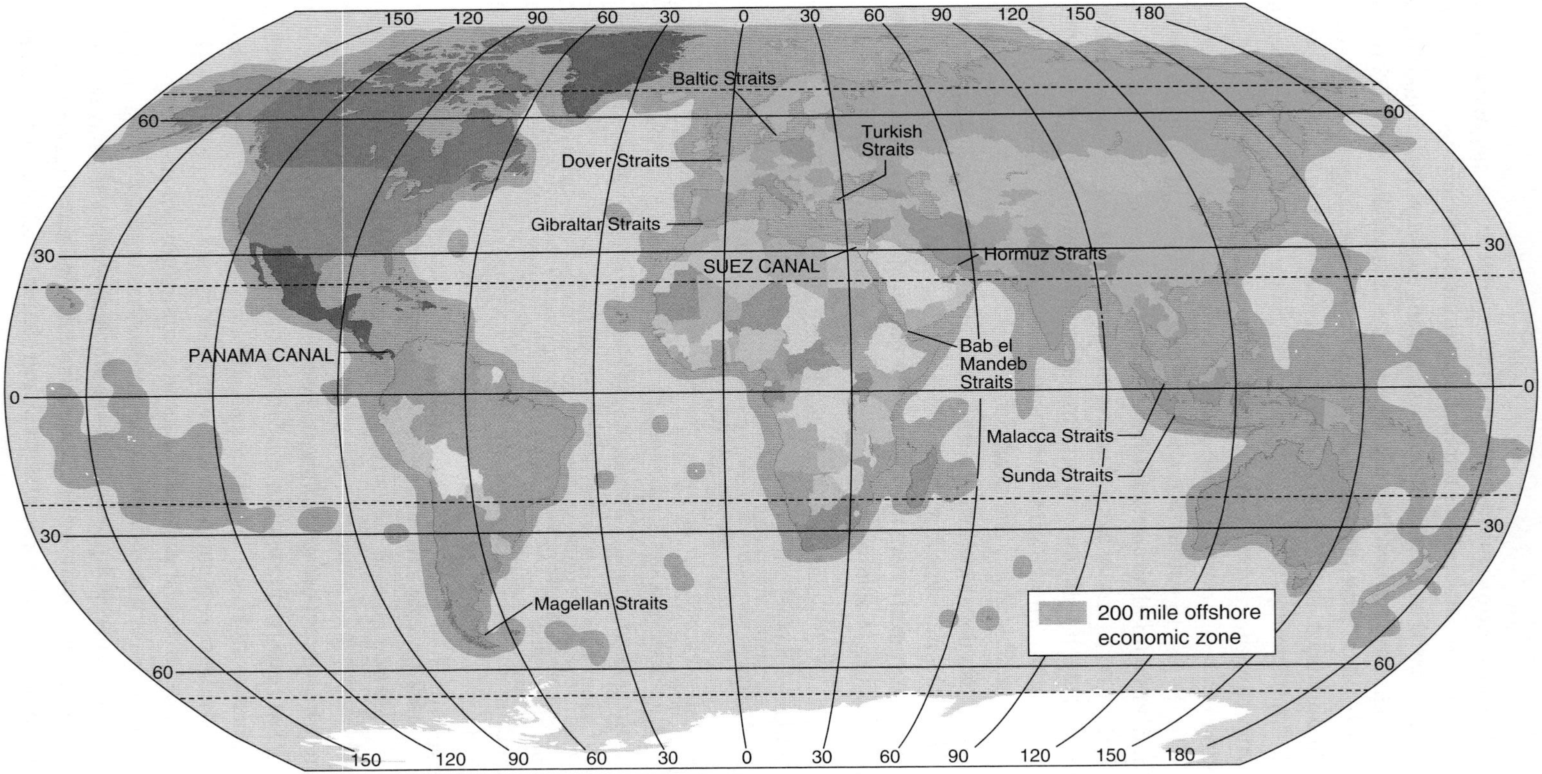

Policy Perspectives
Prime Minister of Ireland, Enda Kenny

PROBLEM *How do you balance environmental and economic concerns?*

BACKGROUND Imagine that you are the president of Ireland. Genetically modified organisms (GMOs) are highly controversial in Europe, and this certainly includes your country. In 1997, for example, Ireland reluctantly approved a permit for the global MNC Monsanto to grow sugar beets near Dublin. After several legal attempts to halt the planting of the crop failed, activists destroyed the crop in the ground before it could be harvested.

Your country has quietly supported several Irish biotechnology firms in the past with joint ventures in research. These have produced a variety of advances that give Ireland a significant advantage over other European states in this field. Several MNCs stand to benefit from this research, providing you with investment and tax income.

DOMESTIC CONSIDERATIONS Unfortunately, this "positive but precautionary" approach is unpopular with the public. Some worry that Ireland's reputation as "the Green Island" will suffer, which could pose a threat to tourism—a major source of income for your country. Others join the chorus of European opposition to

GMOs based on concerns over the possible environmental effects of these products. A recent Eurobarometer poll found that 54 percent of European consumers consider GMO foods "dangerous."

In the spring of 2004, the EU approved an end to the moratorium on GMO product sales (with your country voting in the majority), partially under a threat from the United States to enforce a World Trade Organization (WTO) ruling that found the GMO ban illegal. The United States is your largest single trade partner, but other EU states combined are your most significant export market. Despite the US threat, the European Parliament voted in 2015 to allow individual EU member states to ban the production of GMOs.

SCENARIO Imagine that, in light of the recent EU legislation, interest groups pressure your party to ban GMOs in Ireland. These groups threaten to support opposition parties in the next election should you refuse.

GMO crops could provide economic benefits to your country. Given your comparative technological advantage in this area, your economy stands to profit from expanding GMO use through increased agricultural output and increased business activity from MNCs. The United States has no regulations concerning the importation of GMO products and would be open to exports of these crops.

GMOs carry possible dangers as well. Some environmentalists warn that GMOs could have negative effects on ecology, wildlife, and human health. Many of your EU partners will shun your GMO products, robbing you of a large export market for these goods. Domestically, expanding the production of GMOs will be controversial.

CHOOSE YOUR POLICY Do you continue quietly to encourage the advance of GMO crops? Do you use the new EU legislation as a justification to ban the production of GMOs, due to interest group pressure to respect the long-term environmental concerns raised by these products? Do you work with MNCs to use your comparative advantage for economic gain? How do you balance economic prosperity with a concern for the environment?

In several regions—notably Western and Eastern Europe and the Middle East—states are closely packed in the same air, river, or sea basins. Here, pollution controls must often be negotiated multilaterally. In Europe during the Cold War, the international pollution problem was exacerbated by the inability of Western European states to impose any limits on Eastern ones, whose pollution was notorious.

acid rain Rain caused by air pollution that damages trees and often crosses borders. Limiting acid rain (via limiting nitrogen oxide emissions) has been the subject of several regional agreements.

Several regional agreements seek to limit **acid rain**, which is caused by air pollution. European states—whose forests have been heavily damaged—have agreed to limit air pollution and acid rain for their mutual benefit. In 1988, 24 European states signed a treaty to limit nitrogen oxide emissions to 1988 levels by 1995. After long negotiations, the United States and Canada signed bilateral agreements to limit such pollution as well. These regional agreements have worked fairly well.

Water pollution often crosses borders as well, especially because industrial pollution, human sewage, and agricultural fertilizers and pesticides all tend to run into rivers and seas. For instance, in 2005, a huge chemical spill in northeast China polluted a river that flows into Russia. Long-standing regional agencies that regulate shipping on heavily used European rivers now also deal with pollution. The Mediterranean basin is severely polluted and difficult to manage because so many states border it. In 2010, the largest accidental oil spill in U.S. history occurred in the Gulf of Mexico. The spill resulted from an explosion on an oil platform. The leakage took months to contain and highlighted the dangers associated with deep-water oil drilling. British Petroleum, the company that operated the well, agreed to set aside billions of dollars to pay damages to residents of several southern U.S. states affected by the spill.

Toxic and *nuclear wastes* are a special problem because of their long-term dangers. States occasionally try to ship such wastes out of the country. However, international agreements now ban the dumping of toxic and nuclear wastes at sea (an obvious collective goods problem). But such wastes have been sent to developing countries for disposal, for a fee. For instance, toxic ash from Pennsylvania became material for bricks in Guinea, and Italian nuclear waste was shipped to Nigeria.

Norms have developed in recent years against exporting toxic wastes—a practice seen as exploitive of the receiving country. In 1989, 100 states signed a treaty to regulate shipments of toxic and nuclear wastes and prevent their secret movements under corrupt deals. Forty more countries, in Africa, did not sign the treaty but called for a halt to toxic waste shipments to Africa. Nonetheless, in 2006, a multinational company tried to dispose of toxic waste from a tanker ship in the Netherlands but took it back on finding the cost to run into hundreds of thousands of dollars. Six weeks later, the ship unloaded the toxic sludge in Abidjan, Ivory Coast, where a local company dumped it at locations around the city. Thousands of residents got sick and eight people died. In 2007, the company agreed to pay $200 million to settle claims.

In 1986, a meltdown at the Soviet nuclear power plant at Chernobyl, in Ukraine, created airborne radioactivity that spread over much of Europe, from

Italy to Sweden. The accident exemplified the new reality—that economic and technical decisions made in one state can have grave environmental consequences for other countries. Soviet leaders made matters worse by failing to notify neighbors promptly of the accident.

On the various issues of water and air pollution, both unilateral state actions and international agreements have often been feasible and effective. In recent decades, river water quality has improved in most industrialized regions. Market economies have begun to deal with pollution as just another cost of production that should be charged to the polluter instead of to society at large. Some governments have begun to allocate "pollution rights" that companies can buy and sell on a free market.

In the former Soviet bloc, decades of centrally planned industrialization created severe environmental problems. With staggering environmental damage and human health effects, the economically strapped former Soviet republics had to bargain over limiting pollution and repairing the damage. For example, the severely polluted Aral Sea, formerly contained within one state, the Soviet Union, is now shared by two, Kazakhstan and Uzbekistan. Once the world's fourth-largest inland sea, it shrank in half, its huge fisheries destroyed, after a Soviet-era mega-irrigation project diverted the Aral Sea's inlet rivers and polluted them with pesticides. Former fishing towns found themselves many miles from the shoreline. Local and international political leaders failed to implement plans to address the problem, and thus local populations suffered from the widespread health effects of the disaster.

Natural Resources

8.3   Describe three ways in which the need for natural resources can create international conflict.

The natural environment is not only a delicate ecosystem requiring protection but also a repository of natural resources. The extraction of resources brings states wealth (and hence power), so these resources regularly fuel international conflicts. Because they are mostly located within individual states, however, they do not present a collective goods problem. Rather, states bargain over these vital resources.

Three aspects of natural resources shape their role in international conflict. First, they are required for the operation of an industrial economy (sometimes even an agrarian one). Second, their sources—mineral deposits, rivers, and so forth—are associated with particular territories over which states may fight for control. Third, natural resources tend to be unevenly distributed, with plentiful supplies in some states and an absence in others. These aspects mean that trade in natural resources is extremely profitable; much additional wealth is created by such trade. They also mean that trade in resources is fairly politicized—creating market imperfections such as monopoly, oligopoly, and price manipulation, sometimes by cartels (see pp. 190–191).

World Energy

Of the various natural resources required by states, energy resources are central. The commercial fuels that power the world's industrial economies are oil (about 40 percent of world energy consumption), coal (30 percent), natural gas (25 percent), and hydroelectric and nuclear power (5 percent). The fossil fuels (coal, oil, gas) thus account for 95 percent of world energy consumption. Some energy consumed as electricity comes from hydroelectric dams or nuclear power plants, but most of it comes from burning fossil fuels in electric-generating plants.

Table 8.1 shows energy consumption per person in the nine world regions. The four industrialized regions of the North use much more energy per person than those of the South. North America uses 15 times as much per person as South Asia or Africa. Among industrialized countries, there are differences in the *efficiency* of energy use—gross domestic product (GDP) produced per unit of energy consumed. The least efficient are the former Soviet Republics; North America is also rather inefficient; Europe and Japan are the most energy efficient.

Table 8.1 Per Capita Energy Consumption and Net Energy Trade, 2011

	Per Capita Consumption (million BTU)	Total Net Energy Exports[a] (quadrillion BTU)
North America	285	−4
Europe	135	−37
Japan/Pacific	180	−22
Russia/CIS	155	+28
China	80	−4
Middle East	140	+45
Latin America	60	+3
South Asia	18	−4
Africa	16	+18
World as a whole	75	

[a]Net exports refers to production minus consumption. Net exports worldwide do not equal net imports for technical reasons.
Source: Calculated from data in U.S. Department of Energy. Energy Information Administration. See http://www.eia.doe.gov/iea/.

International trade in energy plays a vital role in the world economy. As Table 8.1 shows, the regions of the industrialized West are all large net importers of energy. The Middle East, Africa, and Russia are exporters of energy. Although all forms of energy are traded internationally, the most important by far is oil, the cheapest to transport over long distances. Russia receives vital hard-currency earnings from exporting oil. Venezuela and Mexico (in Latin America) and Nigeria and Angola (in Africa) are also major oil exporters. But the largest source of oil exports is the Middle East—especially the countries around the Persian Gulf (Saudi Arabia, Kuwait, Iraq, Iran, and the small sheikdoms of United Arab Emirates, Qatar, Bahrain, and Oman). Saudi Arabia is the largest oil exporter and holds the largest oil reserves. Thus, the politics of world energy revolve around Middle Eastern oil shipped to Western Europe, China, Japan, and North America.

The importance of oil in the industrialized economies helps explain the political importance of the Middle East in world politics. Not only is energy a crucial economic sector (on which all industrial activity depends), but it is also one of the most politically sensitive because of the dependence of the West on energy imported from the Middle East and the rest of the global South.

To secure a supply of oil in the Middle East, Britain and other European countries colonized the area early in the twentieth century, carving up territory into protectorates in which European power kept local monarchs on their thrones. The United States did not claim colonies or protectorates, but U.S. MNCs were heavily involved in the development of oil resources in the area from the 1920s through the 1960s—often wielding vast power. These U.S. and European oil companies kept the price paid to local states low and their own profits high, yet local rulers depended on the expertise and capital investment of these companies.

After World War II the British gave up colonial claims in the Middle East, but the Western oil companies kept producing cheap oil there for Western consumption. Then in 1973, during an Arab-Israeli war, the oil-producing Arab states of the region decided to punish the United States for supporting Israel. They cut off their oil exports to the United States and curtailed their overall exports. This sent world oil prices skyrocketing. The Organization of Petroleum Exporting Countries (OPEC) realized its potential power and the high price the world was willing to pay for oil. This 1973 *oil shock* had a profound effect on the world economy and on world politics. Huge amounts of hard currency accumulated in the treasuries of the Middle East oil-exporting countries, which in turn invested them around the world (these were called *petrodollars*). High inflation plagued the United States and Europe for years afterward. The economic instability and sense of U.S. helplessness—coming on top of the Vietnam War—seemed to mark a decline in American power and perhaps the rise of the global South.

In 1979, the revolution in Iran led to a second oil shock. But higher oil prices led to the expansion of oil production in new locations outside OPEC—in the North Sea (Britain and Norway), Alaska, Angola, Russia, and elsewhere. By the mid-1980s, the Middle East was rapidly losing its market share of world trade in oil. At the same time, industrialized economies learned to be more *energy efficient*. With supply up and demand down, oil prices dropped in the late 1980s to historic lows of less than $20 a barrel. A similar cycle saw oil prices climb to $140 a barrel and then collapse with the global economic recession in 2008.

In the late 1990s, the Caspian Sea region beckoned as a new and largely untapped oil source (see Figure 8.4). However, the oil must travel overland by

Figure 8.4 Dividing the Caspian Sea

The Caspian Sea is the world's largest inland body of water. It could be defined under international law as either a lake or a sea.[a] A *lake* has a joint area in the middle (in green on the left panel) that can be exploited only if the countries agree on terms. There are also coastal zones under each country's sole control. In a *sea* less than 400 miles across, the bordering countries' 200-mile Exclusive Economic Zones (EEZs) split up the whole sea (right panel). If the whole area is split as in the map on the right, the sectors can be defined by median lines (dashed line) or by a division into five sectors of equal area (dotted line), giving Iran a larger sector. In 2010, with major oil development underway in all five countries' coastal areas, a summit meeting agreed to give each a 25-mile zone, but most of the border issues remain in dispute. Russia had agreed with its neighbors, Azerbaijan and Kazakhstan, to use the median line on the seabed floor. Iran still wants one-fifth of the lake. In 2012, a naval arms race was underway, and Russia held joint military exercises with Kazakhstan to practice defense of oil facilities from an Iranian attack. But this conflict will be resolved not through dominance, but through reciprocity. Nobody benefits from a war and all five countries benefit from developing their oil resources. Solutions are enormously complicated—in this case factoring in additional elements like shipping, fishing, smuggling, and pipeline routes—and reaching agreement can take a very long time.

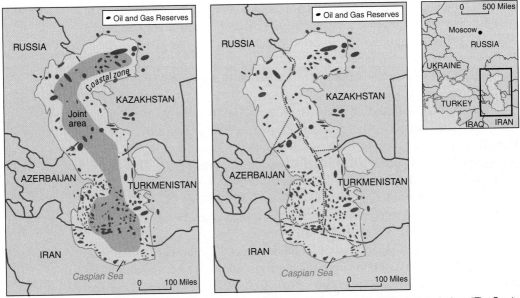

[a]Sciolino, Elaine. "It's a Sea! It's a Lake! No. It's a Pool of Oil!" *The New York Times*, June 21, 1998. Kucera, Joshua. "The Great Caspian Arms Race." *Foreign Policy*, June 22, 2012.

pipeline to reach world markets (the Caspian is an inland sea). But the main pipeline from oil-producing Azerbaijan to the Black Sea (where tanker ships can load) traveled through war-torn Chechnya in southern Russia. The pipeline reopened in 1997, but in 2000, it still carried only a fraction of its capacity. Russia meanwhile built a bypass route around Chechnya that carries a large and growing amount of Caspian oil for export through the Black Sea. Western powers sought other pipeline routes that did not cross Russia, while Turkey sought to control a larger market share and reduce environmental damage to the Bosporus waterway (through which Russian tankers must travel). After long negotiations, states and oil companies agreed to build, in 2002–2004, a large-capacity pipeline, costing billions of dollars, through Azerbaijan and Georgia to Turkey's Mediterranean coast.

Violent conflicts make pipeline routes particularly complex. All three countries on the new pipeline route have recently been at war. Meanwhile in 2003, a new $4 billion pipeline began carrying oil from Chad through Cameroon for export, promising to help both countries alleviate poverty, but as rebels based in Sudan attacked in Chad, oil money was diverted to military purposes. Although borders and geopolitics may be less and less important in communications and business, they still matter greatly in international economic transactions such as oil pipelines.

Minerals

To build the infrastructure and other manufactured goods that create wealth in a national economy, states need other raw materials in addition to energy. These include metals, other minerals, and related materials extracted through mining. The political economy of minerals—iron, copper, platinum, and so forth—differs from that of world energy. The value of international trade in oil is many times that of any mineral. Mineral supply is not so concentrated in one region of the world. Industrialized countries have also reduced their vulnerability by stockpiling strategic minerals.

Most important to industrialized economies are the minerals used for industrial equipment. Traditionally most important is iron, used to make steel. The leading producers of steel are the former Soviet Union, Japan, the United States, China, and Germany, followed by Brazil, Italy, South Korea, France, and Britain. Thus, major industrialized countries produce their own steel (Germany and Japan are the leading exporters worldwide). To preserve self-sufficiency in steel production, the United States and others have used trade policies to protect domestic steel industries (such as the U.S. steel tariffs; see p. 194).

For other important industrial minerals such as copper, nickel, and zinc, the pattern of supply and trade is more diffuse than it is for oil, and the industrialized countries are largely self-sufficient. Even when states in the global South are the main suppliers, they have not gained the power of OPEC. There is a producer cartel in some cases (copper), a producer-consumer cartel in some (tin), and separate producer and consumer cartels in others (bauxite). China currently holds a near-monopoly on the world's supply of rare earth minerals vital (in small amounts) to the production of electronics. China has cut exports at times to boost these minerals' price. Yet in the last five years, countries such as Vietnam have begun to produce some of these elements to challenge China's grip on the market.

Certain agricultural products have spawned producer cartels such as the Union of Banana Exporting Countries (UBEC) and the African Groundnut Council. Like minerals, some export crops come mainly from just a few countries.

These include sugar (Cuba), cocoa (Ivory Coast, Ghana, Nigeria), tea (India, Sri Lanka, China), and coffee (Brazil, Colombia). Despite the concentrations, producer cartels have not been very successful in boosting prices of these products, which are less essential than energy.

Water Disputes

In addition to energy and minerals, states need water. This need increases as a society industrializes, as it intensifies agriculture, and as its population grows. World water use is 35 times that of just a few centuries ago, and grew twice as fast as population in the twentieth century. Yet water supplies are relatively unchanging and are becoming depleted in many places. One-fifth of the world's population lacks safe drinking water, and 80 countries suffer water shortages. Water supplies—rivers and water tables—often cross international boundaries; thus access to water is increasingly a source of international conflict. Sometimes—as when several states share access to a single water table—these conflicts are collective goods problems.

Water problems are especially important in the Middle East. For instance, the Euphrates River runs from Turkey through Syria to Iraq before reaching the Persian Gulf. Iraq objects to Syrian diversion of water from the river, and both Iraq and Syria object to Turkey's diversion.

The Jordan River originates in Syria and Lebanon and runs through Israel to Jordan. In the 1950s, Israel began building a canal to take water from the Jordan River to "make the desert bloom." Jordan and its Arab neighbors complained to the UN Security Council, but it failed in efforts to mediate the dispute, and each state went ahead with its own water plans (with Israel and Jordan agreeing, however, to stay within UN-proposed allocations). In 1964, Syria and Lebanon tried to build dams and divert water before it reached Israel, rendering Israel's new water system worthless. Israeli air and artillery attacks on the construction site forced Syria to abandon its diversion project, and Israel's 1967 capture of the Golan Heights precluded Syria from renewing such efforts. Thus, the dominance principle comes into play in resolving conflicts over natural resources.

Of course, these resources can also be related directly to international security. IR scholars have expanded their studies of environmental politics to study systematically the relationship of military and security affairs with the environment. One side of this relationship is the role of the environment as a source of international conflict. We have seen how environmental degradation can lead to collective goods problems among large numbers of states, and how competition for territory and resources can create conflicts among smaller groups of states. During the 1991 Gulf War, for example, Iraqi forces spilled large amounts of Kuwaiti oil into the Persian Gulf and then, before retreating from Kuwait, blew up hundreds of Kuwaiti oil wells, leaving them burning uncontrollably and covering Iraq and Iran with thick black smoke.

Population

8.4 Explain the demographic transition and why some states are vulnerable to rapid population growth.

World population, 7 billion in 2016, is growing by 80 million each year. Forecasting future population is easy in some respects. Barring a nuclear war or an environmental catastrophe, today's children will grow up and have children of their own. For the coming 20 to 30 years, world population growth will be driven, rather mechanistically, by the large number of children in today's populations in the global South. The projected world population in 2030 will be 8–9 billion people, and there is little anyone can do to change that projection. Of the increase in population in that period, 96 percent will be in the global South. Currently, half the world's population growth occurs in just six countries: India, China, Pakistan, Nigeria, Bangladesh, and Indonesia. Among the world's poorest countries, population is expected to triple in the next 50 years, whereas many rich countries' populations will shrink in that period.

Projections beyond a few decades have a range of uncertainty (see Figure 8.5). New data in 2002 showed that higher women's status and literacy are reducing population growth more than expected in large, poor countries. The actions of states and IOs *now* will determine the earth's population in 200 years. Two hundred years ago, the British writer Thomas Malthus warned that population tends to increase faster than food supply, and he predicted that population growth would limit itself through famine and disease. Critics point out that technology has kept pace with population in the past, allowing more food and other resources to be extracted from the environment even as population keeps growing.

Figure 8.5 World Population Trends and Projections

Source: UN Population Office.

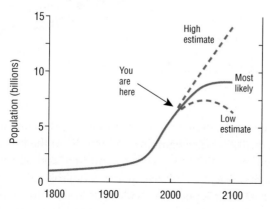

The Demographic Transition

Population growth results from a difference between rates of birth (per 1,000 people) and rates of death. In agrarian (preindustrial) societies, both birthrates and death rates are high. Population growth is thus slow—even negative at times when death rates exceed birthrates (during a famine, for instance).

demographic transition The pattern of falling death rates, followed by falling birthrates, that generally accompanies industrialization and economic development.

The process of economic development—of industrialization and the accumulation of wealth on a per capita basis—brings about a change in birthrates and death rates that follows a fairly universal pattern called the **demographic transition** (see Figure 8.6). First, death rates fall as food supplies increase and access to health care expands. Later, birthrates fall as people become educated, more secure, and more urbanized, and as the status of women rises. At the end of the transition, as at the beginning, birthrates and death rates are fairly close to each other, and population growth is limited. But during the transition, when death rates have fallen more than birthrates, population grows rapidly. One reason poor people tend to have many children is that under harsh poverty, a child's survival is not assured. Disease, malnutrition, or violence may claim the lives of many children, leaving parents with no one to look after them in their old age. Having many children helps to ensure that some survive.

Figure 8.6 The Demographic Transition

As income rises, first death rates and then birthrates fall. The gap between the two is the population growth rate. Early in the transition, the population contains a large proportion of children; later it contains a large proportion of elderly people.

Source: United Nations.

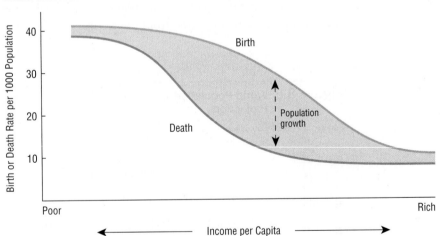

As a state makes the demographic transition, the structure of its population changes dramatically. At the beginning and middle of the process, most of the population is young. Families have many children, and adults do not have a long life expectancy. Because children are not very productive economically, the large number of children in poor countries tends to slow down the accumulation of wealth. But by the end of the demographic transition, adults live longer and families have fewer children, so the average age of the population is much older. Eventually a substantial section of the population is elderly—a different nonproductive population that the economy must support.

The industrialized countries have completed the demographic transition and now have slow population growth. Russia, Europe, and Japan have shrinking populations. Most developing countries are in the middle of the transition and have rapid population growth.

The dilemma of the demographic transition is this: Rapid population growth and a child-heavy population are powerful forces lowering per capita income. Yet the best way to slow population growth is to raise per capita income. Population growth thus contributes to a vicious cycle in many poor states. Where population rises at the same rate as overall wealth, the average person is no better off over time. Even when the economy grows faster than population, so that the *average* income rises, the total *number* of poor people may increase.

The demographic transition tends to widen international disparities of wealth. States that manage to raise incomes a bit enter an upward spiral—as population growth slows, income levels per capita rise more, which further slows population growth, and so forth. Meanwhile, states that do not raise incomes have unabated population growth; per capita incomes stay low, which fuels more population growth—a downward spiral.

Globally, this disparity contributes to the gap in wealth between the North and South (see Chapter 7). Within the South, disparities are also sharpened as a few countries manage to slow population growth and raise incomes while others fail to do so. Even within a single country, the demographic transition sharpens disparities. Cities, richer classes, richer ethnic groups, and richer provinces tend to have low birthrates compared to the countryside and the poorer classes, ethnic groups, and provinces. In countries such as France, Israel, and the United States, wealthier ethnic groups have much slower population growth than poorer ethnic groups.

Recent trends suggest that the global South is splitting into two groups of states. Around 1970, nearly 50 states including China and India entered the phase of the demographic transition marked by falling birthrates. But in nearly 70 other poor states, death rates were still falling faster than birthrates, leading to accelerating population growth. These population trends contributed to disparities within the global South that emerged in the 1990s, notably between Africa and Asia.

Population Policies

The policies that governments adopt—not just economic and demographic conditions—influence the birthrate. Among the most important policies are those regarding birth control (contraception). State policies vary widely.

At one extreme, China uses its strong government control to try to enforce a limit of one child per couple for many years. Penalties for having a second child included being charged for services that were free for the first child. China initially started to encourage wealthy and more educated families to have two children.

For example, in Shanghai, couples were allowed two-child families. In late 2015, China announced it was ending its one child policy and allowing all citizens to have two children. Beyond two children, the penalties escalate. Contraceptives and abortions are free. China's policy has lowered growth rates considerably in the cities but less so in the countryside, where most people still live. Still, in a single decade (the 1970s), China's fertility rate fell from 6 children per woman to about 2.5, a dramatic change. By 2015, the fertility rate was 1.6.

But the Chinese policy has drawbacks. It limits individual freedom in favor of government control. Forced or coerced abortions have been reported. In traditional Chinese society, sons are valued more than daughters. Couples who have a daughter may keep trying until they have a son. In recent years, parents in China (and some places in India) are using ultrasound scans to determine their fetus's gender and abort it if it is female. China's 2000 census showed a sex difference that amounts to a million "missing" girls per year. Many hoped the relaxation of the one child policy in 2015 will bring these gender ratios back to normal.

India's policies are less extreme but have been slower to reduce the birthrate, which fell from nearly 6 per woman in 1970 to 2.5 in 2015. India's government, strongly committed to birth control, has tried to make information and means widely available, but as a democracy it does not have China's extreme government control over society. Like China, India and several other countries have widespread sex-selective abortion and imbalanced sex ratios.

At the other extreme from China are governments that encourage or force childbearing and outlaw or limit access to contraception. Such a policy is called **pronatalist** (pro-birth). Traditionally, many governments have adopted such policies because population was seen as an element of national power. More babies today meant more soldiers later. Today, only a few governments have strongly pronatalist policies, but many do not make birth control or sex education available to poor women. In some such states, population is not considered a problem (and may even be seen as an asset); in other states, the government simply cannot afford effective measures to lower birthrates. According to the United Nations Population Fund (UNFPA), 200 million women do not have access to effective contraception.

Birthrates are heavily influenced by the status of women in society. In cultures that traditionally see women as valuable only in producing babies, great pressures exist against women who stop doing so. Many women do not use birth control because their husbands will not allow them to. These husbands may think that having many children is proof of their manliness. However, as women's status improves and they can work in various occupations, own property, and vote, women gain the power as well as the education and money necessary to limit the size of their families.

According to UNFPA, improving the status of women is one of the most important means of controlling world population growth. Government policies about women's status vary from one state to another. International programs and agencies, such as the UN commission on the status of women, are working to address this issue on a global scale.

pronatalist A government policy that encourages or forces childbearing, and outlaws or limits access to contraception.

Disease

Population growth is determined by the death rate as well as the birthrate. People die from many different causes at different ages. In poor countries, people tend to die younger, often from infectious diseases; in richer countries, people live longer and die more often from cancer and heart disease. The proportion of babies who die within their first year is the **infant mortality rate**. It reflects a population's access to nutrition, water, shelter, and health care. Infant mortality is 4 percent worldwide: 1 percent or less in rich countries but more than 10 percent in the poorest countries and even higher in local pockets of extreme poverty (especially in Africa and in recent war zones).

infant mortality rate
The proportion of babies who die within their first year of life.

Although death rates vary greatly from one state or region to another, the overall trends are stable from decade to decade. Wars, droughts, epidemics, and disasters have an effect locally but hardly matter globally. In the poorest countries, which are just beginning the demographic transition, the death rate declined from nearly 30 deaths per thousand people in 1950 to less than 15 since 1990. In the industrialized countries, the death rate bottomed out around 10 per thousand by 1960 (now around 7). These stable trends in mortality mean that the death rate is not a means by which governments or international agencies can affect population growth—worsening poverty may cause famine and a rising death rate, but this is not a realistic way to control population growth. It would mean moving backward through the demographic transition, which would wreck any chance of lowering birthrates. Nor do wars kill enough people to reduce population growth. In short, most of the world is already at or near the end of the transition in *death* rates; the key question is how long birthrates take to complete the transition.

However, three mortality factors—AIDS, other infectious diseases, and smoking—deserve special attention because they exact very high costs even if they do not much affect global population trends. In these cases, actions taken in the short term have long-term and often international consequences, and once again there are short-term costs and long-term benefits.

HIV/AIDS In the worldwide HIV/AIDS epidemic, one state's success or failure in limiting the spread of HIV (human immunodeficiency virus) affects infections in other states as well. There is a delay of five to ten years after infection by the virus before symptoms appear, and during this period an infected individual can infect others (through sex or blood). AIDS spreads internationally—through business, tourism, migration, and military operations—reflecting the interdependence of states.

By 2014, the HIV/AIDS epidemic had already killed more than 30 million people, and an estimated 35 million more were infected—though most of them did not know it. Two-thirds of them live in Africa and half of the rest in South Asia (see Table 8.2). The epidemic has also left 16 million orphans (over 75 percent in Africa). Each year, about 2.3 million people are newly infected with HIV, and 1.6 million die from AIDS, including almost 200,000 children.

In Africa, already the world's poorest region, AIDS has emerged as one of several powerful forces driving the region backward into deeper poverty. About 5 percent of adults are infected with HIV, more than half of them women. In the

Table 8.2 Population and AIDS by World Region, 2013

Region[a]	Population (millions)	Population Growth Rate 1991–2008	HIV Infections (millions)
World	7,100	1.3%	35
Global North	1,400	0.3	4
Global South	5,400	1.6	29
of which:			
China	1,380	1.0	1
Middle East	450	2.0	0.2
Latin America	610	1.3	2
South Asia	2,150	1.8	4
Africa (sub-Saharan)	930	2.7	25

[a]Regions do not exactly match those used elsewhere in this book.

Source: Calculated from World Development Indicators. World Bank, 2014. UNAIDS Report on the Global AIDS Epidemic. UNAIDS, Progress Report on the Global Plan, UNAIDS.

most affected African countries in southern Africa, one in six adults has HIV (one in four for Botswana, the worst case). Infection is also rampant in African armies, with direct implications for international security.

In North America and other industrialized regions, new drug therapies (which keep the virus in check for years) dramatically lowered the death rate from AIDS starting in the late 1990s. But these treatments were too expensive to help much in Africa and other poor regions. India and Brazil began to export cheap generic versions of these drugs, violating patent rights of Western drug companies. The U.S. government threatened to punish South Africa and other countries if they allowed import of these drugs without compensating U.S. corporations holding patents. It filed a complaint against Brazil with the WTO. In response, AIDS activists demonstrated loudly and mobilized public opinion to get the policies changed.

The United States withdrew its complaint against Brazil in 2001. Meanwhile, drug companies began offering lower prices to poor countries, but delivery of the drugs to millions of poor people remained painfully slow. In 2004, the international community finally initiated the large-scale delivery of antiviral drugs to AIDS patients in poor countries. Now, tremendous progress has been made in delivering these drugs. In the past eight years, the number of people receiving treatment has increased dramatically, with UNAIDS now estimating that nearly 10 million people have access to these drugs. Meanwhile, since 2003, the United States has provided nearly $20 billion to combat AIDS and pledged $48 billion to combat AIDS, tuberculosis, and malaria in 2009–2014.

In some ways, AIDS has deepened the global North-South division. The 2001 UN session also revealed sharp differences between Western, secular states and a number of Islamic states that objected to any reference to gay people. Catholic authorities, furthermore, objected to programs that encourage condom use. But the most effective prevention measures are public education and the distribution of condoms (especially to prostitutes) and clean needles to drug users. All of these are culturally and politically sensitive issues.

States must cooperate with each other if they are to bring the epidemic under control. These international efforts are coordinated primarily by the World Health Organization (WHO) and funded mainly by the industrialized countries. But the entire WHO budget is equivalent to that of a midsize hospital in the global North. WHO depends on national governments to provide information and carry out policies, and governments have been slow to respond. Some governments falsify statistics to underreport the number of cases (lest tourists be driven away), and many governments do not want to condone or sponsor sex education and distribution of condoms because of religious or cultural taboos.

In recent years, HIV has spread rapidly in South Asia, China, Russia, and Eastern Europe, where prostitution and drug use are growing. In China, the government has been slow to act, and a stigma still prevents effective identification or treatment of the rapidly growing HIV-positive population. China had an estimated 1 million infected people in 2014, although these numbers are hard to confirm.

AIDS illustrates the transnational linkages that make international borders less meaningful than in the past. Effective international cooperation could save millions of lives and significantly enhance the prospects for economic development in the poorest countries in the coming decades. But once again, a collective goods problem exists regarding the allocation of costs and benefits. A dollar spent by WHO has the same effect regardless of which country contributed it.

OTHER INFECTIOUS DISEASES   AIDS is not the only concern. Tuberculosis (TB), malaria, hepatitis, dengue fever, and cholera have all reemerged or spread in recent decades, often mutating into drug-resistant forms. TB now kills nearly 1.5 million people per year (in addition to AIDS patients, who also contract TB). Malaria sickens hundreds of millions of people and kills more than 1 million per year, nearly all in Africa. New campaigns have distributed millions of mosquito nets in Africa to reduce malaria—a proven, cost-effective measure. A new vaccine that was approved for widespread use in 2015 could cut malaria cases in half. Vaccination programs have reduced the incidence of both polio and measles in recent years. Measles deaths are down by 80 percent since 2000. But a polio vaccination drive in Pakistan was cut short in 2012 after Taliban militants killed health workers, claiming the vaccine was a Western plot to sterilize Muslim children. Epidemics among animals have major economic effects as well.

In 2014, the world dealt with a significant disease crisis in West Africa. The Ebola virus became widespread in Guinea, Liberia, and Sierra Leone. It is estimated that nearly 10,000 people died as a result of the disease. Concern spread throughout the world as cases began appearing outside Africa, including the United States and Spain. Countries adopted travel restrictions and quarantine policies for those suspected of having the virus. Billions of dollars of aid was provided to these West African states to stop the virus and improve health care for its victims. It was yet another example of how, in the interconnected and

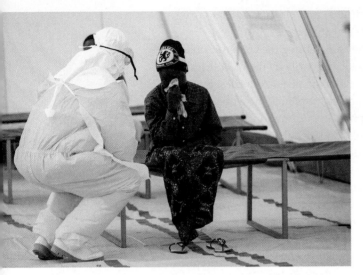

PANDEMIC PREVENTION In 2014, Ebola spread quickly in parts of western Africa. Many states, international organizations, and nongovernmental organizations responded to the epidemic by providing medical assistance. Several states also implemented quarantines for those suspected of coming in contact with the disease. The epidemic was mostly contained within West Africa with a handful of cases spreading to the United States and Europe. Here, a health worker admits a suspected Ebola patient to a temporary clinic in Sierra Leone, 2014.

globalized world, diseases may spread quickly over wide areas, even across oceans.

SMOKING Worldwide, more than 1 billion people smoke, five-sixths of them in developing countries, and more than 5 million people a year die from tobacco-related disease. States that fail to curb the spread of nicotine addiction face high future costs in health care—costs that are just beginning to come due in many poor countries. The costs are largely limited to the state itself; its own citizens and economy pay the price. Nonetheless, the tobacco trade makes smoking an international issue. Tobacco companies' recent marketing campaigns targeting women in the global South could produce a huge increase in smokers in that group, according to the World Health Organization.

In 2001, tobacco companies, with some U.S. support, sought to weaken a new proposed treaty, the Framework Convention on Tobacco Control, but in 2003, the United States dropped its objections and WHO member states adopted the treaty. Member states agreed to ban tobacco advertising and raise taxes on tobacco 5 percent a year above the inflation rate. The United States, alone among the world's major powers, still had not ratified the treaty in 2015.

In managing the daunting environmental and disease threats discussed in this chapter, states and NGOs have begun to use new technologies productively. Information technologies, especially, allow scientists to confirm global warming, NGOs to mobilize public opinion, and MNCs to produce more fuel-efficient cars. This information revolution also has far-reaching consequences for world politics far beyond issues of environmental management. The remainder of this chapter discusses these profound, yet still ambiguous, consequences.

The Power of Information

8.5 Explain two ways in which information can be a tool used by governments and two ways in which information can be a tool used against governments.

Global telecommunications are profoundly changing how information and culture function in international relations (IR). These technological advances, at the center of globalization, are bringing the identity principle to the fore as communities interact across distances and borders. Newly empowered individuals and groups are creating new transnational networks worldwide, bypassing states.

Connecting the World

New international political possibilities are based on technological developments. The media over which information travels—telephones, television, films, magazines, and so forth—shape the way ideas take form and spread from one place to another. The media with the strongest political impact are television, radio, phones, and the Internet.

TV AND RADIO   There are nearly 2 billion TV sets and 3 billion radio receivers in the world. Radio, and increasingly TV, reaches the poorest rural areas of the global South. Peasants who cannot read can understand radio.

Ordinary over-the-air TV and radio signals are radio waves of specific frequencies, which are a limited resource in high demand, regulated by governments. Because radio waves do not respect national borders, the allocation of frequencies is a subject of interstate bargaining. International regimes have grown up around the regulation of communications technologies, centered on the International Telecommunications Union (ITU).

Satellite TV bypasses states' control and fortifies transnational or supranational identity politics by allowing, for example, all Arabs in the world to see Arab satellite TV coverage of the Palestinian issue. The Qatar-based al Jazeera, begun in 1996, is a force in Middle Eastern politics and reaches an influential audience worldwide. In a 2006 poll in six Arab countries, citizens listed al Jazeera as their main source of international news by a large margin over any other satellite TV network. In 2013, al Jazeera bought Al Gore's channel, Current, in a bid to expand its U.S. audience.

TELEPHONE AND THE INTERNET   Even more empowering of ordinary citizens are telephones and the Internet. These are two-way media through which users interact without a centralized information source. In 2014, the world had nearly 7 billion cell phone subscriptions, almost as many as people and far outnumbering the 1.1 billion landlines. More than 2 billion, including 100 percent of the population in Korea and Singapore, had mobile broadband Internet capability. India has more than tripled its number of cell phone subscribers since 2007, while China had more than 1 billion cell phone subscribers as of 2014. The explosion of international phone traffic worldwide and of home and mobile access to the Internet is a clear indicator of globalization (see Figure 8.7).

One of the most politically important features of these technologies turned out to be the cell phone camera. It has empowered ordinary citizens to create visual records, such as videos of political demonstrations in one country that end up on TV in another country. In the 2011–2012 Arab Spring revolutions, especially in Syria, cell phone videos played a critical role in winning support by showing governments brutally murdering citizens. A related technological

Figure 8.7 World Phone and Internet Use, 1995–2014

Source: International Telecommunication Union (ITU) data.

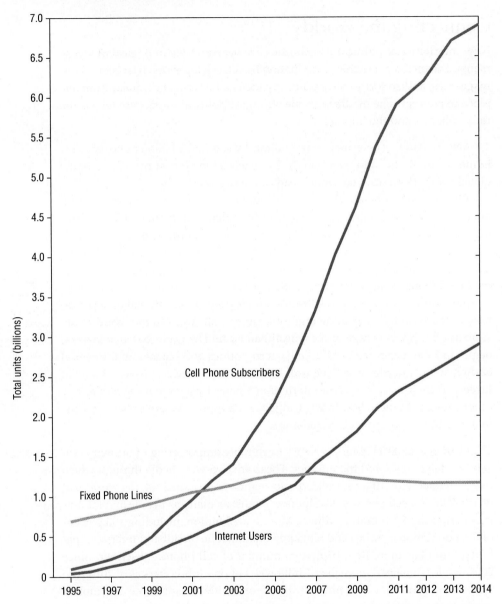

development of paramount political importance is the growth of social media such as Facebook, which helps to build communities and allow sharing of ideas (including those cell phone videos) outside government control and sometimes across international borders.

In Africa, cheap cell phones with cheap prepaid calling cards have let millions of relatively poor individuals communicate. In about a decade, sub-Saharan Africa saw subscribers increase to nearly 600 million by 2014. These phones empower individuals, for example, by letting farmers check market prices before deciding when to harvest crops. In one notable African success, Kenya has become the world's leader in using cell phones for banking. The country has 10 million banking transactions daily (averaging $20), but half the population lacks a bank account, so entrepreneurs developed the M-Pesa mobile payment system. City dwellers can transfer money to their home villages by phone instead of taking a wad of cash for a long bus ride. By 2014, these mobile fund transfers by 17 million users (about two-thirds of the population) made up a quarter of Kenya's GDP.

Deep political divisions over the Internet came into focus in December 2012, at a conference of the ITU in Dubai to develop a new treaty on the Internet and global telecommunications. Russia, China, and others saw the Internet as a system of government-controlled networks, while the United States and others, including Google and various NGOs, saw it as a more amorphous entity to facilitate the free flow of information. The U.S. House of Representatives, in a rare moment of bipartisanship, unanimously opposed the new treaty. In the end, 89 countries supported it but 55 others would not sign.

THE DIGITAL DIVIDE   Taken on its own, the addition of phone and Internet capability in poor countries is impressive. But in comparison with rich regions, the gap persists (see Figure 8.8). A person living in the global North is far more likely than a person in the global South to have a landline, cell phone, and Internet access. This gap, along with the gap in access to information technologies *within* countries, is known as the **digital divide**.

> **digital divide** The gap in access to information technologies between rich and poor people, and between the global North and South.

Figure 8.8 The North-South Digital Divide, 1994–2014

Source: International Telecommunication Union (ITU) data.

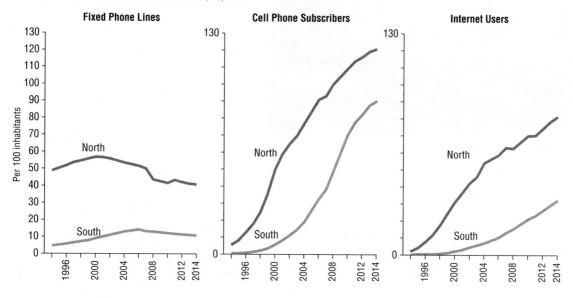

As the Internet connects parts of the world into a tight network centered on the United States, Europe, and East Asia—where most Web users live—other regions are largely left out. Poor countries and poor people cannot afford computers. In 2015, the Internet bandwidth per user was 25 times higher in Europe than Africa. The Internet reached 80 percent of households in the global North but only 30 percent in the global South. The numbers for mobile phone Internet are 80 percent in the North and 20 percent in the South. The explosive growth of Internet use is occurring mainly among the world's richer people.

Some activists hope that the Internet can transform poor villages in the global South, partly by letting them produce traditional goods locally and market them globally, and partly by accelerating education. In 2012, one NGO sent boxes of simple tablet computers to elementary students in two remote Ethiopian villages that had no schools and no literacy. Other than showing some adults how to use the solar chargers, the project included no instructions. In five days, the average child was using nearly 50 apps daily, and within two weeks the children were singing ABC songs and teaching themselves to read. Within five months, they had hacked into the Android operating system to enable a camera and customize the desktop.

COMMUNICATION WITHOUT TAXATION Global communication, a very new capability on the timeline of the international system, is changing the rules of IR and empowering nonstate transnational actors. Telecommunications could change the path of development in poor countries, possibly bypassing traditional infrastructure such as phone lines and leapfrogging to a wireless networked economy. And digital capabilities allow groups to coordinate protest against governments more easily. Here, protesters march against proposed taxes on internet usage in Hungary, 2014.

Information as a Tool of Governments

With more information traveling around the world than ever before, information has become an important instrument of governments' power (domestic and interstate). After the Soviet Union collapsed, leaders of the newly independent republics asked the U.S. secretary of state, "How do I get CNN?" They wanted information. Today, governments can gather, organize, and store huge amounts of information. In this respect, the information revolution empowers governments more than ever. In the past, a wanted criminal, drug lord, or terrorist could slip over the border and take refuge in a foreign country. Today, however, it is more likely that a routine traffic ticket in the foreign country could trigger an instant directive to arrest the person. These technologies are now being mobilized in force to strengthen counterterrorism.

Just as citizens and terrorists find it harder to hide from governments, so are state governments finding it harder to hide information from each other. The military importance of satellite reconnaissance has been mentioned (see p. 153). A powerful state such as the United States can increase its power through information technologies. It can and does monitor phone calls, faxes, data transmissions, and radio conversations in foreign countries. The revelation in 2013 that the National Security Agency (NSA) and other American agencies had mass surveillance programs showed that even democratically accountable governments can use technology to monitor their own citizens.

In the Arab Spring movements in 2011, protesters were not the only ones to deploy Internet capabilities; governments did as well. Egypt successfully blocked a choke point and cut off international Web access. And Syria's government used its own hackers to track down the identities of protesters anonymously posting antigovernment videos and messages on the Web. The U.S. government in response trained democracy activists in Internet and social media technologies and created shadow Internet and cell phone networks inside foreign countries whose governments were trying to shut down communications.

As the cost of information technology decreases, it comes into the reach of more states. Now small states can gain some of the same capabilities electronically. Even sophisticated information is more available and cheaper—high-resolution

satellite photos are now available commercially and are cheap or free. These images can be used for both military purposes and natural resource management.

Most governments (but not the U.S. government) own and operate at least one main TV station, and many hold a monopoly on TV stations. Thus, TV signals often rank with military equipment and currency as capabilities so important to a government that it must control them itself. Indeed, in a military coup d'état, one of the first and most important targets seized is usually the television broadcasting facility.

Information as a Tool Against Governments

Information can be used against governments as well, by foreign governments, NGOs, or domestic political opponents. Governments, especially repressive ones, fear the free flow of information, for good reason. New information technologies have

HOT OFF THE PRESS Information, which easily crosses state borders, is a major factor in both international and domestic politics and may even be laying technological foundations for a global identity. Governments have many ways to try to control information. Here a staff member of Kenya's daily newspaper surveys the damage after police—responding to unfavorable coverage of the president—stormed its offices and burned tens of thousands of copies, 2006.

become powerful tools of domestic opposition movements and their allies in foreign governments. Television coverage fed popular discontent regarding the U.S. war in Vietnam in the 1960s and 1970s, and the Russian war in Chechnya in 1995.

More than 600 million Chinese use the Internet, though not uncensored. In Iran, where millions of people have used the Internet to discuss taboo topics like sex, fashion, and politics, the government was criticized for cracking down on protesters after the 2009 election. That crackdown was broadcast on Internet sites such as Twitter and Facebook as opposition members posted video of beatings and even the shooting death of a female protester. These methods were adopted by the Arab Spring protesters in 2011.

To counteract such uses of information, governments throughout the world try to limit the flow of unfavorable information—especially information from foreign sources. For example, China, like several other developing countries, channels all access to the Internet through a few state-controlled service providers, and filters the hundreds of billions of text messages exchanged annually among 300 million Chinese cell phone subscribers. In 2010, the United Arab Emirates announced it would shut down BlackBerry's services but later reached a compromise allowing users to continue using the devices. In 2015, in response to protests against its president, the Democratic People's Republic of the Congo imposed an Internet blackout to stop protests from growing.

A major controversy over internet freedom also emerged in 2010 when the U.S. company Google announced that it would no longer comply with Chinese law that censored Internet searches by blocking politically sensitive words from its Chinese search engine. Later, Google compromised with the Chinese government, angering some U.S. critics. China continues to place significant limits on many Internet sites and ratcheted up those restrictions in early 2015.

The U.S. government worries that real terrorists could use the Internet to cause massive disruptions in the United States. The Obama administration has invested millions of dollars to increase cybersecurity, out of concerns that hackers could cause significant economic damage to the economy. American military officials have also stressed the dangers of cyberattacks on defense systems.

All in all, the tide of technology seems to be running against governments. Information gets through, and no political power seems capable of holding it back for long. As more and more communication channels carry more information to more places, governments become just another player in a crowded field.

Telecommunications and Global Culture

As the information revolution continues to unfold, it will further increase international interdependence, making actions in one state reverberate in other states more strongly than in the past. Information is thus slowly undermining realists' assumptions of state sovereignty and territorial integrity. At the same time, by empowering substate and transnational actors, information technology is undermining the centrality of states themselves in world affairs.

The information revolution greatly increases *transparency* in international relations. As a result, states do not need to arm against unknown potential threats because they see the real threats. Similarly, the ability to monitor performance of agreements makes collective goods problems easier to resolve because cheaters and free riders can be identified. The ability of governments to bargain effectively with each other and to reach mutually beneficial outcomes is enhanced by the availability of instant communications channels. In these ways, the increased transparency allowed by new technologies strengthens the reciprocity principle as a solution to IR conflicts. The complex monitoring and accounting required in international agreements based on reciprocity—from trade deals to arms control—becomes much easier in a transparent world.

WORLD CULTURE The power of information, opening up a wave of globalization in international business, is also strengthening global communities that cross or even transcend national borders. Some events, such as the British royal wedding in 2011, may be rooted in one nation but become global news stories followed by millions around the world.

Telecommunications, with its ability to connect communities beyond geographic space, is also strengthening the identity principle in IR because people's identities have new sources and new avenues of expression that often transcend national borders. In the past, nationalism tapped into the psychological dynamics of group identity in a powerful way that legitimized the state as the ultimate embodiment of its people's aspirations and identity. Now the information revolution may aid the development of transnational or supranational identities. So far, however, nationalism continues to hold the upper hand.

Although a global culture is still only nascent and the most powerful identity is still at the national level, people have begun to participate in specific communities that bridge national boundaries. Journalists, scientists, and church members work in communities spanning national borders. So do members of transnational movements, such as those linking women from various countries, or environmentalists, or human rights activists. The links forged in such transnational communities may create a new functionalism that could encourage international integration on a global scale.

Sports also create transnational communities. Citizens of different states share their admiration of sports stars, who become international celebrities. The Olympics (run by the International Olympic Committee, an NGO) is a global event with a worldwide audience. The U.S.-Chinese rapprochement of 1971 was so delicate that political cooperation was impossible until the way had first been paved by sports—the U.S. table tennis team that made the first official U.S. visit to China.

Finally, tourism also builds transnational communities. International tourists cross borders 500 million times a year. Tourism ranks among the top export industries worldwide. People who travel to other countries often develop both a deeper understanding and a deeper appreciation for those countries. Added to these contacts are exchange students and those who attend college in a foreign country.

Like international integration and globalization generally, global culture has its downside. The emerging global culture is primarily the culture of white Europeans and their descendants in rich areas of the world (mixed slightly with cultural elements of Japan and local elites in the global South). This cultural dominance has been referred to as **cultural imperialism**. For many people, especially in the global South, the information revolution carrying global culture into their midst is, despite its empowering potential, an invasive force in practice. For example, half of the world's nearly 7,000 languages risk extinction this century.

cultural imperialism
A term critical of U.S. dominance of the emerging global culture.

Above all, the emerging global culture is dominated by the world's superpower, the United States; U.S. cultural influence is at least as strong as U.S. military influence. Culture may be just another economic product, to be produced in the place of greatest comparative advantage, but culture is also central to national identity and politics. The prospect of cultural imperialism thus opens another front in the conflict of liberalism and mercantilism.

Recent trends seem to be moving toward a more multilateral world culture. For example, South Korea's Ministry of Culture has supported the mass-production of a new, fast growing, billion-dollar export product, Korean pop music (K-pop). Boy and girl bands are systematically recruited and developed, then marketed globally via social media. The music video "Gangnam Style" by the Korean artist PSY outpaced Justin Bieber to become the most-watched YouTube video ever (2.2 billion views by 2015). Another highly successful cultural export product can be found in Brazilian soap operas. And the Internet's governing body has started allowing Web addresses to contain non-Latin characters such as Chinese, Cyrillic, Japanese, or Arabic characters.

These supranational cultural influences are still in their infancy. Over the coming years and decades, their shape will become clearer, and scholars will be able to determine more accurately how they influence world politics and state sovereignty.

Conclusion

Ultimately the conflicts and dramas of international relations are the problems of human society—struggles for power and wealth, efforts to cooperate despite differences, social dilemmas and collective goods problems, the balance between freedom and order, and trade-offs of equity versus efficiency and of long-term versus short-term outcomes. These themes are inescapable in human society, from the smallest groups to the world community. The subject of international relations is, in this sense, an extension of everyday life and a reflection of the choices of individual human beings. IR belongs to all of us—North and South, women and men, citizens and leaders—who live together on this planet.

This text has shown that, in IR more than other social settings, collective goods problems pose formidable challenges to successful cooperation among the large number of independent (state and nonstate) actors. With no central government to enforce order, actors in IR have developed three kinds of solutions to collective goods problems—our three core principles. Countries turn to the dominance principle most often in international security affairs, especially military force (Chapter 4). The identity principle matters most in the remarkable process of integration (Chapter 6). Most important, however, is the reciprocity principle, which underlies international treaties; law; and organizations, from the UN to the WTO. Characteristic solutions based on the reciprocity principle are complicated, take forever to agree upon, and require extensive monitoring of compliance thereafter. But woven together, these reciprocity-based agreements offer the basis for an international system that has moved, over centuries, from extreme war-proneness to ever stronger peace and prosperity—notwithstanding the world's many serious remaining problems.

One major theme of this text is the nature of the international system as a well-developed set of rules based on state sovereignty, territoriality, and "anarchy"—a lack of central government. Yet the international system is becoming more complex, more nuanced, and more interconnected with other aspects of planetary society. State sovereignty is now challenged by the principle of self-determination. International norms have begun to limit the right of government to rule a population by force against its will and to violate human rights. Territorial integrity is also problematic because national borders do not stop information, environmental changes, or missiles. Information allows actors—state, substate, and supranational—to know what is going on everywhere in the world and to coordinate actions globally.

Technological development is just one aspect of the profound yet incremental changes taking place in international relations. New actors are gaining power; long-standing principles are becoming less effective; and new challenges are arising for states, groups, and individuals alike.

Technology is also profoundly changing the utility and role of military force. The power of defensive weaponry makes successful attacks more difficult, and the power of offensive weaponry makes retaliation an extremely potent threat to deter an attack. The twentieth-century superpowers could not attack each other without destroying themselves. Today technology plays key roles on both sides in counterinsurgency wars such as in Iraq and the other 15 active wars in the world.

Nonmilitary forms of leverage, particularly economic rewards, have become much more important power capabilities. The post–Cold War era is a peaceful one, yet the peace is fragile. Will this era, like past postwar eras, lapse slowly into the next prewar era, or will it lead to a robust and lasting "permanent peace" such as Kant imagined?

In IPE, we see simultaneous trends toward integration and disintegration among states. People continue to speak their own language, to fly their own flag, and to use their own currency with its pictures and emblems. Nationalism continues to be an important force. Although people identify with their state, they now also hold competing identities based on ethnic ties, gender, and (in the case of Europe) region. In international trade, liberal economics prevails because it works so well. States have learned that, to survive, they must help the creation of wealth by MNCs and other actors.

Environmental damage may become the single greatest obstacle to sustained economic growth in both the North and South. Because of high costs, the large number of actors, and collective goods problems, international bargaining over the environment is difficult.

Meanwhile, North-South relations are moving to the center of world politics. Demographic and economic trends are sharpening the global North-South gap, with the North continuing to accumulate wealth while much of the South lags. Ultimately, the North will bear a high cost for failing to address the economic development of the South. Perhaps, by using computerization and biotechnology innovations, poor states can develop their economies more efficiently and sustainably than did Europe or North America.

The future is unknowable now, but as it unfolds you can compare it—at mileposts along the way—to the worlds that you desire and expect. For example, you could ask questions such as the following (asking yourself, for each one, why you answer the way you do for your desired future and your expected future):

1. Will state sovereignty be eroded by supranational authority?
2. Will norms of human rights and democracy become global?
3. Will the UN evolve into a quasi-government for the world?
4. Will the UN be restructured?
5. Will World Court judgments become enforceable?
6. Will the number of states increase?
7. Will China become democratic?
8. What effects will information technologies have on IR?
9. Will weapons of mass destruction proliferate?
10. Will military leverage become obsolete?
11. Will disarmament occur?
12. Will women participate more fully in IR? With what effect?
13. Will there be a single world currency?
14. Will there be a global free-trade regime?
15. Will nationalism fade or continue to be strong?
16. Will many people develop a global identity?
17. Will world culture become more homogeneous or more pluralistic?
18. Will the EU or other regional IOs achieve political union?
19. Will global environmental destruction be severe? If so, how soon?
20. Will new technologies avert environmental constraints?
21. Will global problems create stronger or weaker world order?

22. Will population growth level out? If so, when and at what level?
23. Will the poorest countries accumulate wealth? If so, how soon?
24. What role will the North play in the South's development?

The choices you make and the actions you take will ultimately affect the world you live in. You cannot opt out of involvement in international relations. You are involved, and year by year, the information revolution and other aspects of interdependence are drawing you more closely into contact with the rest of the world. You can act in many ways to bring the world you expect more in line with the world you desire. You can empower yourself by finding the actions and choices that define your place in international relations.

Now that you have completed the studies covered in this text, don't stop here. Keep learning about the world beyond your country's borders. Keep thinking about the world that might exist. Be part of the changes that will carry this world through the coming decades. It's your world: Study it, care for it, make it your own.

Chapter Review

Summary

- Environmental problems are an example of international interdependence and often create collective goods problems for the states involved. The large numbers of actors involved in global environmental problems make them especially difficult to solve.

- To resolve such collective goods problems, states have used international regimes and IOs, and have in some cases extended state sovereignty (notably over territorial waters).

- Global warming results from burning fossil fuels—the basis of industrial economies today. The industrialized states are much more responsible for the problem than are states in the global South, but countries such as China and India also contribute to the problem. Solutions are difficult to reach because costs are substantial and dangers are somewhat distant and uncertain.

- Damage to the earth's ozone layer results from the use of specific chemicals, which are now being phased out under international agreements. Unlike global warming, the costs of solutions are much lower and the problem is better understood.

- Many species are threatened with extinction from loss of habitats such as rain forests. An international treaty on biodiversity and an agreement on forests aim to reduce the destruction of local ecosystems, with costs spread among states.

- The UN Convention on the Law of the Sea (UNCLOS) establishes an ocean regime that puts most commercial fisheries and offshore oil under control of states as territorial waters.

- Pollution—including acid rain, water and air pollution, and toxic and nuclear waste—tends to be more localized than global and has been addressed mainly through unilateral, bilateral, and regional measures rather than global ones.

- Most Western states import energy resources, mostly oil, whereas the other world regions export them. Oil prices rose dramatically in the 1970s, declined in the 1980s, rose in 2008, and have declined since. Such fluctuations undermine world economic stability.

- The most important source of oil traded worldwide is the Persian Gulf area of the Middle East. Consequently, this area has long been a focal point of international political conflict.

- World population—now at 7 billion—may eventually level out around 10 billion. Almost all of the increase will come in the global South.

- Future world population growth will be driven largely by the demographic transition. Death rates have fallen throughout the world, but birthrates will fall proportionally only as per capita incomes go up.

- The global AIDS epidemic will impose huge costs on many poor states in the coming years. Currently, 35 million people are infected with HIV, and 30 million more have died. Most are in Africa, and new infections are appearing in Asia and Russia.

- Supranational relationships and identities are being fostered by new information technologies, although such a process is still at an early stage. Access to these technologies is very unequal between rich and poor countries.

- Government access to information increases the stability of international relationships. Collective goods problems are made less difficult in a transparent world where governments have information about each other's actions.

- The greater and freer flow of information around the world can undermine the authority and power of governments as well. Information technologies can empower ordinary citizens and contribute to transnational and supranational structures that bypass the state.

- Internet governance is under negotiation at UN meetings, notably one in 2012, where 89 countries supported a new treaty giving governments more power, but 55 others would not sign.

- Telecommunications are contributing to the development of global cultural integration. Transnational communities are developing in areas such as sports, music, and tourism. However, cultural imperialism may result if such a culture is too strongly dominated by the United States.

Key Terms

Critical Thinking Questions

1. Does the record of the international community on environmental management reflect the views of mercantilists, liberals, or both? In what ways?

2. Dozens of poor states appear to be stuck midway through the demographic transition; death rates have fallen, birthrates remain high, and per capita incomes are not increasing. How do you think these states, with or without foreign assistance, can best get unstuck and complete the demographic transition?

3. What are the good and bad effects, in your opinion, of the emergence of global communications and culture? Should we be cheering or lamenting the possibility of one world culture? Does the answer depend on where one lives in the world? Give concrete examples of the effects you discuss.

Appendix
Jobs and Careers in International Relations

Jobs in Government and Diplomacy

Summary

Jobs in government and diplomacy offer team players the chance to affect policy, but these jobs require patience with large bureaucracies.

BENEFITS AND COSTS Both governments and intergovernmental organizations (IGOs) play key roles in international relations (IR) and employ millions of people with interests and training in IR.

Despite differences between careers in IGOs and governments, there are numerous similarities. Both are hierarchical organizations, with competitive and highly regulated working environments. Whether in the U.S. State Department or the UN, entrance into and promotion in these organizations is regulated by exams, performance evaluations, and tenure with the organization.

Another similarity lies in the challenges of being pulled in many directions concerning policies. Governments face competing pressures of public opinion, constituencies, and interests groups—each with distinct policy opinions. IGOs also deal with interest groups such as nongovernmental organizations (NGOs), but an IGO's constituents are states, which in many cases disagree among themselves.

Many employees of IGOs or governments thrive on making decisions that influence policies. Both work environments also attract coworkers with deep interests in international affairs, and the resulting networks of contracts can bring professional and intellectual rewards. Finally, jobs in governments or IGOs may involve travel or living abroad, which many enjoy.

However, promotion can be slow and frustrating. Usually, only individuals with advanced degrees or technical specializations achieve non–entry level positions. It can take years to climb within the organization and the process may involve working in departments far from your original interests. In addition, both IGOs and governments are bureaucracies with formal rules and procedures, requiring great patience. Employees often express frustration that initiative and "thinking outside the box" are not rewarded.

SKILLS TO HONE The key to working in IGOs or government is to get your foot in the door. Be flexible and willing to take entry positions that are not exactly in your area of interest. For example, the State Department is only one of many parts of the U.S. government that deal with IR. Do not assume that you must be a diplomat to work in foreign affairs.

Foreign language training is also important, especially for work in large IGOs with many field offices. The ability to work well in groups and to network within and across organizations is an important asset. People who can strengthen lines of communication can gain support from many places in an organization.

Finally, strong analytical and writing abilities are extremely important. Both IGOs and governments deal with massive amounts of information daily. The ability to analyze information (even including mathematical or computational analysis) and to write clear, concise interpretations will make one invaluable.

RESOURCES

Shawn Dorman. *Inside a U.S. Embassy: Diplomacy at Work*. 3rd ed. Washington, DC: Potomac Books, 2011.

Linda Fasulo. *An Insider's Guide to the UN*. 3rd ed. New Haven, CT: Yale University Press, 2015.

http://jobs.un.org

http://careers.state.gov

http://jobsearch.usajobs.opm.gov/a9st00.aspx

Jobs in International Business

Summary

Jobs in international business offer high pay, interesting work, and demanding hours for those with language and cultural skills.

BENEFITS AND COSTS As the pace and scope of globalization have accelerated, opportunities to work in international business have blossomed. For many large companies, the domestic/global distinction has ceased to exist. This new context provides opportunities and challenges for potential employees.

Careers in international business offer many advantages. Business jobs can pay substantially more than those in governments or NGOs and can open opportunities to travel extensively and network globally. Foreign-based jobs mean relocation to another country to work and immerse oneself in another culture.

Such a career choice also has potential costs, however. Many jobs require extensive hours, grueling travel, and frequent relocation. As with any job, promotion and advancement may fall victim to external circumstances such as global business cycles. And these jobs can be especially hard on families.

International opportunities arise in many business sectors. Banking, marketing (public relations), sales, and computing/telecommunications have seen tremendous growth in recent years. These jobs fall into three broad categories: (1) those located domestically, yet involving significant interactions with firms abroad; (2) domestic jobs working for foreign-based companies; and (3) those based abroad, for foreign or domestic firms.

SKILLS TO HONE One key to landing in the international business world is to develop two families of skills: those related to international relations and those related to business operations. Traditional masters in business administration (MBAs) and business school programs will be helpful for all three types of jobs. Yet for jobs based abroad, employers often also look for a broader set of skills taught in economics, political science, and communications. Thus, not only traditional business skills but also language and cultural skills are essential. Employers look for those who have knowledge of a country's human and economic geography as well as culture. Experience with study abroad, especially including working abroad, can help show an ability to adapt and function well in other cultures. Strong analytical and especially writing abilities also matter greatly to employers.

Research also helps in landing a job. Employers often look for knowledge of a particular industry or company in order to make best use of an employee's language and cultural skills. Of course, while experience in noninternational business never hurts, be mindful that the practices, customs, and models of business in one country may not apply well abroad. Cross-cultural skills combined with substantive business knowledge in order to translate the operational needs of companies from the business world to the global realm are highly valued.

RESOURCES

Edward J. Halloran. *Careers in International Business*. 2nd ed. New York: McGraw-Hill, 2003.

Deborah Penrith, ed. *The Directory of Jobs and Careers Abroad*. 13th ed. Oxford, UK: Vacation Work Publications, 2007.

http://www.rileyguide.com/internat.html
http://www.jobsabroad.com/search.cfm
http://www.transitionsabroad.com/listings/work/careers/index.shtml

Jobs in Nongovernmental Organizations (NGOs)

Summary

Jobs in NGOs provide personally rewarding experiences for those willing to work hard for a cause, but they pay poorly and are hard to obtain.

BENEFITS AND COSTS Nearly 40,000 NGOs exist, and that number grows daily. Thousands of individuals are interested in working in these organizations. Although all NGOs are different, many perform multiple functions: working in developing countries regarding a variety of issues, public outreach at home and abroad, lobbying governments to change their policies, designing projects to solve problems and attempting to find funding for their implementation.

Working for an NGO has many benefits. Workers often find themselves surrounded by others concerned about the same issues: improving the environment, protecting human rights, advancing economic development, or promoting better health care. The spirit of camaraderie can be exhilarating and rewarding.

While working for an NGO can be extremely rewarding personally, it is rarely rewarding financially. Most NGOs are nonprofit operations that pay workers meagerly for long hours. Moreover, many smaller NGOs engage in a constant fight for funding from governments, think tanks, private foundations, or individuals. The process of fundraising can be quite time consuming.

Despite the large number of NGOs, relatively low pay, and long hours, finding a job with an NGO can be difficult. One key is to be specific. Try to narrow your interests in terms of substantive areas (e.g., human rights, environment) and/or geographic region. Also think about whether you want to work in your own country or abroad. Positions abroad may be more rewarding but are in lower supply and higher demand.

SKILLS TO HONE NGOs are looking for self-starters. Most have little time and few resources for training. Basic office skills (e.g., computer expertise) are essential, but employees also need to cover a range of duties every day. Anything and everything is in your job description. Writing and communication skills are key, especially when fundraising is part of the job. Foreign language skills also matter because many NGOs maintain or work with field offices abroad.

Often, NGOs ask potential employees to volunteer for a period while they train, before being hired. Increasingly, some companies place workers in an NGO or volunteer opportunity for a price. By paying to work, you can gain a probationary period to develop your skills and familiarize yourself with the operation and become efficient before going on the payroll.

Finally, in cities where NGOs cluster (e.g., Washington, DC), personal networks play an important role in finding good opportunities. Workers often move from one organization to another. For this reason, many volunteer or accept jobs with NGOs not in their immediate area of interest to gain experience and contacts, which can help future career advancement.

RESOURCES

David Weiss. "Careers in International Development and Humanitarian Assistance NGOs." In *Careers in International Affairs*. 9th ed. Washington, DC: Georgetown School of Foreign Service, 2014.

Richard M. King. *From Making a Profit to Making a Difference: How to Launch Your New Career in Nonprofits.* River Forest, IL: Planning/Communications, 2000.

http://www.ngo.org/links/index.htm
http://www.idealist.org
http://www.wango.org/resources.aspx?section=ngodir

Jobs in Education and Research

Summary

Jobs in teaching and research offer freedom to pursue ideas and work with colleagues, but they require years of schooling.

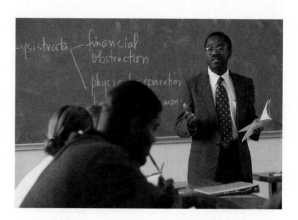

BENEFITS AND COSTS People follow various paths to an interest in teaching and researching in the field of international relations. Your own professor or instructor is likely to have a unique story about how he or she became interested in international affairs.

One advantage of an academic and research career, whether at a teaching-oriented institution or a large research university, is intellectual freedom. One can spend a career approaching a variety of topics that are interesting and constantly evolving, may involve travel abroad for fieldwork, and may let you network with hundreds of colleagues interested in similar topics.

Most research positions (e.g., in think tanks) are different in two respects. First, these jobs often give more direction to an individual in terms of the research to be performed. Second, there is little or no teaching involved. Still, for those interested in IR research, such jobs can result in a wider dissemination of one's work to a broader audience that often includes policy makers.

To teach IR at an advanced level or to perform research for think tanks and government agencies usually requires an advanced degree—nearly always a masters degree, often a doctorate (Ph.D.). Masters degree programs often take between one and two years, while a Ph.D. in international relations usually takes a minimum of five years. Often, students take time off between their undergraduate and graduate educations to travel internationally or get work experience to hone their interests. Of course, many students never return to extend their education if they find a job that allows them to achieve their personal and career goals.

Finally, in completing most advanced degrees, a large amount of self-direction is necessary. Coursework is only one part of masters or Ph.D. programs:

A thesis is also required. Writing a thesis requires you to work on your own time schedule, balancing other duties (such as work as a teaching or research assistant) that can easily crowd out your own work. Many who complete the coursework for an advanced degree do not finish their thesis or take many years to do so.

SKILLS TO HONE Whether one wants to pursue an advanced degree for the purposes of teaching in an academic setting or engaging in applied research, there are important skill sets to develop. First and foremost is critical thinking. Scholars and researchers must consider many alternatives as answers to questions, while being able to evaluate the validity or importance of those alternatives. Second is writing. Before, during, and after producing a thesis, writing is a key skill for academics and researchers. Finally, think about developing a set of applied skills to use as a toolbox while analyzing questions. The contents of this toolbox might include other languages to facilitate fieldwork abroad. It could include statistics and data skills to facilitate quantitative analysis. Or it could include mathematics to use game theoretic models. No matter which tools you emphasize, specialized skills will help you answer research questions, whether as part of the academy or in a private or governmental research organization.

RESOURCES

The Chronicle of Higher Education (weekly). Online at http://chronicle.com
American Political Science Association. *Earning a PhD in Political Science.* 4th ed. Washington, DC, 2004.
http://www.apsanet.org
http://www.apsia.org
http://www.isanet.org

Glossary

acid rain Rain caused by air pollution that damages trees and often crosses borders. Limiting acid rain (via limiting nitrogen oxide emissions) has been the subject of several regional agreements. (p. 346)

airspace The space above a state that is considered its territory, in contrast to outer space, which is considered international territory. (p. 145)

alliance cohesion The ease with which the members hold together an alliance; it tends to be high when national interests converge and when cooperation among allies becomes institutionalized. (p. 54)

Amnesty International An influential nongovernmental organization that operates globally to monitor and try to rectify glaring abuses of political (not economic or social) human rights. (p. 270)

anarchy In IR theory, a term that implies not complete chaos but the lack of a central government that can enforce rules. (p. 44)

Antarctic Treaty of 1959 One of the first multilateral environmental treaties. It forbids military activity, sets aside territorial claims for future resolution, and establishes a regime under which various states conduct scientific research in Antarctica. (p. 343)

arms race A reciprocal process in which two or more states build up military capabilities in response to each other. (p. 61)

autarky A policy of self-reliance, avoiding or minimizing trade and trying to produce everything one needs (or the most vital things) by oneself. (p. 182)

balance of payments A summary of all the flows of money into and out of a country. It includes three types of international transactions: the current account (including the merchandise trade balance), flows of capital, and changes in reserves. (p. 211)

balance of power The general concept of one or more states' power being used to balance that of another state or group of states. The term can

refer to (1) any ratio of power capabilities between states or alliances, (2) a relatively equal ratio, or (3) the process by which counterbalancing coalitions have repeatedly formed to prevent one state from conquering an entire region. (p. 46)

balance of trade The value of a state's exports relative to its imports. (p. 178)

ballistic missiles The major strategic delivery vehicle for nuclear weapons; it carries a warhead along a trajectory (typically rising at least 50 miles high) and lets it drop on the target. (p. 162) See also *intercontinental ballistic missiles (ICBMs)*.

basic human needs The fundamental needs of people for adequate food, shelter, health care, sanitation, and education. Meeting such needs may be thought of as both a moral imperative and a form of investment in "human capital" essential for economic growth. (p. 281)

bilateral aid Government assistance that goes directly to governments as state-to-state aid. (p. 318)

biodiversity The tremendous diversity of plant and animal species making up the earth's (global, regional, and local) ecosystems. (p. 340)

Biological Weapons Convention (1972) An agreement that prohibits the development, production, and possession of biological weapons but makes no provision for inspections. (p. 164)

brain drain Poor countries' loss of skilled workers to rich countries. (p. 312)

Bretton Woods system A post–World War II arrangement for managing the world economy, established at a meeting in Bretton Woods, New Hampshire, in 1944. Its main institutional components are the World Bank and the International Monetary Fund (IMF). (p. 210)

burden sharing The distribution of the costs of an alliance among members; the term also refers to the conflicts that may arise over such distribution. (p. 54)

cartel   An association of producers or consumers (or both) of a certain product, formed for the purpose of manipulating its price on the world market. (p. 190)

cash crop   An agricultural good produced as a commodity for export to world markets. (p. 286)

central bank   An institution common in industrialized countries whose major tasks are to maintain the value of the state's currency and to control inflation. (p. 209)

centrally planned economy   An economy in which political authorities set prices and decide on quotas for production and consumption of each commodity according to a long-term plan. (p. 197)

Chemical Weapons Convention (1992)   An agreement that bans the production and possession of chemical weapons and includes strict verification provisions and the threat of sanctions against violators and nonparticipants in the treaty. (p. 164)

civil-military relations   The relations between a state's civilian leaders and the military leadership. In most countries, the military takes orders from civilian leaders. In extreme cases, poor civil-military relations can lead to military coups. (p. 170)

civil war   A war between factions within a state trying to create, or prevent, a new government for the entire state or some territorial part of it. (p. 118)

Cold War   The hostile relations—punctuated by occasional periods of improvement, or détente—between the two superpowers, the United States and the Soviet Union, from 1945 to 1990. (p. 25)

collective goods problem   A tangible or intangible good, created by the members of a group, that is available to all group members regardless of their individual contributions; participants can gain by lowering their own contribution to the collective good, yet if too many participants do so, the good cannot be provided. (p. 4)

collective security   The formation of a broad alliance of most major actors in an international system for the purpose of jointly opposing aggression by any actor; sometimes seen as presupposing the existence of a universal organization (such as the United Nations) to which both the aggressor and its opponents belong. (p. 73) See also *League of Nations*.

Common Agricultural Policy (CAP)   A European Union policy based on the principle that a subsidy extended to farmers in any member country should be extended to farmers in all member countries. (p. 247)

common market   A zone in which labor and capital (as well as goods) flow freely across borders. (p. 247)

comparative advantage   The principle that says states should specialize in trading goods that they produce with the greatest relative efficiency and at the lowest relative cost (relative, that is, to other goods produced by the same state). (p. 179)

compellence   The threat of force to make another actor take some action (rather than, as in deterrence, refrain from taking an action). (p. 60)

Comprehensive Test Ban Treaty (CTBT) (1996)   A treaty that bans all nuclear weapons testing, thereby broadening the ban on atmospheric testing negotiated in 1963. (p. 168)

conditionality   See *IMF conditionality*.

conflict   A difference in preferred outcomes in a bargaining situation. (p. 120)

conflict and cooperation   The types of actions that states take toward each other through time. (p. 10)

conflict resolution   The development and implementation of peaceful strategies for settling conflicts. (p. 100)

constructivism   A movement in IR theory that examines how changing international norms and actors' identities help shape the content of state interests. (p. 92)

containment   A policy adopted in the late 1940s by which the United States sought to halt the global expansion of Soviet influence on several levels—military, political, ideological, and economic. (p. 25)

convertible currency   See *hard currency*.

cost-benefit analysis   A calculation of the costs incurred by a possible action and the benefits it is likely to bring. (p. 62)

Council of the European Union   A European Union institution in which the relevant ministers (foreign, economic, agriculture, finance, etc.) of each member state meet to enact legislation and reconcile national interests. Formerly known as the Council of Ministers. When the meeting takes place among the state leaders, it is called the "European Council." (p. 249) See also *European Commission.*

counterinsurgency An effort to combat guerrilla armies, often including programs to "win the hearts and minds" of rural populations so that they stop sheltering guerrillas. (p. 149)

coup d'état The seizure of political power by domestic military forces—that is, a change of political power outside the state's constitutional order. (p. 170)

crimes against humanity A category of legal offenses created at the Nuremberg trials after World War II to encompass genocide and other acts committed by the political and military leaders of the Third Reich (Nazi Germany). (p. 271) See also *genocide.*

cruise missile A small winged missile that can navigate across thousands of miles of previously mapped terrain to reach a particular target; it can carry either a nuclear or a conventional warhead. (p. 162)

Cuban Missile Crisis (1962) A superpower crisis, sparked by the Soviet Union's installation of medium-range nuclear missiles in Cuba, that marks the moment when the United States and the Soviet Union came closest to nuclear war. (p. 28)

cultural imperialism A term critical of U.S. dominance of the emerging global culture. (p. 368)

customs union A common external tariff adopted by members of a free trade area; that is, participating states adopt a unified set of tariffs with regard to goods coming in from outside. (p. 247) See also *free trade area.*

debt renegotiation A reworking of the terms on which a loan will be repaid; frequently negotiated by poor debtor governments in order to avoid default. (p. 313)

default Failure to make scheduled debt payments. (p. 312)

democratic peace The proposition, strongly supported by empirical evidence, that democracies almost never fight wars against each other (although they do fight against authoritarian states). (p. 75)

demographic transition The pattern of falling death rates, followed by falling birthrates, that generally accompanies industrialization and economic development. (p. 354)

dependency theory A Marxist-oriented theory that explains the lack of capital accumulation in poor countries as a result of the interplay between domestic class relations and the forces of foreign capital. (p. 298) See also *enclave economy.*

deterrence The threat to punish another actor if it takes a certain negative action (especially attacking one's own state or one's allies). (p. 60) See also *mutually assured destruction (MAD).*

devaluation A unilateral move to reduce the value of a currency by changing a fixed or official exchange rate. (p. 208) See also *exchange rate.*

developing countries States in the global South, the poorest regions of the world—also called third world countries, less-developed countries, and undeveloped countries. (p. 279)

Development Assistance Committee (DAC) A committee whose members—consisting of states from Western Europe, North America, and East Asia—provide 95 percent of official development assistance to countries of the global South. (p. 318) See also *foreign assistance.*

difference feminism A strand of feminism that believes gender differences are not just socially constructed and that views women as inherently less warlike than men (on average). (p. 103)

digital divide The gap in access to information technologies between rich and poor people, and between the global North and South. (p. 363)

diplomatic immunity A privilege under which diplomats' activities fall outside the jurisdiction of the host country's national courts. (p. 265)

diplomatic recognition The process by which the status of embassies and that of an ambassador as an official state representative are explicitly defined. (p. 264)

disaster relief Provision of short-term relief in the form of food, water, shelter, clothing, and other essentials to people facing natural disasters. (p. 324)

discount rate The interest rate charged by governments when they lend money to private banks. The discount rate is set by countries' central banks. (p. 209)

Doha Round   A series of negotiations under the World Trade Organization that began in Doha, Qatar, in 2001. It followed the *Uruguay Round* and has focused on agricultural subsidies, intellectual property, and other issues. (p. 187)

dominance   A principle for solving collective goods problems by imposing solutions hierarchically. (p. 5)

dumping   The sale of products in foreign markets at prices below the minimum level necessary to make a profit (or below cost). (p. 183)

economic classes   A categorization of individuals based on economic status. (p. 96)

economic development   The combined processes of capital accumulation, rising per capita incomes (with consequent falling birthrates), the increasing of skills in the population, the adoption of new technological styles, and other related social and economic changes. (p. 299)

economic liberalism   In the context of IPE, an approach that generally shares the assumption of anarchy (the lack of a world government) but does not see this condition as precluding extensive cooperation to realize common gains from economic exchanges. It emphasizes absolute over relative gains and, in practice, a commitment to free trade, free capital flows, and an "open" world economy. (p. 176) See also *mercantilism* and *neoliberal.*

electronic warfare   Use of the electromagnetic spectrum (radio waves, radar, infrared, etc.) in war, such as employing electromagnetic signals for one's own benefit while denying their use to an enemy. (p. 155)

enclave economy   A historically important form of dependency in which foreign capital is invested in a developing country to extract a particular raw material in a particular place—usually a mine, oil well, or plantation. (p. 298) See also *dependency theory.*

enclosure   The splitting of a common area or good into privately owned pieces, giving individual owners an incentive to manage resources responsibly. (p. 333)

ethnic cleansing   Euphemism for forced displacement of an ethnic group or groups from a territory, accompanied by massacres and other human rights violations; it has occurred after the breakup of multinational states, notably in the former Yugoslavia. (p. 141)

ethnic groups   Large groups of people who share ancestral, language, cultural, or religious ties and a common identity. (p. 125)

ethnocentrism   The tendency to see one's own group (in-group) in favorable terms and an out-group in unfavorable terms. (p. 127)

Euratom   An organization created by the Treaty of Rome in 1957 to coordinate nuclear power development by pooling research, investment, and management. (p. 247)

euro   Also called the ECU (European currency unit); a single European currency used by 19 members of the European Union (EU). (p. 252)

European Commission   A European Union body whose members, while appointed by states, are supposed to represent EU interests. Supported by a multinational civil service in Brussels, the commission's role is to identify problems and propose solutions to the Council of the European Union. (p. 248) See also *Council of the European Union.*

European Court of Justice   A judicial arm of the European Union, based in Luxembourg. The court has actively established its jurisdiction and its right to overrule national law when it conflicts with EU law. (p. 250)

European Parliament   A legislative body of the European Union that operates as a watchdog over the European Commission and has limited legislative power. (p. 250)

European Union (EU)   The official term for the European Community (formerly the European Economic Community) and associated treaty organizations. The EU has 28 member states and is negotiating with other states that have applied for membership. (p. 243) See also *Maastricht Treaty.*

exchange rate   The rate at which one state's currency can be exchanged for the currency of another state. Since 1973, the international monetary system has depended mainly on floating rather than fixed exchange rates. (p. 202)

export-led growth   An economic development strategy that seeks to develop industries capable of competing in specific niches in the world economy. (p. 308)

fiscal policy   A government's decisions about spending and taxation, and one of the two major tools of macroeconomic policy making (the other being monetary policy). (p. 213)

fissionable material The elements uranium-235 and plutonium, whose atoms split apart and release energy via a chain reaction when an atomic bomb explodes. (p. 161)

fixed exchange rates The official rates of exchange for currencies set by governments; not a dominant mechanism in the international monetary system since 1973. (p. 204) See also *floating exchange rates.*

floating exchange rates The rates determined by global currency markets in which private investors and governments alike buy and sell currencies. (p. 204) See also *fixed exchange rates.*

foreign assistance Money or other aid made available to states in the global South to help them speed up economic development or meet humanitarian needs. Most foreign assistance is provided by governments and is called official development assistance (ODA). (p. 317) See also *Development Assistance Committee (DAC).*

foreign policy process The process by which foreign policies are arrived at and implemented. (p. 84)

"four tigers"/"four dragons" The most successful newly industrialized areas of East Asia: South Korea, Taiwan, Hong Kong, and Singapore. (p. 301)

free trade The flow of goods and services across national boundaries unimpeded by tariffs or other restrictions; in principle (if not always in practice), free trade was a key aspect of Britain's policy after 1846 and of U.S. policy after 1945. (p. 177)

free trade area A zone in which there are no tariffs or other restrictions on the movement of goods and services across borders. (p. 247) See also *customs union.*

game theory A branch of mathematics concerned with predicting bargaining outcomes. Games such as Prisoner's Dilemma and Chicken have been used to analyze various sorts of international interactions. (p. 62)

gender gap Refers to polls showing women lower than men on average in their support for military actions, as well as for various other issues and candidates. (p. 106)

General Agreement on Tariffs and Trade (GATT) A world organization established in 1947 to work for freer trade on a multilateral basis; the GATT was more of a negotiating framework than an administrative institution. It became the World Trade Organization (WTO) in 1995. (p. 185)

General Assembly See *UN General Assembly.*

Generalized System of Preferences (GSP) A mechanism by which some industrialized states began in the 1970s to give tariff concessions to poorer states on certain imports; an exception to the most-favored nation (MFN) principle. (p. 186) See also *most-favored nation (MFN).*

genocide An intentional and systematic attempt to destroy a national, ethnic, racial, or religious group, in whole or in part. It was confirmed as a crime under international law by the UN Genocide Convention (1948). (p. 126) See also *crimes against humanity.*

geopolitics The use of geography as an element of power, and the ideas about it held by political leaders and scholars. (p. 43)

globalization The increasing integration of the world in terms of communications, culture, and economics; may also refer to changing subjective experiences of space and time accompanying this process. (p. 18)

global warming A slow, long-term rise in the average world temperature caused by the emission of greenhouse gases produced by burning fossil fuels—oil, coal, and natural gas. (p. 335) See also *greenhouse gases.*

gold standard A system in international monetary relations, prominent for a century before the 1970s, in which the value of national currencies was pegged to the value of gold or other precious metals. (p. 202)

government bargaining model A model that sees foreign policy decisions as flowing from a bargaining process among various government agencies that have somewhat divergent interests in the outcome ("where you stand depends on where you sit"). Also called *bureaucratic politics model.* (p. 86)

great powers Generally, the half-dozen or so most powerful states; the great power club was exclusively European until the twentieth century. (p. 47) See also *middle powers*.

greenhouse gases   Carbon dioxide and other gases that, when concentrated in the atmosphere, act like the glass in a greenhouse, holding energy in and leading to global warming. (p. 336)

gross domestic product (GDP)   The size of a state's total annual economic activity. (p. 13)

groupthink   The tendency of groups to validate wrong decisions by becoming overconfident and underestimating risks. (p. 89)

guerrilla war   Warfare without front lines and with irregular forces operating in the midst of, and often hidden or protected by, civilian populations. (p. 118)

hard currency   Money that can be converted readily to leading world currencies. (p. 203)

hegemonic stability theory   The argument that regimes are most effective when power in the international system is most concentrated. (p. 52) See also *hegemony*.

hegemonic war   War for control of the entire world order—the rules of the international system as a whole. Also called *world war, global war, general war,* or *systemic war.* (p. 116)

hegemony   One state's holding of a preponderance of power in the international system so that it can single-handedly dominate the rules and arrangements by which international political and economic relations are conducted. (p. 51) See also *hegemonic stability theory*.

high seas   The portion of the oceans considered common territory, not under any kind of exclusive state jurisdiction. (p. 342) See also *territorial waters*.

human rights   The rights of all people to be free from abuses such as torture or imprisonment for their political beliefs (political and civil rights), and to enjoy certain minimum economic and social protections (economic and social rights). (p. 266)

hyperinflation   An extremely rapid, uncontrolled rise in prices, such as occurred in Germany in the 1920s and some poor countries more recently. (p. 203)

idealism   An approach that emphasizes international law, morality, and international

organization, rather than power alone, as key influences on international relations. (p. 38) See also *realism*.

identity   A principle for solving collective goods problems by changing participants' preferences based on their shared sense of belonging to a community. (p. 6)

IMF conditionality   An agreement to loan IMF funds on the condition that certain government policies are adopted. Dozens of developing countries have entered into such agreements with the IMF in the past two decades. (p. 314) See also *International Monetary Fund (IMF)*.

import substitution   A strategy of developing local industries, often conducted behind protectionist barriers, to produce items that a country had been importing. (p. 307)

industrialization   The use of fossil-fuel energy to drive machinery and the accumulation of such machinery along with the products created by it. (p. 195)

infant mortality rate   The proportion of babies who die within their first year of life. (p. 357)

information screens   The subconscious or unconscious filters through which people put the information coming in about the world around them. (p. 87) See also *misperceptions*.

intellectual property rights   The legal protection of the original works of inventors, authors, creators, and performers under patent, copyright, and trademark law. Such rights became a contentious area of trade negotiations in the 1990s. (p. 192)

intercontinental ballistic missiles (ICBMs)   The longest-range ballistic missiles, able to travel 5,000 miles. (p. 162) See also *ballistic missile*.

interdependence   A political and economic situation in which two states are simultaneously dependent on each other for their well-being. The degree of interdependence is sometimes designated in terms of "sensitivity" or "vulnerability." (pp. 70, 177)

interest groups   Coalitions of people who share a common interest in the outcome of some political issue and who organize themselves to try to influence the outcome. (p. 78)

intergovernmental organization (IGO)   An organization (such as the United Nations and its agencies) whose members are state governments. (p. 14)

International Committee of the Red Cross (ICRC) A nongovernmental organization (NGO) that provides practical support, such as medical care, food, and letters from home, to civilians caught in wars and to prisoners of war (POWs). Exchanges of POWs are usually negotiated through the ICRC. (p. 274)

International Court of Justice See *World Court*.

International Criminal Court (ICC) A permanent tribunal for war crimes and crimes against humanity. (p. 272)

international integration The process by which supranational institutions come to replace national ones; the gradual shifting upward of some sovereignty from the state to regional or global structures. (p. 244)

International Monetary Fund (IMF) An intergovernmental organization (IGO) that coordinates international currency exchange, the balance of international payments, and national accounts. Along with the World Bank, it is a pillar of the international financial system. (p. 210) See also *IMF conditionality*.

international norms The expectations held by participants about normal relations among states. (p. 223)

international organizations (IOs) Intergovernmental organizations (IGOs) such as the UN and nongovernmental organizations (NGOs) such as the International Committee of the Red Cross (ICRC). (p. 224)

international political economy (IPE) The study of the politics of trade, monetary, and other economic relations among nations, and their connection to other transnational forces. (p. 10)

international regime A set of rules, norms, and procedures around which the expectations of actors converge in a certain international issue area (such as oceans or monetary policy). (p. 72)

international relations (IR) The relationships among the world's state governments and the connection of those relationships with other actors (such as the United Nations, multinational corporations, and individuals), with other social relationships (including economics, culture, and domestic politics), and with geographic and historical influences. (p. 2)

international security A subfield of international relations (IR) that focuses on questions of war and peace. (p. 10)

international system The set of relationships among the world's states that is structured by certain rules and patterns of interaction. (p. 11)

International Whaling Commission An intergovernmental organization (IGO) that sets quotas for hunting certain whale species; states' participation is voluntary. (p. 341)

irredentism A form of nationalism whose goal is to regain territory lost to another state; it can lead directly to violent interstate conflicts. (p. 140)

Islam A broad and diverse world religion whose divergent populations include Sunni Muslims, Shi'ite Muslims, and many smaller branches and sects from Nigeria to Indonesia, centered in the Middle East and South Asia. (p. 130)

Islamist Political ideology based on instituting Islamic principles and laws in government. A broad range of groups using diverse methods come under this category. (p. 130)

issue areas Distinct spheres of international activity (such as global trade negotiations) within which policy makers of various states face conflicts and sometimes achieve cooperation. (p. 10)

just wars A category in international law and political theory that defines when wars can be justly started (*jus ad bellum*) and how they can be justly fought (*jus in bello*). (p. 265)

Keynesian economics The principles articulated by British economist John Maynard Keynes, used successfully in the Great Depression of the 1930s, including the view that governments should sometimes use deficit spending to stimulate economic growth. (p. 213)

Kyoto Protocol (1997) The main international treaty on global warming, which entered into effect in 2005 and mandates cuts in carbon emissions. Almost all the world's major countries, except the United States, are participants. (p. 337)

landmines Concealed explosive devices, often left behind by irregular armies, that kill or maim civilians after wars end. Such mines number more than 100 million, primarily in Angola, Bosnia, Afghanistan, and Cambodia. A movement to ban landmines is underway; more than 100 states have agreed to do so. (p. 150)

land reform   Policies that aim to break up large landholdings and redistribute land to poor peasants for use in subsistence farming. (p. 287)

League of Nations   An organization established after World War I and a forerunner of today's United Nations; it achieved certain humanitarian and other successes but was weakened by the absence of U.S. membership and by its own lack of effectiveness in ensuring collective security. (p. 38) See also *collective security.*

liberal feminism   A strand of feminism that emphasizes gender equality and views the "essential" differences in men's and women's abilities or perspectives as trivial or nonexistent. (p. 103)

limited war   Military actions that seek objectives short of the surrender and occupation of the enemy. (p. 118)

Maastricht Treaty   A treaty signed in the Dutch city of Maastricht and ratified in 1992; it commits the European Union to monetary union (a single currency and European Central Bank) and to a common foreign policy. (p. 251) See also *European Union (EU).*

malnutrition   A lack of needed foods including protein and vitamins; about 3 million children die each year from malnutrition-related causes. (p. 285)

managed float   A system of occasional multinational government interventions in currency markets to manage otherwise free-floating currency rates. (p. 204)

Marxism   A branch of socialism that emphasizes exploitation and class struggle and includes both communism and other approaches. (p. 97)

mediation   The use of a third party (or parties) in conflict resolution. (p. 100)

mercantilism   An economic theory and a political ideology opposed to free trade; it shares with realism the belief that each state must protect its own interests without seeking mutual gains through international organizations. (p. 176) See also *economic liberalism.*

microcredit   The use of very small loans to small groups of individuals, often women, to stimulate economic development. (p. 309)

middle powers   States that rank somewhat below the great powers in terms of their influence on world affairs (for example, Brazil and India). (p. 49) See also *great powers.*

migration   Movement between states, usually emigration from the old state and immigration to the new state. (p. 288)

military governments   States in which military forces control the government; they are most common in poor countries, where the military may be the only large modern institution. (p. 170)

Millennium Development Goals   UN targets for basic needs measures, such as reducing poverty and hunger, adopted in 2000. (p. 280)

misperceptions/selective perceptions   The mistaken processing of the available information about a decision; one of several ways—along with affective and cognitive bias—in which individual decision making diverges from the rational model. (p. 87) See also *information screens.*

Missile Technology Control Regime   A set of agreements through which industrialized states try to limit the flow of missile-relevant technology to developing countries. (p. 162)

mixed economies   Economies such as those in the industrialized West that contain both some government control and some private ownership. (p. 198)

monetary policy   A government's decisions about printing and circulating money, and one of the two major tools of macroeconomic policy making (the other being fiscal policy). (p. 213)

Montreal Protocol (1987)   An agreement on protection of the ozone layer in which states pledged to reduce and then eliminate use of chlorofluorocarbons (CFCs). It is the most successful environmental treaty to date. (p. 340)

most-favored nation (MFN)   A principle by which one state, by granting another state MFN status, promises to give it the same treatment given to the first state's most-favored trading partner. (p. 186) See also *Generalized System of Preferences (GSP).*

multilateral aid   Government foreign aid from several states that goes through a third party, such as the UN or another agency. (p. 318)

multinational corporation (MNC)   A company based in one state with affiliated branches or subsidiaries operating in other states. (p. 213)

Munich Agreement A symbol of the failed policy of appeasement, this agreement, signed in 1938, allowed Nazi Germany to occupy part of Czechoslovakia. Rather than appease German aspirations, it was followed by further German expansions, which triggered World War II. (p. 38)

Muslims See *Islam.*

mutually assured destruction (MAD) The possession of second-strike nuclear capabilities, which ensures that neither of two adversaries could prevent the other from destroying it in an all-out war. (p. 167) See also *deterrence.*

national interest The interests of a state overall (as opposed to particular parties or factions within the state). (p. 61)

nationalism Identification with and devotion to the interests of one's nation. It usually involves a large group of people who share a national identity and often a language, culture, or ancestry. (p. 123)

nation-states States whose populations share a sense of national identity, usually including a language and culture. (p. 12)

neocolonialism The continuation, in a former colony, of colonial exploitation without formal political control. (p. 298)

neofunctionalism A theory that holds that economic integration (functionalism) generates a "spillover" effect, resulting in increased political integration. (p. 245)

neoliberalism Shorthand for "neoliberal institutionalism," an approach that stresses the importance of international institutions in reducing the inherent conflict that realists assume in an international system; the reasoning is based on the core liberal idea that seeking long-term mutual gains is often more rational than maximizing individual short-term gains. (p. 71) See also *economic liberalism.*

neorealism A version of realist theory that emphasizes the influence on state behavior of the system's structure, especially the international distribution of power. (p. 49) See also *realism.*

newly industrializing countries (NICS) Countries in the global South that have achieved self-sustaining capital accumulation, with impressive economic growth. The most successful are the "four tigers" or "four dragons" of East Asia: South Korea, Taiwan, Hong Kong, and Singapore. (p. 300)

nongovernmental organization (NGO) A transnational group or entity (such as the Catholic Church, Greenpeace, or the International Olympic Committee) that interacts with states, multinational corporations (MNCs), other NGOs, and intergovernmental organizations (IGOs). (p. 14)

Non-Proliferation Treaty (NPT) (1968) A treaty that created a framework for controlling the spread of nuclear materials and expertise, including the International Atomic Energy Agency (IAEA), a UN agency based in Vienna that is charged with inspecting the nuclear power industry in NPT member states to prevent secret military diversions of nuclear materials. (p. 167)

nonstate actors Actors other than state governments that operate either below the level of the state (that is, within states) or across state borders. (p. 14)

nontariff barriers Forms of restricting imports other than tariffs, such as quotas (ceilings on how many goods of a certain kind can be imported). (p. 183)

norms The shared expectations about what behavior is considered proper. (p. 44)

North American Free Trade Agreement (NAFTA) A free trade zone encompassing the United States, Canada, and Mexico since 1994. (p. 188)

North Atlantic Treaty Organization (NATO) A U.S.-led military alliance, formed in 1949 with mainly West European members, to oppose and deter Soviet power in Europe. It is currently expanding into the former Soviet bloc. (p. 54) See also *Warsaw Pact.*

North-South gap The disparity in resources (income, wealth, and power) between the industrialized, relatively rich countries of the West (and the former East) and the poorer countries of Africa, the Middle East, and much of Asia and Latin America. (p. 20)

optimizing Picking the very best option; contrasts with satisficing, or finding a satisfactory but less than best solution to a problem. The model of "bounded rationality" postulates that decision makers generally "satisfice" rather than optimize. (p. 88)

organizational process model   A decision-making model in which policy makers or lower-level officials rely largely on standardized responses or standard operating procedures. (p. 85)

Organization of Petroleum Exporting Countries (OPEC)   The most prominent cartel in the international economy; its members control about half the world's total oil exports, enough to affect the world price of oil significantly. (p. 190)

Oxfam America   A private charitable group that works with local communities to determine the needs of their own people and to carry out development projects. (p. 321)

ozone layer   The part of the atmosphere that screens out harmful ultraviolet rays from the sun. Certain chemicals used in industrial economies break down the ozone layer. (p. 339)

peacebuilding   The use of military peacekeepers, civilian administrators, police trainers, and similar efforts to sustain peace agreements and build stable, democratic governments in societies recovering from civil wars. Since 2005 a UN Peacebuilding Commission has coordinated and supported these activities. (p. 237)

Peace Corps   An organization started by President John Kennedy in 1961 that provides U.S. volunteers for technical development assistance in poor countries. (p. 320)

peace movements   Movements against specific wars or against war and militarism in general, usually involving large numbers of people and forms of direct action such as street protests. (p. 101)

positive peace   A peace that resolves the underlying reasons for war; not just a cease-fire but a transformation of relationships, including elimination or reduction of economic exploitation and political oppression. (p. 100)

postmodern feminism   An effort to combine feminist and postmodernist perspectives with the aim of uncovering the hidden influences of gender in IR and showing how arbitrary the construction of gender roles is. (p. 103)

postmodernism   An approach that denies the existence of a single fixed reality and pays special attention to texts and to discourses—that is, to how people talk and write about a subject. (p. 95)

power   The ability or potential to influence others' behavior, as measured by the possession of certain tangible and intangible characteristics. (p. 40)

power projection   The ability to use military force in areas far from a country's region or sphere of influence. (p. 151)

power transition theory   A theory that the largest wars result from challenges to the top position in the status hierarchy, when a rising power is surpassing (or threatening to surpass) the most powerful state. (p. 50)

Prisoner's Dilemma (PD)   A situation modeled by game theory in which rational actors pursuing their individual interests all achieve worse outcomes than they could have by working together. (p. 63)

proliferation   The spread of weapons of mass destruction (nuclear, chemical, or biological weapons) into the hands of more actors. (p. 165)

pronatalist   A government policy that encourages or forces childbearing, and outlaws or limits access to contraception. (p. 356)

prospect theory   A decision-making theory that holds that options are assessed by comparison to a reference point, which is often the status quo but might be some past or expected situation. The model also holds that decision makers fear losses more than they value gains. (p. 89)

protectionism   The protection of domestic industries against international competition, by trade tariffs and other means. (p. 182)

proxy wars   Wars in the global South—often civil wars—in which the United States and the Soviet Union jockeyed for position by supplying and advising opposing factions. (p. 28)

public opinion   In IR, the range of views on foreign policy issues held by the citizens of a state. (p. 79)

"rally 'round the flag" syndrome   The public's increased support for government leaders during wartime, at least in the short term. (p. 82)

rational actors   Actors conceived of as single entities that can "think" about their actions coherently, make choices, identify their interests, and rank the interests in terms of priority. (p. 61)

rational model   A model in which decision makers calculate the costs and benefits of each possible course of action, then choose the one with the highest benefits and lowest costs. (p. 84)

realism A broad intellectual tradition that explains international relations mainly in terms of power. (p. 38) See also *idealism* and *neorealism.*

reciprocity A response in kind to another's actions; a strategy of reciprocity uses positive forms of leverage to promise rewards and negative forms of leverage to threaten punishment. (p. 5)

refugees People fleeing their countries to find refuge from war, natural disaster, or political persecution. International law distinguishes them from migrants. (p. 288)

remittances Money sent home by migrant workers to individuals (usually relatives) in their country of origin. (p. 290)

reserves Hard-currency stockpiles kept by states. (p. 204)

resource curse The difficulties faced by resource-rich developing countries, including dependence on exporting one or a few commodities whose prices fluctuate, as well as potentials for corruption and inequality. (p. 297)

responsibility to protect (R2P) Principle adopted by world leaders in 2005 holding governments responsible for protecting civilians from genocide and crimes against humanity perpetrated within a sovereign state. (p. 270)

satisficing The act of finding a satisfactory or "good enough" solution to a problem. (p. 88)

Secretariat See *UN Secretariat.*

secular Created apart from religious establishments, with a high degree of separation between religious and political organizations. (p. 130)

security community A situation in which low expectations of interstate violence permit a high degree of political cooperation—as, for example, among NATO members. (p. 245)

Security Council See *UN Security Council.*

security dilemma A situation in which actions that states take to ensure their own security (such as deploying more military forces) are perceived as threats to the security of other states. (p. 45)

selective perceptions When individuals are more likely to perceive information that is consistent with their beliefs, while ignoring information that is inconsistent with those beliefs. (p. 87)

service sector The part of an economy that concerns services (as opposed to the production of tangible goods); the key focus in international trade negotiations is on banking, insurance, and related financial services. (p. 193)

Sino-Soviet split A rift in the 1960s between the communist powers of the Soviet Union and China, fueled by China's opposition to Soviet moves toward peaceful coexistence with the United States. (p. 27)

sovereignty A state's right, at least in principle, to do whatever it wants within its own territory; traditionally, sovereignty is the most important international norm. (p. 44)

Special Drawing Right (SDR) A world currency created by the International Monetary Fund (IMF) to replace gold as a world standard. Valued by a "basket" of national currencies, the SDR has been called "paper gold." (p. 211)

state An inhabited territorial entity controlled by a government that exercises sovereignty over its territory. (p. 11)

state-owned industries Industries such as oil-production companies and airlines that are owned wholly or partly by the state because they are thought to be vital to the national economy. (p. 198)

state-sponsored terrorism The use of terrorist groups by states, usually under control of a state's intelligence agency, to achieve political aims. (p. 158)

Strategic Defense Initiative (SDI) A U.S. effort, also known as Star Wars, to develop defenses that could shoot down incoming ballistic missiles. It was spurred by President Ronald Reagan in 1983. Critics call it an expensive failure that will likely be ineffective. (p. 167)

subsistence farming Rural communities growing food mainly for their own consumption rather than for sale in local or world markets. (p. 285)

subtext Meanings that are implicit or hidden in a text rather than explicitly addressed. (p. 96) See also *postmodernism.*

summit meeting A meeting between heads of state, often referring to leaders of great powers, as in the Cold War superpower summits between the United States and the Soviet Union or today's meetings of the Group of Eight (G8) on economic coordination. (p. 28)

supranational Larger institutions and groupings such as the European Union to which state authority or national identity is subordinated. (p. 223)

tariff A duty or tax levied on certain types of imports (usually as a percentage of their value) as they enter a country. (p. 183)

technology transfer Developing states' acquisition of technology (knowledge, skills, methods, designs, specialized equipment, etc.) from foreign sources, usually in conjunction with direct foreign investment or similar business operations. (p. 312)

territorial waters The waters near states' shores generally treated as part of national territory. The UN Convention on the Law of the Sea (UNCLOS) provides for a 12-mile territorial sea (exclusive national jurisdiction over shipping and navigation) and a 200-mile exclusive economic zone (EEZ) covering exclusive fishing and mineral rights (but allowing for free navigation by all). (p. 144) See also *high seas* and *UN Convention on the Law of the Sea (UNCLOS).*

total war Warfare by one state waged to conquer and occupy another; modern total war originated in the Napoleonic Wars, which relied on conscription on a mass scale. (p. 118)

tragedy of the commons A collective goods dilemma that is created when common environmental assets (such as the world's fisheries) are depleted or degraded through the failure of states to cooperate effectively. One solution is to "enclose" the commons (split them into individually owned pieces); international regimes can also be a (partial) solution. (p. 333)

transitional economies Countries in Russia and Eastern Europe that are trying to convert from communism to capitalism, with various degrees of success. (p. 198)

Treaty of Rome (1957) The founding document of the European Economic Community (EEC) or Common Market, now subsumed by the European Union. (p. 247)

truth commissions Governmental bodies established in several countries after internal wars to hear honest testimony and bring to light what really happened during these wars, and in exchange to offer most of the participants asylum from punishment. (p. 120)

United Nations (UN) An organization of nearly all world states, created after World War II to promote collective security.

UN Charter The founding document of the United Nations; it is based on the principles that states are equal, have sovereignty over their own affairs, enjoy independence and territorial integrity, and must fulfill international obligations. The Charter also lays out the structure and methods of the UN. (p. 227)

UN Conference on Trade and Development (UNCTAD) A structure established in 1964 to promote development in the global South through various trade proposals. (p. 242)

UN Convention on the Law of the Sea (UNCLOS) A world treaty (1982) governing use of the oceans. The UNCLOS treaty established rules on territorial waters and a 200-mile exclusive economic zone (EEZ). (p. 343) See also *territorial waters.*

UN Development Program (UNDP) A program that coordinates the flow of multilateral development assistance and manages 6,000 projects at once around the world (focusing especially on technical development assistance). (p. 318)

UN Environment Program (UNEP) A program that monitors environmental conditions and, among other activities, works with the World Meteorological Organization to measure changes in global climate. (p. 335)

UN General Assembly A body composed of representatives of all states that allocates UN funds, passes nonbinding resolutions, and coordinates economic development programs and various autonomous agencies through the Economic and Social Council (ECOSOC). (p. 228)

UN Secretariat The UN's executive branch, led by the Secretary General. (p. 230)

UN Security Council A body of five great powers (which can veto resolutions) and ten rotating member states that makes decisions about international peace and security, including the dispatch of UN peacekeeping forces. (p. 228)

Universal Declaration of Human Rights (UDHR) (1948) The core UN document on human rights; although it lacks the force of international law, it sets forth international norms regarding behavior by governments toward their own citizens and foreigners alike. (p. 268)

urbanization A shift of population from the countryside to the cities that typically accompanies economic development and is augmented by displacement of peasants from subsistence farming. (p. 286)

U.S.-Japanese Security Treaty   A bilateral alliance between the United States and Japan, created in 1951 against the potential Soviet threat to Japan. The United States maintains troops in Japan and is committed to defend Japan if attacked, and Japan pays the United States to offset about half the cost of maintaining the troops. (p. 57)

war crimes   Violations of the law governing the conduct of warfare, such as by mistreating prisoners of war or unnecessarily targeting civilians. (p. 271) See also *just wars*.

Warsaw Pact   A Soviet-led Eastern European military alliance, founded in 1955 and disbanded in 1991. It opposed the NATO alliance. (p. 54) See also *North Atlantic Treaty Organization (NATO)*.

weapons of mass destruction (WMDs)   Nuclear, chemical, and biological weapons, all distinguished from conventional weapons by their enormous potential lethality and their relative lack of discrimination in whom they kill. (p. 160)

World Bank   Formally the International Bank for Reconstruction and Development (IBRD), an organization that was established in 1944 as a source of loans to help reconstruct the European economies. Later, the main borrowers were

developing countries and, in the 1990s, Eastern European ones. (p. 210)

World Court (International Court of Justice)   The judicial arm of the UN; located in The Hague, it hears only cases between states. (p. 260)

world government   A centralized world governing body with strong enforcement powers. (p. 101)

World Health Organization (WHO)   An organization based in Geneva that provides technical assistance to improve health conditions in the developing world and conducts major immunization campaigns. (p. 242)

world-system   A view of the world in terms of regional class divisions, with industrialized countries as the core, poorest countries as the periphery, and other areas (for example, some of the newly industrializing countries) as the semiperiphery. (p. 292)

World Trade Organization (WTO)   An organization begun in 1995 that expanded the GATT's traditional focus on manufactured goods and created monitoring and enforcement mechanisms. (p. 185) See also *General Agreement on Tariffs and Trade (GATT)*.

zero-sum games   Situations in which one actor's gain is by definition equal to the other's loss, as opposed to a non-zero-sum game, in which it is possible for both actors to gain (or lose). (p. 62)

Photo Credits

1: Nasa/Corbis; 3: Doug Mills/The New York Times/Redux; 8: Roberto Neumiller; 12: White House/Reuters/Landov; 18: Xu Xiaolin/Corbis; 27: Bettmann/Corbis; 32: Andolu Agency/Getty Images; 37: Eric Feferberg/Afp/Getty Images; 41: Kaveh Kazemi/Getty Images News/Getty Images; 43: Wally Santana/AP Images; 45: Mark Blinch/Reuters/Landov; 51: Zha Chunming/Xinhua Press/Corbis; 53: Chris Hondros/Getty Images; 59: Dinodia Photos/Alamy Stock Photo; 61: Mandel Ngan/Afp/Getty Images; 67: Andy Buchanan/Afp/Getty Images; 72: Jeremy Piper/Afp/Getty Images; 75: Hassene Dridi/AP Images; 81: Aflo/Nippon News/Corbis; 86: Kcna/Xinhua Press/Corbis; 91: Alexandra Avakian/Contact Press Images; 94: Reuters/Str/Landov; 99: Ammar Awad/Reuters/Landov; 100: Cathal Mcnaughton/Reuters/Landov; 102: Ju Peng/Xinhua Press/Corbis Wire/Corbis; 105: Rune Hellestad/Corbis; 108: Photo by Spc. Jeremy D. Crisp, USA/U.S. Department of Defense; 115: Waseem Andrabi/Hindustan Times/Getty Images; 119: Pius Utomi Ekpei/Afp/Getty Images; 122: Itar-Tass Photos/Newscom; 127: Shamil Zhumatov/Reuters/Corbis; 129: Candace Feit/Epa/Corbis; 137: Stringer/Reuters/Corbis; 138: Mark Ralston/Afp/Getty Images; 141: Matt Dunham/AP Images; 144: Kyodo/Landov; 152: U.S.Department of Defense; 155: Str/Reuters/Landov; 156: Masatomo Kuriya/Corbis; 163: Rina Castelnuovo/Contact Press Images; 166 (top): DigitalGlobe/Getty Images; 166 (bottom): DigitalGlobe/Getty Images; 169: Paula Bronstein/Getty Images News/Getty Images; 174: Toby Melville/Reuters/Corbis; 181: Vahid Salemi/Ap/Corbis; 184: Roberto Neumiller; 192: John Woo/Reuters/Corbis; 199: Rahul Talukder/Demotix/Corbis; 205: Sean Gallup/Getty Images News/Getty Images; 207: Xie Huanchi/Xinhua Press/Corbis; 208: Justin Sullivan/Getty Images News/Getty Images; 212: Pacific Press/Corbis; 214: Wong Maye-E/AP Images; 216: Robin Moyer; 222: Samir Bol/Anadolu Agency/Getty Images; 225: Yannis Behrakis/Reuters/Landov; 227: Atef Safadi/Epa/Corbis; 232: David Karp/AP Images; 239: Timothy A. Clary/Afp/Getty Images; 241: Shamil Zhumatov/Reuters/Landov; 244: Tim de Waele/Corbis; 252: Nacho Guadano/Zuma Press/Corbis; 262: Richard Semik/Alamy; 264: Andy Thornley/Demotix/Corbis; 271: Adam J. Jones, PhD; 273: Isaac Kasamani/Afp/Getty Images; 278: Dan Kitwood/Getty Images News/Getty Images; 280: Narinder Nanu/Afp/Getty Images; 281: John Moore/AP Images; 287: Roberto Neumiller; 289: Pascal Rossignol/Reuters/Landov; 297: Zohra Bensemra/Reuters/Landov; 302: Imaginechina/Corbis; 305: Gautam Singh/AP Images; 310: Qamar Sibtain/The India Today Group/Mail Today/Getty Images; 315: Dylan Martinez/Reuters/Landov; 316: David Karp/AP Images; 321: Roberto Schmidt/Afp/Getty Images; 324: Department of Defense; 331: Michael S. Yamashita/Corbis; 333: Chris Bouroncle/Afp/Getty Images; 339: Ulet Ifansasti/Getty Images News/Getty Images; 345: Francois Lenoir/Reuters/Landov; 360: Baz Ratner/Reuters/Corbis; 364: Janos Marjai/Epa/Corbis; 365: Tony Karumba/Afp/Getty Images; 367: Dylan Martinez/Reuters/Landov; 374: Fabiano/Sipa/Newscom; 375: Andersen Ross/Stockbyte/Getty Images; 376: Vladimir Valishvili/Afp/Getty Images; 377: Bob Krist/Corbis.

Index

Note: **Boldface** entries and page numbers indicate key terms. Entries for tables and figures are followed by "*t*" and "*f*", respectively.